The

Definitive

Christian D. Larson

Collection

6 Volumes
30 Titles

Compiled and Edited
by
David Allen

Volume 6 of 6

Copyright © 2014 by David Allen / Shanon Allen
All rights reserved. No part of this publication may be reproduced, distributed, or transmitted in any form or by any means, including photocopying, recording, or other electronic or mechanical methods, without the prior written permission of the publisher, except in the case of brief quotations embodied in critical reviews and certain other noncommercial uses permitted by copyright law.
Printed in the United States of America

Reprint

First Printing November 2014

ISBN: 978-0-9909643-5-3

Visit Us At NevilleGoddardBooks.com for a complete listing of all our books and **1000's of Free Books to Read online and download.**

Books include: The Power of I AM 1, 2, 3, The Neville Goddard Collection, Neville Goddard's Interpretation of Scripture, The Money Bible, The Creative Power of Thought, The Secrets, Mysteries & Powers of The Subconscious Mind, Your Inner Conversations are Creating Your World, The World is At Your Command - The Very Best of Neville Goddard, Imagining Creates Reality - 365 Mystical Daily Quotes, Imagination: The Redemptive Power in Man, Assumptions Harden Into Facts: The Book, David Allen - Your Faith Is Your Fortune, Your Unlimited Power

First Printing
Copyright © 2014

Foreword

The Definitive Christian D. Larson Collection is a 6 volume set of 30 titles from one of the most renowned and prolific new thought authors and lecturers of his day. No metaphysical, new thought, law of attraction collection would be complete without Christian D. Larson's books. Before Neville Goddard, before Ernest Holmes, before Joseph Murphy and Napoleon Hill and a host of many of the great authors and teachers of today, there was Christian D. Larson (1874 – 1954) who was credited by Horatio Dresser as being a founder in the New Thought movement.

Christian D. Larson books contain hidden secrets (hidden from the conscious minds of those not prepared to receive them) and treasures that you are unlikely to find anywhere else and if you do it is likely it originated from Christian D. Larson.

David Allen

All Christian D. Larson's books are in the public domain.

* Editors note: Some Christian D. Larson books were originally published without chapter titles. They were later added by other editors of Mr. Larson's works. To my knowledge none of them are copyrighted.

Christian D. Larson Titles
Volume - Original Year Published - Title

Vol.	Year	Title
Vol. 1	1913	Brains and How to Get Them
Vol. 1	1912	Business Psychology
Vol. 1	1907	How Great Men Succeed
Vol. 1	1912	How the Mind Works
Vol. 2	1920	Concentration
Vol. 2	1912	How to Stay Well
Vol. 2	1908	How to Stay Young
Vol. 3	1908	The Great Within
Vol. 3	1912	The Mind Cure
Vol. 3	1912	What is Truth
Vol. 3	1912	Your Forces and How to Use Them
Vol. 4	1916	The Good Side of Christian Science
Vol. 4	1912	The Ideal Made Real
Vol. 4	1910	Mastery of Fate
Vol. 4	1907	Mastery of Self
Vol. 4	1916	My Ideal of Marriage
Vol. 4	1916	Nothing Succeeds Like Success
Vol. 4	1916	Steps in Human Progress
Vol. 5	1918	Healing Yourself
Vol. 5	1912	Just Be Glad
Vol. 5	1940	Leave it to God
Vol. 5	1908	On the Heights
Vol. 5	1910	Perfect Health
Vol. 5	1922	Practical Self-Help
Vol. 5	1912	Scientific Training of Children
Vol. 5	1912	Thinking for Results
Vol. 6	**1912**	**The Hidden Secret**
Vol. 6	**1916**	**In Light of the Spirit**
Vol. 6	**1912**	**The Pathway of Roses**
Vol. 6	**1907**	**Poise and Power**

Volume 6

The Hidden Secret	6
In Light of the Spirit	82
The Pathway of Roses	218
Poise and Power	468

The Hidden Secret

The Hidden Secret

Table of Contents

Chapter 1 - With Faith All Things Are Possible	8
Chapter 2 - A Living Faith	10
Chapter 3 - A Faith That Knows	12
Chapter 4 - Faith That Opens the Door	14
Chapter 5 - The Great Within	16
Chapter 6 - Increasing Life	18
Chapter 7 - Unlimited Power	20
Chapter 8 - Live a Larger and Greater Life	23
Chapter 9 - Expansion of Consciousness	27
Chapter 10 - Faith Awakens the New Life	29
Chapter 11 - Through Faith All Things Are Possible	31
Chapter 12 - Have Faith in Yourself	35
Chapter 13 - Have Faith in Mankind	39
Chapter 14 - Have Faith in Your Work, Opportunities and Circumstances	42
Chapter 15 - Have Faith in God	44
Chapter 16 - Have Faith in Faith	48
Chapter 17 - More on Have Faith in Faith	49
Chapter 18 - Desire and Faith	52
Chapter 19 - Entering into the Life Of the Higher Power	56
Chapter 20 - Faith For Everyday Living	65
Chapter 21 - Banish Fear; Have Faith	67
Chapter 22 - The Hidden Secret	71

Chapter 1

With Faith All Things Are Possible

To him who has Faith all things are possible.

Faith is that something in man that transcends every form of limitation and opens the mind to the limitless powers of the soul.

It is faith that emancipates the person; it is faith that unfolds the unbounded greatness of the soul; it is faith that removes the veil of mystery and reveals to man that wonderful world, that limitless world, that divinely beautiful world that is within.

Faith has been the hidden secret of the great souls in every age; faith has been the secret through which all miracles have been wrought; faith has been the secret through which the prophet gained his wisdom and his power; faith has been the secret through which the sons of glory gained their rare and wonderful genius; faith has been the secret through which everything high, everything worthy and everything beautiful has been given to the world.

It is faith that the awakened minds have eternally sought to find, though not always knowing that the hidden secret was faith, and faith alone; and it is faith that will change the world, as the world should be changed, when its inner sanctuary has been entered by the mind of man.

Faith is the hidden secret to everything; the key that unlocks every door that may exist in the universe; faith is the perfect way to that inner world from which all things proceed; faith is the royal path to unbounded power, immeasurable wisdom and limitless love; faith is the gates ajar to that kingdom which first must be sought if all other things are to be added; faith is the hidden secret to every desire and need of man.

Chapter 2

A Living Faith

There is a faith that is faith; there is a faith that can do all things; there is a faith that moves mountains, whatever those mountains may be; there is a faith that rises above every obstacle in the world and reaches the greatest heights that the mind of man may have in view; and it is this faith that is the hidden secret.

When this faith is attained all the ills of human life must take their departure; when this faith is attained every form of poverty must vanish, never to appear again; when this faith is attained every wrong will be righted, the crooked paths made straight, and every wish of the heart satisfied.

This faith is a living faith; it is a faith that works; not a faith that simply consoles. It is not a faith that merely believes things, but a faith that does things.

It is this faith that opens the mind to the limitless possibilities of the great within and gives to man that something through which he may become as great as he ever may desire to be.

It is this faith that the Master Mind referred to when he declared that nothing shall be impossible unto you; it is this faith that gives the word of truth its invincible power; it is this faith that gives birth to the living thought the thought that has healing on its wings.

It is this faith that will emancipate the race, bring peace on earth, goodwill to man; and it is this faith that will reveal to mind the hidden spirit of truth that spirit which, when known, will give man freedom from everything that is human, and the power to attain everything that is divine.

To possess such a faith is the prayer of every spiritual heart, and it is tidings of great joy, indeed, that this prayer may be answered, and answered now.

Chapter 3

A Faith That Knows

To fully define this faith is an effort that will never be attempted, because true faith is far beyond the description of words; the true faith is something that must be spiritually discerned, and the higher one ascends in the understanding of the spirit the larger and more powerful this faith becomes.

Faith is not mere belief; neither is it a doctrine about anything that was, is, or is to be. Faith and belief have nothing in common; they are as different as darkness and light.

Belief is human; faith is more than human; belief knows nothing; faith knows everything.

The true faith is a spiritual state of mind; a state of mind that is very deep, very high, and beautiful beyond description. It is a State of mind that knows; and it knows, because to be in faith is to be upon the mountaintop of intelligence, wisdom and illumination.

The innumerable kingdoms of the great within are known to faith; faith knows everything that is high, everything that is perfect, everything that is limitless, everything that is supreme; faith knows because it has seen; seen with the eyes of the spiritual vision.

Faith is an attitude of mind that turns the superior sense of man towards the inner, the hidden, the unseen, the great beyond, and takes consciousness into those finer realms where everything is perfect, and far more real than that which appears to visible sight.

The Hidden Secret

Faith demonstrates that that which seems unreal is absolutely real; that that which seems hidden can be revealed to any mind, and understood by any mind; and that the invisible becomes visible to all those who will open the full vision that exists within them.

Faith demonstrates that the inner world is far more substantial than the outer world, and that the farther we proceed into the great within the more substantial, the more real, the more perfect and the more beautiful everything becomes.

One of the principal functions of faith is to enter the boundless and awaken the great within; and since all increase in life, power and ability comes from the awakening of a larger and a larger measure of the within, we understand perfectly why all things are possible to him who has faith.

Chapter 4

Faith That Opens the Door

There is a life within that has no limit; it is the life more abundant the life that every awakened mind has sought with heart and soul; it is the life from which all great things proceed; the source of everything that has real value and high worth.

Faith opens the door to this life and takes man into the sacred sanctuary within, to enter this life is to be filled with this life, and gain possession of all that this life may contain.

This does not indicate that faith deals wholly with a life that is apart from daily life; faith finds real life abundance of real life, and what it finds it gives richly to daily life. Faith opens the mind to the influx of limitless life, and every atom in one's being becomes filled with this life.

Faith does not dwell apart from things, but works through things, giving to all things an abundance of the unbounded power from within. Without the spirit of faith, things become lifeless, soulless, purposeless and useless.

Everything is limited when faith is absent; everything breaks bounds when faith appears.

Faith does not work apart from intellect, but gives soul to intellect; illumines the intellect with higher wisdom; inspires the intellect with greater possibilities; permeates the intellect with a power that mind can never measure.

Faith not only gives superiority to the intellect, but elevates the mind to a higher and higher state of comprehension, so that an ever-increasing world of thought and life is incorporated in the scope of mentality. This gives added power and quality to every talent, and opens consciousness to the limitless source of everything that mind may require.

Chapter 5

The Great Within

Whatever we may desire to accomplish, nothing is more important than to possess that rare faculty called resourcefulness. To be able to draw upon the limitless for thought, ideas, plans, methods, wisdom, power, inspiration, in brief, everything that one may require to take advantage of every opportunity to be able to do this is to be able to reach the highest goal that mind may have in view. And faith enables the mind to do this; faith opens all the doors to everything that mind may desire to secure; faith opens the mind to that immense inner world from which everything may be received.

It is being demonstrated more fully every day that all things pertaining to the life of man come from the within; not only great things, but all things. From the within comes all wisdom, and the mind that has awakened the largest measure of their within has the greatest wisdom.

The same is true of power; we do not receive power from what we eat or drink, nor from the air we breathe; power comes from an inner world; therefore, he who would become strong in body, mind and soul must awaken more and more of the great within.

That rare insight that something that leads and guides with a superhuman understanding that also comes from the illumined within, and develops as consciousness gains a higher realization of the inner world. By entering this superior state of mind one will live perpetually in the light, and thereby eliminate all mistakes from daily existence. And he who enters faith enters this superior, illumined state.

The Hidden Secret

The other forms of understanding, perception, conception, and comprehension also have their source in the inner mind, and will increase in power and efficiency as the within unfolds.

The powers that create, the forces that build, the elements that promote the growth of mind and soul all of these come from the same inner source, and will come in greater abundance as the inner world is awakened in the mind of man.

The love that loves everything with real love also comes from the wonderful within; likewise, purity, virtue, kindness, harmony, joy and the peace that passeth understanding. All of these may be obtained in boundless supply through the living of life in faith.

Every form of health and wholeness, and all perfect conditions of mind or body have their origin in the within; therefore, he who would banish all the ills of life must, through faith, unfold the perfect life from that limitless, inner world.

Whatever we may require for attainment, advancement, or the enlargement of life, we may secure from the great within; and since faith is the royal path to this marvelous realm, we understand again why all things are possible to him who has faith.

Chapter 6

Increasing Life

To obtain complete emancipation, to perpetually ascend in the scale of life, to become something, to accomplish something, to secure results, to do things, to move forward, to make every effort count, to make the fullest use of everything that one may be, or possess, to live a life worthwhile and to secure from life the very best that life has the power to give these are some of the ruling desires among the better minds of today; and we know of no desires that are more worthy, nor more indicative of a superior understanding of real existence.

It is therefore a great privilege to gain possession of that something through which all of these desires may be realized; and since that something is faith, everyone may henceforth fulfill his desires all of his desires, because anyone can obtain faith. In fact, everyone has faith, to a degree; when anyone ceases to have faith he will cease to be. Before man can do anything he must have faith; he must have faith even before he can begin to perpetuate existence.

To live is to move forward; to do anything, or attempt anything is to move forward; and to move forward is to enter the great unknown, unknown to the senses, but not to faith. Faith knows that the seeming void of the great unknown is solid rock; faith knows that man may safely proceed, and by what faith man may possess he does proceed.

If there was nothing within him to give him this assurance, this feeling that he may proceed with safety, he would not proceed: he would bring the whole of existence to a standstill, and cease to be.

The Hidden Secret

This, however, no one will ever do, because faith is a part of the soul; it is inseparably united with the soul; one can never lose all his faith, but one can increase its power without end; and as the power of faith is increased, by having more faith, the expression of life will increase, and everything that comes from life will increase.

The life of man is large or small in proportion to his faith, because it is through faith that he touches the source of life and receives life.

Likewise, all the attainments and achievements of man are large or small in proportion to his faith.

"According to your faith," that is the law that determines everything.

Since faith is the hidden secret of all life, and is absolutely indispensable to existence, we all have faith just as we all have life; to find faith, we are therefore not required to search for something we never knew; we are simply required to have more faith in the faith we already possess; the greater things will invariably follow.

Chapter 7

Unlimited Power

Through faith every desire can be realized, and every object in view can be accomplished, because faith places mind in touch with the power that can do all things.

Faith opens the mind to the unbounded power from within and creates in mind the conscious realization of that power. When you are in faith the power that you feel is so great that nothing seems impossible; you feel strong enough to do almost anything, and what you feel is the truth.

You can do anything while you are absolutely in faith, because while you are in faith you are in a world where unlimited power is at your command.

There is a world of limitless power; that world is within us and all about us, but in ordinary consciousness we are not aware of its existence; at those times, however, when we transcend ordinary consciousness we gain glimpses of this marvelous world.

It is during such moments that we feel strong enough to move mountains; it is then that we receive our inspirations, when new truths are revealed, when new discoveries are made, and when immortal deeds are done.

This world of limitless power is an inner world permeating the outer world, and is revealed through faith; it is through faith that we enter into this world, and it is through the growth of faith that we realize its limitless power, thereby gaining possession of a greater measure of this power.

The Hidden Secret

The fact that we live and move and have our being in a world of unlimited power, that we can become conscious of this world through faith, and thereby place unlimited power at our command the fact that this is the truth is a fact so extraordinary, so far-reaching and so enormously important that it should be proclaimed with a loud voice to all the world; and not a single soul should live another day without hearing this wonderful message proclaimed.

This is one of the greatest truths of all truths, and should not only receive profound attention from every mind, but it is a truth that should be constantly held in every mind. To live, think and act in the spirit of this truth the truth that you live and move and have your being in a world of unlimited power and that through faith all of this power is placed at your command to live in this truth, with faith, is to open the mind more and more to the perpetual influx of this power, until you gain so much of this power that nothing becomes impossible to you henceforth and forever.

That there is such a world no one can doubt; that faith is the hidden path to that world anyone can demonstrate; anyone can also demonstrate that we gain possession of an immense power while we are in that world, and that the power continues to be our own so long as we remain in the full faith; it is therefore evident that those who will continue permanently in the full faith will accomplish everything they may undertake to do.

Through the growth of faith the real faith, the mind becomes more and more aware of this inner world, and consciousness opens more and more to receive its limitless power; the entire personality becomes filled with the power, and before long you feel that an immense power is with you every moment of existence. This brings the realization that nothing is impossible; you never hesitate to undertake anything that is worthy, no matter how great and extensive the undertaking may be, because you know there is a power with you that can do all things. You feel that this power is working through you; you feel that it is your power; therefore, anything worthy that you may undertake, the same shall be done.

To enter this realization is to gain more power from the very beginning; therefore, he who enters faith will begin at once to accomplish greater things and better things, whatever his work may be; and as for his future, it is as great, as wonderful and as beautiful as he may desire to make it.

Chapter 8

Live a Larger and Greater Life

By entering the immensity of superior mental worlds, faith enlarges the mind, thereby increasing capacity, ability and every substantial quality contained in the world of intelligence.

Through the same process faith expands consciousness beyond all present limitations and adds rich domains to the kingdom of mentality. To live in faith is to live a larger and a greater life perpetually, because it is the nature of faith to enlarge, expand and develop everything that pertains to the mental and spiritual life.

Faith penetrates the great unknown and makes it known; faith goes out upon the seeming void and finds the solid rock; faith always finds the solid rock because the solid rock is everywhere.

Everything is real and substantial; the fathomless depths and the immeasurable heights contain worlds within worlds; all real, all substantial, all perfectly safe for mind to enter and explore. Faith knows this, therefore never hesitates to go out upon the seeming void; never hesitates to go on with every worthy undertaking. Faith knows that all is real and all is possible, and acts accordingly.

Faith demonstrates conclusively that you may go out in every direction, or enter into any depth of soul-existence, you will find the Infinite everywhere; you will find real life everywhere; you will find beautiful souls everywhere; you will find love and peace everywhere; and wherever you go you will find unlimited possibilities, unbounded power, and innumerable opportunities to arise in the endless scale of existence.

Again it is most evident that all things are possible to him who has faith.

Through the action of faith new worlds are discovered in every part of mentality, and valuable qualities, talents, capabilities and powers constantly added. Through the revelations of faith we discover that the most prodigious minds we know are but infants compared with what we all may became now, if we will simply have faith in faith, and follow faith into these greater mental worlds that we even touch at every movement of thought.

We are all on the very verge of rare genius, superior talent and limitless worlds of extraordinary intelligence; but faith alone can lead us on; faith alone is the hidden secret to the wisdom and power that knows no bounds.

Every faculty of the mind can be enlarged and expanded indefinitely; there is no end to the possibilities that may be unfolded and developed through the enlargement of the various faculties of the outer mind; even the physical senses may expand their spheres of action far beyond the widest stretches of the imagination.

The world of color, the world of sound, the world of feeling all the worlds of sense are limitless. That the physical senses have limitations is not the truth; they may appear to be limited because they have not been developed beyond their present spheres of action; but through faith we discover that the spheres of action of the physical senses contain possibilities for enlargement that have absolutely neither limitation nor end.

The Hidden Secret

Through faith we also discover how this development of the senses may be promoted on the largest possible scale.

Innumerable kingdoms of marvelous beauty lie hidden within the world of color; the same is true of the world of sound; and as to the possibilities that are latent in the sense of feeling, we have not dreamed of a millionth part.

We may think the world is beautiful; and it is, but our perception of the beautiful is in its first stages only; it remains for the further development of physical sight and the discernment of color to reveal to us worlds of splendor such as mind has never been able to picture.

We may be charmed into ecstasy with certain tender strains of music, but the sweetest music is not heard; the most tender strains do not touch the soul; we pass them by, not even knowing of their existence. The world of sound with its innumerable symphonies is almost entirely closed to the average mind. He may be charmed with what little he does hear, but what will he be when he hears it all?

It is through the further development of the physical senses that many of these beautiful worlds will be realized and enjoyed; and it is through faith that the physical senses will reach that higher state of development; because it is faith that enters the unknown; it is faith that penetrates the within; it is faith that transcends all limitations and gives to mind greater and greater measures of the immensities still in store.

Faith is the secret to all that is hidden; and to him who follows faith, all things will be revealed.

What faith can do for the enlargement of the physical senses and the outer mind, it can do far more extensively for the spiritual senses and the inner mind. We therefore understand perfectly why all things are possible to him who has faith.

Chapter 9

Expansion of Consciousness

We all realize that unlimited possibilities are latent in the great within; and we are all in search of the best and most thorough methods through which these possibilities may be developed; but it has been discovered that the within is unfolded only through the expansion of consciousness; how to expand consciousness, therefore, becomes one of the greatest problems in the life of man.

It is solved, however, through faith; faith expands consciousness; in fact, it is only through faith that consciousness may be expanded. This is a fact of extreme importance, a fact that every metaphysician and psychologist should note with care, and act accordingly. The absence of real faith among psychologists is the reason why the greatest part of their efforts are of no practical value to the world; and the deficiency in faith among metaphysicians is the reason why all the sick are not healed, why all who have troubles do not secure complete emancipation.

Add faith, real faith, to practical metaphysics, and failures among those who are seeking to remove the ills of human life, would almost entirely disappear.

Do not simply speak the word of truth, but have faith in the truth and the truth shall make you free.
It is not the literal statement of truth, but the soul of truth that contains the healing power, the emancipating power, the power that can do all things; and when we have faith we enter the soul of truth.

That we must have faith before we can become conscious of the new, the larger, the better, the higher, the spirit of things, is very evident when we realize that it is faith alone that goes out upon the seeming void; it is faith alone that breaks bounds and demonstrates the existence of a greater life; it is faith that takes the first step forward always, but wherever faith may go, consciousness invariably follows.

We therefore understand clearly that to awaken the great within, and develop the unlimited possibilities that are latent within us, faith is the hidden secret. Through faith the mind gains a greater comprehension of all things, whether those things be physical, intellectual or spiritual.

The greater the faith the larger the view and the better the view, whatever the subject of thought may be; and the more thorough the understanding. Faith is therefore a priceless gift to every mind in existence; for there is no place in life where faith will not be a great and wonderful power for good.

Through faith the mind ascends into that state of being where the life more abundant the spiritual life, the eternal life is realized and received; and among all the powers of faith, this is the greatest. The unfoldment of the inner life prepares the way for the unfoldment of the soul, and places every high spiritual attainment within reach of the growing mind.

Among the many methods that have been given for soul-unfoldment, pure spiritual faith is by far the greatest; other methods may become aids to faith, but without faith they have no value.

A great truth to remember is this, that no soul-unfoldment or spiritual development is possible without faith; and that no system of higher culture or attainment has any value whatever unless it is based upon faith.

Chapter 10

Faith Awakens the New Life

Faith awakens the new life, the healing life, the emancipating life, the purifying life, the regenerating life, the life that is power, health, wholeness and freedom; therefore, through faith anyone may attain complete emancipation from all the ills of human existence.

The coming of the strong, pure life from within will dispel every form of physical disease or mental distress, as light dispels the darkness; and to have faith is to open the entire human personality to the coming of those higher powers of the soul that have healing on their wings.

No disease can remain in the system after these higher spiritual forces have come forth into mind and body; and whenever the real, interior faith is entered into, these forces are awakened with all their purity and power.

When disease threatens, have faith; and have faith in faith; feel the very soul of faith in every atom of your being and the healing power of the soul will fill your system through and through.

Faith is the hidden secret to the power that can do all things; therefore, to have faith in faith is to enter the hidden life of that power; to feel the very spirit of that life, and to permeate that spirit with every conscious action of mind.

When we realize that faith is the hidden secret, and enter into the innermost life of that secret with every thought we think, the invincible powers within will awaken at once; and whatever we desire to do, the same will be done.

The Hidden Secret

The effect of faith upon the intellect is most beneficial in every way, the reason being that the attitude of faith elevates mind above all confusion, doubt, fear, uncertainly and limitations, and actually illumines the entire mental domain.

To enter faith is to enter the crystal sea of pure intelligence, and to steadily grow into that superior understanding that knows because it is the light of truth and wisdom.

He who lives constantly in the attitude of faith will, before long, develop remarkable intellectual brilliancy.

He who lives in faith will not only increase his ability, and the power that does things, but will also acquire that rare and most excellent faculty of doing the right thing at the right time. Faith does develop higher mental insight, thus giving mind the power to act with real wisdom, keen judgment and superior understanding.

Chapter 11

Through Faith All Things Are Possible

Faith is the hidden secret to the real, the true, the genuine and the superior in all things; therefore, to enter faith is to gain possession of the highest truth about everything.

Faith ignores all the limitations of objective intelligence and enters the larger mental world of superior intelligence; faith knows that the dark unknown will be found to be filled with light after we have entered its luminous splendor, and by entering this more brilliant mental world, faith proves that its faith was true.

In the development of the various mental faculties faith is indispensable; the reason for such a far-reaching statement is found in the fact that it is the finer creative energies of mind that build talents; and that we must enter the inner mental world to awaken those energies; but it is only through faith that consciousness can reach the inner realms of mind.

When we are in faith we are in the conscious realization of the finer forces those forces that are required in every form of physical, mental or spiritual development.

Faith is the hidden secret to all the higher powers; therefore, when we enter faith we enter the conscious possession of those powers, and may employ them for any purpose that is before us now.

As we grow in faith the finer creative energies increase in power, because the more faith we have the more power we receive from within; we thereby promote the development of talent, genius and rare ability on an ever-increasing scale.

In the development of any faculty the circumscribed must be transcended, and that phase of consciousness that acts within the faculty must be widened and heightened; this faith does invariably, thereby, not only give every faculty a larger sphere of action, but also greater power and superior quality.

The higher consciousness ascends in the mental world of any faculty, the higher and finer becomes the quality of that faculty; and since faith always promotes the ascension of consciousness, superior mental quality will invariably follow the attainment of faith.

This truth will be better understood when we realize that the larger, the greater and the superior is to be found in the within on a higher plane, and that to gain possession of the superior we must develop the consciousness of the within; that is, consciousness must be expanded to such an extent that it reaches into the within and comprehends the within as well as the without.

Since faith is the only path to the within, and since it is only through faith that consciousness can be expanded, faith therefore becomes indispensable to all forms of development.

Faith is the hidden secret to the true, the perfect and the limitless in everything; therefore, to find faith is to find everything. Nothing is hidden from him who has faith, because he who enters into faith enters into that which was hidden, and it is hidden no more.

The Hidden Secret

Since faith is a hidden path, it can be entered into only when our thinking enters the inner meaning of faith, and as a conscious effort is made to inwardly feel faith.

By concentrating attention upon the inner meaning of faith, trying to feel the spirit of faith, we find the path to faith and steadily enter more deeply into the real soul of faith.

To exercise faith is to consciously enter the inner and the finer essence of everything in which we may have faith; not to menially dwell on the surface of things, but to dwell on the inner life of things the hidden secret of things.

When we understand the inner meaning of faith, and realize that faith is the hidden secret, the mere thought of faith will take the mind into faith; while in faith the mind is opened to the unbounded powers that come through faith, and all limitations and seeming impossibilities disappear from consciousness completely.

When we exercise faith, all doubt, all fear and all anxiety are absent; should these undesirable mental states appear, we may know that our minds are thinking about the surface of things instead of the spirit of things.

To be in faith is to think about the spirit of things, to mentally dwell within the spirit of things, to feel the spirit of things and to be filled through and through with the unbounded power of this spirit.

Faith never pays any attention to appearances; faith has information from a higher source; faith knows that all things are possible now, because to be in faith is to be in that power that can do all things now.

The Hidden Secret

When we try to enter faith we must give full right-of-way to this power; we must permit this power to thrill every atom in being, and we must give this power the privilege to do whatever we now may desire to have done.

The more we depend upon this power the more of this power we shall receive, until our capacity becomes enormous.

The more we exercise faith the more faith we shall secure; and the more faith we have in faith the more deeply we shall enter into the very soul of faith.

Chapter 12

Have Faith in Yourself

To secure the largest and best possible results from the practical application of faith, it is necessary to have a perfect faith in everything with which we may come in contact, both on the visible and invisible sides of life.

Have faith in yourself, have faith in man, have faith in the universe, have faith in God, and have faith in faith.

To have faith in everything is to develop the power of faith in every direction, and it is the full faith that opens the mind to the power that can do all things.

The principal reason why faith sometimes fails is because we exercise faith in some things while we have doubts about others.

It is the faith that has faith in all things and at all times that is real faith; and it is the faith that has faith in the full faith that makes all things possible.

There is a power for good in everything; in everything something may be found that has true value and real worth; something that can add to the welfare of man; but this something is found, not on the surface, but within the soul of things. It is therefore necessary to enter into perfect touch with the inner life of everything to secure the best from everything; and this is possible only through faith.

When we have faith in all things we enter into absolute oneness with the real life of all things; we place ourselves in touch with the universal, and may consequently draw upon the limitless for anything the heart may desire.

The Hidden Secret

The universal can supply all things; therefore, he who lives constantly in perfect touch with the universal will never want for anything.

When you have faith in yourself you awaken the immensity of your own interior life, arid bring into expression your better self, your superior self, your limitless self.

There is something in man that is more than human; something that is far greater than the personal man; something that transcends every form of visible existence; something that is created in the image of the Supreme; and it is faith that unfolds this higher being, causing the Word to become flesh, thereby permeating the visible form with the beauty and the divinity of the soul.

It is the nature of faith to enter the higher, the larger and the boundless; therefore, by living in faith you will mentally dwell in a growing consciousness of superiority. This will develop superiority in all your talents and faculties, because whatever we become conscious of, that we express through our own mind and character.

Have faith in yourself and you will always be at your best; you will constantly express the best that exists in your conscious nature, and your work will be the result of your greatest capacity and highest efficiency.

By having full and constant faith in yourself you place every part of your system in the best possible working condition; and besides, you promote in yourself the process of continuous improvement.

To live in faith is to move forward every single moment; because it is one of the functions of faith to press on to ceaselessly press on.

The Hidden Secret

The man who has the most faith in himself invariably does the best work, and consequently secures the most remunerative places in the industrial world. Faith elevates mind to the highest state of ability and awakens the necessary power from within to sustain the high position.

The man who continues to have a perfect faith in himself can never fail, because it is worth that wins, and faith never ceases to develop worth.

By having faith in yourself you bring to the surface the best that you possess, and then proceed to gain conscious possession of better talents and greater powers than you have ever known before.

There is a genius asleep in the subconscious of every mind; in the great within of every mind, unbounded capacity and ability may be found; and it is faith that awakens this genius; it is faith that unfolds the limitless possibilities within.

Faith is the hidden secret to greatness, because faith takes man into the inner life of that power that produces greatness. Therefore, he who has faith in himself may become anything, attain anything and accomplish anything.

To have faith in yourself is to feel the life and power of that something within yourself that is limitless; that something that is created in the image and likeness of the Supreme.

To grow in that faith, never think of the surface of your system, but think of the strong soul that permeates every atom of your being; mentally dwell upon the inner side of your life, and train your thought to act only upon the finer energies, the finer substance and the real spirit that fills your body, mind and soul.

To develop faith in yourself have faith in the faith that declares that you are the image and likeness of the Supreme, therefore limitless. Aim to be your best and live in the faith that you always will be your best; then have faith in your every word, your every thought and your every deed.

Most important of all, whenever you try to have faith, whenever you think of faith, mentally feel the inner meaning of faith. This will invariably produce results.

Chapter 13

Have Faith in Mankind

When we have faith in man we enter into the most harmonious relations with the better side of man; we mentally live with the real man, the superior man, the true man. We consequently will think, not of human weakness, but of the supreme power and the divine life that exists in man.

What we constantly recognize in others we develop in ourselves; and we steadily grow into the likeness of that which we think of the most.

When we have faith in all people we attract better people, and will have the privilege to live with those who are as we wish them to be.

What we constantly hold in mind that we invariably attract to ourselves; and receives our undivided attention. We shall consequently have the privilege to associate with those who express the real and the true in the highest and most perfect measure.

He who has the most faith in mankind has the most friends and the best friends; he receives the truest love from the largest number, and the best that the world can give will constantly flow into his life.

When we have faith in others we inspire others to have faith in themselves; they, consequently, become more competent and more highly developed, thereby helping to make life better for everybody concerned. The more faith we have in people the more they will do for us, the more they will do for themselves, and the more valuable they become to the whole world.

Have faith in the world, and the wrongs of the world will be righted. Have faith in everybody, and you inspire everybody to have faith in everybody; and when everybody has faith in everybody, sin, sorrow and sickness will vanish from this planet.

This is a scientific statement, because when we all have faith in each other, the life of the whole race will be a living faith; the life of every person will be lived in faith, and to live in faith is to live in that life that knows neither sickness, sorrow nor sin. To live in faith is to enter the life of that pure spiritual power that not only can, but does, banish the ills of human existence.

When things seem to go wrong, do not complain about the incompetence of man, but have faith in man, and the better side of everybody with which you are connected, will appear to set all matters right.

The complaining mind goes down into more confusion and denser mental darkness, thereby making more mistakes and misleading everybody concerned to a lesser or greater extent.

It is the truth that the more we complain the more we shall find about which to complain; and the more we contend with things the more things we shall have with which to contend.

The more faith we have in man when in the midst of adversity, the sooner we shall find the way out, and the sooner we shall find the help required under the circumstances.

The Hidden Secret

Faith keeps the eye single upon the better, the right and the true; and he who keeps the eye single upon the better rises into the realization of the better. This is an absolute law through the use of which anyone may find emancipation; and faith is the hidden secret to that law and its perfect use.

The man who has faith in everybody will never have much to complain about; the best of everything will come with him into his way, and all things will work together for his good.

There is nothing that will smoothen the pathway of life, and harmonize all the conditions of life more perfectly and more rapidly than a full, strong, living faith a faith that has faith in everybody and in everything.

When we have faith in everything we are brought into closer touch with the best of everything, and will thus secure the best from every source.

This is perfectly natural, because whenever we enter into the life of faith we enter into the best, the highest and the truest that there is in life. Faith lives in the superior world, and to enter into faith is to enter that world.

What we enter into with mind, that we become conscious of; and what we become conscious of, that we express through our own mentalities and personalities. Therefore, by entering the inner realms of superiority we develop in ourselves all the qualities of superiority.

Chapter 14

Have Faith in Your Work, Opportunities and Circumstances

Have faith in your work, and your efforts will produce far greater results; because through the attitude of faith you give your very best life and power to your work. In addition you enter into a more perfect harmony with all the elements contained in your work, thereby producing that unity of purpose which invariably culminates in great achievements.

Have faith in every opportunity and the richest treasures that may be hidden within that opportunity will be given to you. Faith enters the soul of things and gains possession of the very essence of all worth. Wherever there is a secret, faith will find it.

Have faith in every circumstance, in every phase of environment and these will give only their best to you. When you have faith, adverse environments will trouble you no more; they will, on the other hand, become open gates to pastures green.

Nothing but the best can come through faith, therefore it is the hidden secret to the best that anything in the world can give.

If you cannot understand this, have faith, and faith will reveal to you the reason why. The hidden secret of faith is revealed only to those who live in faith.

Have faith, even in adversity; believe with the whole heart that adverse circumstances are simply opportunities to a larger life for you; and as your faith is so shall it be.

The Hidden Secret

There is a power in every form of adversity a power that can be turned to good account. Faith enters into harmony with this power, gains possession of it and transforms adversity into a most powerful friend.

Live in the faith that all things are working out right, and you will draw all things into the pathway of right; all things will go with you and do the right things for you.

There is nothing strange about this, because the power of faith is invincible. Faith is in touch with the world of unbounded power, therefore can do all things.

Have faith in all the elements and forces of nature, and their hidden secrets shall be revealed to you. Faith can find anything; faith goes into the soul of things, and through superior vision discerns everything that may exist in life.

Live perpetually in the full faith, and you shall discover many things that the world has never known; things that may add immeasurably to the welfare of the race.

When we have faith in all things our attention is subconsciously concentrated upon the best; we thereby think the best, create the best, and enter into the world of the best. By entering into the world of the best we shall have the privilege to associate with the best, appropriate the best and live the best.

The secret of high thinking and right thinking is therefore found in faith; and as man is as he thinks we again realize the unbounded value of faith.

Chapter 15

Have Faith in God

When we have faith in God we enter into oneness with God, and with everything in the universe that is good.

It is only through faith that we may know God; it is only through faith that we may enter the presence of God and walk with God; it is only through faith that we may enter the spirit and dwell in the secret places of the Most High.

Faith removes the gulf that seems to exist between God and man by demonstrating that there is no gulf, but that man is one with God now, in the highest, truest and fullest sense of divine unity.

To enter faith is to know that "My Father and I are one", and to feel that the power to do the greater things are even now at hand.

To enter faith is to enter into the conscious realization of the great truth that man is created in the image and likeness of God; to enter faith is to inwardly feel that "I AM the Son of God," and that "all that the Father hath is mine."

When we have faith in God we are with God, and realize perfectly that to him who is with God all things are possible.

No one can fail when God is with him; and God is with everybody who unites his mind with the infinite mind.

"Come with Me, and I AM with thee," thus speaketh the Voice Divine in the soul of every man. Those who have faith can hear this voice, and will invariably act accordingly.

The Hidden Secret

Have faith in God and you will live with God, and you will feel that God is with you in everything you may undertake to do.

Do not simply believe in God. Have faith in God. The difference is immense.

He who simply believes in God stands apart from God; but he who has faith in God enters into the very spirit of God; he is filled with the power of God; the purity of God; the wisdom of God and the peace of God; and he rests eternally in the arms of Infinite Love.

To have faith in God is to take God absolutely at His Word; to believe so thoroughly that all things are created in the image of God, and that all things are good, because created by God, that we proceed to act accordingly.

Everything that God has created is good, and he who lives in faith finds that all things are good.

He also finds that the imperfections of man's creations disappear completely when we realize the perfections of God's; creations.

When we have faith in God we can doubt nothing; we know that infinite power, infinite wisdom and infinite love are within all things, and that the final results will be wonderful, marvelous, indescribably beautiful.

When we have faith in God our fears and worries disappear; what we ourselves cannot overcome or accomplish, we place in the hands of God living in the faith that God can and will make all things well; and as our faith is, so it is always done unto us.

The Hidden Secret

When you feel that you live and move and have your being in God you will never have any fear; you know that you are safe and secure; fully protected at all times; and that nothing but good can come to you. Again, as your faith is, so is it done unto you.

To eliminate fear of every sort, simply have faith in God; it is a remedy that never fails. Glad tidings of great joy, indeed; something that is worth all the wisdom in the world.

Again, do not simply believe in God; have faith in God.

When you have faith in God you enter so completely into the spirit of God that you actually feel that He is "closer than breathing, nearer than hands and feet."

To be in this state is not only supreme joy, but it is to be in a state of superior wisdom, superior ability and superior power. While in this state you realize that "My Father worketh and I work." You feel that the hand of the Infinite works with your hand, and that neither weariness nor failure can possibly follow.

While in this state, you think the thoughts of the Infinite after Him; your mind is illumined with the Word of wisdom, and the spirit of Truth reigns supremely in all your world. You are in the peace that passeth understanding; you have forgotten evil because you know only the good; you are within the pearly gates and are living with the souls of shining glory.

You have entered that state wherein the Christ entered when his face did shine as the sun, and his garments were white as the light.

The Hidden Secret

You have entered the presence of God, you have been glorified with His spirit and His love; you have seen His Kingdom God's perfect world that world in which we all may dwell now, providing we not simply believe in God, but have faith in God.

Chapter 16

Have Faith in Faith

To find the hidden secret of faith the principal secret is to have faith in faith.

To have faith in faith is to enter into the very soul of faith, thereby increasing all the powers of faith, and giving mind that inner secret through which everything that is great and extraordinary may be accomplished.

To develop the power of faith, realize that faith is the hidden secret; then direct the whole of attention upon the soul of the hidden secret until you feel that you are in the very life of life itself.

While you are in the very life of life, you are in faith; it is then that you have faith in faith because you are within the within; you are in the secret chamber of the hidden secret; you are in the spirit of the very soul of all existence.

It is in this state that you find the perfect peace, the limitless power and the supreme joy. It is in this state that you find the beautiful calm, the heaven within and the life eternal. It is in this state that the personal will gives way to the divine will, and where we can hear the gentle voice. "Ask what thou will and I will answer thee."

To be in this state is to have faith in faith; we can therefore understand why all things are possible to him who has faith; and why all things shall be according to our faith.

Chapter 17

More on Have Faith in Faith

Whatever you attempt while you have faith in faith that you shall surely accomplish; the power of faith is limitless, and to have faith in faith is to work in the limitless power of faith.

To gain that understanding of truth that knows the real truth the truth that makes man free, the secret is to have faith in faith. More real wisdom comes through having faith in faith than through all other sources combined; though the other sources must not be neglected.

The usual sources of knowledge supply the body, the vehicle, the instrument of wisdom; faith supplies the light, the power, the life, and the soul of wisdom.

By having faith in faith our own faith becomes stronger, larger, higher and more perfect, until we are in real faith; and to be in real faith is to be within the gates of the soul's unbounded domain; to be within the very innermost chamber of life; to be in the spirit itself.

It is therefore evident that nothing can be impossible to him who has faith; and the perfect path to more faith is to have faith in everything and to have faith in that faith.

To have faith in faith is to keep the eye single upon the greater in every kingdom of life; to open the mind to see the greater in all things. The mind that is constantly seeing the greater is constantly entering into the greater, and is therefore eternally becoming greater.

The Hidden Secret

The thoughts we create while in faith are always strong, because the attitude of faith gives higher power to everything; more evidence to prove that faith can do all things.

Faith enlarges all the faculties and spheres of action in the mind of man, and expands consciousness to such an extent that it perpetually breaks bounds and penetrates even those realms that objective man has never known.

The mind that has faith may discover anything at any time, because faith dwells eternally upon the borderland of greater things. Therefore, to develop the power of faith train consciousness to act constantly upon the borderland of the unknown; and train every action of mind to touch the limitless in every part of mental life.

In all these actions, however, the mind must act in faith and must inwardly feel that the seeming void everywhere is solid rock. This removes all timidity about pressing on, into the great unknown, and makes the great unknown a splendid world of reality, even more real than the world that is tangible to the physical senses.

Faith has no fear because faith does not grope blindly in the dark; faith knows; faith can see; faith is in the light and demonstrates that the entire universe is full of light. Through faith we can see much farther than we can reach, therefore know how to proceed. We know where to go, how to go and when to go in order to enter the greater life, the more beautiful life the life that is fairer than ten thousand to the soul.

Every step in advance that may be taken is the result of faith; it is faith only that can lead mind on into larger realms, superior ability and greater powers; therefore, we should give faith the full credit for every increase that appears in life. By doing this the power of faith will increase; and as we receive more faith we shall receive more of everything else that is good in the world.

When faith grows, all good things grow, and there is nothing that promotes the growth of faith more rapidly than to give faith credit for what faith has done; and without faith nothing has been done.

Nothing is accomplished without faith, because every step taken in advance must be preceded by the faith that it is possible.

Faith always leads the way; nor does faith disappear with the improvement of the intellect; it is faith that makes it possible for the intellect to improve. What faith sees the intellect enters into and proceeds to analyze, understand and comprehend; but the intellect never goes where faith has not first revealed a new world of possibility to study and explore.

Chapter 18

Desire and Faith

The greatest power that can be expressed through the mind of man comes from the united actions of desire and faith. This power is actually irresistible; therefore, whatever we desire in faith, that we shall positively receive.

Have faith, and no true desire shall remain unfulfilled; not that we shall always receive the very identical thing desired, because that would frequently prove undesirable; but the desire will be fulfilled. When we do not receive the very thing desired we shall receive something that will serve our purpose far better.

When we express a strong desire, and leave it to faith to fulfill that desire, the very best will be secured; faith lives in a higher light and can see far better than the personal man what would give us the greatest good and the greatest joy. Faith, therefore, acts accordingly, when we have faith in faith, and does not always give us what we ask for, but gives us something better.

The prayer of faith is always answered, and it is the only prayer that is always answered.

The true prayer is the prayer that is expressed while we are in the spirit; and since it is the function of faith to open the way to the spirit and take us into the spirit, the prayer of faith will always be in the spirit.

To pray is not to stand apart and ask God, but to take our desires to God; to enter into the presence of God and receive directly through the spirit whatever we may desire and need.

The Hidden Secret

The prayers that are sent to a distant God are never answered; but the prayers that we personally take to God, through faith, these prayers are always answered. To ask for something is not the only essential in prayer; we must personally enter into the presence of God and personally receive the answer.

To receive from the Infinite what we may desire, or pray for, we must enter into that state where we feel that He is "closer than breathing, nearer than hands and feet;" but it is only through faith that we may enter that sublime state.

While in faith we know that the Infinite is just as desirous to give as we are to receive; and this is absolutely necessary to know and feel, because if we doubt the desire of God to give, or believe that He must be persuaded and implored, our thought of God is wrong; we are out of harmony with God, and cannot enter into His presence to receive what we have asked for.

It is for this reason that the prayer of the righteous availeth much; the righteous is in harmony with God, in perfect oneness with God, in right relations to God, and is therefore in the spirit, in the presence of God.

To be righteous means to be living the right life; and to live the right life is to live with God, to be so near to God that we feel His peaceful and loving presence at all times.

The righteous man has entered into such perfect oneness with the spirit that he can feel that he is living, moving and having his being in the very life of the Supreme. He is, therefore, in the secret places of the Most High, and is so near the throne that he may receive whatever he desires to ask for.

The Hidden Secret

All things that are necessary to the perfect life of man have already been given to man; they are in store for man, in the spirit; and by entering the spirit he may receive them now.

"Whatsoever ye ask and pray for, believe that ye have received, and ye shall have it." No prayer is answered unless we believe that we have received; but faith believes because faith knows. Faith lives in the spirit and knows that anything that man may ask for is already in store for him. To pray is therefore not to stand apart from God and implore, but to enter into the spirit of God and receive from His loving kindness what He is more than willing to give.

Whatever we receive in the spirit, that we also shall receive in the personal life, because whatever comes from the within draws unto itself its own from the without.

We receive from the within only that which we realize we have received in the within; we must feel convinced that all our needs have already been supplied, and that the supply is waiting, in the great spiritual domain, for us to come and take possession; but this conviction comes only through faith, because faith is in the spirit and knows what the spirit has in store.

It is therefore simple to understand why the prayer of faith is always answered; and why those who live by faith have all their desires supplied.

Faith will invariably supply all your needs if you are doing something to justify those needs.

If you are engaged in a large undertaking, and are doing something that has value and worth, everything that you need to carry on that undertaking will be supplied, if you have faith.

Have no fear to begin any good work, no matter how great and extensive it may be; all the essentials will be supplied; your prayers will be answered if uttered in the spirit of faith.

In every phase of personal life the same is true; live a worthy life; live for something worthwhile, and everything you may need to make your own life as large, as ideal, as perfect and as beautiful as you may wish it to be, shall be supplied, and supplied without delay, if all your prayers are uttered in the spirit of faith.

It is prayer and faith united as one that produces the greatest power in the life of man; it is a power that is invincible, therefore, whatever we desire in faith, that we shall positively receive.

Desire wisdom, desire power, desire ability, desire gold and silver if you need them, desire everything necessary to a great and successful life, and have the faith that all your prayers will be answered.

Give your whole life to your desire, and express every desire through the very soul of faith; your desires shall be fulfilled, absolutely without fail. As your faith is, so shall it be unto you.

The Hidden Secret

Chapter 19

Entering into the Life of the Higher Power

When we enter the inner spirit of faith we discover that there is a higher power in man, and all about the being of man; in brief, we live and move in an infinite sea of higher power.

No matter how far we may go in the ascending scale of life, there is always a higher power that we may realize and appropriate for personal, tangible use.

To gain possession of this higher power, faith is the secret; because faith transcends all limitations; faith perpetually transcends; therefore, to live in faith is to pass eternally from the superior to that which is greater than the superior; from that which seems limitless to that which is infinitely larger and more sublime.

In the mind of the average person there is a belief that he is a limited personality, endowed with a certain amount of physical and menial energy; he believes that there is no way to increase that amount, therefore, stamps upon the subconscious the idea of the limitation he has fixed for himself.

The result is that he receives from the limitless source only as much power as his limited, circumscribed mentality can receive and appropriate; he is not aware of the fact that what he does receive comes from the limitless source; nor does he know that the supply received is limited simply because he thinks that his power is limited.

The law is that we receive from the source of limitless power only as much power as we think we possess; therefore, by expanding consciousness so as to realize a larger measure of power we begin to receive this larger measure.

The average person is also unaware of the fact that the supply of power will increase as he prepares to receive the increase, and that he may receive from the limitless source as much power as he can possibly hold in consciousness.

However, when the mind, through faith, rises above its previous circumscribed states, and enters more closely into touch with the Supreme, the truth concerning the entire subject of power is realized.

We then find that we are not endowed with a certain limited amount of life and power that remains fixed, and that perpetuates itself through physical processes during a temporal, personal existence; we find, to the contrary, that we receive daily, and hourly, from the boundless, as much power as we can consciously comprehend at the time; or as much as we have the capacity to receive and appropriate in our present state of consciousness of power.

As consciousness ascends into a higher and a more perfect realization of the eternal and the limitless, the mind is opened more and more to the power that exists in the boundless state; and as the nearness between the individual mind and the Supreme is perfected, the greater capacity to live, to think and to do is realized.

The nearer we feel that we are to the Infinite, the more life and power we receive from the limitless source; and it is through faith that this nearness is attained.

The same law holds in the worlds of freedom, purity, health, harmony, wisdom, joy and love. The nearer we feel we are to the Infinite, the more of these qualities we receive.

The Hidden Secret

The nearer we feel we are to the higher realms the more fully we are conscious of what exists for us in those realms; and the more we are conscious of the more we receive, because whatever we become conscious of that we bring forth into possession and expression.

Every soul should learn to open the mind fully to this higher power, and should never undertake anything without securing the largest possible measure of those energies that come direct from the limitless source.

We shall find that our best and largest work is always done while we are conscious of the immensity of this power within us, and all about us.

All great minds have been inspired and pressed on to remarkable achievements through feeling the presence of this superior power; and it is this power that is responsible for the greatest deeds that the world has seen.

When you realize the presence of this power you feel that you are something more than human; you feel that you are not only a genius, but that you are a giant in mind and soul: you feel that there is a supreme something within you, and this something thrills your entire being with the conviction that nothing is impossible; you feel that you are able to be everything you ever imagined yourself to be, and infinitely more. You are in that world where the limitless actually does exist, and you feel as one that is limitless.

By entering into the life of this higher power, and by depending upon this power at all times, you will positively achieve greatness; and you will discover that this power is your own; your own unbounded power, awakened from the great within.

The Hidden Secret

By depending upon higher power you are depending upon yourself your whole self: you are recognizing the great truth that what is in God is in you, and that all things that belong to the Supreme belong to Man the image and likeness of the Supreme.

To depend upon higher power is not dependence, but the opening of the mind to the limitless life from within. It is therefore the direct path to the highest individual development.

Through the constant appropriation of higher power the small mind becomes great, the ordinary mind becomes a genius, and those who already have ability may double and treble the rare talents they now possess.

To constantly live in the consciousness of higher power will give this power to every thought that mind may create; a fact of extreme importance, because every man, in the personal sense, is the product of his thought.

Through the power of thought anything in the personal life can be changed; but the power of the thought must be equal to every occasion.

It is through thought that man changes himself, changes his environment and creates his own destiny; therefore, if he is to do all that he desires to do, the power of his thought must be limitless.

To live and think in the consciousness of higher power will give unlimited power to thought, and enable the mind to exercise complete mastery over life; and it is through faith that the consciousness of higher power is gained; therefore, nothing is impossible to him who has faith.

The Hidden Secret

When every thought is filled with higher power, nothing but good will come from thought, however powerful the thought may be, because all higher power is constructive, elevating and emancipating. This power is harmony, peace, health, purity and perfection, and gives richly of itself to everything with which it may come in contact.

Since man is constantly thinking, the good that will come when every thought has higher power, can never be measured.

The thought that has power is the thought that is created in faith; the thought that is formed while we feel the presence of higher power.

The strong thought is born of the spirit, and of the spirit only; and it is through faith that we enter the spirit.

It is such thought that heals, and when we learn to create all our thought in the realization of higher power, every person to whom we may give our healing thought will find emancipation.

It is the strong thought that heals, but the strong thought is not that thought that is driven by will-force; thoughts that come from will-force are the weakest of all, and seldom accomplish anything.

The strong thought is the thought that is created in the silent realization of unbounded power.

Such thought has healing on its wings; such thought will fill the body with health, purity and power; such thought will produce complete emancipation wherever its power may be directed; such thought will smoothen the pathway of life, harmonize all the elements of existence, and build for a man a vigorous body, strong character, a powerful mind and an invincible soul.

Be still, and know that you are in the presence of a power that is supreme, a power that can do all things, and every thought you think will contain this power, and will do with this power whatever your heart may desire to have done.

To secure more power do not try to force the power you may already possess, but enter those higher spiritual realms, through faith, where power is limitless; and when you enter that state your thoughts not only become enormously strong, but thinking becomes so smooth and so gentle that you think the most wonderful thoughts and the most powerful thoughts, even without any effort whatever.

When we have great and difficult undertakings before us, we should remain calm, and permit supreme power to enter our thoughts; difficulties will instantaneously disappear, the work will almost do itself, and the goal in view will be reached with as perfect ease as the simplest task we ever performed.

The great achievement will be the result of higher power; not a power coming to us from some separate, outside source, but a higher power all our own — our own unbounded power, awakened from the limitless within.

Experience teaches that it is neither strenuous nor laborious thinking that produces the greatest results in life, but those high, strong thoughts we create while we are in the secret places — in the peace that passeth understanding.

The hidden path to these secret places is faith; to enter faith is to enter the life of higher power, supreme power, limitless power; to enter faith is to enter the very soul of existence and gain possession of that something that produces all the worth, all the goodness and all the beauty of eternal life; to enter faith is to enter that rare and wonderful something that is prepared for them that love Him.

Eye hath not seen, nor ear heard; neither has it entered into the heart of man; but faith knows; faith has found the hidden way; and those who follow faith shall pass through the gates ajar and shall meet Him face to face.

Not in the distant future, in some other sphere of existence; but now, today; the kingdom of heaven is within you, and faith is the hidden secret to its splendor, its glory and its infinite joy.

To have faith in faith is to open the mind to an inner world of sublime existence a life of indescribable beauty and unfathomable joy. It is this life of which we gain occasional glimpses while we are on the mountain top of spiritual thought; and it is in these states that we behold that something that tongue can never picture nor the mind of man understand.

At rare intervals we pass within the pearly gates; we touch the hem of His garment; we are transformed by the presence of His shining glory, and life is not the same any more. We have been in the cosmic state; we have seen real life; and we offer eternal thanksgiving because we are blessed with the privilege of existence; a privilege so great, that to live simply to live that is sufficient.

As we grow in faith we come nearer and nearer to this sublime state of existence, until we dwell on the borderland of its splendor nearly every hour. Later, we may pass the

The Hidden Secret

borderland whenever we so desire, and live almost constantly on that fair eternal shore.

Again, we must remember, that this life is not for some future state of existence; this life is for today; and faith is the perfect way; faith is the hidden secret to the marvelous splendor of the cosmic state.

To train ourselves to live in these beautiful serene realms, where simply to live is everlasting joy, we must learn to be still; never to force anything, but to so live that we constantly depend upon infinite power to come forth and do what the heart may desire to have done.

It is while living in this state that we feel the real presence of higher power invincible power; and it is by giving full and free expression to this power that we transcend all limitations and demonstrate the great truth that all things are possible.

To enter this state faith is the secret the hidden secret; but hidden no more from those who have faith in faith.

To enter faith, turn mind upon the inner side of life, and mentally dwell upon the inner reality that permeates all things. This reality may be termed a shining reality because it is the very essence of light, purity and perfection.

When you are in faith your mind actually enters into this essence, and thereby awakens the unbounded life that absolute reality contains.

It is for this reason that faith can see you through anything; no matter what your obstacles or difficulties may be, simply have faith; faith will see you through. Live in the faith that everything is coming the way you desire, and as your faith is, so shall it be.

Do not permit fear or doubt to enter mind when things fail to look as bright as you may wish; judge not according to appearances; have faith; faith can change anything in your favor, and turn everything to good account for you.

When faith seems to fail, have more faith; and have more faith in faith; you will thereby produce a turn in the lane, because faith can produce anything; faith opens the mind to limitless power, therefore, we can never doubt the power of faith.

When in doubt, have faith, more faith; enter into the very soul of faith and what you have been waiting for shall immediately appear.

Whatever the indications may be, they signify nothing in the presence of faith; faith can turn any failure into the greatest success; faith can lay its hands upon anything that is going backward, and cause it to move forward more rapidly than any undertaking has moved before.

Let not your heart be troubled in the presence of unfavorable indications; simply have faith; faith will see you through; faith never fails; faith can do anything, providing we continue ceaselessly in faith, and have abundance of faith in the limitless power of faith.

Chapter 20

Faith For Everyday Living

Faith is not for a part of life; faith is for the whole of life; therefore, the power of faith should be applied to every phase of practical everyday living; but to secure the best results from faith in daily, objective work we must not look upon external success as a material, inferior product.

All things are good when turned to good account; and all success will be turned to good account when we live, think and work in faith.

Faith does not stand apart from the physical world, waiting to minister to certain obscure spiritual wants only; faith is ready to turn its power into everything and has the power to produce success through everything; but faith will not cooperate with those things that are looked down upon and condemned by man.

The power of faith does not work apart from present physical means and methods; but uses these methods for the attainment of the highest results that are possible now.

You do not have to change your occupation to introduce faith into practical life; if your occupation is legitimate, remain where you are; use the methods you have used before, no matter how material they may seem to be; make no startling changes in the without; meet the world in the usual way, and deal with the world in a way that the world can understand, knowing that all things are good that are turned to good account; but make this change give your occupation soul by working in faith.

The Hidden Secret

By working in faith you bring forth a greater power from within, a power that will permeate every part of your occupation, a power that will expand, enlarge, and develop your business, a power that will purify your business and elevate the entire undertaking to a higher plane.

Upon this higher plane your efforts will be promoted on a far more extensive scale, you will have greater success than ever before, the products of your work will be superior in worth, value and quality, and your usefulness to the race will become greater and greater in proportion.

The industrial world will not be purified by making changes in the without, but by awakening the higher powers from within; the man who enters the industrial world may not expect to reach his goal in view by hard work on the surface, but by permeating his work with limitless power from within.

This he may do by having faith in his work; by thinking of his work as good, not material, and by having such a perfect faith in faith that fear concerning results is entirely eliminated from his mind.

The greatest obstacle to real, true success in any sphere of human endeavor is fear, fear concerning results; faith removes this fear absolutely, therefore, faith is indispensable in the industrial world.

No man is equipped for any undertaking in life unless he has faith the real, living faith; the faith that does things; the faith that can make all things possible.

Chapter 21

Banish Fear; Have Faith

In the attitude of faith the mind sees the ideal, the real, the perfect, and patterns all thinking according to the vision or that greater life; and since man is as he thinks, by thinking greater thoughts he becomes a greater man.

In the attitude of fear the imagination pictures all kinds of false, imperfect, inferior and even monstrous forms of thought; all of these work themselves out in mind, character and personal life, thereby burdening the system with all kinds of detrimental conditions. Such conditions interfere so seriously with everything that man may try to do, that the failure he feared must inevitably follow.

To follow faith is to move forward steadily and surely, even under the most adverse and trying conditions; to follow fear is to go down to failure and defeat even under the most favorable conditions in existence.

To banish fear, have faith; the only infallible remedy for fear is faith; faith in all things, and at all times.

Faith sees the substance and gains the substance; fear sees the shadow and is soon left with nothing but the shadow.

The man who fears looks upon the lesser, thereby becoming lesser for every passing day; the man who has faith keeps the eye single upon the larger, thereby entering the path of perpetual increase.

The Hidden Secret

Fear, by looking down, compels the mind to create the lower; faith, by looking up, causes the mind to create the superior.

Fear expects the human side to prevail, and believes the worst is coming, thereby causing the weak human side to prevail, and bringing the worst to pass. Faith continues to believe that the divine side will prevail, thereby causing the divine side to gain supremacy.

When mind is in the attitude of faith there is no fear of adversity; there is not even any thought of adversity, because while in faith the mind is above all adverseness; it is in peace, harmony and rightness; it is in the life of that power that can, and does cause everything to move smoothly, and all things to work together for good.

While in faith the mind has no fear of failure; faith never thinks of failure; faith sees the possibilities of success; faith knows that success in every instance is possible because it knows that all things are possible; faith does not ask if success will come, but opens the mind to the great power within that positively will produce success.

When in the attitude of faith the mind has no fear whatever, because fear, in any form, is absolutely out of the question when you realize that you live and move and have your being in the spirit of the infinite; and to enter faith is to enter completely into this high and wonderful realization.

When the mind is in fear, attention is centered upon evil; when the mind is in faith, attention is centered upon the good; therefore, fear creates evil in mind and character, while faith creates only the good. We always think about that upon which our attention is centered; and what we think about that we create in our own mentalities.

The Hidden Secret

This being true, we can readily understand why the things we fear come upon us, and why we always receive the things we desire in faith.

To desire, with the whole heart and soul, what we need or wish for, and to place unbounded faith in that desire, will in every instance produce results.

This principle can be applied to everything on all planes of life; there is therefore, no reason why anyone should ever want for anything.

Faith is the hidden secret to all supply, and he who enters faith, by having faith in faith, will find the world of limitless supply.

To the mind of mere reason this may not seem true, but it is true; faith knows it to be true, and the light of faith is higher than the light of reason. It is, therefore, well in the beginning, not to reason too much about the why's and the wherefore's of faith.

To reason about that which the outer mind cannot understand will confuse consciousness and prevent that serene state of perfect assurance which is necessary to faith.

Know that faith can do everything: and know that faith will reveal to you exactly how it is done; then have more faith; before long, faith will become so strong that even reason will be convinced, and will cooperate with faith in demonstrating to the outer mind that the claims of faith are true absolutely true.

What you do not understand leave to faith; faith is the hidden secret to all understanding, and by having faith in faith, the secret of everything will be revealed to you.

The Hidden Secret

Since faith is the hidden secret, to enter into faith is to enter into this same secret; henceforth, nothing will be hidden from you.

To him who lives in faith there are no problems; life is clear, the purpose of life is clear, the law of living the life is clear, the path to endless ascension in life is clear everything is clear; and it is also clear that all things will be according to the measure of faith.

Chapter 22

The Hidden Secret

Faith knows; faith is not blind; faith is in the real light and sees everything; faith is never misled, because it is a superior vision, a keener insight and a higher understanding. It is therefore safe to follow faith, and whenever we follow faith wherever faith may go, whatever comes will be good very good.

All things will work together for good when we live in faith, and constantly follow the light of faith.

Whatever you undertake to do, expect to be guided by faith, have faith in the superior wisdom of faith, and depend upon faith to give you the insight that knows when to act, and the power required to secure the very best and the very greatest results. You positively cannot fail, because as your faith is, so shall it be.

When you have found your work, have faith, and press on. Do not stop to wonder if you are to succeed; have the faith that you will succeed, and nothing in the world can prevent you from reaching the very highest goal you may have in view.

Do not wonder what is going to happen, but proceed to create those events and circumstances that will be favorable to the purpose you have in mind. This anyone can do who works with the Infinite, and works in faith.

Do not wait for things to come your way; take hold of things and turn them the way they ought to be; faith will give you the power.

The Hidden Secret

When things go wrong, have faith; depend upon faith to set them right, and the limitless power that is back of faith will appear to fulfill your desire.

When in the midst of changes expect every change to be an open door to better things than you ever knew before; live in that faith; permeate your whole heart, your whole life and your whole soul with that faith, and as your faith is, so shall it be.

When you have obligations to meet, bills to pay, and have not the essentials required, have faith; never worry nor feel anxious for a moment; know that faith can open to you the realms of limitless supply, and know that faith will do this if you have faith in faith.

Whatever you need place the matter in the hands of faith; faith will find a way; faith will reveal to you the necessary opportunities through which you may accomplish what you desire and meet your obligations. Do not ask how, simply depend upon faith; you will soon know how; have faith in faith and the hidden secrets of faith will be fully revealed to you.

Never be disturbed if results should fail to appear at once; know that faith will open the way before it is too late; and the same shall positively be done.

Again, we must remember not to depend simply upon a mere belief in faith, but to mentally dwell in the very soul of faith.

When you have faith in things, take heart and mind and soul into the real spirit of things and you enter the spirit of faith; you enter real faith the hidden secret, and the great secret is hidden to you no more.

The Hidden Secret

Faith never fails when you enter into the soul of faith while having faith; this is one of the greatest of all truths; and the man who accepts this truth will have unlimited power placed at his command.

To enter faith is to enter the life of the limitless power that is within us and all about us; to have faith real faith, is to open the mind to the influx of that power from within that can do all things; therefore, to have faith the deep, strong, soul faith, is to reduce failures to nothing.

This is another great truth that should be proclaimed from every housetop, and reechoed throughout the world.

Have faith, and whatever you may undertake to do, that you shall surely accomplish. Limitless power cannot fail, and faith opens the mind to that power.

This proves conclusively that faith is the hidden secret the very secret of all secrets. Faith has the secret, therefore it pays no attention to appearances nor external indications; faith works upon the principle that whatever we have the desire to accomplish, that we have the power to accomplish; faith works upon this principle because it knows that there is unbounded power in man; and faith also knows that man can gain conscious possession of this power by having faith in faith.

One of the greatest essentials to the attainment of the more beautiful life is to realize the reality of the real; and to produce this realization is one of the principal functions of faith.

Faith is interior understanding; faith can look beyond the world of sense and see things as they are; faith can see what is in the real, what can be done through the realization of the real, what ought to be done to express the real, and how this may be done now; or what should be done now to work up to the high ideals we may have in view.

If you wish to realize your ideals follow faith; faith will guide you perfectly, and provide everything you may require to reach your lofty goal.

Faith always brings us into harmony with the inner, finer essence of things; hence its enormous power.

Faith opens the door to the great unknown, and proves that the great unknown is simply an extension an endless extension, of that which is known.

Faith is the evidence of things not seen, because faith does see what has not been seen; faith knows that the unseen is real and substantial; faith proves that the unseen can be seen by those who will awaken the superior mind within; therefore, by entering into faith we enter into the realization of the real and see all things as they are in the perfect state.

Faith proves that the great unknown is unknown only to those who have not begun to live the larger life; but to follow faith is to enter the new life, because faith goes on and reveals the wonders and the powers of the larger spheres of existence; not simply those spheres that may exist beyond the scope of sense, but also those spheres that exist all about us, here and now, within the very world of sense.

In every vocation, in every study and in every field of thought, there are new worlds of unbounded possibilities, which when discovered and developed will add immeasurably to the real worth of life.

The Hidden Secret

Never yearn for new worlds to conquer, nor complain because there are no opportunities at hand for you; there are a million worlds rich, marvelous worlds at your very door; turn your attention to these and you shall have opportunities without number, not simply for the present, but for ages yet to be.

The hidden secret to these new worlds is faith; enter faith and a new universe shall be given to you; a universe that is more real and substantial than anything you have known before; a universe that is marvelous in beauty, and filled with possibilities more numerous than the sands of the shore.

In faith consciousness is constantly on the verge of the great unknown, receiving glimpses of the great beyond; when faith disappears our visions of greater things are gone; but when faith returns again we see the same marvels, and know that we shall tangibly possess them in the coming days.

To try to become conscious of something that is beyond the present capacity of consciousness, produces a shock to the mind; a fact that everyone knows who has tried to comprehend the universe with the limitations of the personal mind; but when the mind works and thinks in faith, consciousness expands constantly, naturally and of its own accord, thus producing perpetual and normal growth of mind.

To understand the universe, to understand God, to understand life these things are impossible without faith; to try to do so simply shocks the mind; but in faith these things are readily understood without the slightest mental effort. High truths come as clear, vivid revelations to the mind that thinks in faith.

Faith does not simply believe; faith knows; real faith is a superior understanding, and deals with tangible facts on all planes.

It is not the function of faith to blindly accept, but to give man the wisdom, and the power to do greater things. Real faith goes to work, but asks no questions about results. Faith knows that all is possible now, and acts accordingly. Faith enters the larger life and takes up the greater undertakings as if there were no obstacles, and discovers that obstacles cannot exist anywhere.

The only semblance of obstacles that can be found are the limitations that we believe to exist within our own conscious actions. Consciousness goes out so far, reaches so far, and where it ends today we imagine our obstacle to be. We fear to go on farther because beyond the reach of present consciousness there seems to be nothing. There seems to be nothing because we have not gone on any farther to see; but when we follow faith and press on, we find the seeming void to be solid rock.

Faith knows that the obstacle we think we see is an illusion; it does not exist in reality; it is only a belief produced by our inability to reach any further than we do; but faith dispels this belief; faith leads consciousness on in every direction, and proves to mind that we may go as far as we like anywhere, we shall find substantial footing everywhere, without a single obstacle in the way.

Faith knows that there is something everywhere; and to him who has faith this something is revealed.

For this reason faith is the substance of things hoped for; faith enters into the very life and substance of that which

The Hidden Secret

is desired, thereby finding the substance and gaining possession of the coveted treasure.

Faith is the hidden secret, therefore is in the substance of all things; to have faith in things is to enter into the substance of things, into the secret life of things; faith is the soul, the inner substance of all mental actions, of all desires and hopes; therefore faith is the substance of things hoped for, and brings that substance into tangible possession.

No thought should end in hope; the thought that ends in hope produces failure; the thought that passes from hope to faith will succeed under any and every circumstance. The reason why is most evident.

Hope stands on the outside, faith walks in; hope waits to be guided, faith trusts in its own light and proceeds; hope expects to receive external help, faith awakens its own limitless powers and produces results without help; hope is ever waiting for things to come right, faith goes to work and turns all things into the right; hope hopes for the best, faith lives and works in the faith that the best must come, thereby creating the best and the best only.

Faith can do all things because it uses all things and works in harmony with all things. Faith enters into the very life of life, and is therefore in the soul of life; to be in the soul of life is to feel, realize and receive the life that contains all power, all wisdom and all love.

Through faith man can do all things, because faith awakens that something in man that can do all things.

If ye have faith as a grain of mustard seed, ye shall say unto this mountain, Remove hence to yonder place; and it shall remove; and nothing shall be impossible unto you.

The Hidden Secret

This remarkable statement, coming from the greatest mind that has appeared upon earth, offers more evidence absolutely conclusive evidence, to substantiate the assertion that faith is the hidden secret.

No attainment is therefore greater than the attainment of faith; neither can any other attainment reach its highest state of efficiency, perfection and power, unless it is based upon faith, animated by faith and developed through faith. The Highest and best can never be reached without faith, because faith alone is the hidden secret to all that is high, worthy and superior in man.

Faith does not come to take the place of other attainments; faith comes to give real soul and higher power to every attainment; and to awaken in many possibilities he has never known before.

Faith does not come to supersede skill, intellect and ability, nor to reduce work to a minimum; faith comes to unite all work, all skill and all ability with the limitless powers of the great within; therefore, the man who unites these three — work, ability and faith — shall accomplish everything he may undertake to do. When these three are made One, failure is annihilated completely, and the greatest success is positively in store.

Work with the most perfect skill that you can possibly develop, but fill your work with the limitless power of unbounded faith; become as learned, as intellectual and as highly cultured in mind as possible, but illumine that prodigious intellect with the radiant spirit of faith; make the fullest use of all physical functions and all mental talents, but animate every action of mind and body with the invincible power of faith.

The Hidden Secret

Give faith to everything, have faith in everything, unite faith with everything, and everything shall be filled with that power that makes all things possible.

If you wish to reach the highest places that life has in store for man have faith, and your wish shall positively come true. It is faith that awakens the higher and greater within you, thereby elevating all your faculties to the highest state of efficiency; it is faith that opens the mind to that superior power that alone can create the prodigy and the genius; it is faith that gives such a rare quality to everything you do that both you and your work are stamped universally with the mark of high worth.

It is faith that fills the soul with that strange determination that carries you on and on through all sorts of conditions, and finally brings you to the very mountaintop of attainment and achievement.

It is faith alone that produces real greatness; that greatness that can never die, but forever remains as an inspiration to all the world.

What the personal man is today matters nothing; where the personal man may live today matters nothing; faith can change everything.

Have faith, and sorrow, sickness, trouble and misfortune shall vanish completely; all mountains shall be removed, and nothing shall be impossible unto you.

Have faith, and all your desires shall positively be fulfilled; faith and desire united as One can bring anything, produce anything, create anything, and cause anything to transpire in the life of man.

The Hidden Secret

Faith gives invincible power to everything; faith is the hidden secret to all power; therefore, to enter faith is to enter the secret of faith, and the secret is hidden from you no more; the great within is opened before you, and unlimited power is at your command.

"Come where glory waits thee," this is the call of faith; not in some other sphere of existence, but here and now. Follow faith, and you shall enter greatness and power, wealth and glory, wisdom and genius, worth and superiority, peace and joy.

Enter faith the very soul of faith, and you enter into the very presence of the Infinite, thereby placing yourself in the very life, the very power, the very wisdom and the very love of God. God will therefore be with you in everything you may undertake to do; and when God is with you, nothing is impossible. You feel His presence, and you are filled with His life at all times; this life is supreme, limitless, invincible; therefore, everything must pass before it that your prayer may be answered and His will be done.

To enter into the very soul of faith is to speak to the Infinite in the beautiful language of faith; and this is the prayer of faith; Infinite Father. I thank Thee that Thou hearest my prayer; I thank Thee that Thou hearest me always. I thank Thee that Thou hast already given me all that my heart can wish for, all that my life may need, for the time that is and the eternity that is to be; and now, with supreme joy and unspeakable thanksgiving, I come to Thee to receive Thy gifts, and receive from Thy loving hands the divine blessings that Thou hast, from all eternity, treasured for me.

This is the prayer of faith; this is the prayer that is always answered; this is the prayer without ceasing; the

The Hidden Secret

prayer that becomes a consecrated life the life that is lived with God.

Faith is in the spirit; faith knows that God has given us everything now, and that it is His will that all our prayers should be answered now. Everything that we may need to live the full life, the perfect life, the beautiful life the life that is fairer than ten thousand to the soul everything that is necessary to this life, is ready for us in His kingdom now; but we must enter into His presence to receive our own, and faith is the gates ajar.

Faith is the hidden secret to every desire and need of man; therefore, all things are possible to him who has faith; and all things desired shall come to him who lives, thinks and acts in the very soul of that faith that is faith.

In Light of The Spirit

In Light of the Spirit

Table of Contents

Chapter 1 - Leave it to God	84
Chapter 2 - The Highest Prayer	87
Chapter 3 - The Religion of the Soul	91
Chapter 4 - The Spiritual Side of Life	98
Chapter 5 - The Mysteries of the Kingdom	109
Chapter 6 - The Secret of Spiritual Power	122
Chapter 7 - The Use of Spiritual Power	127
Chapter 8 - The Light of Inner Consciousness	131
Chapter 9 - The Power of Spiritual Transparence	135
Chapter 10 - Upon the Path Where All is Good	145
Chapter 11 - The I AM is the Way	159
Chapter 12 - I Go Unto the Father	169
Chapter 13 - I AM With You Always	181
Chapter 14 - It Is Well With the Soul	193
Chapter 15 - The Spiritual Borderland	201
Chapter 16 - When God So Wills	209
Chapter 17 - Regions of Infinite Repose	214

Chapter 1

Leave it to God

When you are confronted with problems that you cannot solve, or find yourself in the midst of conditions that are distressing and adverse, do not permit yourself to become disturbed for a moment. There is a simple secret that will invariably set you free and change everything for the best. And the secret is this "Leave It To God." When you do not know what course to pursue, leave it to God. When you do not know where to turn, or how to dispel the darkness that may surround you, then leave it to God. When you do not know where the path to the greatest good may lie, and have not become conscious of that supreme light of the soul through which all things may be discerned rest serenely in the faith that you can leave it all to God. In His hands everything is safe; and whatever we place in His hands, will be disposed of in the best conceivable manner.

It is remarkable how soon darkness takes flight, how soon confusion is stilled, how soon conditions adjust themselves and how soon adversities change into blessings, when we can say, in perfect faith, and in perfect sincerity of soul "Leave It To God." For thus we place everything in the keeping of a Wisdom that knows what should be done, and in the hands of a Power that can do what is best for all concerned. It is the best for everybody that we all desire; it is the happiest outcome of everything that we pray for as the most perfect ideal of visible existence; and we know full well that such an ideal will surely be realized when we leave it to God. The Infinite can solve our problems, and so arrange all things in life, that the greatest good will come to pass, regardless of time, place or circumstances. And we should not hesitate to seek the superior guidance of the Infinite in this regard, whether our problems be great or small, momentous or insignificant.

Whatever the matter may be, we should leave it to God. The sun will soon shine once more, and all will be well again. There are many things we may wish to do, but do not know whether to begin now or later. There is someone, however, who does know; and if we leave it to Him, something will happen to delay the matter, if that is best, or to bring about a speedy beginning, if that is best. And afterwards, when we see how delightfully all things worked out, we will be glad very glad, that we did say, when in doubt "Leave It To God."

We frequently come to places where the whole world seems to be against us; when every friend seems to be gone; and when adversity seems to make life a useless desert of waste and desolation. But at such times we should not be disheartened or dismayed. There is a way to freedom. There is a Light that is stronger than all the darkness in the world. There is a Power that can change everything in our entire destiny. There is a Love that can bring to us the friendship and the sympathy of all mankind. Then why should we ever be discouraged or sad? There is a royal path that leads out of, and away, from all adversities. And we may find that path if we leave it to God.

When we can say, in perfect faith and sincerity of soul, that we will leave it to God, we place ourselves in that state of being where the power of the Infinite can work for us, and through us, to the end that the best may surely come to pass. The Infinite is always at hand, waiting to be of service; but we must be willing to accept such service; and we do accept when we can say with depth of sincerity "Leave It To God."

Then we must know, and fully believe, that what we leave to God to do, will be done right; and we must realize that when anything is done right, every trace of evil, sin, pain or sorrow is eliminated completely. God will never bring sickness, pain, want or death to any human soul. It is not the will of God that any human being should suffer, or be deprived of anything that is good in the world. The ways of the Infinite do not lead into pain and privation, but always into greater freedom, greater good, greater power, greater joy.

When we leave anything to God, we may know that the wrong alone will be taken away; the good will remain and be multiplied again and again, without end and without measure. We may rest assured, therefore, that nothing that is worthy or good or beautiful will be lost when we leave things to God. The kingdom of the Supreme, with all its riches and glory, is for man; but man must be willing to receive; and he does express perfect willingness when he can say, with the faith of the soul, that he will, henceforth, leave everything to God.

Whatever there is in life that we wish to change, remedy or perfect, the simple secret is this "Leave It To God." And we should make this statement in that deep feeling of the soul that knows that feeling that seems to say to us that our wish will be realized, our prayer will be answered the best will come to pass. In truth, how could it be otherwise? God would not have it otherwise; therefore, when we leave all things to Him, we may know that the outcome will be all that we could have wished for and infinitely more.

Chapter 2

The Highest Prayer

We know that the prayer of the righteous availeth much; but we also know there are many prayers that seemingly are not answered prayers that are sincere, and that come from souls that we know to be righteous. And accordingly, the question arises again and again, how we should so pray that we may not pray in vain.

When we consider the subject of prayer, however, and examine the true spiritual significance of prayer, we find that we have, in the past, mistaken both the purpose of prayer and the attitude of the Infinite toward the needs of man. We find, in the first place, that God has already given His kingdom to man; and therefore we need not ask for anything whatever. There is nothing we can ask for that we have not already received. Why then should we ask again, or pray in any form or manner?

We find in the second place, that although God has given us everything, still we do not always gain personal possession of the gifts of his infinite kindness and love. And therefore, this entire theme becomes, for the time being, exceedingly mysterious. But the mystery disappears completely when we consider this theme through the understanding of the highest prayer. And the highest prayer may be expressed, in the simplest and most beautiful manner, through this remarkable statement: "My Father, I thank thee that thou hearest me always."

The highest prayer does not ask, directly, for anything that may be desired; but gives constant, and deep spiritual recognition, to the great truth, that the Infinite has, from the very beginning, given all things to man that may be needed for growth and ascension throughout eternity. And in addition to this recognition, gives expression to ceaseless gratitude, and sincere, unending thanksgiving. In the language of the highest prayer, we do not ask God to give us what we need or desire; we affirm, in spirit and in truth, that God is giving us all these things now. And we add, to all our affirmations, this beautiful, inspiring statement: "I thank thee that thou hearest me always."

When the body is ailing, we do not ask for health. We affirm, "God is now and forever giving me perfect health." And, "The perfect health of the Infinite fills me through and through, because I AM in God, and God is in me." We affirm, "God is giving me power"; "God is giving me peace"; "God is giving me increase"; "God is giving me the gifts of the spirit." In brief, whatever we find that we need in life, physically, mentally or spiritually, we affirm that God is now giving us all these things. And this is absolutely true. God is closer than breathing; therefore knows what we need every hour, and supplies every need at once, whatever that need may be.

We shall find a remarkable difference in the working out of all our circumstances, material and spiritual, when we change our mode of prayer; that is, when we no longer implore the Infinite to give us what we need, but affirm, with sincere thanksgiving, that God is giving us all these things now.

God is eternally giving to man the all good of life; and God is giving to each human soul every day what is needed for that day. It would therefore be wrong to implore God to do what He already is doing. Instead, we should recognize His goodness by speaking this truth "God is now giving me all that I need." And in addition, we should give expression to our most sincere and heartfelt gratitude.

In Light of the Spirit

When we recognize, in spirit and in truth, what God is doing for us, we enter into harmony with the act of His giving; and accordingly, we receive every day everything that is given to us for that day. But when we do not recognize this great truth, we are not in harmony with anything that the Supreme may be doing for us; and therefore we do not receive, at the right time and place, what has truly been given to us as our very own. And possibly we may never receive those gifts in this life, but may have to depend altogether upon our own efforts for everything efforts that are sometimes disappointing, and frequently ineffectual.

The truth is, however, that no soul is destined to depend upon personal efforts alone. We all must, indeed, use our powers and talents well; but we can accomplish but little if we work entirely alone, that is, apart from higher power and divine guidance. Great souls invariably seek constant assistance from the Supreme; and wherever they go, they always "walk with God." Such souls invariably recognize the great law, "My Father worketh and I work," and enter into the spiritual realization of that law absolutely. We must take God with us in all things, if we would rise above mere existence, and be true to the wonderful life we have been given the privilege to live. And we do take God with us in all things when we constantly recognize the truth that God is with us always, and that He is giving us every hour what we need to make that hour full, perfect and complete.

When we understand this law, that God is constantly giving to man everything that is necessary to make life all that we wish it to be, and place ourselves in perfect harmony with that law, we shall find that every need will be supplied in its true place and time. The right way will always open through which we may gain what we desire, and realize the ideals that the great eternal now holds in store.

In Light of the Spirit

Every day will be full to overflowing with blessings of every conceivable state or being. Every succeeding day will become richer and larger than the days that have gone before, as we become more and more conscious of the great truth, that God is giving us everything today that is needed to make this the greatest day we ever knew. And in all our efforts we will be guided, to the end that we may invariably do what is best knowing that higher power will be with us so long as we live and work for the larger life and the greater good.

Chapter 3

The Religion of the Soul

Religion is always of the soul; its purpose invariably is to save the soul; and it is only insofar as it is absolutely true to that purpose that any form of religion can retain its influence and power. Whenever a religion no longer lives and works exclusively for its original purpose, it begins to fail; and there is nothing else that can ever cause religion to fail, whatever its form or creed may be. If it is true to its purpose, it will live and grow, and advance in its methods according to the changing needs of a growing humanity. What it means to save the soul, however, is something that resolves itself largely into what each individual may have realized in his own spiritual attainments. But as most individuals develop in groups, we find the human race separated into a number of spiritual divisions, all having the same purpose in view saving the soul but differing, more or less, both as to method and as to the meaning of this one common purpose.

When we examine these spiritual divisions more closely we find that they naturally arrange themselves into two special divisions, one of these much larger than the other. The larger division takes the literal view, believing in literal methods with which to save a literal soul from literal suffering, in a literal, localized future. The smaller division, however, takes the spiritual view, giving the literal phase of all life an insignificant position.

In all ages we have found these two special divisions, the two sometimes blending in places so that a distinct line of demarcation could not be readily drawn. But regardless of this interblending, the two principal factors the literal and the spiritual have always been prominent; the one always standing apart from the other. And the reason for this is readily found when we know that we have had, in every age, what may be called children in the faith; that is, men and women whose spiritual understanding has not been developed sufficiently to enable them to go beyond the literal significance of things. And we have also had, in every age, the enlightened, who could discern the spiritual elements that are within all things.

We all are familiar with the literal conception of the soul and its salvation; and we know that it contains but a fragment of the whole truth. It is the best, however, that the children in the faith can understand; therefore we must be tolerant, and also thankful that they have actually entered upon the great spiritual journey the goal of which is complete emancipation, soul mastery and spiritual illumination. But we are not so familiar with the spiritual conception of this eternal theme. And as the spiritual conception will henceforth become more and more prominent in all the great religions the advancement of the race towards the spiritual having become more pronounced than ever before in history it will be well to give closer attention to its real or interior significance.

According to the spiritual understanding of life and its purpose, the saving of the soul means the living of a life which will prevent the soul from stepping outside of the path at any time; in brief, saving life from all those adverse consequences that invariably follow when the soul, even for a short time, steps out of the true pathway of life. Salvation therefore according to the spiritual view, is not merely for the future, or for the great eternal now, but for every moment in eternity.

The true pathway of life is the eternal path of an endless ascension the soul rising ever and ever into higher and higher states of existence. It is the path of wisdom and light, the path of freedom and truth the straight and narrow path the path leading directly towards the spiritual heights; but it is not a path of suffering. There is neither suffering nor bondage upon this path. It is only when we step outside this path that we suffer. So long as we are on the path, then all is well, and we are daily rising into more perfect realizations of larger joys, higher states of being and a greater measure of all that is worthy and good.

This being true, we have everything to gain, both of things temporal and of things eternal, by so living that the soul is always on the path. And what is more, every soul was created to follow the path must sooner or later begin to follow the path absolutely in order to work out its own sublime destiny. Knowing this, we realize that we have nothing to gain through delay. Every moment spent outside the path simply means more suffering for the near future; while every moment spent upon the path means more real enjoyment, more wisdom, more power, a greater measure of freedom and a larger life for the near future.

It is absolutely true that what time we spend outside the path is time wasted, for what experience we may gain on the outside is of no value to the soul in its advancement towards mastership and illumination. On the contrary, such experience is a burden that will have to be cast aside before we can proceed on our upward journey. Here we must remember that the only experience that will prove of value is that which we gain while living uncompromisingly upon the true eternal pathway. It is only sound principles that will avail when we meet problems for solution. It is only light that can add to the measure of light. And it is only on the path that light can be found. When the soul steps outside of this path, it is lost; and continues lost so long as it remains outside the path. But the moment the soul returns to the path, it is saved, saved for the present, but not necessarily for the entire future. We are living only for the now the great eternal now, and every moment in the future must care for itself. The steps we take today are sufficient for this day; therefore all our prayers must be, "Just For Today."

Salvation therefore is a spiritual process that must ever be present something we shall need every hour. For although we may be saved now on the path now we may at any time step out again if we do not continue to live absolutely according to the principles of divine truth. And when we step out of the path, the soul is lost again for the time being; it has gone astray, and is going wrong, going contrary to the laws of its being. The result will be pain and suffering, so that the lost soul is more or less in torment; and that torment never ceases so long as the soul continues to be lost, or continues on the outside of the path. Here then we find the origin of the belief in ceaseless or endless torment for the lost soul; for torment is ceaseless on the outside of the path. But the other side of that same truth is this, that the soul can be saved at any time can at any time in eternity step in on the path again and be free.

The cause of all suffering is found in this tendency of the soul to step outside of the path the path provided by the infinite laws of eternal ascension. And the cause of this tendency is found in the soul's natural desire for growth, this desire, in its undeveloped stages, prompting the mind to seek all places for experience and truth. Thus the misdirection of mental action is originated, and the soul turns frequently, both to the left and the right, hoping to find the one thing we all seek the life more abundant, knowing instinctively that a greater measure of life will bring a greater measure of all other things needed in the living of a full life.

The life more abundant, however, can be realized only as our living on the path becomes more and more perfect.

In Light of the Spirit

Therefore, the functions of a true religion are to help man live continually on the path, and to live the life on the path more and more perfectly. Every effort made by real religion must have this one object in view to help every soul to live on the path continually. It is only in this way that a religion can be true to its purpose to save the soul and to be what it was founded to be a religion of the soul.

This gives us a new view of religion a much larger view; and it is a view that makes religion indispensable. It makes, religion the greatest power in the life of man, both in the temporal and the spiritual; for if religion applied its full power, then every soul would be saved now, would be on the path now, and therefore would neither produce suffering for itself nor for others. Every soul would be living for the good, would be building for the good, and would constantly add to the peace, the joy and the welfare of all. And this is the very condition of life we have all hoped to see established upon earth; but we have not given sufficient attention to the principal thing.

The principal thing is to keep the soul on the path continually to keep every soul on the path continually. And this is the work of religion the true religion the religion of the soul. We realize therefore what a tremendous power the religions of the world would become if they would rise out of the literal into the spiritual; if they all would work ceaselessly to save every soul now not from future torment, but from wrong living in the present; if they would give less attention to the helping of man to die, and more attention to the helping of man to live to live on the path, here and now in this world. The coming religion, which will be in every, sense of the term a religion of the soul, will concern itself directly with this great work the greatest work of all the world that of guiding the soul of man so perfectly that we all may live continually on the path, and thus be saved from every pain and ill now a complete salvation both for time and eternity.

In working for such a salvation, however, the coming religion will not forget the great truth that the soul must, in order to continue on the path, continue to move forward on the path. For we know full well that we almost invariably step out of the path the moment we cease to move forward. Therefore, the true religion of the soul must be prepared to teach the human race all the principles of a continuous spiritual attainment; and must possess a science of living through which any individual can learn the sublime art of living on the path. Thus we realize that religion in the future will become a far greater factor in human life than it has ever been in the past. And instead of dying out, as some believe, religion is being born again born into the consciousness of its real mission that of helping the human race to live On the Path here in this world saving the soul of man from all the ills of life in the great eternal now.

The spiritual conception of the saving of the soul is in perfect harmony with the central idea of salvation that of going to heaven; for the soul, when on the path, is going directly to heaven; in truth, is in the beginning of a heavenly life, and is steadily rising into higher and higher heavens eternally.

To be on the path is to be one with God; and to be one with God is surely a foretaste of heaven; it is the beginnings of the joys that cannot be measured, of the peace that passeth understanding, of the bliss that angels alone can know. Then we must remember that to be on the path is to be free from every ill in the world; and that in itself is heaven enough for many and many a day.

In Light of the Spirit

To live on the path, however, is not merely a secret to freedom from the ills of temporal life as important as that may be. It is far more than this, for it is a path the only path that leads to the spiritual heights, to all the glories and splendors of cosmic existence, to all the sublime attainments of the master state to that higher world of wisdom and power wherein the soul of man shall be able to fulfill the great promise, "What I have done, ye shall do, and even greater things."

It is such a goal, high and wonderful as it may be, that lies before us all. It is such a future that is in store for every human soul. But to reach that goal, and realize that future, we must follow the path. Is it not important then more important than all else in the world that we live on the path continually, never for a moment turning to the right nor to the left. And it is indeed time that all religions and all spiritual movements consecrate themselves absolutely to this great and wonderful work.

The world is awakening to the spiritual vision. The race is no longer satisfied with the limitations of the letter. And the individual wants a plan of salvation that will save the soul both for time and for eternity that will give complete emancipation now. And the religion of the soul is coming to answer the call a religion that will help the soul of man to live, On the Path, here in this world, in the great eternal now.

Chapter 4

The Spiritual Side of Life

When we examine our mode of living, we shall find that we dwell upon the spiritual side of life only upon rare and occasional intervals, while most of the time we permit consciousness to come out into the personality and sometimes remain for days, weeks, or months, upon the personal side of existence; we find that during this period soul activity becomes passive, and in consequence the personality does not have the benefit of that greater spiritual power which is necessary in order that we may meet and overcome every problem and condition in life.

This being true, it is most important that we learn to live, more and more, upon the spiritual side of consciousness so that we may gain possession of a larger measure of this higher power which alone can give emancipation to the personality and higher wisdom to mind and intellect.

We realize that we are not here to drift with the stream, or to fold our arms passively and say that we will let the best come to pass. The truth is, that if there be anything we want, we must work for it. If we wish to make life ideal, we must make it so ourselves. These things do not come to us simply through mere passivity or expectation. We know that we are living in an imperfect world, a world which is in the process of growth; therefore, we necessarily meet undeveloped conditions on every side; and if we remain in a passive condition, or simply drift with the stream, many of those undeveloped conditions will come into our own world, and not only disturb the order of our personal existence, but produce a great many adverse conditions, both within ourselves and in our environment. For this reason, we must make ourselves stronger than all those conditions; that is, we must rise above adversity both in wisdom and in power; and this is made possible only through the continuous expression of the soul.

To this end we must permit the spiritual side of life to have full and continuous expression, both in mind and in body; and we shall find, under those circumstances, that we will continue to have that mastery of self, of life, of feeling, of conditions, of tendencies, that will always enable us to be equal to any condition that may arise, and that will enable us to state positively that "none of these things move me." In brief, we will be above them all, and stronger than them all, because we have permitted the life and the power of the spiritual side to come forth in greater and greater measure. Herewith a question of vast importance will arise; and it refers to the idea of whether or not it is desirable to live wholly upon the spiritual side. There is a belief current that we may weaken the personal side if we live too much in the spiritual; but nothing could be farther from the truth. We know that when we are functioning on the spiritual side we are constantly placing in action more and more of those higher spiritual forces that we become conscious of upon the spiritual side; and in consequence we give expression to more life than we ever realized before. The result will be, that both the life and the power of the personality will increase remarkably; and we shall have more strength, vitality and energy, both in mind and in body, than we ever had before.

Realizing this truth, we know that if we wish to meet a personality that is thoroughly filled with life we must always look for a personality with soul; and a personality with soul is a personality where the soul has begun to express itself to a much larger degree than usual. But when we meet a personality without soul, we find the reverse condition. True, the soul is there, but it is not expressed; and the greater powers are there, but they are not expressed, simply remaining in passivity. So therefore, the reverse of the above belief is the truth; and in consequence, the more attention we give to the spiritual side, the stronger and more powerful we become, not only in soul, but also in mind and body.

There is, however, truth in the belief that certain people sometimes appear to become physically weak when they begin to give marked attention to the spiritual side; but we shall find that those people are in reality not giving attention to the spiritual side. When we analyze their minds we will find that they have not come in contact with real spiritual power, but have simply been dreaming of the mystical; and such states of mind are not conducive to physical, mental, or spiritual power.

When you become conscious of the soul you come in contact with powerful forces; and you will have to take control of them all and hold them in your possession if you wish to realize every gain that is made possible through the consciousness of such forces. However, if you do not take hold of those forces and control them perfectly nothing will be gained. This is the reason why a great many people, who touch the spiritual at frequent intervals, simply have a pleasing experience, but do not gain in spiritual power.

Considering this subject further, we should remember the principle involved; that is, that the building up of life on the personal side and on the mental side, as well as on the spiritual side, can be carried forward only through the training of consciousness to make the spiritual side its chief place of functioning; and we may well ask what we should do first in order that this goal may be realized. To begin, we must study the spiritual side just as thoroughly as we have been studying the physical side; and accordingly we must begin at once to apply the scientific method to the spiritual side; in other words, we should take up the other side of science.

We know that we cannot function on the spiritual side to any extent until we become thoroughly familiar with the life and the nature of the soul; for the truth is, as long as the inner kingdom is a vague, mysterious something, we cannot consciously function there. But when we begin to analyze and explore the great spiritual kingdom, and proceed to study all its elements and principles, trying to get hold more and more of the fundamental qualities involved, we shall find that consciousness will gradually transfer itself to the spiritual side; and as this is being done, we shall find that increased power and increased life will come forth into mind and personality. When this great change begins, we will find ourselves gaining a deeper and deeper understanding of the mysteries of the kingdom. We will become familiar with our own spiritual nature; and we may continue this process of higher and greater understanding of the upper side of existence for any length of time. Then we shall find that whenever we take another step in that direction, thus increasing the power of consciousness to function spiritually, the soul will express itself, both in mind and in body, in added measure to correspond.

Returning to the original idea when the soul is fully and completely expressed in the personality, the physical or visible side of life will be filled with the light and the power of the spirit; and the more perfectly we understand this truth, the more fully we realize that physical weakness, as well as weakness of character or of mind, will naturally disappear as we advance in the expression of the soul through the life of the personality. And we shall also find that the tendency of the human mind to drift with the stream, or to go under, when in the midst of adversity, is due entirely to the fact that consciousness functions too much on the outside, thereby being limited both in wisdom and in power; that is, the personality under those circumstances is not strong enough to overcome adversity, or to create its own conditions and its own life.

The great change begins, however, when we step over the border, and proceed to direct consciousness to function more and more upon the spiritual side; for the truth is, that the moment consciousness begins to function in that higher realm, the coming forth of the spiritual elements and powers will begin in no uncertain manner. Accordingly, from that time on there will be steady increase in the power of mind, character, physical existence, and the life force in general. The great influx from the soul will proceed, and the personality will be filled more and more with life and power from above.

When we so live that this process may continue indefinitely, and that consciousness may secure positive hold of the higher side of life, the expression of the soul will become stronger and will be continuous under every circumstance. Then we will always live in the strong, masterful state; we will always realize the power of the spirit living in us; and we will feel, more and more, that power surging through us, animating and inspiring every atom, fiber and vein. Thus we shall be able to transcend all discord, all inharmony, all disease, all weakness, and in fact, anything that does not belong to the true order of a perfect state of being.

In order to further this study and train consciousness in this wonderful work, we shall find the scientific method indispensable; and even though we may not comprehend this method perfectly in the beginning, we shall find, if we apply the principle involved, that we shall succeed remarkably and upon an ever-increasing scale. However, even if we do not go any farther than simply taking this one step, that is, training consciousness to live more and more upon the spiritual side, the gain will be nothing less than extraordinary; and here we should remember that consciousness invariably tends to enter into those realms that we think of continually, or that we think of deeply and with persistent desire.

Therefore, our purpose henceforth must be to give continuous thought to the spiritual side with a strong, persistent desire to become more and more conscious of the spiritual life with all its elements, qualities and powers. The gain will be unusual, and will appear in many forms, because the training of consciousness to enter into the spiritual realm will not only enable us to understand more perfectly the mysteries of the kingdom, but the experience will enrich the mind to a remarkable degree. In addition, this mode of living will add immensely to the joy of life; indeed, we shall find upon the spiritual side an ever-increasing measure of that which is perfectly beautiful and sublimely ideal. Furthermore, we shall find in this mode of life the secret of the Great Life.

In every generation, and in every time, men and women have appeared who were in possession of remarkable power; but they all did not seem to gain their power from the same source. Among them were many who depended upon the infinite alone, while others made no secret of the fact that they were the instruments of invisible entities. And in many instances the latter seemed to exercise just as great a power, and just as high a power, as the former. Much inquiry therefore has arisen among all who are in search of higher spiritual power, as to what course to pursue; whether to go directly to God for this power, or to go to mediators in the realms of the invisible. In all these things there is one infallible guide "by their fruits ye shall know them" but in searching for the fruits or the consequences, we must not examine isolated circumstances only; we must examine the whole life, from beginning to end, of the one who has the power; and also examine the results of that power upon all that have come directly under its influence.

When we pursue such a course, we shall find that all those who are in possession of remarkable power, naturally array themselves into two separate and distinct groups; the one group depending absolutely upon the Infinite for all spiritual power, and the other group depending principally upon "invisible orders," "invisible helpers," or invisible entities of some kind. And as we pursue this course to its ultimate state or condition, we find that the one group follows unmistakably the right-handed path, leading directly into eternal light, while the other group follows the left-handed path leading eventually into utter darkness.

To all appearances, both groups may seem to be, in the beginning, on the same path the path of true spiritual power; and they all may seem to be prompted by the highest and purest motives; but as the two groups advance, farther and farther, upon their respective pathways, a marked difference begins to arise between them; and this difference becomes greater and greater until it finally becomes an impassable gulf. At first sight, there may seem to be nothing wrong in receiving higher power directly from invisible entities; and there may be certain temporary periods, or conditions, when such a course may be permissible; but no soul can continue very long to receive, or "borrow" spiritual power from other souls, in the invisible, without drifting directly into the left-handed path. And the very moment anyone finds himself upon the left-handed path, the temptation, and the inclination, to use higher power for unholy ends, becomes stronger and stronger until the conscious self gives in almost continually. Besides this, a marked weakening of character and principle begins almost at once the soul drifts into this path; and finally the desire to resist the temptation to misuse such power almost entirely disappears.

The principal reason why it is wrong to seek spiritual power from groups, or "orders," or invisible entities, and why such a course leads directly and inevitably into the left-handed path, will be clearly understood when we realize what it truly means to grow and advance in spiritual things. Then we shall be fully convinced of the great truth that there is only one way to the light and the power of the spirit; and that one way may be defined briefly, in the flaming words of the prophet, "Return Ye Unto God." We advance spiritually by becoming more and more conscious of our oneness with the Infinite; and all true spiritual growth depends directly upon the realization of higher and higher degrees of this very consciousness. But when we proceed to depend upon invisible entities for higher power, we turn our attention away from the realization of oneness with God, and seek, instead, a more perfect unity between ourselves and those invisible groups from which we expect to receive greater power. We turn away from the One Source of power; and whenever we turn away from that Source we step out of the right-handed path into the left-handed path.

We cannot depend upon God unless we depend upon Him absolutely. Our eye must be single; otherwise we cannot see the light. We must follow the Supreme in all things, or we cannot follow Him truly in anything. We must turn either to the right or to the left. There is no intermediary path. If we turn to the left we turn away from God. But we cannot turn to the right unless we are prepared to depend upon God, absolutely, for all spiritual wisdom, for all spiritual power, and for all the gifts that pertain to the spiritual life.

In Light of the Spirit

The way is simple, and the inner truth is so clear that all can understand. Know that you are one with God, and you are on the way. Realize that God is "closer than breathing, nearer than hands and feet," and the dawn of spiritual consciousness will have begun in your own life. And as you grow in that consciousness you will find yourself gaining possession, in greater and greater measure, of higher spiritual power. Your spiritual vision will open, more and more, to the great eternal light; and you will know, in your own soul, that you have found the way, the truth, and the life. When we pursue this wonderful study we shall meet many minds that will reason in this fashion: "We know that we are receiving our power from invisible entities; but we are convinced that the power is pure; and we feel that our acceptance of this power will prepare us for a higher life and a greater work. In the meantime, we are doing a good work; we are helping many; we are thoroughly sincere, and our purpose, both in our life and in our work, is the very highest conceivable."

In reply, however, to this mode of reasoning, plausible as it may seem to be, we must consider the truth as it is for all time, and not judge merely from a certain amount of good work that may be carried on in the present. We cannot judge from motives or intentions either, and judge wisely, for we all know that anyone can have good motives; anyone can be sincere; but in the midst of his sincerity he may be mistaken. He may be good and kind today, and still he may gradually be drifting in the wrong direction.

The truth is this, that if you wish to be helpful to the world, you need not go to invisible entities for your power. You can gain greater power and higher power by going directly to God. You have no excuse, therefore, in that respect, for attaching yourself to invisible groups, or "orders," the true existence of which has been, and always will be, very doubtful. For here we must remember that invisible entities who really know God, will never undertake to "lend" spiritual power to man. Enlightened entities in higher realms will forever seek to inspire man to go direct to God for all spiritual power, for they well know that any other course will inevitably lead into ages of distress and darkness. When we consider this phase of the subject, we realize, in a most positive manner, that we cannot "borrow" spiritual power from enlightened entities in higher realms; and we would not want to receive power from those who are not enlightened.

We can, however, receive remarkable power from invisible entities under circumstances favorable to that end; but such entities do not know God; they do not know the way, the truth and the life; if they did know, they would not lead man away from God, by encouraging him to accept power from them, instead of from the Supreme. They are therefore "spirits of darkness"; and they themselves are already on the left-handed path. But even the "power of darkness" can perform miracles at times, and do "good work" for a season. Therefore, we must not be misled by "signs," "wonder works" or remarkable "appearances." We must first inquire the source of their power; then we shall know, whether or not, they are on the path that leads to eternal light. Your work may at present be good, and your intentions may be good; but if you are not receiving your power directly from the Infinite, you are gradually and surely drifting away from the true Source of light, power and truth. And before you may be aware of it, you will find yourself on the left-handed path. In truth, you may continue for years on this downward path without knowing where you are drifting, for the way to darkness does not always reveal its true nature to the human soul, or warn anyone from going farther. Such warning must come from the way of light; but there is a simple secret that will always inform us, truthfully, where we are. Ask yourself from whence you receive your power. If you know that you are receiving your power from the Supreme, and if you are trying to so live that you may realize, more and more perfectly, your oneness with the Infinite then you are on the path of the light. But if you must admit to yourself that you are depending principally upon other sources, both for power and guidance, then heed instantly these inspiring words of the prophet "Return Ye Unto God."

The first and greatest principle in all spiritual advancement or attainment is this "Enter more and more perfectly into the conscious realization of your oneness with God." This is the way; this is the truth; this is the life. The whole of human existence, therefore, must be so constructed that every thought and act will tend directly to increase and deepen this conscious realization. Our one greatest purpose must be to know absolutely that we are eternally in the Spirit of God, and forever one with God. And everything in life that may, in any way, interfere with the constant advancement of that purpose, must be eliminated completely.

Herein we find the full meaning of the great commandment, that we should seek no other gods but the one only supreme God. The power we may gain from lesser lights in the invisible world, is but temporary; and their guidance leads inevitably away from the light and the truth. They alone are on the true spiritual path, who depend absolutely upon the Supreme. They alone are worthy to lead mankind who follow implicitly the guidance of the pure, white light of the One Spirit.

Chapter 5

The Mysteries of the Kingdom

When we inquire as to the greatest need of mankind, our answer must invariably be, to know more and more of the truth; and this answer is based upon the principle that it is the increased understanding of truth that alone can provide the human soul with those essentials that are required to the living of life and the fulfillment of destiny. The need of more and more truth has been deeply felt in every soul at every time; and therefore we find the human race constantly in search of the truth, although it is quite evident that the majority do not realize, most of the time, why they do want to know the truth. The soul, however, does know; and it is this prompting from within that causes the mind to go out in every direction, and employ every possible means to the end that a greater measure of truth may be realized.

The truth that we may know at any particular time, provided it is all the truth that we can understand at that time, will satisfy our purpose for the living of a full life in that special period; but the very moment we come to a place where the needs of life have been enlarged and made more extensive, we shall feel at once the need of a greater measure of truth. This leads the soul into an attitude that we all have experienced an attitude that may be described as the hungering and thirsting for something within, or for something higher that we do not seem able, at the time, to gain possession of; but what we really do want at those times is more truth; and the moment we find the greater truth we are in search of, the soul is satisfied, and the greater needs of life, for the moment, are perfectly fulfilled.

When we examine the relationship that the knowing of truth sustains to the living of life, we find that the truth of today is for today only; and that new truth and a greater measure of truth becomes absolutely necessary as the soul grows or advances into larger and higher states of existence. We find therefore that whenever a new step is taken, or something higher is undertaken, the truth that we have known in the past will prove insufficient. We find that we must have new truth, and that we must gain a higher and a larger understanding of life before we can proceed with the new step or undertaking in view.

However, if we do not succeed at once in gaining this larger understanding, we shall experience a deep dissatisfaction with almost everything in life; and we have all had this experience at various times; but now we know what it means; and we can avoid such experiences in the future if we will make proper provision for the greater needs of the future by learning to search the truth in all places, and by learning the art of entering into a higher understanding of truth according to the demands of human advancement. In our search for the truth in the past, we have confined ourselves almost exclusively to ways and methods that have been more or less uncertain; that is, we have not developed a definite system for the seeking of truth, or for the finding of truth, and this is especially true of spiritual truth. Accordingly, the race has not advanced spiritually to any degree of satisfaction, although great advancement has been made along other lines, because the search of truth in the material world has been carried on more thoroughly, according to science and system.

The soul must have more truth, however; and therefore we find large masses of people coming, at frequent times, to places where they do not know where to turn because the understanding of the past does not serve any longer; and they do not know how to find the greater understanding that is demanded. In brief, they wish to discard old conditions and old beliefs, but do not know where to go for new ones; therefore they find themselves in conditions that are anything but favorable to the highest welfare of man.

We find that this very thing has happened in history, again and again; and during such seasons of change and uncertainty, there have been prolonged periods of spiritual darkness. The cause of this we can readily understand, because when the light of the past proves insufficient, and the greater light desired is not at hand, the soul must of necessity find itself in a state of darkness, or at least in a state of confusion; and mental confusion almost invariably produces more or less spiritual darkness. To avoid this, because it should be avoided by all means, we must seek to work out a more definite system for the search of the greater and the greater truth, as demanded by the growth and advancement of the soul. In brief, we must provide for ourselves a method of growth in the truth that will enable us to continue in the spiritual light constantly, without meeting at any time those periods that invariably follow when the supply for the higher is not at hand to provide for greater demand.

We all realize the situation, and the needs of such a situation; but the question is, how a more thorough system can be provided through which we may find, for each day, all the truth that we need for that day; but here we must remember that it is not a system of belief that we are in search of. We do not desire systems of belief, but rather a definite system for mental and spiritual growth into a higher and higher understanding of truth. The finding of such a system, however, will not prove so difficult as we might think, because we have the principle in our very, midst.

When we look into the material world, we find that in that world a perfect system has been evolved for the search of more and more truth; and that system is based upon the scientific method a method which is practically infallible, and which can be applied in any domain, even the spiritual domain. The value of the scientific method in the material world becomes very evident when we discover the fact that the world knew practically nothing about the material universe previous to the coming, of the scientific method; but since that method has been employed so extensively, in connection with all visible and tangible objects and forces, the material universe has become almost like an open book. We can read nearly all its secrets at the present time; and its mysteries are no longer hidden, but have been clearly revealed to all intelligent minds. The fact is, that the scientific method has revealed the material universe to us in such a wonderful manner that we are now able to perform miracles almost every day in connection with tangible forces and elements; and still we realize that we are simply in the beginning of real knowledge in connection with material things. The discoveries that have been made in connection with the tangible, and the inventions that have been perfected, are nothing less than extraordinary; but greater things in connection with the visible universe will be evolved and perfected from this time on, because we are learning to apply the scientific method more perfectly every day, and upon a much larger scale.

The advancement and the changes that have been made upon the physical side of life since the scientific method appeared, have been so numerous and so wonderful that we really do not appreciate them all. The reason is we have become so accustomed to miracles in everyday life that we do not stop to consider the principles and laws through which all these things have been accomplished. Those principles and laws, however, are based upon the scientific method; and it is that method that deserves the credit for every comfort and every mode of advancement in life that we enjoy at the present time.

Realizing this great fact, the question is, if we can apply the same method to the spiritual universe. We have searched the mysteries of the physical kingdoms, and we have found thousands of invaluable facts; we are finding more and more every day, and we are working them out in a practical manner for the greatest good of man; but can we understand the mysteries of the spiritual kingdom in the same way? Can we enter the vastness of higher realms, and find greater and greater truth in those realms, through the same method that we have employed in the physical or tangible world? If we can, then the mysteries of the kingdom will not be mysterious much longer; we shall soon learn to understand them all, and gain possession of wisdom such as we have never dreamed.

We are familiar with the physical side of science; and our minds have been so engrossed in this physical side that we have never paused to ask ourselves the question if there might not be another side to science a side that would relate itself directly to the spiritual realms. For this reason, we have failed to appreciate the power of the scientific method in connection with higher and finer things. But now we know that there is another side to science, and that this other or higher side can be applied as successfully in the spiritual world as the physical side of science has been applied in the tangible world. However, we do not refer to any special kind of science, but refer to the scientific principle itself, without any modifications or specifications whatever; that is, it is the idea involved in the scientific method the only method known for the finding of truth with which we are concerned; and we have now come to the conclusion that it is pure science that we must apply, not only to the physical, but to the metaphysical, and also to the spiritual, if we would know all truth and place ourselves in a position where we can constantly rise in the understanding of a greater and greater measure of truth.

Appreciating this fact, the problem will be, how to apply the scientific method in the search of truth in the spiritual world. The Great Master Mind declared, "It is for you to know the mysteries of the kingdom;" but until recently we did not give serious attention to that remarkable statement; and the reason may possibly be found in the fact that our spiritual needs had not become sufficiently strong to arouse our minds in a manner where we really could not tolerate our limitations any longer. In recent times, however, most of us have come to places where we felt that we simply would have to secure new light; and the whole world almost is in that position at the present time.

Nearly everybody feels the need of a new life and a higher state of existence; but the majority do not know how to proceed in the search of what their souls demand. They have a fear of going out upon the seeming void, not realizing that this seeming void is nothing less than a greater world of substantial and finer reality. But there are many who have eliminated that fear, and who have begun to get out upon the seeming void, finding there the solid rock of greater truth, as all will do who take that most important step.

We must remember, that in the search of truth, there is no need of having fear of anything, because while we are in the search of truth, we cannot go astray. If it is the truth that we want, and if we are applying the best methods that we know, we shall gain at least a measure of greater truth; and we will not go astray; we will not be lost even though we leave behind us all the beliefs of the past. We need not think that we will enter the desert of uncertainty simply because we leave the lesser in search of the greater; for the fact is, we cannot go very far in any direction, if we are in search of truth, without finding something that will prove of greater value for the advancement and the enrichment of life than anything we possessed before. Our ruling purpose therefore from this time on should be, to go out more and more into the vastness of the higher and the greater realms of the spiritual world, knowing that the farther we go into that world, the more truth we shall find; and as we grow in the truth, life will become larger, richer, more enjoyable and more beautiful; and in addition, we shall become living examples to the thousands who are in search of those higher things that we have found.

When we consider the mysteries of the kingdom, we must remember that we are dealing purely with the spiritual side of life; and we must realize that the spiritual side, or the seeming unreal, is the most real of all states of existence. There is far greater reality in the life of the spirit than there is in the life of the material; indeed, it is only in the spiritual that we find reality in its true state of being; and when we realize this, then it is that we shall begin to gain, not only a higher understanding of all life, but a greater degree of mastery, both of the mental world and of the material world.

We are subject to physical conditions only so long as we continue to believe that the body is more real than the soul. The very moment, however, that we know absolutely that the soul is more real than the body, then the soul will begin to gain mastery over the body; and when the soul does gain mastery over the body, all imperfect conditions in the physical life must disappear. The principle is the same as that of turning on the light; when the light comes, then darkness must go.

We find that physical conditions are always similar to the nature of the spiritual expression that is taking place at any particular time; that is, if the spiritual expression in your life is full and complete, every condition in your body will, of necessity, be full and complete, or similar to the expression of the spirit; and as the spirit is always in a state of harmony, peace, health, wholeness and the fullness of life, conditions in the physical life must be the same when the spiritual expression is full and perfect. The spirit is always in a state of divine perfection; therefore, we must of necessity conclude that the body would enjoy the same state of divine perfection if the expression of the soul were full and complete during every moment of personal existence.

The reason why there are imperfect conditions on the physical side of mind or body is because the spiritual expression of life is only partial in most individuals; and in a great many individuals the spiritual expression is actually insignificant, so that it can hardly be spoken of as a true expression; that is, the soul is simply passively alive in a great majority of people, and really does not express itself or its qualities in any form or manner. And the cause of this condition is due to the fact that we have looked upon the body as more real than the soul.

Herewith we must remember that so long as we live in the belief that the body is more real than the soul, the soul will be looked upon in our consciousness as a negative factor. It will simply be passive, because our material belief does not permit of active expression from the spiritual side. And when we look at the life of the great majority, we discover at once that the spiritual life in them all is purely passive; life in them is simply a state of existence; they do not live in the true sense of the term; they do not express real life; and the expression of the spiritual or the divine reality within them has not begun. It is true, however, that the very moment material belief is eliminated, spiritual expression will begin. But we do not eliminate material belief until we begin to live in the soul; and we begin to live in the soul the very moment we realize that the soul is more real than either mind or body. It is in this very place that we find the parting of the ways in the life of every individual, or the beginning of a new order of things in the world of any individual.

When the human entity begins to realize that the spiritual side is more real than the physical side, consciousness will begin to function more definitely upon the spiritual side; that is, life will be lived, not from the body, but from the soul; and when we live in the soul, and from the soul, we will give expression to an ever-increasing measure of life, wisdom and spiritual power.

When we consider our past consciousness, we remember that our conscious existence was concerned almost entirely with the outer life of the personality; that is, we really lived in the body, and looked upon the soul as a vague something that no one could understand. We could consciously feel the existence of the body, but we did not have any conscious realization of the existence of the soul. We possibly believed that we had a soul, but it was merely a belief; and we did not possess sufficient conscious realization of the spiritual life to prove to ourselves that such a life had actual existence.

In the present age, however, a large percentage have come to a wonderful change in consciousness. These human entities know that the soul has existence; they do not simply believe it, but are beginning to know it as an absolute truth. And if you are a member of this fortunate company you realize exactly what has brought about this change. You are being to feel inwardly that you are a soul, and you are beginning to live consciously in the soul world. Your chief abode is no longer in the body, but is in the spiritual state of your life. You have moved, literally speaking, from the external to the internal, or from the lower to the higher; and you are now living, actually and truly, in the higher. The result is that you are giving expression to the elements and powers that exist in the higher; and as a consequence, you are finding that physical conditions are changing to respond more and more perfectly to this expression of finer life from above.

And here it is well to remember that we cannot give expression to the powers of the soul, and to the superior qualities of the soul, unless we live in the soul. So long as we live in the body, we have to depend exclusively upon material conditions, material forces and material things; but the moment we begin to live in the soul, we become actually conscious of the greater power; and the higher qualities that exist in the soul; and whatever we become conscious of, that we invariably express in the personality. The result of these higher conditions we all have experienced. We all have proven conclusively the great truth that we can eliminate adverse physical conditions by entering a higher spiritual realization; for the moment we enter the spirit we become conscious of the power of the spirit, and according to the law, give expression to that power through every part of mind and body; in brief, we send forth the light from the soul, and the darkness of the body must disappear.

We have also found that this higher spiritual realization will invariably eliminate discord and adversity from the mind, increase the richness of life in every manner, and enlarge consciousness, both in the visible and in the invisible, so that new kingdoms are added again and again to the world in which we live. We all have experienced and proven this great truth; and all these experiences are based upon the principle that we invariably give expression to the higher and the finer life of the soul the moment we begin to live in the soul.

In Light of the Spirit

The principal idea to be considered in our study of this important theme is, that conscious activity, invariably takes place wherever we feel that we live; that is, if we feel that we live in the body, our consciousness will act principally in the body, and we will deal almost exclusively with the physical side of life. But when we begin to feel that we live in the soul, consciousness will become active among the spiritual elements and forces, and we will place in action more and more of those higher forces. Accordingly, we are no longer confined to the limitations of the physical, but may proceed to enter more and more into the conscious realization of the limitless life of the spiritual.

The truth is, that the moment we transfer the principal place of conscious functioning from the body to the soul, we find that the higher spiritual forces will begin to express themselves, and thereby enlarge, enrich and perfect the entire domain of human existence physical, mental and spiritual; in other words, wherever you are conscious, there you awaken activity. This is the simple truth that underlies this entire field of study. Therefore, when you are conscious on the spiritual side, you awaken spiritual activity; and when you awaken spiritual activity, you cause the expression of spiritual life and spiritual power, and in fact, the expression of everything that pertains to the wonders of the spiritual world. You have taken conscious possession of that higher, richer life, and have begun to bring forth that life into every part of your entire being. Thus your entire being will be lifted up, perfected, made better and higher, and existence itself, on all planes, more beautiful and more enjoyable.

When we understand this great truth in all its fullness, we will begin to realize its many possibilities, and we must come invariably to the conclusion that if we should actually live for a number of years on the spiritual side of our consciousness, the spiritual expression of everything pertaining to the soul would become so strong that it would be impossible for adverse conditions to ever find place in the body; that is, the body would be so thoroughly filled with the life and the power of the spirit that no adverse condition could ever begin for a moment upon the physical side. This would be only one of the many wonderful things that would happen; and another would be the continuous enlargement of the mind, because the expression of the soul has a tendency to build up, to develop, and to further the growth of everything that is natural and true in any part of the mental world. All in all, therefore, we would realize perpetual health and physical perfection on the tangible side, and become giants of character, power and talent on the mental side; but such a remarkable realization could not take place unless we lived for a number of years on the spiritual side exclusively, and during every moment of existence.

But there are many who may say that they have tried for some years to function entirely upon the spiritual side, and yet have realized neither physical emancipation nor higher mental attainments a situation that may appear to contradict the truth of the statement just made; but we must remember that when we face the fact as it is in our own life, and ask ourselves if we have always functioned on the spiritual side during every moment of existence, we must invariably reply, that we have functioned on the spiritual side only at rare moments. We have not made the spiritual side the principal place of conscious activity; and that is the reason we have not gained the results that we think should have followed our efforts in that direction. If we would realize all the fruits of the spirit, we must give every moment to the spirit; and this we can do without interfering with the duties and privileges of the physical side of life. We can live continually on the spiritual side of consciousness, and at the same time give full justice to everything that may demand our attention on the tangible side. Besides, the more perfectly we live in the spiritual, the more life and power we will give to the body, due to the fact that greater spiritual activity in consciousness will arouse a greater abundance of life; and the more life we have, the more power, the more virility, the more strength and the more harmony we shall have, and the better will be the health both of mind and body.

The first step to be taken in the further understanding of truth, and in the search of the secrets of the kingdom, is to train consciousness to live more and more upon the spiritual side of life; and here we must remember that we cannot understand the mysteries of the kingdom, no matter how much we may study or investigate the subject, until we consciously live in the soul. If we live in the body, or in the mind, we cannot understand the spirit, and the mysteries of the kingdom will continue to be mysterious in every form and manner; but the moment we begin to realize that we are spiritual beings, and begin to live in the soul, so that we actually feel that we are living upon the spiritual side, we become conscious of spiritual things; and the moment we become conscious of spiritual things, we gain the power to understand spiritual things.

The consciousness of the spiritual must come first; that is, we must actually be in the spiritual world before we can study the spiritual world; and therefore we must live in the soul, and consciously function in the soul, before we can proceed further in the search of truth. Having taken this first step, we will not only gain immensely, both physically and mentally, but we will also have entered consciously the real light of the spiritual world; and when we have entered that light, we shall be able to see clearly how to proceed farther, how to apply the other side of science to all the mysteries of the kingdom.

Chapter 6

The Secret of Spiritual Power

In every age spiritual giants have appeared wonderful souls, that have almost continually been in perfect touch with that vast, inexhaustible world of supernal light and transcendent power that surrounds us all, and that permeates the entire cosmos in all its unbounded domains. These rare and exceptional souls have been the prophets of the race, and have been the saviors of mankind; they have beheld the vision; they have proclaimed the kingdom of higher and greater things; they have revealed the light of "another and a better world;" they have prepared the way for the whole of humanity "to come up higher" and enter the joys and the riches of pure, spiritual existence. And they have also manifested marked possession of spiritual power, the secret of which has been a mystery to the greater part of the race.

In years gone by we did not consider it possible for man to understand the inner mysteries of the kingdom; but now we know that it is for all mankind to understand these mysteries; and therefore we have begun a ceaseless and unlimited research, the end in view being nothing less than the full realization of the one eternal truth. And among the many higher and finer domains, upon which we are turning the wonderful eye of the soul, the secrets of these spiritual giants is in no wise the least.

When the soul is awakened, there comes a strong and increasing desire for higher wisdom and higher power. The spirit within begins to hunger and thirst for more light; and there is a feeling in the deeper depths of consciousness, that proclaims unmistakably the nearness of a power that is truly akin to the power of the Supreme. In truth, the awakened soul can almost touch this power, it seems so near; but many a soul continues for years on the verge of touching this power, but never being able to lay hold upon its elements, or realize its conscious possession even to a slight degree. And the cause of this strange delay has been a deep mystery to many.

To fathom this mystery we have turned our attention to the spiritual giants of every age, thinking we might find in them the secret; and we have not gone to them in vain. Their lives have revealed to us what we sought to know. They have prepared the way; and we may pursue the same course if we will learn to understand the state and the motive of the interior, spiritual life.

To begin, we must know and feel that we "live and move and have our being" in an infinite sea of pure spirit. And we must enter so deeply into the consciousness of this omnipresent spiritual world that we can actually feel the "presence" of the power in every element of body, mind and soul. In brief, the spiritual world must become so real to us that the material world appears to be mere mist in comparison. We may know the presence of the spirit, and continue in this knowing all through life without gaining possession of the power; but when we begin to "feel" the presence of the spirit, then indeed shall we be able to lay hold upon the power, and make it our very own.

Herein we find the secret of the prophets and the mighty in spirit. They could feel the presence of this higher power in every fiber and vein; they could touch it with their hands in the atmosphere all about them; they could charge their very thoughts with the elements of this power; they could direct the tremendous forces of this power into every word they might utter or declare; and they could, through the use of divine will, give expression to this power through the higher laws of nature, and thus perform what, to the world, has seemed miraculous.

When we can feel the presence of spiritual power, then we know that we actually have entered into the real, interior life of that power; and the law is, that whenever we "enter into" any measure or state of spiritual power, that measure of power becomes our own. Another great law that we find herein is this, that the power of the spirit obeys implicitly the desire of the higher human will. And therefore, whenever we feel the presence of the power, that power will act for us upon any purpose or goal towards which the higher will of the soul may be directed. When we actually feel the power of the spirit, that power will invariably do whatsoever we may will to do, provided the desires and motives of the will are inspired by the pure and lofty aspirations of the soul.

The first and great secret, therefore, is to feel the presence of the spirit, and enter into the very life of higher spiritual power. Having taken this important step, the steps that follow can in no wise be difficult; and the reason for this we shall understand when we find how readily these higher forces respond to the masterful attitude of the soul. The soul should be and, in truth, is the ruling principle in the human domain. And every awakened soul does lay positive hold, more and more, upon this divine prerogative. The awakened soul therefore soon comes to a place where the absolute right to govern life and destiny is fully recognized; and at that period the need of higher power becomes very great indeed. When the awakened soul arrives at this, the parting of the ways, and learns that life can no longer drift with the stream, but must be directed, with wisdom and power, towards the supreme goal of the illumined spiritual heights when the soul comes face to face with this astounding truth, the desire for the necessary wisdom and the necessary power becomes invincible. And there is no rest until this indispensable need

In Light of the Spirit

is supplied. If the supply is not forthcoming, both mind and soul will continue in a state of inconsolable distress, a state that, in many instances, fails to depart during existence in this world. The cause, however, is simply the failure to gain the higher power required for the new order and the new time.

Herein we find the reason why so many among awakened souls have not realized the perfect peace of the spirit and the higher joys of divine existence. They are living in a period of unrest and distress, that frequently becomes unendurable pain; and the cause is always this, that they have awakened to the need of higher power, but have not gained conscious possession of that power. They have entered upon the responsibilities and privileges of a higher life, but have not gained the necessary power to partake of the privileges or meet the responsibilities. Their spiritual sight is opened, and they can clearly see the supreme goal of human destiny; but they have not the power to press on towards those sublime and radiant heights. They have awakened to the true meaning of life, but have not the wisdom or the power to live according to the higher light they have received. In consequence, the soul is in distress, yearning eternally for that wonderful something that seems so near, and still so utterly unattainable.

This wonderful something, however, seems to be unattainable for no other reason than this, we have not found the simple secret of entering into the very life of the spirit. We may know that we live and move and have our being in an infinite sea of pure spirit; but we may not feel the "presence" of the power. It is the "presence" of the power that we must, feel; and when we do feel this presence, then indeed will the pain of the soul disappear. The great need will be supplied. The wisdom and the power that is required to live the life will be out of reach no more; and the soul can begin in earnest to press on towards the spiritual goal of glorified human destiny.

Chapter 7

The Use Of Spiritual Power

When you accomplish something that is remarkable, or unusual, through the use of spiritual power, do not permit yourself to think or say that you were the author of this work. In truth, do not consider yourself, in any form or manner, as having done what has seemingly been done by you. Keep the eye single upon the Source of the power, with which this great work was performed, and give all honor and glory to the Supreme Author of all that is great and wonderful in the world.

When we consider the great truth, that he who exalts himself shall be humbled, that he who humbles himself before the Most High shall be exalted, we are dealing with one of the greatest of laws in the spiritual kingdom. And when we understand this law, we shall know the inner secret of the seers and the prophets, and of all the spiritual giants that have appeared upon any planet in the cosmos.

There is but one Source of true spiritual power; and that Source is the Infinite; but the man who exalts himself does not look to the Infinite for his power; he looks to his own mind and soul. But here we must remember that although the human soul can give expression to marvelous power, still all of that power must come from the Supreme. And no one can receive power from the Supreme unless the eye is single upon the Supreme throughout the period of conscious existence. We receive from the Source only when we think constantly of the Source, and open mind and soul to the divine influx from On High.

When we humble ourselves before God, we do not depreciate our own worth; we still know that we are created in his image; and we realize most keenly that we are forever one with God; but we recognize the great truth that all power comes from above, and that God is the source of everything that is real and true in life. We do not exalt ourselves and say, "I have power of my own; I can depend upon myself." Nor do we think of ourselves as poor, insignificant creatures; for how can the noblest creation of the Supreme be insignificant? In truth, how can those creations be otherwise than wonderful? They are indeed wonderful; far more wonderful than we have ever dreamed.

This we realize perfectly; but in the midst of this realization, we know that all power comes from God, and that we receive from God only as we depend absolutely upon Him for all things we may need or desire. When you exalt yourself, you do not depend upon God; you do not look to God; you turn away from Him, and therefore disconnect yourself from the only source of power. The result will be, that you will steadily decrease, until you are poverty-stricken in body, mind and soul. Then you shall have to begin once more on the upward path, and from the very beginning. But when you look to God for all your power, you enter into more perfect harmony with His spirit and His life; in brief, you draw nearer and nearer to God; and in consequence, you become filled more and more, with His power until you become a giant in mind and soul. The very moment you draw nearer to God, you begin to increase; and the nearer you come to Him, the more power you receive. Thus we understand why they who have exalted themselves have been humbled, while they who have humbled themselves before the Most High, have continued to rise, higher and higher, finally becoming joint heirs with Christ in all the power and glory of the kingdom.

There is one thing herewith that we positively must understand; and it is this, that we cannot receive power from

In Light of the Spirit

the Supreme unless we fix the whole of heart and mind and soul upon the Supreme. But the moment we think of ourselves as "having the power," or as "doing the work," we transfer attention from the Supreme to our own personality. Then we no longer receive power from above, and will soon begin to weaken. This we all realize, for how can we be in touch with the Source after we have turned away from the Source? And how can we receive more and more from the Source unless we draw nearer and nearer to the Source?

Absolute oneness with God is necessary if we are to gain possession of remarkable spiritual power; and this oneness we all can realize if we look to God for everything, and depend upon Him for everything in the faith that all our prayers will be answered without a single exception whatever. But the moment we begin to think of ourselves as sufficient, we turn away; we separate ourselves, to a degree, from the Infinite; the open door between our own soul and the world of spiritual power begins to close in more and more; and if we continue in our self-sufficiency, that door will close almost entirely until the light and the power of the spirit is, for the time being, shut out from our world.

Your own personality may be the channel for the expression of marvelous spiritual power; but never say that "this is my work;" and never think that you are the author. Your work is to seek oneness with God; the power will follow. And it is the power of the Most High, living and working in you, that is the author of that wonderful work that seemingly comes from your mind and soul. This truth we must know. This truth we must realize more and more perfectly; and the more perfect the realization of this truth becomes, the deeper will become our realization of oneness with God. More and more will follow. Gradually and surely we will rise towards the sublime spiritual heights. The riches of the kingdom will come into our world in greater and greater measure; and whenever we are prepared to receive our full inheritance, then everything that heart and mind and soul may desire, shall become our own. All things belong to God; but we are the heirs; and our full inheritance is ready for us to enjoy whenever we are fully prepared to receive. And when we are willing to depend upon God for everything, then we are prepared to receive everything that God has to give.

Chapter 8

The Light of Inner Consciousness

When we function through outer consciousness only, we are able to appreciate only those things that appeal to the physical senses, or to reason, or to the usual states of emotion; that is, we live almost exclusively in the material world, and therefore can have no real understanding of things spiritual. We may believe in the spiritual, and be more or less conscious of the finer things in life; and yet, if we look upon all things through the light of outer consciousness, we can have no true conception of the spiritual world, or the spiritual life. We do not realize, in the least, what it means to be spiritual, or what it means to be in touch with higher, spiritual power; and, for this reason, can neither possess spiritual power, nor respond to the healing or emancipating influence of that power.

To possess spiritual power, we must be able to function, at least to some degree, through the elements of inner consciousness. And the same is true if we wish to respond to such power. If we wish to be healed by spiritual power, we must live largely in the world of inner consciousness, because spiritual power acts only through that world. When our minds are living and moving in the world of inner consciousness, we can be reached by spiritual power; that is, we are, more or less, in that world where spiritual power naturally finds expression, and therefore, this power may work through us fully and freely as we desire.

There are many who seemingly cannot be healed by spiritual power; and the reason why is simply this, that they have not entered inner consciousness. They are living on the outside of the spiritual realm; they do not come in contact in any way with the finer, spiritual forces; and therefore they are never touched by these forces in any mode or manner. Everybody can, however, learn to enter inner consciousness; and this is indeed something we all should learn to the most perfect degree this very day.

They who do live, to some degree, in the world of inner consciousness, can be healed of anything through the full and proper administration of spiritual power; and they may proceed, at any time, to employ that same power in the building of a richer, larger life, for body, mind and soul. They will respond invariably to the influence of higher spiritual power, whatever the need or the goal may be. And it is well to know, that the number of human souls who are in touch with inner consciousness, is very large, although many of them are not aware of the privilege they enjoy. However, the very moment they give their attention to the spiritual side of life, they find that they can be helped, and helped wonderfully, by spiritual means. They were ready to receive higher power; and they were ready because they were living largely in that finer realm through which the spiritual forces live and move and have their being. Great souls live constantly, both in the world of outer consciousness and in the world of inner consciousness. They are therefore in possession of higher spiritual power at all times, and may give that power expression in any way desired. It is not necessary, however, to live absolutely in the world of inner consciousness in order to respond to spiritual power; but this is necessary before we can personally possess and employ spiritual power.

Even though but a corner of your mind should extend, ever so little, into the world of inner consciousness, that would mean that the door was open. Spiritual power could then come into your mind and body; and if fully administered, could act in you with sufficient force to banish every ailment, weakness or wrong that might exist in your system.

If you should wish, however, to gain possession of remarkable spiritual power to be employed in the emancipation of others, and for the furthering of your own higher development, it would be necessary to extend your whole mind into the wonderful world of inner consciousness. In brief, you would find it necessary to enter so fully into that consciousness that you could actually feel the tremendous forces of the spirit, surging through your entire system, like a mighty, invincible current. And you would always be conscious of the all-powerful Presence.

To learn to enter more and more deeply into the world of inner consciousness, we must consider the great law, that the human mind tends to develop in that direction where we express our deepest desires, our strongest thought and our highest faith. The way therefore is simple. There are no mysterious methods to employ, or rigid rules to follow. The first step is to know that inner consciousness is the consciousness of that interior life that per all life; and the consciousness of the spiritual world a world that is to the visible cosmos what the soul is to the visible form of man.

When you enter interior consciousness, you not only become conscious of your own soul, but you also become conscious of the soul of the universe. You gain the power to discern the spiritual side of all things, because your mind has been extended into that vast interior realm where the spiritual elements and the spiritual forces forever have their being.

The second step is to desire inner consciousness with a deeper and a stronger desire than you have ever felt before. In truth, this desire should become a soul passion continuous and invincible; and the power of that desire will draw the mind farther and farther into the world of interior consciousness until you actually live and move in that world. Then to the power of this desire we must add the power of our strongest and most concentrated thought. "Think on these things;" and think with such power and feeling that your whole mental life enters into the very spirit of those things into the very soul of the spiritual world. Then crown your efforts with faith pure, interior, unbounded faith. Know that your mind is entering more deeply and more perfectly into the illumined world of interior consciousness. Believe this absolutely, and enter into the spirit of that belief into the very life of that faith that has limitless faith in faith.

Chapter 9

The Power of Spiritual Transparence

When we examine those conditions that are usually spoken of as evil, and trace them back to their possible origin, or last analysis, it is impossible to find any actual evidence in support of the belief that evil is real, or that it has independent existence. On the contrary, all evidence is on the other side, and we are impelled to accept the idea that evil is nonexistent. But the question is, why does evil seem to be real; and why is it here affecting the life of man in such a positive manner?

Deep thinkers in every age have given the larger parts of their lives to these questions; and naturally various conclusions have been formulated. Among the best known of these conclusions is the belief that evil is merely a condition arising from the misuse of the good; but in the full analysis of this belief a difficulty is met with that no thinker along that line has as yet overcome. And it is this, that if evil has no real existence, there can be no natural evil in man; and if there be no natural evil in man there can be no desire or tendency to misuse anything.

But the good is misused as we all know; then from whence comes that tendency in man to want to misuse the good? Such a tendency cannot be good; and therefore cannot originate in the good. However, if all is good, where are we to find that from which the tendency to misuse can originate? There is a great difficulty here that must be overcome or explained if we are to demonstrate the belief that evil is merely the misuse of the good. But this difficulty has not thus far been explained; and yet when we examine evil closely we find that it certainly is nonexistent.

In Light of the Spirit

There is another belief, not so well known, that will prove itself far more satisfactory to the pure reasoned, and that will, not only explain the various difficulties that are met with in its analysis, but that also presents a method for eliminating evil that is far more perfect than anything else ever conceived of by the mind of man. It will be interesting therefore to consider this belief; although it will be necessary to be brief, the subject being so large that a volume would be required for a full and complete elucidation.

According to this new belief, evil is but a shadow a shadow that is cast by the life of man himself when he is in the light, and only when he is in the light, it being impossible to cast a shadow when in the dark. In other words, evil exists only as a shadow, it having no reality or permanency in itself. Thus evil is known only to those who have evolved sufficiently from the lower states of consciousness to have come up into the light, as it is not possible for those to know shadows who have never been in the light.

If we are to accept this belief and there is nothing to disprove it, while all the evidence obtainable is in its favor we must, in one sense, rejoice in the fact that there is evil in the world that our lives do cast a shadow, for this at least proves that we are in the light. But although we may rejoice in the fact that we are in the light, still we cannot rejoice in the fact that our lives do cast a shadow, and that these shadows have occasioned so much misunderstanding, so much stumbling and so much pain in the world. We must find, therefore, the reason why the life of man does cast a shadow. When we go in search of this reason why, we soon discover that the life of man casts a shadow because the light does not pass through his life his life is not transparent. If the light of truth and goodness and perfection in brief, the divine light of being, could pass through his life, there would be no shadow, and man would not know evil in any form.

In Light of the Spirit

This is self-evident. But before we can go further in the demonstration of this belief, we must find the reason why the life of man is not transparent. This is our greatest problem; and although the solution cannot be made so clear that it will be intelligible to everybody, still it is in our possession, and can be proven, by any thinker of spiritual insight, to be the exact solution. The many, however, may not concern themselves so much with the reason why the life of man casts a shadow as they may with the finding of practical methods for the elimination of the shadow. And here this particular belief has a decided advantage over all others; it does present methods for the elimination of the shadow that all can understand and apply.

The principle is that if the life of man is to cease to cast a shadow, his spiritual nature must become transparent; his life must attain unto spiritual transparence; and the way to spiritual transparence can be found and followed by any earnest, awakened soul. When we proceed to examine the problem of evil more closely, and from the viewpoint of this belief, we come to several self-evident conclusions. We find that the life of man does cast a shadow; that some lives cast a darker and a heavier shadow than others; and that this shadow not only causes our minds to believe in darkness and evil, its presence being always with us, but it also gives origin to all the ills known in the world. This last statement may seem to be too far-reaching, but it can be proven to be true.

When we look upon this shadow, our thoughts are created in the image of darkness; and any thought that is not created in the image of light must necessarily be an evil thought a thought that will affect human life adversely. Such thoughts darken the mind, confuse the mind, misdirect the mind; and we have, in consequence, a number of mental actions that can only end in undesirable results. Thus, by thinking of the shadow, believing it to be real, the mind is prevented from doing all its thinking in the light; and here we find the final cause of good and evil in man. The good in him comes from his thinking in the light; the evil in him comes from: his thinking in the shadow, and by following the shadow during a large portion of his daily existence. It is clearly evident therefore that if there were no shadow, all the thinking of man would be in the light; and as such thinking can result only in the good, there would be no further evil in his life or in his world.

Our reasoning thus far is on solid ground, and our conclusions, as far as we have gone, cannot be gainsaid. But we still have to find the reason why the life of man does cast a shadow; or why the light of divine being does not pass through the human being. True, a number of the rays of that light do pass through the nature of many, and there are not a few who are approaching spiritual transparence, or who are on the verge of such transparence at frequent intervals. The lives of these are, at certain periods, almost like windows, through which we discern quite distinctly the majestic glory of the spiritual side of existence. That spiritual transparence can be attained, is being attained by a constantly growing number, we know therefore full well; but before this attainment can be completed by the few and made possible by the many, we must know the original cause of the shadow.

It is evident that the life of man cannot become transparent so long as he thinks in the shadow; and he will think more or less in the shadow so long as he believes the shadow to be real; for the truth is that we shape our thoughts largely after those things we believe to be real; and also, what we believe to be real we make a part of our own minds. Thus the shadow has come into the mind of man, due to the fact that he has considered the shadow, believed in it, thought of it as real because it was always with him.

But we can well understand that no mind can think clearly so long as there are shadows in that mind. Under such conditions thinking would be confused; and it is impossible for the light to pass through a confused mind. Thus the mind, by believing in the shadow, and by making the shadow a part of itself, becomes instrumental in producing that very condition in the life of man that casts a shadow, or that prevents the divine light from passing through. In other words, the windows of such a mind will not be clear; they will not transmit the light. And the atmosphere of such a mind will be shadowy and dense, so that the mental sky will be overcast, more or less, with dark and heavy clouds. The light therefore cannot pass through, and the life of that man will cast a shadow.

From these facts we learn how man, through his recognition of the shadow, making it more or less a part of his mind, actually perpetuates in himself those very conditions that caused his life to cast a shadow in the first place. But why did his life cast a shadow in the first place? Simply because he did not understand the light when he first came up into the light. He came up from simple states of consciousness; in fact, from the darkness, and therefore could not think in the language of light the very moment he came into the light.

Man was not created a finished being. He was created with certain powers and possibilities all of them marvelous and limitless; but he was left free to use his gifts in the making of himself, in the unfoldment of what was inherent in his nature, in the finishing of that remarkable piece of work that the Supreme had, through the laws of nature, begun in him. We realize therefore that man could not, at first, be in the spiritual light. He came up gradually into this light, and earned every step of the way. But as he came into the light he naturally would be ignorant of the nature of that light, and in consequence would form many wrong conclusions, which in turn would confuse the mind. And as a confused mind does not transmit the light, his life would at the very beginning cast a shadow. Besides, his mind would be literally filled with imperfections as he came up in the scale; in brief, he was, in a sense, crude in his mental nature when he began to awaken to his birthright, and a crude mental nature will not transmit the light, but will instead cast a shadow.

We clearly understand therefore how the life of man came to cast a shadow as he began to rise from darkness into light; and we can naturally understand how this shadow came to attract his attention; how he came to think of it as real; and how he came to make it more and more a part of his own mentality, thereby confusing the mind and perpetuating those very conditions in himself which caused his life to cast a shadow in the first place. In this way then evil has continued; but it has continued only as a shadow, and has caused pain and sorrow in the world in this way, that by attracting the attention of man it has prevented him from doing all his thinking in the light. And thinking that is not in the light will naturally produce conditions that are incompatible with living in the light. Wherever we live, all conditions must be in harmony with the sphere in which we live. If we live in the dark, all our conditions will be of the darkness and cannot confuse each other. But if we live in the light we cannot permit conditions that come from the darkness or there will be confusion and disorder, which mean pain, sorrow and tribulation.

The problem of evil therefore resolves itself into this, that since man is now in the light he must live wholly for the light, giving no thought whatever to darkness or to the shadow that may follow his life for a time. He must begin now to think wholly in the light; and by doing this his mind will soon become so harmonious and, clear that the divine light will pass through; in brief, he will become spiritually transparent and his life will not cast any shadow any more.

If we are casting a shadow, be it very dark or very faint, we are obstructing the light to that extent, and thereby interfering with the best welfare of the world, Besides, we are not fulfilling our purpose in life; for we are not here simply to see the light; we must also transmit light; therefore, to eliminate the shadow must become one of our leading aims in life; and to begin, we must consider the cause of the shadow first, and then means through which it may be removed.

We find that the cause of the shadow is found in confused thinking, thinking partly in the light and partly in the dark; and we find that we think in the dark much of the time because we believe the shadow to be real. Therefore, at the very outset we must refuse absolutely to think of the shadow as real. We must know that it is nothing but a shadow, and that it will disappear the very moment we begin to think wholly in the light.

In like manner, we must refuse to think of any evil as real in itself, coming as it does from no other cause than that of our believing a shadow to be a reality. In other, words, we must take consciousness above and back of our usual mode of confused thinking, and begin to think only in the terms of light knowing that the shadow, with all its train of shadows, are one and all mere shadows, not to be considered or recognized in the least. Then we must also know that when we begin to think wholly in the light, that entire train of shadows will disappear as completely as if there never had

In Light of the Spirit

been such things in the world. In training the mind to abandon the old way of thinking, thinking both in the darkness and in the light, and to adopt the new way of thinking in the light only, we must mentally face that state of being which will be realized when the conditions desired have been attained. In other words, if we wish to eliminate the shadows we must turn all the actions of the mind upon that state in which we shall find ourselves when we no longer cast a shadow. And that state is spiritual transparence.

Our strongest desire therefore must be to become spiritually transparent; for as that desire becomes an active part in all the workings of the mind, every power in the mind will be directed upon the ideal of spiritual transparence. Accordingly, the entire mind will begin to transform itself into a finer and finer degree of transparence; for the law is that the mind invariably tends to become like that ideal to which all its powers are directed, provided all the actions of those powers are inspired with an invincible desire to attain unto that ideal.

Thus, by placing spiritual transparence before our mental vision as the one supreme state we wish to realize, we cause everything within us to conform more and more with the law of transparence. In consequence, these conditions that obstruct the light will gradually disappear, not being produced any more; the mental atmosphere will be cleared; and our thinking will become so clarified that every part of the mind will transmit all the light that may come upon us from higher realms. The result will be that more and more of the divine light will shine through our lives and natures; the shadows therefore will become less and less evident until they do not appear again. Then we shall be surrounded entirely by the light; we shall live in the full light; all our thinking will be in the light; and when every thought is born of the light, in the light, there can be no evil, no sorrow, no wrong any more. Then will begin the emancipated life, the glorified life the life we shall live when "our eyes are stayed on Thee" when we live so deeply in the spirit and in the truth that we know only that which is wholly, completely and eternally of the truth.

When we consider the lives of those who have lived largely, who have lived richly, who have lived beautifully, we find that they have invariably transcended the mere demands of the senses; they have taken higher ground; they have gone up into the lofty, the sublime, the empyrean, and have trained their minds to be in constant touch with the finer elements of the soul world. In consequence, their minds have continually reached out for those vast worlds that lie beyond the realm of sense; and in these worlds they have found a universe, the richness, the beauty and the splendor of which no tongue or pen can ever describe. There indeed have they found something to live for; in truth, they have literally reveled in gorgeous mansions of celestial luxury.

They have not, however, lived apart from the world of things. On the contrary, they have lived more closely to things than before because they have learned to see the finer world in all things. They have learned to hold that secret communion with the soul of nature's visible forms they have entered into that sweet and strange relationship with the beautiful everywhere which has always been the privilege of the great soul, and which has always added so much to the loveliness, the joy and the real worth of life.

When we have learned to live constantly in touch with that finer world, we have learned a great secret a secret that will serve us wonderfully well whatever conditions may be in that external world in which we now may live. If we are bountifully supplied with everything in the visible and the tangible, we shall be able to enjoy these things infinitely more if we can also see and appreciate the finer elements of worth and beauty which those things may contain. In truth, no one can enjoy the things that are seen unless he can also discern the glory and the splendor of the unseen.

Then if all external sources of supply and enjoyment should fail us, as they sometimes do temporarily where all is change and reconstruction, we need not be affected thereby in the least if we are in touch with the greater good in the finer world. This higher source never fails and we may draw upon it sufficiently to make life wonderfully rich and beautiful regardless of the absence or presence of external possessions. We may enjoy the finer things to the full wherever we may be. And he who enjoys the finer things to the full is living a life that is not only great and wonderful, but is also sublimely beautiful.

We must not infer, however, that we need neglect the worthy and the beautiful in the external world in order that we may enjoy the greater riches of the finer world. On the contrary, we find that if we would live largely in the world of finer things, it is a great advantage to give our attention to the perfecting and the beautifying of external things. Our great aim must be, the best, the richest and the most beautiful for everybody on all planes. But the finer things must hold the first place in all that we think and do, because the world of finer things is the richest world and the most beautiful world of all; besides, it is only as we live for the finer things that we gain the power to enjoy the good and the beautiful that may exist in all other things. And to rise perpetually into the purity, the light and the glory of the finer world this is how we attain to spiritual transparence; this is how we so refine and clarify the mind that the Great Light may shine through; and our own thinking and living will cast no shadow any more.

Chapter 10

Upon the Path Where All is Good

At the present time the statement that all is good is heard frequently, and as it seems to be a contradiction of human experience, it has naturally led to many arguments and much research into metaphysics, as well as the fundamental cause of things. There is, however, a large number that is convinced that in some form or manner all is in reality good; but the majority still cling to the idea that much is evil and wrong. When we consider the subject from the standpoint of what we may call eternal reality, defining the term "reality" as consisting of that something from which everything proceeds, it is not difficult to prove that all is good in its original state; in other words, that all that is real is good just as we might say that all substance is good, and that all law is good. We know that no law has evil intentions, fundamentally, and we realize that every law has possibilities for good, in one or many directions, although the results from the use of any law will depend upon whether the original purpose of the law was applied, or whether there was a misuse of the original purpose. We know that the same is true with regard to principle, and with regard to all the elements and forces in nature. They all are good in themselves, and we must naturally conclude that all things, wherever they exist, must necessarily be good in themselves. We realize, therefore, that when we deal with reality, or the fundamental side of things, we find that all is good.

However, when we deal with the whole of life, or life as it appears in its various forms of expression, the question is if we can say, in this broad and general manner, that all is good. To answer this question, we shall have to ask ourselves what we are living for, or what we are here for; and we need not go very deeply into the analysis of that phase of the subject before we convince ourselves that we are here to learn some most important lesson. We are here to acquire certain qualities, certain attainments, and to develop towards a certain supreme goal; and we soon find, in viewing the subject in this manner, that we shall, in order to fulfill our purpose in this life, find it necessary to follow a certain path; that is, the one path that naturally leads to the goal we have in view. This path we may speak of as the straight and narrow path; and although it is not narrow in the sense that it restricts us to an extent where we do not have privileges outside of a certain system of life or thought, still it does restrict us from the enjoyment of those things that are not conducive to the great purpose we all have in view.

Here we must remember that the enjoyment of life is a part of the great purpose of life; and therefore the great pathway must necessarily provide, not only for enjoyment, but for the highest form of enjoyment, and at every step of the way. When we learn this, we find that the principal reason why we have not had more happiness in the past is because we have been drilled so long to believe that the moment we were becoming happy we were on the wrong path. We were of the opinion that happiness and pleasure lead to destruction; but the new doctrine declares that you cannot be good unless you are living in the highest form of happiness that you can appreciate at the time. The contrary of the old doctrine declares that if you are not happy you are not good; that is, if you are not thoroughly enjoying life you are not living upon the great pathway of life.

Knowing this, we realize that if we are unhappy there is something about our living that is contrary to the great law of the ever ascending life; or we may be practically off the path, so that the remedy would be to seek the great path once more; and we shall find, after we have entered into the realization of this new idea, that it will be much easier to gain that fullness of happiness and joy that we all desire so much. We may begin our analysis of this subject, therefore, by making the statement that we are here to learn a great lesson, a lesson that is so large and so wonderful that the objective mind cannot possibly comprehend it under any circumstances; but as we develop the higher form of understanding, we realize more and more the fullness of its meaning, and we also realize that this lesson can be learned or worked out only as we follow the great path.

To proceed further therefore in our study, we must understand the meaning of the great path; and we find that it is not some restricted mode of living, but a mode of living that we enter into when our whole attention is directed upon the great light of Supreme Wisdom. In other words, we are on the path when the whole of life has been consecrated to the best, to the highest, to the truest, to the richest and to the ideal, including the best that can be found everywhere on all planes of life. Briefly stated, we are on the path when we are inspired with that great and wonderful purpose. But do we always follow this path? We find that we step outside frequently. We turn to the right and to the left almost every day, and in fact, almost every hour; and when we do step outside we experience pain, adversity, sickness, want and all those conditions that we have spoken of as evil.

Now the question is, if those things really are evil. We have thought of them as such, but we must analyze further before we find the real truth upon this important subject. We all know, through experience, that whenever we step outside the path we have pain, and we also know that this pain reminds us of the fact that we are off the path. Is this pain therefore an evil? It cannot possibly be an evil if it reminds us of our duty to our highest light. On the contrary, it is a good friend, and the moment we take the advice of this good friend and return to the path, there will be no more pain.

From this brief analysis we must conclude that pain is good; that is, it acts as a friend under every circumstance to encourage us to return to the path. We shall find that the same is true of all these other conditions that we call evil; they are reminders, some existing on the left side of the path, others on the right side of the path; and whenever we step outside, then these reminders inform us that we are off the path. Therefore, we must think of them as good, for indeed they are very good. If it were not for those reminders we would possibly remain outside of the path for ages, and thus be deprived, for all that time, of the wonderful realizations that are in store for us as we advance in the scale of eternal ascension.

The truth is that all of these reminders, or so-called evils, are good; and we shall need them just so long as we continue to step outside the path. They are necessities for the time being; but the very moment we decide that we will never step outside of the path again, we shall never know those reminders anymore; we meet them only when we step aside, and they are there to tell us to return; therefore they are good.

We all have had periods of experience proving the fact that when we continued on the path for some length of time we realized that we were not, during that time, in touch with adversity, sickness or pain on any side. We knew nothing about those things in our own experience. The reason was we were on the path; and those conditions do not exist on the path. But when something happened that caused us to step outside the path once more, we met pain, adversity and other reminders, informing us instantly that we had stepped aside from the true way of existence.

The question then will naturally be why we step off the path; and the answer is, that we are learning our lesson; and a mind that is learning is not complete in its knowledge. Such a mind may form misconceptions now and then, and may secure impressions that are not in harmony with what we speak of as absolute truth. In other words, those impressions or ideas are fragments of what is really true; and such ideas may cause the mind to turn, occasionally, from the path of the absolutely true. We understand this perfectly; and even though we shall not be able, for a long time, to see the whole truth upon any subject, still we know that no matter how many imperfect impressions we may form in the future about life, law or existence we know that the very moment we step outside of the path, whether we do so through the suggestions of adverse impressions, imperfect impressions, or whatever the cause may be, we have a group of good friends on either side that will tell us to return to the path at once. Those good friends are pain, sorrow, trouble, adversity and their companions. To act according to wisdom, therefore, we would take their advice and return, and henceforth so live that we shall never step outside the path again.

We all know, through experience, that these so-called evils produce effects upon mind and body that are anything but pleasant; then how can we think of these things as good. But here we remember that if those conditions produced a pleasant effect upon us we would not return to the path. We would remain on the outside and never accomplish what we are created to accomplish. So therefore, the fact that these so-called evils, or good friends, are painful in their effect is also a positive good. It is quite necessary that their effect should be such, otherwise we would not accept their advice and return to the great work we have in store.

In this connection it is most important to consider the fact that if we would always look upon those conditions as good friends, instead of thinking about them as evils, thereby filling our minds with a mass of useless impressions if we changed our attitude in this matter, we would find that several things would happen. In the first place, we would find that all the energy that we had been sending out to annihilate those good friends to no purpose whatever could be used to build up soul, mind, character and life on the great path. We all have experimented along this line, living for weeks and months in an attitude where we did not antagonize anything or anybody in any form whatever; and we discovered that, during such a period, we had more energy and life than ever before, and we accomplished far more than in the past; besides, our work was better, and we enjoyed life to a far greater degree; in fact, we had more life to enjoy, because we were not wasting life trying to remove evil, or trying to remove those conditions that are absolutely necessary where they are, acting as eternal reminders to the human race in order that no individual may remain on the outside of the path for any length of time.

We know the value of the great law, "Resist not evil;" and if we would never resist these so-called evils, never turn energy out to the right, or to the left, where it cannot be used for any purpose whatever, but on the contrary, use all our time, energy and attention in building for a greater life and in learning the great lesson, we would find the greatest difference in the world; we would find that where we took one step forward under the old mode of living, we would be able to take ten or twenty under the new mode.

We all know the effect of periods of grief and worry, how those conditions use up life and energy to no purpose; and the cause is simply this, that we are turning our energies out against conditions that cannot be removed, and therefore, all such energy is wasted. Instead of trying to remove evil, we should let it alone, and return to the great path. Evils do not exist upon the path; but they do exist outside the path; and it is absolutely necessary that they do exist there. No one, however, need turn to the left or to the right; therefore, no one need meet evil if living be always on the path. We shall meet them, however, just as long as we make it a practice to turn to the left or to the right at frequent intervals.

Accepting this idea, we will proceed to turn our energy where it can be used for some purpose; that is, in building for the great life that lies before us. And when we realize that every pain or adversity may have some good advice, some information that we need, we will, if we seek such information, gain decidedly; we will learn something of importance whenever we meet one of these good friends; and instead of antagonizing the so-called evil, we would ask what it all means, and what good advice this friend has to give us at this particular time.

Whenever we meet any condition that is not pleasing, we may know there is something for us to learn. We know that we have stepped outside the path, and we must investigate, so as to ascertain the reason why. We should meet these good friends, therefore, as monitors on the way, for that is what they really are; and if we look for information whenever we meet evil, instead of resisting and deploring our experience, we shall find what we are looking for and learn much. Under those circumstances we should be scientists, and proceed to investigate instead of being anxious or permitting grief and worry. We should look for the facts in the case, the lesson to be learned, for the law to be discovered; and in every instance, these so-called evils will prove to be instructors, giving us valued and timely information along many lines.

When we learn to look upon these conditions on the left or on the right as necessary advisers, knowing that we are here to continue on the path, training ourselves to see that in the ultimate, or in the fundamental, all things are good, the effect upon the mind will be wonderful. The moment we begin to live in the conviction that all things have a good purpose, whether we may see it now or not, we will find the mind becoming more wholesome, becoming stronger and more active, and that life will be elevated and enriched in many ways. We then enter into what has been called healthy mindedness, and we all appreciate the fact that such an attitude holds immense power for greater things. We shall also find the mind becoming more constructive, because, instead of a large percentage of the elements and forces of the mind being turned aside, warring with outside conditions to no purpose, these energies will be used in building for the greater enrichment of existence. Thus the mind will be enlarged, consciousness expanded, and life become deeper, higher, more beautiful and more perfect in every form and manner.

We all know the value of filling the mind brimful of good thoughts; we know what a difference it makes; we know how much it adds both to joy and power; and there is no better way in which we can do this than to live in the conviction that all is good. And we shall not find it difficult to live in this conviction when we know that after all, the so-called evils of the world are good friends existing on the right and on the left of the path to remind us when we step aside, so that we may return at once. Another important gain is this, that if we realize that all is good, we will want to look for the real good and the greater good that must necessarily exist within all conditions, beyond all conditions, above all conditions. If we train the mind in this manner, complying with the great law, "He who seeks shall find," making it a practice to look for the greater good in everything and in everybody, we will find that consciousness will steadily expand, reaching out more and more, coming in contact with more desirable things, more things of value and worth than we ever were conscious of before.

We understand that when the mind dwells continually in an attitude where attention is concentrated upon the imperfect, we are not coming in contact with greater worth nor meeting the superior in life anywhere. Such a mind may be satisfied in a certain sense, for a brief time, but can gain nothing from life that will have a real or permanent value; and in every instance, the temporary satisfaction that was secured from contacting with the imperfect will give way to a state of mental and physical disease, due to the fact that such a mind will soon find itself outside the path.

It is the mind that touches the worthy, the superior, the higher, the finer and the richer on all sides that really gains happiness, and that really gains possession of the highest and the best that life can give. If we seek for the greater good in all places and in all modes of life, we will not simply find the good, but the greater good and the greater worth; and if there is one thing that we all need very much, it is this training of the mind to reach out for the greater, the worthier, the superior in all thought and action. We frequently ask ourselves what might be the greatest need upon this planet at the present time; and the answer is simple a larger number of superior men and women.

We need more such men and women in order that they may become inspirations to the race. The entire world, almost, is now convinced of the truth that our destiny is upward and onward. The race can advance, and must advance to be true to life; but the question is, how we are to find those elements and methods through which continuous advancement may be realized. Here we should remember the statement, "When I AM lifted up." It is the same with every individual; it was not simply true of Jesus Christ, although true of him to a larger degree than anyone else. We know, through experience and observation, that whenever any individual takes higher ground, that individual becomes an inspiration to scores, to hundreds, to thousands.

Therefore, we want more superior men and women in the world, men and women who have found the real worth of life, who have found the upper side, the real side, the true side, the superior side, the lofty side that side of life that is teeming, we might say, with the rich, the beautiful and the ideal. We want more such men and women to become inspirations to the race; and to that end we should give more attention to this wonderful law of seeing the greater good everywhere.

However, we are not going to find this greater good if we give most of our time and attention trying to eliminate those conditions that exist on the outside of the path. If we think that those things are bad and try to remove them, we are wasting time. They are perfectly harmless where they are; and we need not go out where they are. It is not intended that we should go out where they are; it is intended that we should remain on the path where we shall never find pain, trouble, sorrow, sickness or adversity in any form or manner.

Henceforth, therefore, our object should be to let those harmless things on the outside alone; and instead of trying to remove them, we should give our time and attention to the training of the race to remain on the path. That would solve the great problems of evil all over the world.

In analyzing the subject further, we find that, although all things are good, fundamentally speaking, some things are better; that is, there are many things that contain possibilities for greater and greater good; but we cannot find the better or the greater anywhere unless we consecrate life absolutely to the idea that all is really good that all things can and do, in themselves, serve a great purpose.

When we look at human society and note the so-called ills and troubles of certain modes of life, we may ask what we are to do about those things. We may also ask if it is necessary that people live in those adverse realms of society; in brief, if those people need such a life. But the answer to all these questions is very simple. The fact is, that every individual is in contact with the path, and whether he may be in the first step on the way, or higher up in the scale, he will be absolutely free from pain, adversity and ailments of all kinds the very moment he steps into the path. It is not necessary to be a mastermind or an illumined soul in order to continue on the path. It is only necessary that we live on the path where we are, whether we are at the early stages of growth or upon the sublime heights.

The fact that thousands and thousands of people are ignorant of this great truth should convince us of the importance of dealing scientifically with this great subject. We all are more or less responsible for every condition that exists in the world; and therefore we must all work together to the end that every individual may find the path, and also that every individual may be trained to continue uninterruptedly upon the path; but this will necessitate an absolute revolution of practically all the ideas that we have inherited from the past, and a large percentage of more recent ideas. However, the moment we understand that we are here to learn a great lesson, and that we can learn that lesson by remaining on the path, and also that we suffer pain and adversity only when we step off the path, we shall not find it difficult to solve the great problem before us.

But this idea is not a recent revelation. The truth is that all the illumined souls of history have declared this very same thing. We cannot find a single exception. The wise men and women of all ages, including all the prophets, all the scientists and all the students of the higher life, whether they were in the first stages of wisdom or higher in the scale they all declared that we are here to learn a great lesson; we are here to find the kingdom; we are here to rise in the scale; we are here to find and continue upon the great path. That is the message of every great soul that has ever lived; and the corresponding truth of this message, that is, that we suffer pain and adversity only when we are off the path this has also been declared by every mind in history who saw the light.

We should therefore, once and for all time, accept this great message as absolutely true because we can prove it to be true; and we should eliminate from mind and thought every doctrine in the world that contradicts this message in any form or manner.

If we could conceive of human society waking up to the realization of this great message, we can readily imagine the result. The great mass of humanity would at once return to the path, and suffering from pain, sickness or adversity would speedily be reduced to a minimum.

The great purpose of the future must be to convey this message to all the world, and to teach mankind how to find the path. We know full well that there is not an awakened soul upon earth who would want to remain on the outside of the path. Every awakened soul can see what lies on before; and such a soul will not care to step out even for a moment. There is nothing to be gained by turning to the left or to the right, even though such experiences may appear tempting at times. It is all loss and no gain; and the very moment we do step out, our good friend on the outside evil will declare at once, "You are off the path, return this very moment."

In Light of the Spirit

From whatever point of view we may consider the subject we invariably come to the same conclusion; that is, that the purpose of life is good, as it leads to greater and greater good, to greater happiness and to more and more of everything that can add to the worth and joy of existence; and although if we should for the time being, in our study of life, gain imperfect impressions and sometimes step outside, or be tempted to investigate darkness, as learners are liable to do, we shall always find these good friends on the outside declaring, "This is no place for you; you belong on the great path; you are a Son of God; you are destined for glory; therefore return unto God." This is invariably the message of pain and of all the so-called evils of the world; and we cannot speak of those things as evil when their one advice to every human soul is this, "Return ye unto God."

But again, we shall not need the advice of those good friends on the outside after we have received this great message that the awakened of every age have received; that is, that we all belong on the path; and that we meet sin, pain and adversity only when we step outside of the path. Knowing this great truth, we shall want to give our whole time and attention henceforth to a better understanding of how we may so live that we shall always continue on the path; but as we proceed we must not come to the conclusion that this path is so narrow that we are necessarily restricted from the majority of those things that we meet in life upon this planet. The fact is, that me can enjoy everything in life as we proceed upon the path, provided we are true to the purpose of life; that is, provided our one purpose is, through all life and through all enjoyment, to reach out for the higher, the better, the truer, the richer, the more wonderful, the ideal, the sublime.

We are entitled to all the pleasures of physical, mental and spiritual existence; and we can enjoy them all and remain upon the path; but the spirit of all such enjoyment and all modes of life must invariably be upward and onward. And when life is inspired through and through with a desire for the highest and the best on all planes, we shall find that every atom in our being will work steadily and surely for the true, the perfect, the wholesome, the beautiful and the ideal. The result will be that the upward current of life will become so strong that we will invariably be drawn upward and onward by an irresistible force; and thus the inclination to turn to the left or to the right will disappear completely.

When the desire of life for the higher becomes so strong that the whole of life is inspired by, that desire, there will no longer be any desire in mind or body to step outside of the path. The one desire will be to live on the path; and that desire will be supreme. It is possible therefore, through the development of that powerful spiritual desire, to place the human system in a position where it will be protected from temptations on all sides; and then, regardless of what may come or transpire, we shall always continue on the path always ascending towards the greater life, the greater glory, the greater light, the greater joy.

Chapter 11

The I AM is the Way

When we consider the many statements that were made by Jesus Christ during his life upon earth, we find that those statements separate themselves into two distinct divisions; and the difference between the two is so marked that we come naturally to the conclusion that they were made in two different states of consciousness. The first division seems to emanate from a consciousness that is almost human, or at any rate, so close to the human that we might say it was human nature in its highest form giving expression to its thought and feeling. The outer division, however, seems to emanate from a consciousness that is so lofty that we conclude that it is the Supreme that is speaking.

The reason why the statements made by Jesus Christ separate themselves into these two divisions is easily explained, because he did possess two distinct forms of consciousness, consciousness of the human and consciousness of the divine. When we consider the human race we find that the majority are conscious only of the human, and therefore give expression only to thoughts that are decidedly human. A few, however, among the more advanced in the human family are developing the consciousness of the divine; and many are learning to understand this consciousness more and more, so that there are moments when we reach such a high and such a fine state of realization that we almost feel as if the wisdom of the Divine were thinking in us or speaking through us. The greater part of the time, however, we are conscious only upon the human plane, and are chiefly concerned with the manifested side of existence.

In Light of the Spirit

With Jesus it was different, because he had developed that higher spiritual side of his life, and therefore could live consciously, and in fact absolutely, both in the human and in the divine. He could, when he so desired, come down into the life of the human personality, although his human living was indeed of a very high order. Then, at other times, he could ascend to such heights of spiritual wisdom and power that his words were indeed expressions of the eternal I AM; and one of the most remarkable of those expressions is this, "I AM the Way, the Truth and the Life."

In considering this statement we are referred to a corresponding statement that appears earlier in sacred literature; that is, "Be still and know that I AM God," or paraphrased might read, "Be still and know that the eternal I AM is God"; and indeed the eternal I AM is the Way, the Truth and the Life. We know that it is the eternal I AM that is in reality God, the term "I AM," being but another term for the Divine, the Supreme, the Most High; and therefore we can readily appreciate the great statement, "I AM the Way, the Truth and the Life."

We must remember that the I AM, which indeed is the Way, the Truth and the Life, does not dwell exclusively in any one personality. The I AM may find expression through any personality, and indeed does dwell in the soul of every human being. The eternal I AM is enthroned in the spiritual life of every individual soul; and when we enter into the perfect stillness of the soul the peace that passeth understanding that peace that does pass understanding because in that state there is no understanding large enough or wonderful enough to measure the peace we realize it is in that state of peace which is above reason, which is above ordinary mental activity, which is even above what we usually call thinking, where we may know or discern the presence of the I AM.

In Light of the Spirit

When we are in that peace we are in absolute Light, and we do not really think about anything, for the truth is that when we are in the Light we know. It is not necessary to think there in the usual sense of that term, because we know; and here let us remember that there is a marked distinction between thinking and knowing, and between understanding and realization. The process of thinking is a process through which we create thoughts about something that we are trying to understand; but when we know, then we do not have to try to understand or create temporary thoughts about what we are seeking to know. When we know, then the mind is in a state of illumination, and dwells serenely in the perfect realization of the Great Spiritual Light.

We understand therefore that when we are in the peace that passeth understanding, we are above actual mental activities; we are in a state where all these things are felt and realized as absolute states of being; and it is in that realization that we become conscious of the presence and the power of the Eternal I AM.

If we should try to define the I AM to objective intellect, we might liken the I AM to a great White Light enthroned in the soul, and giving expression to its wisdom and power through those higher states of consciousness into which we enter when we are in the glory and light of the soul world. We realize therefore that when we ascend in our consciousness, higher and higher into our own spiritual being, we draw nearer and nearer to the Great White Light that exists upon the spiritual heights of that realm in which the soul forever dwells serene.

When we enter into this lofty state, we meet a wonderful experience; and it is this, that as we become conscious of the life and the presence of the Great White Light, we enter in a measure into that Light, and we feel that we are so perfectly in that Light that we partake of the consciousness of the Eternal I AM. In brief, we feel as if we have become one with the I AM, and can actually make the same great statement, "I AM the Way, the Truth and the Life." In a measure this is true, because we all are one with the I AM in spirit; and when we become conscious of that sublime unity, we partake of the same wisdom and the same power, and also become channels, so to speak, through which the Most High may speak the Word of Eternal Truth.

The statement that "My Father and I are one," illustrates this same experience, because every human entity, spiritually speaking, is one with the Supreme; and when this oneness becomes a reality in consciousness, the Infinite does speak through us, or we give expression to what is in reality the Word of God.

The eternal I AM is individualized in every soul, and therefore we can say that the I AM in ourselves, that is, the Great White Light of the soul, does constitute the Gates Ajar, in our own spiritual being, to the Way, the Truth and the Life. What is more, we find that it is the consciousness of the I AM in our own spiritual existence that constitutes the only secret path to that lofty state wherein we find the Way, the Truth and the Life. We cannot find the Way, the Truth and the Life through any external source not even through the personality of Jesus, or through the personality of any extraordinary soul that might have appeared, or that may appear upon earth. The secret path to the Way is found only in our own interior consciousness of the I AM individualized in us, or our own spiritual consciousness of the Great White Light enthroned in the secret realms of our own soul. If we would find the Way, we must become conscious of the I AM in ourselves; and it matters not how we may proceed, what system of thought or religion we may follow; those things are of secondary importance. The one thing of supreme importance is that we have this great object in view in every effort, or study of life to become conscious more and more of the I AM the Supreme Spiritual Light reigning supremely within our own spiritual kingdom. When our attention is concentrated entirely upon that goal, it does not matter what we may call ourselves or what systems of thought we may follow. If we all have that goal, we all are moving in the same direction; and we all are realizing an ever-increasing measure of that Great Light into which we someday shall enter perfectly, and there meet, face to face, the I AM the Infinite the Most High.

It is the truth that so long as we all have that lofty goal in view, our minor differences are of no importance whatever; and therefore we should lay them all aside, and try to serve each other more perfectly, so that we may rise in the scale of consciousness to a far greater degree than ever before. Thus we shall gain more and more of that wisdom and realization that constitutes the key to the mansions of Freedom, of Truth and of Light.

Where the human race has erred in the past is in this, that we have sought the Way, the Truth and the Life through the existence of some personality instead of seeking it through the consciousness of the I AM in our own spiritual kingdom; and the race has also mistaken in trying to gain spiritual power through various external methods, or by means that are not identified with the consciousness of the Great White Light within our own spiritual existence; that is, we have gone out on bypaths, so to speak, and have sought wisdom and power through various external sources, thinking that we might climb up some other way. But there is only one way; and the I AM is the Way the consciousness of the I AM enthroned in our own spiritual kingdom.

In Light of the Spirit

The more spiritual we become the more perfectly we realize that those who try to seek spiritual power or wisdom through any other source than through the consciousness of the I AM, are trying to climb up some other way; and Jesus did make some very strong statements in that regard, emphasizing, in no uncertain terms, the uselessness of such a course.

When we study history, especially the spiritual side of history, we discover that those who have tried to seek spiritual power in some other way have invariably come to grief; and they have in all ages been looked upon as the "black sheep" of the fold. It is always true, that whenever we turn away from the one central path and try to gain higher power in some other way, we enter into a state of living that becomes more or less uncanny. In other words, we become abnormal, both mentally and physically, and the world tends to shrink from us, feeling instinctively that we are on the wrong path, and therefore will have nothing to do with our doctrines or our personalities. The world as a whole may be more or less in the dark, but humanity does instinctively feel whether an individual is on the path to the Pure White Light, or is living on one of the bypaths, which is indeed a violation of spiritual law; and no one can violate spiritual law without surrounding himself with an atmosphere that is repulsive to sensitive human souls.

On the other hand, it does not matter what our religious beliefs may be, if we are sincere in that connection and do proceed with the one lofty purpose in view that is, to find the Spiritual Light within ourselves, seeking that Light neither, through signs and manifestations, nor through the study of the psychical, the occult or the mystical, but proceed directly and sincerely through the highest light of spiritual consciousness that we may have if we proceed in that manner, there is something about us that the world invariably regards with respect. And even though the world may disagree with us in a measure, still there is that feeling on the part of the world that we are sincere, and that we are seeking the highest good. In brief, the world discerns intuitively that we are on the right path, and that our consciousness of the Light, as far as we have gone, is the consciousness of the Pure White Light.

We shall find a marked difference in all our efforts when we make this our supreme purpose; that is, to become more and more conscious of the Eternal I AM enthroned in our own spiritual kingdom; and when we follow Jesus Christ we do so, not in the sense of depending upon his personality, or expecting to gain anything through his personal existence, but we follow him in this sense, that he revealed, in his life and in his wonderful teachings, the secret path to this sublime consciousness within ourselves through which we may find the I AM which indeed is the Way, the Truth and the Life.

We can readily understand that the consciousness of the I AM as outlined above, must necessarily constitute the true way, because when we are looking for the Way, we are looking for that path that leads into higher states of consciousness, into great spiritual wisdom, into the illumined state, and into the conscious possession of that sublime power that will enable us to understand life to make life as rich, as high, as beautiful, as wonderful and as ideal as the true spiritual life can and will be made. When we become conscious of the I AM we become conscious of the Light of Wisdom and Truth; we become conscious of that Higher Power that exists inherently in every human soul; and we know that whatever we become conscious of, that we will manifest in mind and body. When we ascend into higher realizations of this same consciousness we find that the mind will go higher and higher into the Light, into the

Wisdom and into the Power; and thus we find those very things that do indeed constitute the Way the Way to the Christ consciousness, the Christ life and the life of sublime unity with the Most High.

We also realize that this same consciousness of the I AM must indeed be the truth, because the light of the I AM is the Light of the Eternal, and it is the Pure White Light the Light that reveals the absolute Truth, and Truth of the All in All.

In like manner, we understand how this same consciousness of the I AM within our own spiritual kingdom must reveal to us the life we seek the life eternal, the glorified life, the spiritualized life, the life more abundant, the life that is, was and ever more shall be. We knew that the nearer we draw in consciousness to this deeper, higher state of spiritual being, the more fully we realize the existence and the expression of the life that is real life; and therefore our growth in that consciousness must necessarily be followed by larger expressions of all that abides within that life.

We all have experienced, while in silent moments, something in this connection that illustrates clearly the idea that we here have in mind. While resting in those silent moments, we have felt something wonderful within ourselves, within the kingdom of the soul, inspiring the mind to take wings so that we have arisen to those sublime states of realization where we have felt the presence of a power and a life that we knew at once to be the life and the power of the spirit. This life and power thrilled every atom of our being, and we felt as if we were surcharged with a living essence that could not be otherwise than immortal and eternal.

It is in that state that we have become conscious of the life more abundant; for in truth, a great influx of higher spiritual life has entered consciousness, mind and personality, sometimes to such a great degree that we were literally overwhelmed with glory and power from On High. It is in this experience that we fully realize the meaning of the great statement, "I came that ye might have life, and that ye might have it more abundantly"; for the truth is, that when the I AM comes into consciousness; or in other words, when we ascend in consciousness so that we meet the presence of the I AM in us, it is then that this wonderful influx of spiritual life appears in our own being. When we touch the I AM within ourselves, we naturally receive the greater life of the I AM; and we always touch the I AM within when we enter into the spiritual consciousness of the I AM.

The same great truth is emphasized by the statement "Follow Me"; because we must follow the Christ or the Christ consciousness if we would enter into this wonderful realm of spiritual illumination. But it is not the personal man, or the personality of Jesus that we are to follow. It is the Great Light that the Christ revealed that we are to follow; and we follow that light when we consecrate thought upon the marvelous spiritual within, and seek the kingdom of God in our own interior life and soul.

The one thing of importance to be considered herewith is this, that we may find the Way, the Truth and the Life only through the inner consciousness of the I AM that sublime expression of the Most High that is enthroned in every soul. The I AM is the Great Eternal Light centralized in the soul and enthroned in the spiritual kingdom of every individual soul. We must look to that light, consecrate attention upon that light, and never try to find the secret path in some other way.

We must enter through the door of the I AM; and we do enter through the door of the I AM when we become conscious more and more of the life, the power and the spirit of the eternal I AM existing within our own spiritual being. Every moment that we might spend in trying to secure these things in some other way is so much time and effort lost.

We realize therefore that we all might advance wonderfully, both in mind and spirit, and rise remarkably in the scale of existence, if we would give every attention to this one sublime source. Our purpose in the future must be to consecrate attention upon the real door of the Spirit, the consciousness of the I AM; and seek the Way, the Truth, and the Life through the spirit of the I AM as it Is upon the heights of our own spiritual world; and to this end we must learn to understand the great statement "Be still and know that I AM God," for the Eternal I AM is indeed God.

When objective thought or objective reason is stilled, it is then that the soul may ascend into that calm serene attitude in search of the Light in its purity, in search of the peace that passeth understanding, in search of supernal heights, in search of the Great White Light. And when all these things are found, then the soul does find the Way, the Truth and the Life the soul does meet in reality the radiant countenance of the Christ, the Glorified Presence of the Most High.

Chapter 12

I Go Unto the Father

When we consider the statement "Greater things than these shall ye do," we must not omit the second part of the statement, "because I go unto the Father," although this second part is usually not quoted. However, it is the second part of the statement that explains why the greater works shall follow; and we shall understand presently the reason why.

There are two interpretations that can be given to this statement, and both of them are true, although the one is necessarily only a part of the whole truth.

We know that Jesus had taught his disciples and friends the mysteries of the kingdom, and therefore they understood these higher laws and these higher powers that we, in this age, have rediscovered, and are trying so faithfully to study and apply. He had performed remarkable things, and some of his disciples had also performed what would seem miraculous to the people at large. However, he declared that they should perform still greater things later; and he gave as a reason, "because I go unto the Father." At first thought, we discern very clearly the reason why they should accomplish more after he had gone, because while he was with them they naturally depended very largely upon him to do what they themselves might do if left upon their own individuality; and here it is worthy our time to pause a moment to consider a very important principle.

If we want to do the greater works, whatever they may be, or if we want to gain higher power and enter into higher discernment, we must not depend too much upon individuals aside from ourselves; we must not be dependent, but on the contrary must try to give expression to all the life, power and talent that we, ourselves, possess.

We know that there has been a tendency all along in the history of the human race, especially among those who have tried to understand higher things, to select some great soul upon which to depend; and we know that a very large portion of the world is depending upon the personality of Jesus for everything pertaining to the spiritual life. We find, however, among the millions and millions that depend absolutely upon Jesus, but very few who have any spiritual power of their own. They are, spiritually speaking, negative entities, and they have no control over physical ailments or conditions, and are unable to master any situation in their environment to any satisfactory degree. They are largely entities drifting with the stream of fate; and with regard to spiritual understanding, most of them have not even entered the "a b c" class. They are depending upon that wonderful personality, and depend so absolutely upon that personality that their own spiritual powers continue to be latent, having in most instances never been awakened in the least.

In this connection we realize that if the vast Orthodox world, with its perfect organizations, would add spiritual power to its many factors, we would soon experience one of the greatest revivals the world has ever seen; and it would be a permanent revival, transforming practically the entire race from materiality to spirituality, and thereby eliminating from this planet practically all the ills and wrongs that may exist in the world today. But the vast Orthodox world is not manifesting any degree of spiritual power, and it is practically impossible to find a soul among them who is doing the greater works. Their spirituality, as it is called, is nothing more than a passive goodness, which in most instances, is not strong enough to maintain itself in the midst of temptation without a constant supply of external aid. We have here, therefore, a powerful illustration, and a far-reaching illustration, of the mistake of depending upon any personality, or worshiping any personality, no matter how wonderful that personality may be.

The truth in this regard is, that we should not depend upon any entity whatever that may have appeared in manifestation; but should depend exclusively upon the Infinite; and in reality we find that we do not depend absolutely upon the Infinite, because the act of depending upon the Infinite becomes rather an act of cooperation with divine power; that is, we are simply uniting with God, instead of depending absolutely upon his wisdom and power. When we enter into the spiritual understanding of this divine unity, we realize the full meaning of the statement, "My Father worketh and I work"; and this is the attitude we should assume. The human soul should enter into harmony with higher spiritual power that power that is gained through this higher consciousness of oneness with God. We should not assume the attitude that our whole personality is acted upon by Higher Power, for the fact is we must do our part just as positively and continually; that is, we must work, doing our utmost in the fulfillment of the purpose we have in view; but if we are conscious of oneness with the Infinite while we work, we are constantly receiving aid and assistance from Higher Power; and we live according to the statement, "My Father worketh and I work."

We know that the great prophets of all ages, as well as the seers and the wonderful souls that have appeared upon earth, all walked with God. They were constantly living in such close spiritual contact with the Supreme that they could truthfully consider the Supreme their companion under all circumstances. They did not leave everything to be done by the Supreme; they did not fold their arms and say, "I AM an instrument in the hands of Higher Power; do with me what you like." On the contrary, they sought constantly to give expression to their own individuality, trying to ascend in the scale of spiritual life and illumination; but whatever they were doing, they always walked with God, and whatever they attempted to do, they always sought divine aid.

We find that an awakened soul never assumes the attitude of a mere instrument in the hands of Higher Power; an awakened soul is not a mere instrument to be played upon by any power; and it is not the will of God that any soul should be a mere passive entity, to be used by outside forces, regardless of the purpose or consequence. The truth is, we are here to work out a wonderful destiny, and it is only as we do something ourselves, and work for this purpose ourselves, that we reach the high goal in view. However, we never go alone. The moment we are awakened and assume the true attitude towards this theme, we find that we are constantly walking in conscious oneness with God, and that higher power is being given to us continually as we may require.

In this connection we must remember that man alone can do very little; and we also know that if any individual assumes the attitude of a mere instrument, to be acted upon by outside forces, he is placing his own talents in the ground; and Jesus clearly emphasized the mistake of such a course.

Under every circumstance we must use the talents we possess, and must try to develop those talents as far as possible, and all through life; but as we continue to use and develop our talents, we shall find that our advancement will be far greater, and the results far greater, if we assume the attitude of unity with the Supreme.

The proper course to take, therefore, is to enter into harmony with the Infinite, and to walk with God; and while in that attitude, which should be perpetual, we should proceed to work out our own destiny, using all our own powers, and working individually, as well as in harmony with the Supreme, for the great goal we have in view.

In brief, we should give expression to all the power that we are conscious of, and try to awaken more; but in all our doing, we should always be conscious of the one great truth, that God is with us, and it matters not what our work may be, whether it be material, mental or spiritual, if we proceed with our work in the consciousness of that wonderful truth, that God is with us, and that "My Father worketh and I work," we will realize that we are in touch with something that adds immensely to our power, to our wisdom, to our courage, to our determination, to our inspiration, and to our faith. We shall find, therefore, that much is added from higher sources to that which we already possess; and whatever our work may be, we will accomplish more, and in less time; and instead of our work being wearisome, it will become a pleasure.

The results of such an attitude will make all the difference in the world; but we are not depending upon the Higher; we are not asking the Higher to do everything for us; we are doing our part, and doing all that we possibly can, giving full expression to all that is in us, and yet, at the same time, we realize that the Higher is working with us, and that we are filled and surrounded with the limitless power of the Supreme.

We know that there can be nothing greater than the realization of this wonderful truth; and they who have learned to work in that realization have certainly reached a place in life that is valuable far beyond any price.

Understanding this important truth, we realize that when Jesus went away, he left his friends and disciples upon their own resources; henceforth, they would have to depend upon themselves, and upon the wisdom they had already received; that is, it would be required of them to make full application of their own life and talent instead of depending on their master.

We know that every soul is a teacher; and that every soul is a learner. We can teach everybody and learn from everybody; and the soul that takes this attitude, trying to gain wisdom from every source, and at the same time trying to add to the light of every mind, either by word or by individual living, has taken a position where the gain will be great in every possible form or manner. But in each instance, this soul must give first attention to its own individuality, and must depend directly upon its own efforts and powers to apply in life and in destiny what may have been gained in all these many ways.

In pursuing this study, we shall find very soon that the most valuable truths come to us through our own extension of consciousness, or through our own effort to find greater truth according to the laws and methods that have been suggested to us by great souls of any age. When your own soul is in touch with the vast sea of wisdom, and yet not depending upon any personality for wisdom, that is the attitude through which the highest light is received. In other words, it is the light that we can see with our own vision that illumines the mind to the greatest degree, although we are permitted to be instructed by others, for a period, as to the most perfect methods in the finding of the light. The spirit of truth is everywhere, and we all may open our minds to the light of the spirit of truth, regardless of who we are, or where we may be in the cosmos.

In Light of the Spirit

The first interpretation, therefore, of this statement, would infer that the greater things must invariably follow when we learn to depend upon our own higher wisdom and power, and thus assume that attitude of life where we may give expression to the highest and best that is within ourselves, while at the same time living and working in harmony with all that is good, all that is high and all that is sublime anywhere in the world.

The second interpretation of this remarkable statement is much deeper and goes much farther; and this interpretation does not refer to Jesus as a personality, but refers to the Christ as the only begotten son of the Most High. Let us try to forget, therefore, for the time being, the personality of Jesus, and let us try to think of Christ, the Eternal Spirit, that is enthroned' in every soul, and one with the Father.

To try to differentiate between God the Father and God the Son, and also to try to understand the distinction between the first and second person in the Trinity, and the third person, or the Holy Spirit will lead us into a very deep metaphysical study; and yet, as we grow in spiritual understanding, we shall be able to discern how these three are one, and yet in a certain sense distinct. The usual conception of the Trinity has been so materialistic that we have failed to find the real truth involved; but the spiritual understanding will give us the full light on this wonderful theme.

In an external sense we find that the term "three in one" is merely a wonderful symbol; but as every external symbol is related to a corresponding truth, in the absolute of the spiritual, we realize that the triune idea is by no means a metaphysical speculation only, but in fact a spiritual truth of wonderful meaning.

To try to analyze, through spiritual consciousness, the difference between God the Father and God the Son would require much time and much fine analytical thinking; but we can simplify the matter and state it briefly by saying that God is the Infinite, the Omnipresent Spirit, and that Christ, being the Son, is God individualized in every soul. The Christ, is enthroned in every soul, and is, therefore, God made manifest in man; and that is how the idea of mediation originates; how we reach God through Christ, although it is not through the personal Jesus, but through the Universal Christ, the purely spiritual Son, because the Christ is the Spirit of God living and manifesting in the human soul.

When we grow in spiritual consciousness, we realize how the Christ is related to God by being the individualization of God, and in every human soul, and how we are related to Christ through the wonderful truth that the Christ is enthroned in every soul. And in the same way, we shall understand the significance of the Holy Spirit, and why our growth in pure spiritual truth must come through the ministrations of the Holy Spirit. Turning now to this wonderful statement, "Greater things than these shall ye do, because I go unto the Father," we realize that the higher our consciousness of the Christ, within us, ascends towards the consciousness of the Infinite, the greater becomes our spiritual power.

The meaning of the term, "because I go unto the Father," is this, that the consciousness of the human soul ascends towards the consciousness of the Supreme; and we know that our own spirituality depends upon how high we can go in. the consciousness of the Christ that is enthroned within us. The truth is, that our own consciousness of the Christ is eternally going to the Father; this consciousness is eternally ascending into higher and higher realizations of the Omnipresent Spirit of God; and we may continue eternally to go deeper and higher into the real spiritual life of the Infinite, or into the Kingdom of God, because there is neither limit nor end to the vastness of that life in the kingdom.

We do not simply go at a certain time to the Kingdom, and then remain forever in a certain place in the spiritual life; that is the materialistic view; but the materialistic view never contains the whole truth, although it may contain an indication of the truth. The purely spiritual view declares that the human soul, created in the image and likeness of God, is eternally going to the Father, eternally rising in the wonderful spiritual scale; and the spiritual cosmos is so vast that we may rise for all eternity to still higher states, and still there will be greater and greater glories on before.

But here we must remember that the human soul, ascending eternally, higher and higher, into the spiritual life of the Infinite, can do so only through the Christ that is enthroned in the soul; that is, we must become conscious of the Christ, within us before we can begin to go to the Father. So that the very moment the Christ begins to go to the Father, or our consciousness of the Christ within us is gained so that we may go with the Christ, in consciousness, into the higher spiritual realization of the Divine, this wonderful change begins to take place. We no longer live in materiality, and we no longer depend upon that which is personal; but we begin to advance steadily and surely in higher spiritual consciousness, and thereby secure possession of higher spiritual power. The result must be that the greater works will inevitably follow.

When we realize that the Christ is God enthroned in the human soul enthroned in every soul in the vastness of the cosmos; that the spirit of Christ is the central principle of every soul; and that the human soul is the real man, the you, the me, the "I AM," we discover that it is impossible to separate ourselves as spiritual entities from the Son or from the Father. There is a unity there that cannot be defined in words; but there is also a differentiation there that cannot be defined in words; but those who are spiritually awakened can spiritually discern how we are eternally individuals, and eternally spiritual entities, and at the same time, realize that the chief principle in every soul is the Son of God, the Christ God enthroned in the real spiritual man.

When we grow in spirituality, and discern that wonderful unity on the spiritual side, uniting the soul with the Christ, and the Christ with God, and all spiritual life with the Holy Spirit in manifestation, we discover the wonderful meaning of the Holy Trinity; and therefore, that term is no longer a mere phrase, or a mere expression, but a divine truth of wonderful meaning a truth that can be discerned only by those who are spiritually awakened. And they who do discern the real meaning of the Trinity have wisdom indeed; and still the understanding of that sublime truth is simply the beginning of real spiritual wisdom. We remember the statement, "To know God is the beginning of Wisdom," and we know God for the first time when we discover this interior spiritual relationship how we, as spiritual entities, have the Christ enthroned within us, and how the Christ is God in manifestation, God living and reigning in every soul in the vastness of the cosmos.

Returning to the original statement, that the greater works must follow when the Christ goes to the Father, we find that this is not something that begins in us at any particular time. The Christ does not begin to go to the Father at any certain time, because the Christ is eternally going to the Father; but the discovery, however, of this eternal truth may come to our consciousness at any time. The fact is, that there are a great many things that have been taking place for eternity, and yet those things have seemingly been hidden from us; in other words, we are just awakening to the realization of the wonderful things that have been going on upon higher planes for ages and eternities.

God has been giving everything to this countless number of human souls for all time, but we may not have known this great truth. However, at a certain time we all awaken to that truth; and at our first awakening, it seems as if God just began to do these things for us. But as we become more fully awake in the spirit, we learn that God has been doing these things for us during all eternity, although we were not ready to accept His gifts or enter into unity with Him in working out the wonderful destiny that we all have in store.

Knowing this truth, we realize that higher spiritual power has been pouring down upon us for ages and ages; but we did not receive that power, not being spiritually awakened. When we awaken in the spirit, however, then we begin to appropriate more and more of this power, and the greater life and the greater work must follow. The same is true of the Christ going to the Father. The Christ in us is eternally rising in the vast spiritual world; and when we become conscious of this, we enter into harmony with that wonderful ascension, that is, the ascension of the Christ eternally taking place in our own soul; and when we make this discovery, or when we awaken to that wonderful spiritual process, it is clearly evident that great spiritual power is added; accordingly, greater works must follow.

What these greater works are to be will depend largely upon our own ability and power in life. There are very few of us who really feel the need of what may be called miracles, although as we grow in spirituality, we are liable at any time, to experience demonstrations in our very presence that are truly miraculous. But the greater works, in many instances, will be the greater awakening of spiritual consciousness, the elimination of ailments and imperfection, the overcoming of the world and of all things that pertain to this world, the complete mastery over mind and body, and the conscious possession of those greater powers within us through which we may attain and accomplish the highest purpose or the most wonderful goal that imagination can picture in the lofty world of the ideal.

Whatever the greater work may be in the present life of each one of us, the essential principle is this, that we gain the power to do the greater things because the Christ enthroned in us is eternally going to the Father. However, we must become conscious of that eternal ascension, because it is only as we become conscious of that ascension that our own consciousness takes higher and higher ground.

We know through our own experience, that as we ascend spiritually into loftier realms, into higher states, that the power is greater, the light more brilliant, and the wisdom more wonderful; we realize gain in every conceivable manner. We grow in wisdom, in understanding, in power and in spirituality; and the result must always be that the greater works will follow; and this is the spiritual meaning of the great statement under consideration.

The whole truth of this statement is purely spiritual; but this whole truth is so vast that we may ascend into it, higher and higher, for all eternity, forever rising into the greater power, the greater wisdom and the greater light; and forever manifesting the greater and the greater works that invariably follow. There is no end to that life, to that attainment, to that ascension in spirituality; and therefore, we can truthfully say, that however great the work of any exalted soul may be today, that soul will perform still greater work in the higher life of the wonderful future.

Chapter 13

I AM With You Always

To know the Christ the real Christ to understand the full significance of the first coming of the Christ and to know when and how the second coming is to take place these are vital and living themes among all who are deeply and sincerely interested in the realities of the spiritual world.

In order to know the real Christ, we shall find it absolutely necessary to make a clear distinction between Jesus of Nazareth and the universal Christ. We know that the Christ was incarnated in Jesus of Nazareth, but there is a distinction between the two that must not be ignored. We know that Jesus of Nazareth was a personality, but the Christ is not a personality, although spoken of as the second person in the Trinity. We also know that Jesus of Nazareth did not claim to be the savior; but we know that the Christ is the savior, so that what we have been taught in this regard is practically true, although our spiritual conception of salvation is very different from the literal conception.

To appreciate the mission and need of a savior, we must understand that God creates man for a certain purpose; or rather sends the human soul out into the manifested world to create an ever ascending destiny. For a time the soul is seemingly separated from God, or from the Creator, and it appears as if the soul was left alone for the time being to work out its own life; but here we must not forget that beautiful statement, "God so loved the world that he gave his only Son."

However, this giving of His only Son does not simply refer to the appearance of the Christ through Jesus of Nazareth two thousand years ago. The truth is that God is eternally giving his only Son to every soul in the vastness of the cosmos. Whenever a soul is sent out into the world to work out its destiny, the Christ invariably goes with that soul; and although there are times in the life of that soul when it seems to be drifting upon the sea of existence, and that the Christ is apparently asleep in the ship; or to state the exact truth the soul itself is not awakened to the presence of the Christ in the ship; but the Christ is there; and whenever the Christ is called upon he will arise in the life of that soul and still the storm.

When we enter spiritual consciousness, we realize that the Christ is the Universal Spirit; that is, the only begotten of God, God manifesting himself going forth to follow and be with every soul upon the great journey of life. And here we should remember another beautiful statement: "I will not forsake thee nor leave thee; I AM thy redeemer; I will care for thee." And this is literally true. The Christ never forsakes a single soul. The Christ is always with us and is always waiting at the door of consciousness to be of service to us whenever we are ready to change our life and return to the higher states of existence.

In this connection, we find the ancient doctrine of the second person in the Trinity as the savior, to be absolutely true, although the spiritual understanding of that doctrine is far different from what we have been taught in the literal sense. It would be very interesting to enlarge extensively upon this phase of the subject, but here we need simply remember that every soul, as it goes out into the vastness and richness of life's domain, does not go alone; the Christ goes with every soul; the Christ may be found in the ship of every life; and there is a wonderful reason why.

The soul goes into the manifested life to work out a marvelous destiny. The soul is potentially divine, and is

In Light of the Spirit

endued with power from on High; but as the soul is born in materiality, the light of the Spirit may for a time be partly or seemingly hidden; and in order that the soul may work out its wonderful purpose, it must not be wholly separated from its divine source. It must not be left alone; it must not be permitted to go astray; and God so loved the world that he brought forth his only Son the only perfect manifestation of his own divinity and declared that this only Son should follow every soul upon the great journey of life to guide and lead, so that every soul might be saved from going astray the wonderful destiny of every soul finally perfected the individual soul in time comes forth upon the spiritual heights, clothed with the glory of sublime victory.

In this very place we might consider the fact that it would have been possible for the Infinite to have created us all perfect; that is, not simply perfect in potentiality, but perfect in actuality; but when we ask ourselves the great question, "Would we rather be created perfect, or would we rather be given the privilege to work out our own perfection?" we all would answer, "Give me the privilege to earn what I receive; give me the privilege to work out this wonderful life myself; and when I have reached the supreme heights, let me be able to say that I, myself, have lived and worked for every step of the way, and am the personal creator of the great victory and triumph that I now have realized."

When we look at life in this manner we invariably conclude that the plan of life is very good. There are some dark moments in existence; still we would not have the plan changed. We feel like saying with the Creator in the distant past, "Behold, it is all very good."

We are given the privilege to work out this wonderful destiny that lies before us; but we are not left alone. The spirit of the Christ the only begotten of God is watching over every soul, always ready, to lead, guide, direct, save; and although the soul frequently becomes confused while still living in materiality, nevertheless, there need be no anxiety as to the future, because the Christ is here with us all; and his promise is ever the same, "I will not forsake thee nor leave thee, I AM thy redeemer, I will care for thee."

When we consider the first coming of the Christ we shall have to come to a somewhat different conclusion from the one to which we are accustomed. We all have heard a thousand times the story of the birth of Jesus of Nazareth, and we know the world in general looks upon that birth as the first coming of the Christ. However, the truth is that that wonderful birth was only a part of the first appearance. The first coming of the Christ is that coming of the Christ that we discern when the Christ spirit manifests to us through other personalities; and there have been, and now are many partial manifestations of the Christ everywhere in the world.

Wherever you see tenderness, kindness, love, forgiveness, sympathy, or the finer things in life expressed through any personality; or whenever you discern those higher and more beautiful human traits, it is the manifestation of the Christ Spirit that you discern, appearing to a limited degree through human entities here and there. It is a portion of the first appearance that appearance that can be discerned only by the physical sense of man.

When you go about in the world you may see many a human soul that happens to be in an attitude where the Christ Spirit is given an opportunity to express itself wonderfully; and you feel that you have witnessed an appearance that is higher than that of mere man; and we know that there is not a single human being, no matter how far down in the scale that being may be, that does not at certain times give expression to the Christ Spirit; and the reason is evident, because the Spirit of the Christ, the only begotten, is in the ship of every life. The Spirit of the Christ is hovering over every soul, waiting for every opportunity to manifest, and thereby lift that life to higher realms.

We have frequently looked upon the faces of those that we have considered depraved, and at certain times we could see something beautiful there, a finer touch, a more sublime expression, indicating unmistakably that Divinity was not far away; and whenever we have met such experiences, our faith in humanity and the future glory of the race has been wonderfully renewed. The truth is, when the beautiful spirit of the Christ can find expression, even through those personalities that are at the very lowest place in the scale of life, then what may we not expect from those who are on the way to the lofty heights of pure, spiritual illumination?

Many a time we meet people where the Christ Spirit is manifesting wonderfully where their sympathy is universal where their spirit of forgiveness is sublime where the tenderness and sweetness of character and life is something that is too high and too beautiful for words to define; and again it is the Christ leading the soul into the beautiful pathways of sublime existence. It is the Christ appearing through another personality. It is another instance of the first coming. All of this is perfectly natural, inasmuch as the Christ Spirit continues to go with every soul everywhere; and it is perfectly natural that the Christ Spirit should give expression to the lofty, the pure and the beautiful whenever sublime moments appear in the life of the soul.

In this connection we realize that if we would give greater opportunity for the manifestation of the Christ Spirit; in brief, train ourselves to live more and more in touch with the lofty, the sublime and the spiritual, we would find that the

Christ Spirit would manifest far more frequently, and in a far more wonderful manner.

The appearance of the Christ through Jesus of Nazareth was, in truth, the most wonderful in history; that is, when we consider the first appearance; but it differed only in degree from the Christ appearance in other personalities. It was indeed the highest expression of the first appearance the only begotten Son manifesting through a human personality; and the reason was that Jesus of Nazareth lived in a personality that gave permission to the fullest manifestation of the Christ.

When we realize that the first coming of the Christ simply means the appearance of the Christ through any or every personality in such a manner that this Spirit becomes evident to the physical senses, we may think for a moment that the appearance of the Christ through Jesus of Nazareth does not occupy as important a position as we previously believed; but we need not come to any such conclusion, because that appearance was nothing less than marvelous; and the effect upon the world for all time was extraordinary.

We do not lose any of the beauty or the power of this remarkable first coming by accepting the idea that the first coming of the Christ is constantly taking place in every human personality, whenever the divine is given expression. The truth is, we gain immensely by accepting this idea, because it is, indeed, both beautiful and consoling to know that the Christ did not leave the world two thousand years ago, after manifesting in that wonderful manner for a few years only, but continues to dwell constantly as before, with every human soul "I will not forsake thee nor leave thee" always ready to lead and inspire always at hand, manifesting in many places, manifesting through all souls at certain times. And if we would draw more closely to the realization of this wonderful truth, our salvation from materiality, from limitation, from bondage to things, would be realized instantaneously.

We know that while we are out upon the sea of life, the ship is tempest tossed; and not knowing that the Christ is there with us, we try to work our way as well as we possibly can; but it is frequently difficult. It may take years and years before we succeed in coming out of the stormy conditions; but if we would remember that the Christ is in the ship, and call upon him, he would arise at once and still the storm.

We remember the statement, "Man's extremity is God's opportunity," and we all have come to places where we realized that we could not do anything anymore personally. Then we turned to God; we remembered, "I AM with you always," and we called upon the Christ who was asleep in the ship; we gave up absolutely to the guidance of the Spirit; and in a wonderful and seemingly miraculous manner, things took a turn.

Something unusual happened, and we were set free. We found ourselves emancipated from bondage, and we found ourselves in the presence of new conditions, new environments, new experiences; and. everything became beautiful and ideal.

There is remarkable power, as well as consolation, in the great truth that the Christ is always with us that the Christ goes out with every soul upon the journey of life, frequently manifesting in various ways through the personality of every soul; and all such manifestations, manifestations that are evident to the physical sense of us all such manifestations we speak of as the first coming the first appearance of the Christ to the human race.

The second coming of the Christ is purely spiritual, and takes place within the higher states of consciousness of every individual soul. When you can turn consciousness upon the spiritual within, or upon the reality of your own soul, you will awaken to the great truth that the Christ is within; and the Christ will appear to you in the spiritual within. This is the second coming, and is the final coming of the Christ to you, because everything that we can realize from within is final; that is, it leads us to the highest that we can know in this realm of existence.

The more perfectly we understand the lofty significance of the second coming, as a purely spiritual appearance of the Christ to the soul, the more wonderful it becomes; but before passing further in that spiritual study, it is well to speak more definitely about Jesus of Nazareth.

There is one thing that adds immensely to our spiritual experience; and it is this, that whenever we can see the spiritual meaning of things, we find that the literal meaning is not eliminated, but rather illuminated. There are thousands of people today who believe in the literal coming, and believe in both the first and second coming as purely literal; and the reason is evident. The human race thus far, living largely in materiality, has a tendency to demand the literal expression of everything; the tendency is to want to see this wonderful coming in the sky; and such people demand a literal, tangible appearance. Then there is another class that looks upon every appearance of the Christ as purely spiritual. They declare that Jesus did not live, that the Virgin Mary was only a symbol, and that the resurrection, as well as everything else spoken of in the life of Jesus all were spiritual symbols.

However, when we discern the spiritual meaning of it all, we realize that the spiritual side is universal, and that the literal or tangible manifestation is only one out of many manifestations, all having their source in the spiritual; but the literal manifestations, even though temporary and partial, are nevertheless real.

Jesus of Nazareth did live, and he was so inspired by the spirit of the Christ, the only begotten Son, that his personality and the Christ Spirit became for the time being as one; but here we must not forget that other great souls may reach the same height; that is, become so inspired by the Spirit of the Christ that their personalities may appear to be as one with the Christ.

The Virgin Mary lived, and was the natural mother of Jesus; and here let us consider, what is indeed one of the greatest revelations in history; but it is a revelation that has scarcely been recognized. When the Christ comes or appears to the human soul, we cannot discern the Christ, or spiritually conceive of the Christ, unless our mental and spiritual conceptions are immaculate, that is, absolutely pure. "The pure in heart shall see God." The pure in mind can conceive of these lofty spiritual truths; and every mind must be pure and immaculate in its mental and spiritual conceptions before it can discern the Christ. This is the real Immaculate Conception; and it is both mental and spiritual absolutely necessary if the Christ is to be born into the life of any individual.

However, we find this same truth manifesting upon the physical plane in a certain way; and herein we shall discover something of unusual importance. We know that God created nature and its laws, and it is not necessary for God to change the laws of nature in order to bring a remarkable soul into the world; but here we should remember what was said of the Virgin Mary. "She was overshadowed by the Holy Spirit"; and that is the reason she became the mother of that great and illumined soul; and it is indeed true that if every mother would enter into that sublime state of consciousness, where she could realize the presence of the Holy Spirit during the prenatal period, every child born into the world would be endowed with higher spiritual power, and would be gifted in a wonderful manner.

We can understand perfectly that if the maternal mind is material during the prenatal period, that is, thinks only of tangible things, and lives only in the world of things, the unborn child will have nothing but materiality upon which to draw for physical, mental or spiritual sustenance; and it does not require any logic to prove that such a child will be just an ordinary child. On the other hand, if the maternal mind would, during that period, be overshadowed by the Holy Spirit if the maternal mind would live in the consciousness of the high, the sublime, the lofty and the beautiful, constantly communing with wonderful spiritual realms, and continuing in this sublime state of mind, feeling, life and consciousness during that important period we can readily understand that the child would be remarkable. Such a child would, during the formative period, have the privilege to be nourished by thoughts that were rich, elements that were inspired, forces that contained within themselves all that is high and wonderful in human life; in brief, Higher Power would constantly thrill the unborn creature; finer elements would go to make up the substance of the body, the power of the mind and the nature of the soul. That child, therefore, would certainly appear as a prodigy, or as a great mastermind, or as a marvelous genius, or as a great prophet, or illumined soul.

The Virgin Mary lived in that lofty state during the prenatal period of the child Jesus. She was in constant touch with the sublime world of the spirit, and she was spoken of as a Virgin because she was pure, meaning that she lived in the purity of the lofty, the beautiful, the spiritual and the sublime. The Holy Spirit, therefore, could enter into her life and into the life of her unborn child. In truth, every thought, every feeling, every element and every vein in her entire being all were thrilled and inspired by power from on High. The result was that Jesus of Nazareth appeared as the highest and the most wonderful personality that was ever born into the world.

We realize in this connection that the human race has been given a wonderful truth, one of the most wonderful and most sublime that has even been revealed to human consciousness. And in recent years this great truth is being recognized; we are beginning to understand the spiritual meaning of the coming of the Holy Spirit to the mother of every unborn child. We are fast coming into this remarkable understanding; and when we begin to realize the full meaning of this truth, we cannot fail to understand that motherhood is indeed the greatest privilege upon this planet, and will be considered as such by everybody in coming days.

We know that we are here upon this planet to work out a wonderful destiny; in brief, we are here to bring the kingdom of heaven upon earth; and one of the greatest essentials to that end is to bring forth upon this planet a finer race of people loftier minds, more refined and more beautiful bodies, more perfect human entities, and in truth, master minds and spiritual giants. We need them all if we are to convert this planet into the wonderful world which we know it is destined to become; and here we have the secret a most powerful illustration of which took place two thousand years ago. But the meaning of it all has been misunderstood, due to literal interpretation; and the race thus far has gained but little from that remarkable revelation. However, we know, that with the Supreme, one day is as a thousand years, so that even though the race may have neglected this revelation for two thousand years, we need not be disturbed, inasmuch as we have eternity before us. But, whenever we do receive a great revelation, and understand it, we should proceed at once to make use of it in real life.

We must proceed, therefore, to make this revelation a part of real life upon this planet from this day on; and we know that there is nothing more wonderful, or more inspiring than to meet a human entity that is highly developed, filled with the lofty, the marvelous and the sublime. There is nothing upon this planet that is superior to a real man or a real woman; and the experience of the Virgin Mary has given us the secret through which such men and women may appear on this planet by the thousands, tens of thousands, and by the millions.

Considering again, the true significance of the second coming, we must remember that this coming is never an external event, but an internal and purely spiritual event; an event that transpires again and again in the finer consciousness of every highly developed soul.

The spirit of the Christ will come to you, in your own soul, whenever you are spiritually awakened, and lead you on and on, to greater and greater heights, until you reach the power and the splendor of the master state when you can say, in truth, "My Father and I are One" when you know that, "All that the Father hath is mine" and when your own life becomes so wonderfully illumined by the glory of His presence, that your face will shine as the sun, and your garments become white as the light.

Chapter 14

It is Well With the Soul

When we enter the innermost and uppermost realms of the soul, we find a wonderful world of peace, of joy, of light, of splendor seemingly apart from all other worlds in existence. And it is a world wherein all things are always well. This wonderful and sublime world has been spoken of, by the illumined of all ages, as the Secret Places of the Most High; and this is what it is in truth. It is a secret place because when you are in that world you are apart from all else; you are free from all conditions and things; you are alone with the Most High, in the glory of His radiant presence. It is evident therefore that when you are in that world you are where all is always well.

The existence of this secret place is not known to many; but it is something, concerning which, all the world should know. Everybody should know that there is a place somewhere in the upper regions of our own spiritual existence where the ills of life can never enter, but into which we may enter now, today, or at any time. And more, we may learn to live in that sublime state almost continually, and thus gain the perfect freedom of the soul now, and realize, all through life, the peace that passeth understanding.

This secret place is the abiding place of the Most High in us; it is that world of light within our own soul existence where we may enter and meet the Infinite face to face; it is that transcendent state of spiritual realization in which we always feel that God is closer than breathing, nearer than hands and feet; it is that inner consciousness of the singleness of all life wherein we can say with the Master Mind, "My Father and I are one"; it is that exalted height of spiritual attainment where we behold, for the first time, with our own vision, what God has prepared for them that love Him; it is the kingdom of heaven in us wherein the Christ reigns forevermore.

This secret place is not merely a place of which we can speak during our lofty moments; it is a place of which we can speak whenever the soul looks unto the heights a place to which we may go whenever we feel the need of God. And all consecrated souls feel the need of God every moment of every day. For it is the truth that without God no moment can be complete no hour can be what the highest and best holds in store. It is only when God is taken into the life of every moment into the tangible activities of every hour, that we can say that the best has come, and that the greatest good possible today has been realized.

The entire world should know of the existence of this sublime state, because it is the one place of refuge, of freedom, of peace. When we are in this state we are absolutely free; we know nothing of physical ills for we are where ills can never enter. We are not affected by external conditions; nor do the coming or going of things disturb us in the least. We are where all is always well; we are above everything that is passing, that is temporal, that is imperfect, that is wrong. We are where God is; and while there with Him, in the secret places, we can truthfully say, "It is well, it is well, with the soul." But it is not only well with the soul when we are there in that wonderful, beautiful world. It is also well with all else in our world, internal and external. For here we must know a great truth. It is this, that when we enter where all is well we cause things to become well, not only in the soul, but also in body and mind. When we enter where pain can never come, we cause all pain to cease throughout our entire being, physical, mental and spiritual. When we enter where there is always perfect freedom, we secure at the same time complete emancipation from all wrongs and ills in our state of existence. When we enter where all is wholeness and purity, we cause all things to become whole and pure in us in body, mind and soul at the self same moment. For the truth is that we cause all things in our own world to become as we are; therefore, all will be well with all things in our world when we are in the secret places, because in these places all is always well.

How important therefore that all mankind should learn to enter this innermost and uppermost realm of the soul. And what a change would come over the world if all could know how to enter this secret place whenever the need or desire was present. It would mean the passing of all ills, and the coming of the Great Day the Day wherein every soul shall find rest, emancipation and light. It would mean the coming of the Golden Age an age of which every prophet has dreamed. And this age will come; that dream will be realized; but it will not come through repeated attempts to change conditions in the without; it will come when we learn to find the kingdom within when we learn to enter this wonderful world in the soul where all is always well.

However, we shall not give all our attention to the dreams of the future, but rather consider what we may realize in the present as we learn, more and more perfectly, to enter these secret places of the lofty within. Knowing that all is always well within these secret places, we must know that emancipation from every ill must follow the very moment the gates for us swing ajar. And as we pass within, and find ourselves in that world of peace and light, we are free, free absolutely in all things. None of "these things" move us anymore. We are not anxious about anything, because we are where all is well; and to be where all is well is to cause all things to continue to be well.

In this realm we consider only that which is good, and the good that is everywhere in a state of becoming. We do not consider, in the least, that which does not seem to be good; for the truth is that while we are in the secret places, there is nothing that does not appear good. We see things from the upper side. We can see the real. We see that upon which the eternal light is ever shining. We do not see the shadow; nor is it necessary that we should, for a shadow holds nothing, is nothing, means nothing. In this upper realm we see the real, the true, the eternal; and although we are aware of imperfections, they are not imperfections to us; they are simply roses in the bud. Then why should we be anxious or disturbed? Why should we doubt the coming of the bloom, or try to force each individual flower to bloom in advance of its own time and day?

The ways of the world, or the thoughts of the world, do not affect you so long as you live in the secret places; for in these places all ways are good ways, and all thoughts are in the image of truth. You are in the right, living in the full realization of that which is right; you are in the truth, thinking the truth; and therefore the ways and thoughts of the world can no more be where you are than darkness can be where all is light. Thus you are at peace, regardless of what the world may think, say or do.

The coming or going of external possession does not disturb you while your life is fixed on high among the marvelous riches of the soul. You have found the most precious and costly of all precious things you are in the consciousness of the wealth untold, compared with which all the riches in the world are mere trifles indeed. Nor can you ever be disturbed by external places or environments. You have found the secret places of all that is good and beautiful and ideal; you have found the blessed abode of sublime existence; you have found the peace that passeth understanding, and the contentment that is deeper than the depth of the fathomless sea. You have found that glorified state wherein your soul delights forevermore, and therefore cannot be downcast if external environments should fail to please the desires of sense. If those environments do please your senses, you are glad; but if they do not please just now, you are not displeased in any form or manner. You have found that which pleases infinitely more than all the delights of the external world you have found the secret places you have met Him face to face, and you now live in the splendor and joy, of His glory.

We must remember, however, that although we may live constantly in this sublime state of peace in this uppermost kingdom where all is always well we are not indifferent to things about us, nor do we neglect the needs of others. This wonderful meeting with God does not separate us from man; nor does this freedom from the ills of the world take us away from our spheres of helpfulness to mankind. The truth is that after we have found that place where there are no ills, we devote far more attention than ever before to the gaining of the same emancipation for others. We are far more watchful of the needs of others, but we are above their sufferings and ills; we are not affected by their pains or tribulations; we have taken higher ground; we are living where pains can never come; we have arisen from the lowlands of weakness and ailment; we have gone up into the majestic heights of freedom and strength; and therefore we are far more able than before to help those who are still in bondage. And also, our desires to help others to reach the same lofty places of rest and peace, are infinitely stronger than in the past. Thus we realize that whenever another soul finds entrance into the secret places of the Most High, a new savior has been given to the world.

In Light of the Spirit

In considering this wonderful message for daily use, the great truth to be always held in mind is this that there is an upper realm in every soul where all is always well. There is such a realm in your own spiritual world; and you may enter at any time. You may live constantly, or almost constantly, in that realm of peace and freedom now while here upon this earth. In that realm no ill can ever enter. Therefore, take refuge there, and free yourself from suffering, tribulations and pain. These do not belong to you. Go where they are not. Live where you will be above them. Depart from them even now, and the moment you say to them, farewell, they exist to you no more. There is a sacred kingdom within us where all is sweetly serene. It is a land of indescribable delight, so far above the world of pain and wrong, that the storms of unenlightened life can never beat upon its fair elysian shore. It is the paradise we long have sought. We must learn to live there. All the world must learn to live there. Then shall indeed the reign of peace and righteousness come down upon the world, and the glories of heaven shall cover the earth as the waters cover the sea.

And it must be so, for ills and wrongs can exist only so long as we reproduce them. But when we go and live where ills and wrongs can never be, we shall neither produce them nor reproduce them anymore. Thus we shall have risen above ills; we also shall have put out of existence those conditions from which ills have sprung in the past. We shall have gone from the world of darkness, and with the same act given light to all that world.

But how shall these things be? What must we be that we may find the way to that sacred realm of freedom, peace and joy? What secret wisdom must we search and understand before those gates will turn ajar? What must we become, attain or achieve before our spiritual strength becomes sufficient to scale those heights of splendor, beyond whose brilliant glories this world of light is found? We must do much; we must do all that any soul that is sincere can ever do, if we would always live beyond those heights, and thus abide forever where all is always well. But now, even before we have attained to that majestic state of wisdom, light and power where we can rise at will to those supernal heights, we may step in beyond the gates, and feel the joy, the peace, the life, the bliss that this fair kingdom holds in-store. And all we needs must do is simply this, to know that this most sacred realm is here within the spirit of us all.

Know that the secret places are within the highest spirit of your soul, and you have found the way. But there must be no doubt never the least shadow of a doubt. If there be doubt the knowing is not complete; and knowing is not knowing unless it is complete. Know therefore that there is a world within you where all is always well, and you have found the key that can unlock the gate. Henceforth, you may, at any time, take refuge there within the soul, where ills and pains can never come where grief and wrong can never enter where sins and tribulations are as naught. The only barriers to that fair kingdom are made of mental states that do not know. Therefore, to him who knows, and knows so deeply and so well that doubt has ceased to be, such barriers are no more. To him the way is cleared; the gates are wide ajar; and he may go and come according to his will.

The first great truth that we must know is this, that all is possible when we know. And the second is akin to this, declaring with conviction and with power, that all things are truly possible, even now. The only obstacle in the world is doubt; the only barrier is not to know. It is only doubt and mental darkness that holds the human race in weakness, and that causes man to live in limitations. These therefore must be put away; and when they are, the soul of man shall rise to greater heights and richer splendors than even seers have seen before. The visions of the prophets shall be surpassed, and the highest regions of life that thought has ever pictured for the future goal of man, shall prove to be no more than early steps in the soul's triumphant flight. It is when we know that we know the way; for, when we know, it is then we are in the light; and he who is in the light can see most clearly where to go, and how and when. Know therefore that there is a sacred realm within where all is always well, and you shall see the way. It is this knowing that has given you the light; and he who has the light will need no further guidance.

Wherever we may be today, this message should be taken to the heart, and made a part of life. For it is true that man can even now be free; there is a realm within his soul where freedom is and ever more shall be. And every soul, by knowing this, can enter there today. It is what all the world should know. It is a message we should all proclaim declaring with conviction and with power there is a realm within us all where all is always well. It is the secret places where God abides in man, and where we meet Him face to face. It is where God and man commune in spirit and in truth where all that is in God is given unto man where the soul comes forth in wisdom and in glory, knowing that the human is divine. And that which is divine must needs have peace and joy and freedom evermore.

Chapter 15

The Spiritual Borderland

We have learned much concerning the subjective, or the subconscious that immense world of mentality that lies beneath the waking consciousness of man; but we have not learned much concerning the superconscious that far greater world of mentality that is above the usual or waking consciousness of man. And although the subconscious is a great marvel, the greatest marvel known to science, still the superconscious is a far greater marvel in truth, so great that it is beyond the reach and comprehension of modern science. It is only those minds therefore that are highly developed in spiritual or transcendental consciousness, and who can clearly discern the higher and finer things, that can reach and comprehend the superconscious. And to these minds, this upper realm in the mental world is marvelous indeed, far beyond the power of words to describe.

If we would know more of the superconscious, we must develop greater spirituality and train our own minds in higher and finer lines of thought; for the superconscious is a world that those alone can appreciate who can go up among its indescribable wonders and see for themselves. But regardless of this fact, there is much that can be said, concerning the superconscious, that will be intelligible to all minds who live more or less on the borderland of the spiritual world.

To state something definite concerning this upper world of the mind of man, it is well, at the outset, to make a general comparison between the superconscious and the other two fields of consciousness; that is, the conscious and the subconscious. And here we must remember that there are three fields of consciousness in the whole mind of man.

The first is the conscious, that field in which the mind functions during its usual waking activities. The second is the subconscious, that field into which the mind enters more or less during the waking state, whenever thought or feeling is deep, and into which the mind enters completely during normal sleep. The third is the superconscious, that field into which the mind enters when it takes wings, so to speak, and ascends to the upper realms of the wonderful mental world.

Whenever our thoughts are very high, and we feel that the mind is sailing about among the glories and splendors of empyrean heights, we have, for the time being, gone up into the superconscious. In truth, we are frequently very high in the superconscious whenever we know that we are in mental touch with the transcendent and the sublime; and we are frequently lifted into such realms by music that is truly of the soul. We are also lifted into these realms by a number of other things in life that tend to inspire the mind towards the lofty, the beautiful, the ideal, the noble, the majestic and the true.

In comparing these three phases of consciousness we may liken the conscious mind to the moving billows on the surface of the sea always in action, but only on the surface. We may liken the subconscious to the deep waters beneath the surface of the sea; and we may liken the superconscious to the vaulted sky above seemingly having limitations, yet being in reality so great in height and so far-reaching in extent that no limit, so far as we have gone, can possibly be found.

From this illustration, even if taken literally, we secure a clear idea of what a vast immensity the superconscious world really is; but when taken spiritually, with its internal meaning, which we must to secure the true idea, it becomes greater still; in truth, it is then we fully realize that the superconscious is surely as high as the heavens, and as limitless, in mental reach, as the vastness of the vaulted blue.

Accordingly, we conclude that the mind may reach out, farther and farther, higher and higher, into this lofty, expansive realm, and never reach its highest possibilities, or its greatest marvels. And consciousness itself may be expanded perpetually into the same wonderful vastness, and never come to a place where it may not be expanded still farther. This fact is extraordinary indeed, but it becomes far more so when we remember that all of these things are in the great within both the subconscious and the superconscious exist in the great within, the one being beneath, the other above; and the great within, with all these astounding marvels, does exist in every individual mind. How this can be possible we know when we begin to realize that direction in the great within goes, not away from the center, as it does in the great without, but towards the center; and also that the center, in the great within, is as far away from any given point as the boundary line of the sky is from any point in external space.

But to understand this we must have spiritual discernment; we must be able to understand the inner meaning of things, and comprehend the life of the inner world. And when we do, these seemingly incomprehensible marvels become as clear as the light of the day.

The fact that consciousness can be expanded indefinitely, into the great superconscious world is of far-reaching value and interest; and proves conclusively that there is no end to the upward and onward advancement of man; for the truth is that the more we expand consciousness, the larger the mind becomes, the greater our measure of life and power becomes, and the richer and more wonderful becomes the mental and spiritual worlds in which we live.

We may live in a very interesting world today a world holding a thousand things of most remarkable fascination; and yet, we may, by simply expanding consciousness another measure into the superconscious, find ourselves living in a world many times as large and many times as fascinating as the world we lived in the moment before. In brief, where there were a thousand wonders before, there would now be ten thousand; and all of them would be far beyond the most wonderful of anything known in the past.

It is well known that souls having the power to enter frequently into the superconscious, meet such experiences almost continually. At times they live for days in the full consciousness of a higher universe that can only be described as a thousand wonder worlds blended into one. And not infrequently they ascend to heights from which they behold a sight so incredibly marvelous that it can only be thought of as a million thoroughfares extending from one end of the cosmos to the other, with all the splendors of the most gorgeously described heavens, arrayed in shining glory on every side. Thus we can imagine what experiences such souls meet on their "ten million mile" journeys through the inner universes of the superconscious world. And our interest in all these things will be heightened remarkably when we learn that such experiences are not imaginary, but are actual journeys of consciousness in realms that have actual existence in the vastness of the superconscious mind.

Considering the subject from the practical viewpoint, we may employ another illustration with a still further comparison of the three phases of the mind. We may liken the conscious mind to the sower, the tiller of the soil in the great mental garden; we may liken the subconscious to the fertile soil in which every seed is placed where every seed, that is, everything we think, say or do, is to grow, develop, multiply itself, come forth and express itself in the outer world of actual living and being. And we may liken the superconscious to the sunlight from above that great power from higher realms coming down upon the mental garden with its warmth, its light and its life-giving elements, so that every seed in the garden may grow freely and develop into the full grown flower of understanding, character and spirituality.

But here we must remember that if the conscious mind the sower, does not make a wise selection of seed, there will be thorn bushes and other objectionable growths in the mental garden; because the subconscious gives its fertility to every seed, and the superconscious gives its light and life to every seed, be it good or otherwise. It is highly important therefore that the conscious mind, the tiller of the garden, be scientific both in the art of seed selection and cultivation. And it is unthinkable that any mind should be negligent any more after learning what marvelous powers and possibilities the subconscious and superconscious hold in store. With such extraordinary powers at our command powers that we can use and control as we will, we positively cannot give too much attention to the science and art of thought selection and mind cultivation.

From the illustration just given we realize, first, that the conscious mind is always the sower of the seed. The mind we use in our daily wide-awake experiences is the mind that selects the seed and that places every selected seed in the subconscious field. And as we are fully awake when using the conscious mind, and have full control over all its actions, we can select whatever seed we may desire, thereby determining absolutely what we would reap what we would become what we would have for our future. We realize, further, that since the subconscious is the field in which every seed is placed to take root, grow, develop and ripen, we must cultivate that field both deeply and well. In brief, our mental actions must not be on the surface only, but must be deeply felt so that more and more of the subconscious life and fertility is liberated for the growth and development of every flower in the garden. And all such mental actions must be scientifically applied; that is, in perfect harmony with the laws of right thinking, so that the cultivation of the subconscious may be according to the highest art known in the field of true mental culture.

We realize, finally, that it is from the superconscious that we receive the sunshine required for the growth of this garden; and therefore our mental sky must be clear. The clouds of doubt, fear, discontent, ignorance, misunderstanding and materiality must be removed completely, so that the great sun of truth may send its life-giving rays upon every flower and tree growing in this remarkable garden. And it is materiality that is the heaviest cloud that attitude of the mind that closes all consciousness to the light from above, and dwells only in the contemplation of the earth, earthy. Such an attitude will also cause the mind to direct its actions towards the limitations of things and towards the lesser, thereby turning all faculties and talents away from the real light of wisdom from above. In consequence, but very little of that light will be received, and the mental garden will bring forth but meagerly.

If we would receive the full light of the sun of wisdom and truth, and thus expand our minds perpetually in the realization of greater light in all ways, we must turn the mind fully upon the vastness of the superconscious world. We must look up, look unto the hills, turn all thought towards the high places, so that the strong light from the great Eternal Sun may come upon us, fully and directly, thereby giving us, not only its sunshine and life-giving powers, but also its brilliancy and inspiring illumination. In the field of attainment we find it most important to enter into closer and closer touch with. the superconscious, and to reach out continually into the brilliancy and the mental richness of that higher world. And the reason is that it is from the superconscious that we receive our inspiration, our greatest thoughts, our most brilliant ideas, our original concepts and our higher understanding of truth. It is thus evident that it is the mind that can go the farthest up into the superconscious that is the greatest mind, the richest mind and the most inspired mind.

The mind that is in harmony with the superconscious, and that is turned fully towards the light of truth from above, receives its thought directly from the supreme fountain of truth; such a mind therefore speaks as one having authority; speaks as the prophet and the seer; speaks as one who has seen the divine light with his own awakened vision. And in the thought of such a mind there is both depth and height, and a superior quality that reveals most clearly its higher source.

Therefore, we need never be mistaken as to the source of anything that is expressed. And whether it be expressed now, or was expressed in the distant past, we may know whether or not it has a higher source. If it comes from above, through the marvelous superconscious world, the thought expressed invariably reveals a higher something that no one can mistake. It is inspired, for all inspiration comes through the same channel through the light and wisdom of the superconscious. For this reason we cannot give too much attention to our study of this upper mental world. It holds untold possibilities, and in every imaginable direction that the mind may wish to reach out or develop. But a marked degree of spiritual development, combined with the mental discernment of the finer things in life, is necessary before we can go very high in that world. These essentials, however, we all can acquire; and when we secure them we shall be able at any time to go, both far and high, into the wonder world of the superconscious; for a wonder world it is in truth, ten million wonder worlds, each one more extensive and more marvelous than the one we passed through before.

Then who shall say that man, who is in possession of such a mind, is not created in the image of the Most High? The truth is that when we really know man we find that he is far more wonderful than we ever could in the past imagine God to be. And from this larger vision God becomes infinitely more wonderful than we could think before. But this vision shall become even larger than it is now. Where then is the end? And again we may ask, "Eternity, what has thou in store for me?"

Chapter 16

When God So Wills

Your aspirations may be lofty and wonderful; you may have begun to dream the great dream; you may feel tempted to wish for everything conceivable; you may feel an irresistible desire to pray for the very highest that the soul can discern. And if so, you have seen the vision. You are no longer living with mere man. You have become a friend and companion of the gods.

This you know; but what of the future? Will your prayers be answered? Will your innumerable wishes come true? Or, will your only reward be in this, that you have had your dream. Sometimes you may think that this is all; but during your lofty and inspired moments you think differently. Something seems to speak to the soul at such moments; and in answer to your questioning mind, the Voice seems to say, "When God So Wills."

You may not be able, however, to find the secret interpretation of that wonderful statement, and therefore may continue to hover between faith and doubt as to your realization for the future. But you cannot give up your lofty aspirations. Regardless of adversity or fate, you will continue to cling to the clouds; you will continue to reach out, in every conceivable mode and manner, for that invisible sublime something that you feel you must have that alone can satisfy. You have taken the upper pathway, and you cannot, would not, return not for everything that the world might offer or contain.

These are your convictions; and yet you feel that you should receive everything that the world can give; you almost feel it is your privilege to wish for everything, everything in the visible life and everything in the spiritual life. And indeed, why not? That all is not too much for those who have become companions of the gods. Surely there can be neither restrictions nor limitations upon the upper pathway.

In your personal effort to live life as it should be lived, you meet many things that seem necessary, not only among higher things, but also among material things; and when obstacles intervene so that these things seem to pass out of your world forever, you may think that you have wished for that which was not best; and although the passing of these ideals may cause your life, for a time, to be nothing more than a desert of distressing emotions, nevertheless you decide, sooner or later, that you will leave it all to God.

You are on the upper pathway and cannot become wholly disheartened. Even when the clouds on every hand are black and heavy, you know that the light is shining above. You have seen the vision. You still have your wonderful dream.

There is much pleasure in this fact; more than that, it is a rare privilege; but your mind will question again and again if dreams were not made to come true. Therefore, when you see passing out of your world those very things that you wanted more than all else, should you give up hope? Could it be possible that God might will to bring all those things back to you at another and a better time.

You know that nothing is impossible; nevertheless, what assurance do you have that the future will smile sweetly upon your every wish and desire. When things are gone, they seem to be gone forever; when you cannot, at present, have what you want, you can only try to be strong, and send up to the heavens some other prayer. When obstacles intervene that seem to be insurmountable, what are you to do but try to find peace and joy and love some other way?

In Light of the Spirit

These may be your thoughts; but are you wholly right in this regard? Is it not true that everything you have wished for shall come to you when God so wills? And might it not be possible that God is waiting to will you everything, provided you will prove that you merit everything.

Again, is it not true that you can, through your own faith and life, cause the Supreme to come on your side not on your side against someone else, but on your side for everything that you have wished for and prayed for. And when the Supreme is on your side, is there anything that can prevent your dream from coming true?

When God declares that "this" shall come to pass, then the great Word will be spoken; and when the limitless power of the Word comes forth, is there anything that can stand in the way? Indeed, difficulties, confusions, misunderstandings, complexities and unthinkable obstacles may seem to intervene, but what are these before the invincible onrush of Higher Power?

We imagine that we may as well cease our prayer when all hope seems to be gone; but why judge according to the seeming? It is not a matter of whether there is much hope or no hope. Your prayer will be answered when God so wills; and God is waiting for you to be worthy of your prayer.

The very thing that you desire may be on the other side of the earth; but the Supreme is everywhere. Higher Power can, at any time, bring about a series of events that will cause you and that which you desire to meet face to face. The hand of God may work mysteriously, but when it is decreed that certain things shall come to pass, they will come to pass, regardless of circumstances or fate.

In Light of the Spirit

Your dream may seem impossible today; but tomorrow everything may be changed in your favor. Your own deeds, your own thoughts or your own life may have wrought those changes, and because you were true to your prayer; you continued in the faith; you paid heed to the guidance of the Voice; you placed yourself in accord with Higher Power; you were prepared to act when God so wills.

But it is not the Supreme that decides what God is to will for you; it is you, yourself, that decides all these things. It is your own soul that writes upon the book of destiny, and decrees therein what shall come to pass; and when you have proven that you are worthy of that which was written, then your prayer will be answered. The Great Word will be spoken for you. Higher Power will appear upon the scene and utterly banish every obstacle or adversary. Then what you wanted will become your own, and what you saw in the heavens will come to dwell upon earth.

There is no longer occasion, therefore, to hover between faith and doubt, or to think that you have prayed for that which was not best. If you feel in your own soul that your dearest wish was inspired, and that it should be realized, then live in the faith. God will find a way. God can do everything, even to change the minds of every entity upon earth. God will answer your prayer, if you really want the answer, and prove that you are worthy of that prayer.

God is your God, and will serve you in every conceivable manner; but you must decide what you wish to have done; and you must, without fail, be as great, as good and as wonderful as your wish. Continue therefore to dream the great dream to wish for everything conceivable to pray for the very highest that the soul can know. When God so wills, then everything shall come to pass; and God wills everything to those who make themselves worthy of everything. This is the principle and the law; but we need not wait for the distant future to fulfill this extraordinary law; for indeed, the soul, being limitless in power and possibility, can so live in the great eternal now that personal existence may deserve and merit everything now. What the vision may reveal in the present, that very thing our own inherent power, working with God, can make real in the present. Therefore, we all may rejoice with infinite joy; we are on the upper pathway, and may, at any time, find that greatest something which we have longed for, prayed for, lived for when God so wills. And God does not live in the future, but in the never-ending present.

Chapter 17

Regions of Infinite Repose

There is a wonderful realm somewhere in the upper regions of spiritual consciousness, far beyond the ever-moving thoughts and feelings of man, where silence is absolute and eternal; where the soul can be still and know; and in this wonderful realm all life abides in a luminous state of unending repose.

To find this charmed state or region this is ever the purpose of those who have taken higher ground those who have discerned the nearness of the spiritual calm, and who have felt, during exalted moments, the presence of the peace that passeth all thought and speech. And they who seek shall always find, even though it be not until the eleventh hour.

In the finer and the higher worlds of soul and spirit there are no disappointments. No effort is in vain. Every endeavor brings its full and expected consequence. Every desire and prayer is granted. Every dream and vision is fulfilled to the uttermost. Therefore, they who are in search of the wonderful realm of unending repose shall, at the right time, find the goal of their heart's desire.

There are so many states and regions within the vastness of this wonderful realm; and the higher we go, the greater becomes the stillness and the calm, until we reach the sublime heights of spiritual being there we find the very soul of Silence the apex of infinite repose.

We may realize many varying stages or conditions of stillness, and experience states of serenity that are very deep and very high; but all of these may merely give peace and rest to mind and personality nothing more, although peace and rest in full measure have value beyond computation. When we approach the sublime heights of stillness, however, we find more than merely peace and rest; we also find light and power.

The mind of the greatest wisdom is the mind that is forever still the mind that is so completely in the light of the spirit that no effort is required to think or know. Such a mind is illumined with the light that is all of The Light the light that does not shine forth through action, but that abides in the perfect calm in the luminous states of unending repose.

The mind of the greatest power is the mind that can remain for all time in that wonderful realm where silence is absolute and eternal. To be alive and at the same time to be still absolutely still in thought, feeling and consciousness that is the secret of power. And the longer the mind can continue in absolute stillness, while being fully and tremendously alive, the greater becomes the power, until the soul becomes a spiritual giant.

They who would find the path to the greatest and the most wonderful that man can become or attain, will remember that the gates ajar are these: To increase the measure of life and to deepen the realization of stillness the life more abundant and ever more abundant, and constant approach towards the soul of the Silence these are the gates that open upon the wonderful pathway.

The higher we go in the realization of the One Life and the soul of the Silence, the greater becomes our wisdom and power. The more completely we can live; and the more deeply we can feel the spirit that is ever still the higher we rise in the scale, and the more wonderful we become in everything that pertains to human worth and spiritual attainment.

Thus we may go higher and higher in the realization of life and the realization of stillness, until we enter the soul of the Silence, the deepest and highest conceivable state of Silence where life is so absolutely still that being abides upon the very heights of unending repose the apex of infinite repose. And in that most lofty realm we find the all wisdom and the all power.

The deeper and the higher the silence of a living soul, the greater the power. Therefore, when the soul abides in the deepest and the highest silence, the all power is inevitably realized. In like manner, the all wisdom, Life is not merely in touch with the One Source, but actually abides in the One Source. Hence, infinite repose, for the One Source is forever still, being within itself the all in all.

It is only limitation that calls forth effort, effort to overcome limitation and enter the boundless. That which lives in part must work to live more so as to finally live the all. But that which does live the all can abide forever in perfect repose. And the One Source does live the all. Likewise, the soul. The personal man lives only in part; therefore, must work and express effort. But the soul lives the all, and need not express effort. The soul can be still and know. The soul can enjoy the ecstasy of unending repose. The soul can, now and forevermore, abide at the very apex of infinite repose. And you are the soul.

To know that you are the soul, living in the upper regions of that wonderful realm, and that the personal man can, during moments of pause and serenity, draw so near to those upper regions that consciousness can actually touch the hem of the pure white garment of peace the peace that passeth understanding and for the moment partake of the same infinite repose what a joy and a privilege. And when the personal man will learn to take advantage of that sublime privilege, the days of weariness and sadness will have gone forever.

Whatever may transpire in the outer world, there is no need of sorrow or despair. Far beyond the ever-moving thoughts and feelings of man there is a realm where all is still, and where all is forever well. Consciousness may go for rest and refuge at any time to that wonderful realm on high, and abide there for a season with the soul.

And when consciousness returns to its work in the outer world, it will return illumined with wisdom and clothed with power. For, indeed, the soul lives in the very spirit of the One Source; and, therefore, one moment with the soul, and all is well. Consciousness is thus prepared for any life, for any fate; and the personal man may resume his divine mission upon earth.

In due time that mission will be fulfilled; and consciousness will arise to abide for ages and eons with the soul abide in the very life of the Silence, the Silence of sublime and luminous heights abide in the glory and the ecstasy of infinite repose that repose that contains within itself the fullness of all life, all wisdom, all light, all power, all joy the unending peace of God.

The Pathway of Roses

The Pathway of Roses

Table of Contents

Chapter 1 - Paths to the Life Beautiful	221
Chapter 2 - The Way to Freedom	229
Chapter 3 - The Supreme Point of View	239
Chapter 4 - The True Order of Things	243
Chapter 5 - The Good That is in You	249
Chapter 6 - Give Your Best to the World	254
Chapter 7 - Giving Much and Receiving Much	261
Chapter 8 - And All Things Shall Be Added	270
Chapter 9 - When Life is Worth Living	278
Chapter 10 - The Way, the Truth and the Life	290
Chapter 11 - To Know and Think the Truth	295
Chapter 12 - Finding the Lost Word	307
Chapter 13 - The Royal Path to Wisdom	316
Chapter 14 - The Golden Path to Increase	322
Chapter 15 - The Life More Abundant	330
Chapter 16 - Human Nature Becoming Divine Nature	337
Chapter 17 - A Sublime State of Existence	343
Chapter 18 - A Foretaste of Heaven	350
Chapter 19 - The Vision of the Soul	357
Chapter 20 - The Infinite Revealed	364
Chapter 21 - Return Ye Unto God	370
Chapter 22 - Prayers That Are Answered	377
Chapter 23 - The Faith That Moves Mountains	392
Chapter 24 - The Winds and the Waves Shall Obey My Will	410
Chapter 25 - For I Have Overcome the World	421
Chapter 26 - The Supreme Purpose of Life	430
Chapter 27 - The Psalm of Rejoicing	437
Chapter 28 - God's Beautiful Gift to Me	459

To live always in the Secret Places of the Most High. To think only those thoughts that are inspired from above, To do all things in the conviction that God is with us, To give the best to all the world with no thought of reward. To leave all recompense to Him who doeth all things well. To love everybody as God loves us, and be Kind as He is Kind, To ask God for everything and in faith expect everything, To live in perpetual gratitude to Him who gives everything. To love God so much that we can inwardly feel that My Father and I are one. This is the prayer without ceasing, the true worship of the soul.

Chapter 1

Paths to the Life Beautiful

The thinking world of today is being filled with a phase of thought that has exceptional value. True, some of it is in a somewhat chaotic condition, but most of it is rich, containing within itself the very life of that truth that is making the world free. But in the finding of this truth, and in the application of its principles, where are we to begin? What are we to do first? And after we have begun, and find ourselves in the midst of a life so large, so immense and so marvelous that it will require eternity to live it all, what are the great essentials that we should ever remember and apply? "What are the great centers of life about which we may build a greater and a greater life? These are questions that thousands are asking today, and the answer is simple.

First, recognize the great truth that every individual can live his own life exactly as he may desire to live. Man, himself, is the real master of his own existence, and he, himself, may determine how perfect and how beautiful that existence is to be.

Your life is in your own hands. You may live as you wish. You may secure from life whatever you desire, because there is no limit to life, and no limit to your capacity to live. The elements of life can be modified, changed, developed and perfected to comply with your own supreme demand; the increase of life can be realized in the exact measure of your largest need; you are in living touch with Infinite life, and there is neither limit nor end to the source of your supply.

To live in the constant recognition of this great truth, is to rise continually into higher and higher degrees of that mastery of life that gives man the power to live his life according to his most perfect ideals. To reach the goal that every ascending mind has in view, this truth, therefore, must ever be recognized and applied. It is one of those principles that we shall always require, no matter how high we may rise in the scale of divine being.

Second, desire that which you desire, and desire with all the power of mind and soul. We invariably receive what we desire, no more, no less. We get what we wish for if the power within that wish is as strong as we can make it.

The fact that we can have an ideal, proves that we have the power to secure it. The fact that we can formulate and appreciate a desire for something larger and better, proves that we can fulfill that desire. The great essential is to desire with the whole heart; that is, to give our desires all the life and power that we can possibly arouse from the depths of invincible being.

The true desire and the true prayer are synonymous. The true prayer is invariably some immensely strong desire expressed when the human mind feels the sublime touch of the Infinite mind; and the true desire must be in perfect touch with Infinite life in order to be filled with the invincible power of that life.

To cause every wish to come true, we must express all the power of mind and soul through every wish; but we cannot give expression to all the power within us until we awaken our spiritual natures, and we cannot awaken our spiritual natures until we begin to live with the Infinite. The largeness and immensity of the supreme spiritual life within us comes forth only as consciousness is spiritualized, and we gain spiritual consciousness by living and thinking constantly in the lofty state where we actually feel that God is closer than breathing, nearer than hands and feet.

We cannot desire too much, and when we desire with all the life and power that is within us, our desires shall positively be fulfilled. The wish must be wholehearted, not halfhearted; it must contain all the power we have, not simply the limited actions of shallow thinking; and it must contain soul, not simply emotion, but that deep, spiritual feeling that touches the very spirit of limitless life and power.

Third, have faith in God, have faith in man, have faith in yourself, have faith in everything; and have faith in faith. When you have confidence in yourself you arouse everything that is stronger, greater and superior in yourself. In consequence, the more confidence you have in yourself, the more you will attain and accomplish. But the power of self-confidence is but an atom in comparison with the marvelous power of faith.

Faith takes mind and soul into the greater realms of life. It goes out upon the boundless, and awakens those interior spiritual forces that have the power to do anything. This is why all things become possible when we have faith.

It is the nature of faith to break bounds; to transcend limitations, and take life, thought and action into the universal. It is the nature of faith to unite the lesser with the greater, to unite the mind of man with the mind of God. Therefore, we shall always require faith; however far we may go into the greater, the superior and the boundless today, faith will take us farther still tomorrow. And that is our purpose; to realize our largest and dearest desires in the present, and then press on to the realization of other and far greater desires in the future.

Fourth, depend upon the superior man within for results, and give this greater man the credit for everything you accomplish. When you depend upon the personal self, you place yourself in touch only with the lesser forces on the surface; you therefore will accomplish but little; but when you depend upon the supreme spiritual self, you place yourself in touch with the greater powers within, and results will be greater in proportion.

When you give credit to the personal self, you ignore the interior spiritual man; you thereby fail to secure that greater wisdom and power that the spiritual man alone can supply. Instead of being led by that inner light that knows, you are led by the confusion of outer thought; you are turned away from the path that leads to truth, freedom and the perfect life, and your mistakes are many. Instead of being taken into the current of that invincible life that can carry you through to your very highest goal, you remain in the hands of mere physical energy, that energy that can do nothing more than simply keep your body alive.

Whenever you accomplish something worthwhile, and give the praise to your own outer personal self, you immediately lose your hold on those powers through which those results were gained; in consequence, failure will begin, and you will have to retrace all your former steps to again gain possession of that power that can do whatever you may wish to have done.

To constantly depend upon the greater self, to constantly expect the desired results from the greater self, and to always give credit to the greater self, is to constantly draw upon the limitless wisdom and power of the greater self — the supreme spiritual man within you. You thereby become larger and stronger in all the elements of your being, rising ever in the scale, gaining ground perpetually, and passing from victory to victory. What you desire you will receive because higher power is working through you, and as you ascend in the scale, there is nothing that you will not attain and accomplish.

The principal cause of failure among those who are trying to live in harmony with real truth, may be found in the general tendency to think of the outer person as the power that does things on the visible plane. But it is the interior man that gives the power, though the outer person is required to apply it. And the more thought we give to the interior man, the more life and power we bring forth from within.

The interior man is the man, created in the image and likeness of God; it is therefore evident that when you begin to live with the life and the power of the interior man, the expression of real greatness and real spirituality will begin. And from that moment you will not be limited to the power of the personal self; instead you will fill the personal self with that divine power from on high that is limitless, inexhaustible and invincible.

Fifth, live for a great purpose, and hold the central idea of that purpose constantly before mind. Do not live for the mere sake of prolonging existence; live for something that magnifies, on the largest possible scale, all the elements of existence. To live for a great purpose is to live a great life, and the greater your life, the greater the good that you will receive from life. The ruling desire of every living soul is to have life, and have it more abundantly; therefore, to fulfill that desire we must continue perpetually to live for that which produces more life. No matter how rich we may become in the real, spiritual life, here is a principle that we must ever remember and apply.

Do not work for yourself; work for the great idea that stands at the apex of your greatest purpose. The greater the idea for which you work, the greater will be your work; and it is he who does the greatest work that does the most for everybody, himself included. When your work is great you become a great power for good among thousands, and at the same time you do more for yourself than you could possibly do in any other manner.

When you begin to live and work for a great purpose, you get into the current of great forces, great minds and great souls. You gain from every source; all the powerful lives in the world will work with you; you become a living part of that movement in the world that determines the greater destiny of man; you become one of the chief elements upon which will depend the future of countless generations yet to be; you become one of the chosen of the Most High.

To live for a great purpose is to live in the world of great ideas, and great ideas awaken great thoughts. Man is as he thinks. Great thoughts produce great minds; from great minds proceed great works, and great works constitute the building material with which the kingdom upon earth is to be constructed.

When we begin to live for a great and good purpose, we place in action that law that causes all things to work together for good. Henceforth, nothing is in vain; every person, thing or event that comes into our world will add to the welfare, the richness and the beauty of that world. All things become ministers of the life that is real life, we have been giving our best everywhere, and we are receiving the best from every source in return.

To live for that which is high, lofty and sublime, is to walk with God; the love, the life, the power and the wisdom of the Infinite will ever be with us, and to have such companions is to be blessed indeed. Every moment will give us the peace that passeth understanding, every hour will be filled with the joy everlasting, and every day will be as a thousand years in celestial kingdoms on high.

To give the world emancipation is the ruling desire of all minds that are spiritually awakened; and these should remember that to overcome evil with good is the only way. Forget the wrong that may appear in the outer world of things, and give all your thought to the great good that is inherent in all things. You thereby place in action the greatest emancipating power that the human race will ever know.

We are in bondage because we have lived to please the person. Follow the soul and freedom shall come quickly. Then we shall please the person better than ever before. To follow the soul is to enter the greater domains of life, those domains from which we may secure everything that is rich and beautiful and superior in human existence. The soul leads, not only into the life more abundant, but also into the actual possession of all the spiritual riches that the greater life may contain. And when we find the kingdom that is within, all that we may desire in the without shall be added.

The soul that lives most perfectly in the present, creates most nobly for the future. Be yourself today, regardless of what happened yesterday. Be all that you are or can be today, and you will live in a fairer world tomorrow.

Chapter 2

The Way to Freedom

There is only one will in the universe just as there is only one mind. The one mind is the mind of God, the one will is the will of God. The mind of individual man is an individual or differentiated expression of the Infinite mind, and the largeness of this human mind depends upon how much of the one mind man may decide to appropriate. Man has the freedom to incorporate in his own individual consciousness as much of the Infinite mind as he may desire; and as the mind of the Infinite is limitless, the mind of man may continue to become larger and larger without any end.

The will of the individual mind is a partial expression of the will of God, just as the force of growth that is in each branch is a part of the same force that is in the vine, and the power of the individual will depends upon how perfectly the individual mind works in harmony with the Infinite mind.

There is no limit to the power of the will of God, the divine will; therefore, when the human will is as large a part of the divine will as the individual mind can appropriate and apply, the human will necessarily becomes immensely strong; and since the individual mind can appropriate a larger and a larger measure of the divine will, there is no limit to the power of will that can be developed in the mind of man.

To develop the true will, the first essential is to realize that there is but one will, and that we will with the one will just as we live the one life and think with the one mind, though in our thinking, living and willing, we do not, as a rule, do justice to that part of the whole which it is our privilege to use. We think, live and will too much as isolated entities instead of as divine beings eternally united with the Supreme.

The second essential is to realize that the divine will works only for better things and greater things. The path of the divine will is upward and onward forever, and its power is employed exclusively in building more lofty mansions for the soul. Therefore the will of God does not produce sickness, adversity or death; on the contrary, the will of God eternally wills to produce wholeness, harmony and life.

The ills of personal life are not produced by divine will; they are produced by man's inability to properly use that part of divine will that is being expressed in his mind, and his inability comes because man does not always apply his will in harmony with divine will.

When man uses his will as his own isolated power, he separates his mind more and more from the source of his power; in consequence, the power of his will becomes weaker, and he necessarily fails to accomplish what he has in view. He also falls apart from the one ascending current of life; he gets out of harmony with the true order of things, and sickness, trouble, adversity and want invariably follow.

The true use of the will is to apply the will in the full recognition of the oneness of the human will with the divine will. My will is as much of the divine will as I AM using now, and it is my privilege to use as much of the divine will as I may desire. To constantly think of my will and the divine will as the same will, is to place my mind in such perfect harmony with limitless power of divine will that I can appropriate this power in larger and larger measure, and the more I appropriate, the stronger becomes the power of will in me.

The Pathway of Roses

When the individual mind is in such perfect harmony with the Supreme mind that the divine will can be given free and full expression, the will of the individual mind becomes invincible; the secret therefore of developing a powerful will is found here, and here alone.

The true will is never domineering nor antagonistic; neither does it ever apply the force of resistance. If you are antagonistic or have a tendency to resist everything that is not to your liking, it is proof conclusive that you are not in harmony with divine will. You are misdirecting your power, and are forming obstacles and pitfalls for yourself.

The divine will does not attempt to overcome evils and obstacles with antagonistic or domineering forces; the divine will does not fight wrong, it transforms wrong. It works in silence and serenity, but goes so deeply into the elements of things that it undermines the very first causes of all adverse or detrimental conditions. It does not resist the surface, but goes calmly beneath the surface and transforms those undercurrents from which surface conditions proceed.

The divine will, by going into the deeper life of all things, transforms all things into harmony with itself; and can transform all things because its power is supreme. Therefore when we are in the midst of adversity, we should not rail against fate nor antagonize those conditions that seem to work against us. We have within us the power of divine will, and this will can change everything for good.

But it not only can, it will. It is not the will of God to keep any person in adversity. It is the will of God to set every person free, and every person will be set free when he places his life completely in the hands of divine will.

When the individual mind can say, from the heart, Thy will be done, the individual life has been placed in the power of divine will and that life will at once begin to pass out of adversity, sickness, trouble and want, into the world of freedom.

However, we do not give up our individuality when we give our mind over to divine will; we do not become automatons in the hands of some superior power; on the contrary, we open our minds to that power that alone can produce individuality. The individuality we now possess has been formed by whatever measure of divine will that we have incorporated in our own conscious existence, and by opening our minds completely to divine will, we shall gain sufficient power to make our individuality infinitely stronger and superior to what it now is. Our purpose is not to be used by the Supreme, but to use the power of the Supreme.

To live the life of God, think the thought of God, and will with the will of God — that is the secret path to the highly developed individuality; and it is such an individuality that becomes a master mind, a Son of the Most High.

When the individual mind declares, Thy will be done, consciousness must fully recognize the presence of Supreme power, and must realize, with depth of thought and feeling, that Supreme power invariably leads to higher ground — the world of freedom and superior existence.

When the mind gives up to divine will in an indifferent, submissive, self-surrendering attitude, it is not giving up to divine will; it is simply giving up to the surrounding forces of fate. Such a mind will permit the forces of adversity to have their way, thinking that it is the will of God that much suffering must still be endured, and will consequently drift with circumstances, accepting whatever comes as a necessary chastisement.

This method, however, weakens the mind, and places the individual more out of harmony with God than ever before. We always place ourselves out of harmony with God when we accept evil as coming from Him, and we weaken our own ability to use divine will when we permit adversity to exist thinking that it was sent from God.

To give the mind over to divine will is not to give up at all, in the ordinary sense of that term; we simply place ourselves in that position where we can use the power of the one true will instead of a mere imitation. We blend our own desires and aims with that power that we know can see us through, and we work in the realization that whatever is detrimental in our plans will be eliminated as we press on towards the great goal in view.

The mind that is aimless, waiting for the will of God to take him where he belongs, will drift with fate. He is not in the hands of divine will, he is in the hands of circumstances because he has not given divine will something to do. God does not tell us what to do; He has given us the wisdom to know our own desires and our own tendencies, and He has given us the power to fulfill those desires, but we must take individual action; this is why we have individuality and free individual choice.

However, when we do take individual action, God will work with us if we enter into harmony with Him, and when He is with us, failure is impossible.

To use divine will, we must first have a lofty purpose in view; we must have something high and something definite that we wish to attain; we must have something upon which to apply the limitless power of divine will, and we must desire to reach that goal with the very deepest and strongest desires of heart and soul.

Then we must will to press on, knowing that we are using divine will, the Supreme will of the Most High, because this is the only will in the universe. It is the will that eternally wills the higher, the greater and the better — the will that is invincible, and always does what it wills to do.

To the minds of the many the true meaning of the will of God has not been made perfectly clear; therefore the majority, even among those who have strong spiritual tendencies, hesitate to give up to the absolute direction of higher power. There is a slight dread in the mind of the average person whenever he thinks of entering the uncertainty and the mysteriousness of the seeming void, and as long as things are reasonably well he does not care to give up to some power he knows nothing of. And as a true understanding of higher power cannot be found among the many, there are, accordingly, but few who can actually declare, with the whole heart, "Thy will be done." We frequently pray for His will to guide us, nevertheless we inwardly expect to use our own wills in mostly everything we do. But such prayers are not true to the spirit, and therefore they prevent the soul from actually discerning the real meaning of God's will; and also prevent the mind from becoming a perfect channel for the expression of His will.

The universe is orderly from center to circumference, and everything is established upon the firm foundation of eternal right and universal good. There is a power that lives and moves throughout this vast immensity, and all those things that have a permanent place in the cosmos, or that are instrumental in any way, in promoting the purpose of life, have their source in this one power. All the laws and forces in existence spring originally from this power; it is therefore the center and source of all that lives and moves; and this power is the will of God. Accordingly, to do the will of the Father is to enter into harmony with the universal order and promote the great eternal plan.

The laws of life are all expressions of Supreme will. God wills eternally the right and the true, and the act of His willing originates and perpetuates the sublime plan of life that harmoniously thrills the entire cosmos during endless eternities. God's will is constant and changeless; therefore all the laws and principles in existence remain ever the same, as they are all the expression of the One Will. All that we see in the life of the universe is the eternal coming forth of Divine Will, and the perpetual returning to the One Source.

The true will in every soul is an individualization of Infinite Will, and the true use of the individual will means the doing of the will of God. The Infinite Will does not seek to control things, but seeks eternally to give itself to things. And here lies the secret in correctly using the human will, and in placing the human will in perfect harmony with God's will. When you can say with the whole heart, "Thy will be done," you are not giving up your own will, but you are placing your own will and the whole of your life in oneness with God and in harmony with the universal order. Therefore, when you do the will of God your own will becomes right, and becomes infinitely stronger than it ever was before.

When we act in perfect accord with the laws of life on all the planes of being, we are doing the will of God because what we call law in life is the will of God in expression in life. He who lives in perfect harmony with nature, who fully appreciates her grandeur and her beauty, and who daily seeks to be inspired by the loveliness of her presence is doing the will of God in the natural world. He who rightly employs all the elements of mind and body, and who furthers the purpose of his own being in constant growth and unfoldment is doing the will of God in the human world. He who searches the deep things of God and enters into that high state where God becomes "closer than breathing, nearer than hands and feet;" he who lives and moves and has his being in the infinite sea of divine light, and ever ascends higher and higher into the greater glories of God's kingdom, is doing the will of God in the spiritual world.

Whoever can say with his whole heart "Thy will be done," has placed the whole of his life in perfect accord with God; and henceforth he will seek to live in perfect harmony with all that is, because all is of God. To do the will of God is not only to place one's life in the hands of God, but to be at peace with all the world, and to give one's whole life to all the world. The will of God seeks eternally to give itself to things — all things; the will of man, to be in harmony with the will of God, must do the same.

However insignificant a law may seem to be, it is God working in that part of His universe; and as He is everywhere, manifesting His power everywhere, we must live and work with Him in all things, even the most trivial, if we would be in perfect accord with His life and always do His will. A law in life is a path to greater things; in truth, an open door through which we may pass more closely into His presence. We can meet God at every expression of life, and whenever we are in the highest state of harmony with our expression of life, we have met God in that place. And also, when we use that expression of life in entering into a larger measure of life, we do the will of God in that place. Therefore, whoever meets God everywhere, and does His will in every place, will realize the fullness of life at all times and under every circumstance. And to realize the fullness of life is to realize the allness of the good.

The Pathway of Roses

The incompleteness of human life, in general, is caused by our failure to enter into perfect accord with all the laws in our sphere of existence. We may be wholly right in some things while the very opposite in other things. We may be) scrupulous in regard to the right use of some laws, and at the same time continually negligent in regard to others. There are many who take perfect care of their bodies, and comply most rigidly with all known physical laws, yet they violate the laws of mind nearly every hour of their existence. Others are very careful so as to think only the truth, and do their best to remain continually in the most beautiful states of mind; but while aiming to live in mental ideals they are wholly indifferent to the welfare of the body. Not infrequently we find people who live in perfect accord with intellectual laws but violate daily the moral laws. Also, too many who are the reverse. In brief, the majority do the will of God in some realms while living entirely at variance with His laws in other realms. And here we find the simple answer to many perplexing questions.

When some misfortune comes to you that you do not think you deserve, do not think that God is unjust or that fate is unkind. You have simply failed to do His will in all things. Do not blame others, do not blame fate, do not even blame yourself; simply proceed to readjust your life so that you may become one with Him in all things. Then all ills shall disappear, and you shall not only regain what you have lost but you shall, in addition, receive much more. Live in accord with all the laws of life physically, mentally and spiritually; do all things in the consciousness of God; do all things to the glory of God, and follow the light of His spirit in every thought and deed; then you will always do the will of God.

The Pathway of Roses

Though you may dwell upon the mountain tops of the spirit, though you may glory in the splendors of the cosmic realm, though your mind may go out upon the vastness of the limitless and your soul ascend to empyrean heights, still, do not for a moment deprive the body of anything that is rich and beautiful in physical existence. The great goal is the spiritual life, and in the spiritual life all the joys of sense, all the joys of intellect and all the joys of the highest heavens are divinely blended into one. The physical life is sacred. The earth is the footstool of the Most High. God lives in His heaven, but every atom in the visible universe thrills with the glory of His radiant presence.

Chapter 3

The Supreme Point of View

When we are upon the mountain top of life and look upon things from this lofty point of view, we discover that all is well. Wherever we may turn our vision we find the same — all is well. We can see all things and yet all is well with all things; the good alone is in evidence; everything is in the likeness of God, and we conclude that everything actually is as it was originally created by God — very good.

But when we descend to the valley we find many things quite different, and the problem is whether the scene on the mountain top was simply a beautiful vision, or the scene in the valley an unpleasant illusion.

To the mind in the valley the life of the valley alone seems real; to the mind on the heights the beauty and glory of sublime life alone seems real, while the regions below are but the undeveloped beginnings of some better day.

To decide which of these two minds is right is not necessary; we cannot know the truth by what seems to be true from a single point of view. It is results that demonstrate, therefore we must find what effect life in the valley has upon the whole of life, and what effect life on the heights has upon the whole of life.

To live in the valley alone, ignoring everything that may come from lofty realms, is to live in darkness, trouble and pain. This we know. To him who secludes himself in the lower regions of existence, nothing seems to be wholly well; there is usually something wrong or defective with everything with which he may come in contact, and life at best has but little to give.

The Pathway of Roses

How different, however, everything becomes when we begin to live on the heights. We not only find that all is well in these upper regions but all things become well in the lower realms the moment we begin to live in the upper. We must therefore conclude that all is well when we are well, but that we are not well unless we live on the heights.

We also conclude that the vision of the soul is true, that the ideal alone is real, and that man can see all things as they are only when entering sublime existence. And as all is well from the viewpoint of sublime existence, to think the truth man must always think that all is well.

To live in the lower realms is to live in pain; to live in the upper realms is to live in peace, freedom and joy. Then why should we continue to live in the lower, while wholly ignoring the upper? Why should we declare that the lower alone is real, and that the upper is but a pleasant dream? Is pain more real than joy? Is bondage more real than freedom, death more real than life?

True, daily experience sometimes seems to contradict the vision of the soul, but if darkness be present now, does that prove that light is always a mere dream? When we are wholly out of harmony we cannot understand, for the time being, how there can be any harmony; all seems to be discord; but the moment we fully recognize the absoluteness of universal harmony, discord is no more.

When all does not seem to be well in daily life, we may not feel that we can truthfully say that all is well, but there is a marked distinction between the outer appearance of discord and the inner reality of harmony; and it is the inner reality that we should live.

The Pathway of Roses

When discord appears on the surface, the cause may be found in the fact that we have descended from our true place; we have tried to go away from harmony and have thus produced discord. But the moment we return to harmony, the discord disappears, and all is well.

We must conclude therefore, that so long as we remain in the reality of harmony, all will be well, because all is always well in the world of harmony, and the world of harmony is the true world, the only true world — the world in which man was created to always live.

And we must remember the great truth that so long as man lives in the world of harmony there can be no discord anywhere; so long as he lives in the upper regions nothing can go wrong in the lower regions. The lower states of life are but effects of what man does, and when man is on the heights he will do only that which is well because all is always well on the heights; therefore, since like causes produce like effects, all will be well in the valley so long as man lives on the mountain top.

This being true, every person should always think that all is well, and should always live in that sublime life where all is absolutely well. Thus, that which is well, will manifest in every part of life, while that which did not seem to be well will pass away. Live in the true, and the whole of life becomes true.

Whoever discerns clearly the spiritual essence or divine substance which is the basis or soul of all reality, will manifest in the form, not only purity, but absolute immunity from all disease and from all adverse actions among physical elements and forces. His body will be spiritualized in proportion to this understanding, and will establish itself more and more firmly in that state of being where divine nature reigns supremely. To spiritualize the body is to give greater strength, more perfect health and more youthful vigor, as well as higher quality, to the body. To establish the body in the consciousness of the spirit is to give the body absolute protection from weakness or disease; in the spirit we find all the elements of perfect being for body, mind and soul, and we place the body in the spirit when we realize that every atom in the body is filled, through and through, with the real substance of spirit.

Make yourself a living example of the power of spirit. Do not permit a single weakness to continue for a moment. Do not say that you will be in the future; say that you are now; and you are, because you are the exact image of the Supreme.

Chapter 4

The True Order of Things

What the individual life is to be, as a whole, or in any of its parts, depends upon where the consciousness of being is established, and there are three distinct planes in which this consciousness may be established; viz., the physical, the psychical and the spiritual.

To establish life in the physical is to become a materialist; there will be no consciousness of the finer things of existence, and the understanding of things in general will be one-sided; in consequence, the mind cannot see anything as it really is, and will make mistakes at every turn.

The materialist lives for the body alone, and depends upon the physical senses exclusively, both for knowledge and enjoyment; but the physical senses are never wholly reliable unless when employed by mental faculties that are above the physical; therefore the knowledge of the materialist is composed principally of illusions and half-truths, and his enjoyment is but an inferior imitation of real happiness.

The life of the materialist is necessarily full of troubles and ills because he cannot be in harmony with the true principle of life so long as he is living on the surface of life instead of in real life itself. In brief, all the ills of life can be traced to materialism, in one or more of its various forms; therefore, the materialist is not simply one who denies the existence of the soul; the materialist is anyone who lives in the body, who has established his life in physical existence, and who employs objective senses and faculties only, regardless of what he may believe about God, the soul or the future.

Though a person may be thoroughly religious, as far as he knows, and may believe everything that sacred literature may say about things spiritual, if he cannot comprehend the spiritual except as it is expressed in physical acts, physical ideas, physical rites or physical symbols, he is still a materialist; he is living in the world of tangible things, and has no consciousness of that higher power that produces things.

To be spiritual he must discern the spirit that is within things, back of things, above things; while his senses admire the outer symbol, his spiritual discernment must understand the interior significance of that symbol, otherwise he has not found real religion or real spirituality.

The mind that has not entered into real spirituality, is living in materiality, and to live in materiality is to be in bondage to the ills of this world; therefore true existence cannot be realized so long as life is established in the physical plane.

To establish life in the psychical plane is to be guided almost entirely by feeling and emotion; but no feeling is absolutely true unless it originates in the soul, and our feelings cannot originate in the soul unless we have established life in the spiritual plane. Therefore, the person who is living in the psychical plane, is living in a world of feelings, emotions, desires and sensations that are more or less abnormal. His mental world is artificial, composed principally of imaginations that are patterned after things from without instead of the understanding of absolute truth from within.

The imagination is always influenced a great deal by the play of the emotions; and when the emotions are the results of external suggestions, as they always are unless when we live in the spirit, the imagination will likewise be under the control of things, good and otherwise. This means that our thinking will be worldly, materialistic and more or less disordered, because as we imagine, so we think.

Therefore, to live in the psychical world is to live in a world of abnormal feeling and misdirected imagination; but true being cannot find its foundation in such a world. True being can be established only in the consciousness of truth, and the consciousness of truth can be gained only in the spirit.

When life is established in the spiritual state, the physical ceases to be materialistic, and the psychical ceases to be a troubled sea of conflicting emotions. Instead, the physical becomes an orderly expression of the pure, wholesome life of the soul, and the psychical becomes a world of the richest thought, the most sublime feeling and the highest mental enjoyment.

The spiritual state of being is the true foundation of being, because the spiritual alone has the necessary qualities. To establish life in any other state or upon any other plane is to act contrary to the true order of things, and trouble must necessarily follow. There is only one place for man to live, and that is in the soul. When he tries to live elsewhere, in mind or body, he separates himself from his great inheritance and does not receive what he has the right and the privilege to receive.

When there seems to be nothing in life, the fault lies with the man himself, not with the laws of his being. Instead of living in the spirit, where he could receive everything, he has gone to live in the emptiness of the material, where there is nothing to be had but the undesirable consequences of wrongdoing; and wrongdoing is the direct result of wrong-going, going away from the true state of being.

To live in the spiritual state is to give expression to everything that is in the spirit, because what we actually live we bring out into tangible existence; and the spirit contains everything that may be required to perfect the whole of existence — physical, mental and spiritual.

The belief that the spiritual life is apart from the mental and physical is not true; it is the spiritual alone that can make the physical and the mental complete; in brief, we do not begin to enjoy the body and the mind until we begin to live in the soul.

We cannot attain the most perfect physical health and the most perfect physical development until we can begin to draw upon the inexhaustible life of the spirit, nor can we attain the greatest intellectual power and the highest mental brilliancy until our minds are opened to real spiritual illumination.

To have health and wholeness of body, we must have an abundance of that life that is health and wholeness, and that life comes only from the soul. To gain that life we must live in the soul, and the life that we live we invariably bring forth into mind and body.

To perfect the beautiful in the physical form, we must, likewise, receive the necessary elements from the spiritual state. Beauty of form is produced by harmony in formation and soul in expression; but we can give forth neither harmony nor soul until we actually live in the soul.

The true development of mind, character and life, all depend upon our ever-increasing expression of the perfect qualities of the spiritual life; therefore the truest, the best and the greatest results from physical existence and mental existence can come only when we actually enter spiritual existence.

But to enter the spiritual is not simply to provide those essentials through which we may realize the ideal in the physical and the mental; to enter the spiritual is to enter another and a greater world — the transcendent kingdom of the soul — the sublime world of cosmic consciousness. It was into this world that Jesus entered when" his face did shine as the sun and his garment became white as the light." We can therefore imagine what is in store for those who open their eyes to its splendor and glory.

"Be not therefore anxious for the morrow. Sufficient unto the day is the evil thereof." The term "evil" signifies incompleteness, or that which needs perfecting, development and fulfillment now. The statement therefore means that you have sufficient to do to make the present moment full and complete, without giving any thought to what we are to be or do in the future. When the present moment is filled with the most perfect life that we can possibly realize, the seeming incompleteness of the present moment will simply become a perpetual growing process. Incompleteness will thus become a real step in growth; it will be like a growing bud, and will not be evil, only lesser good on the way to greater good. When the bud ceases to grow it decays, and becomes unwholesome, disagreeable. Likewise, when the buds in human life are checked in their growth they produce disagreeable conditions. And here is the cause of all the ills of the world. The remedy is to so live that all the power of life is centered upon the present moment. To give the whole of life to the present moment is to promote the growth of everything that exists in the life of the present moment. To live a full life now is to live more and more life now.

Chapter 5

The Good That is in You

The good that is inherent in everything is infinitely greater and more powerful than any imperfection or undeveloped condition that may exist in the outer world. And therefore when this good is recognized and brought out into real life, that which is not good must disappear. To apply this great truth to yourself, to others, to circumstances, is to place mind and soul in that attitude where conscious contact with the divine perfection in all things will be gained. In consequence, the good that is within will increase, while undesired conditions in the without will decrease. To recognize the greater good that is inherent in all things is to cause that good to become a greater and greater power in you, until it becomes just as strong in action as it previously was in realization.

Live in the conviction that "I AM greater than all my ills or failures; that I AM greater than the limitations of my circumstances, and greater than any condition that I can possibly meet." When you feel that you are greater than your ills, those ills cannot long remain, because what you inwardly feel, you realize, and what you realize, you bring forth into living expression. To open the mind to the great thought that the health that is within you is greater than any disease than you can ever know, is to open your life to the power of that health; and when the greater power of the health that is within you comes forth into the life of every atom in your being, the lesser power of disease, weakness or adverseness must vanish completely. No disease can long remain in your system after you begin to live in the constant conviction that the absolute health that is within you is infinitely greater and more powerful than all the sickness in the world. Nor can failure continue after you begin to realize that you, in the reality of your whole being, have the power to turn the tide of any circumstance that may ever appear in your world. The good that is within you is larger and more powerful than all the troubles, misfortunes or disappointments in existence; and this good, when fully recognized by you, will begin to work for you. It will work for your good, and will turn to good account everything that can happen.

When you know that you are greater than any undeveloped condition that may exist in mind or body, you gain the power to transcend limitations. Your consciousness begins to break bounds, and you find yourself in that larger, richer mental world that you so long have desired to reach. You are placed in touch with the universal and begin to draw upon the limitless for wisdom and power and joy. You no longer feel cramped, but realize that you are absolutely free to live the largest, the best and the most beautiful life that you can possibly picture. The ideals that you discover during the highest flights of mind and soul, are no longer considered impossibilities; you know that you can realize them all; to you there is no failure because the good that is within you is greater than all failure. You are above limitations; you are master of limitations, and have the power to transform every undeveloped condition into the highest form of completeness and superior worth. The lesser is passing away, and the greater is being realized in an ever increasing measure.

The good that is inherent in others is infinitely greater than all their faults, shortcomings or imperfections; therefore we can readily forgive them for all these. There is more in man than the undeveloped surface, and it is this more that we will recognize, love and admire. When anyone goes wrong we will not criticize or complain; we cannot criticize anyone without harming everybody concerned, ourselves included; nor can we think well of anyone without helping everybody concerned, ourselves included. And everybody wants the best to happen to everybody. To live in constant recognition of the weaker side of human nature is to open the mind to weakness, discord, failure and unhappiness. We steadily grow into the likeness of that which we think of the most. But to live in constant spiritual touch with the great good that exists in everybody, is to open the mind to strength and happiness that cannot be measured. The most beautiful moments in life are realized when we feel that we are one with God and one with that something in man that is created in the image of God. And these moments may become eternal.

Whatever we may meet in life we should always remember that the good within all things is far greater than anything that may appear on the surface; and that this greater good will finally rule the day. When this good is to reign supremely in our world will depend upon us and us alone. The superior within us is always ready and will come forth into tangible expression whenever we are ready to receive it. But we are not ready until we give the greater good in all things the first thought, no matter what the circumstances may be. Whatever may come, meet it all with the thought that the good within is greater still. The good that is inherent in all things is always greater and more powerful. The greatest things in the without are insignificant in comparison. Therefore, we can readily understand how easily the circumstances and conditions in the external world could be changed for the better, provided the all powerful good within us was called forth into tangible action. And now we smooth the pathway of life when we realize that there is a greater good in everything we meet. How kindly we feel towards all persons and all events; nothing seems adverse anymore and what we previously looked upon as obstacles are now stepping stones in attainment. By recognizing the greater good in all things, we open our minds to the wisdom and the power that is contained in this greater good; and, in consequence, we are inspired by every circumstance and enriched by every experience. We gain something from everything we pass through, and every event, however adverse, simply tends to arouse more and more of the real greatness within. Even evil, in all of its forms, becomes a lifting power in our world, because we are in constant touch with the great good that is back of and above all evil. We are not crushed by the ills and the wrongs that may exist about us, but instead we are inspired to greater thoughts, greater deeds and a greater life. All things serve us because we have found that greater good in all things that is ever waiting to serve. We have become friendly with the best that is in the world, and the best is becoming friendly with us in return.

The Pathway of Roses

The great and good are many, but he who loves with such a love that with his love some other soul has scaled the heights and there beheld what life eternal holds in store for man, has wrought the noblest of them all. Then give me such a love in boundless measure. Give me the love of some inspired soul whose living presence, fair and strong, can spur me on and on to greater heights than human life has ever reached before — some pure and tender heart who knows the sacred longings of that life supreme within that must ascend and evermore ascend — some fair illumined soul whose spirit dwells within the vision of transcendent realms on high and knows that I AM made for such a place. Then life shall be a life indeed to me; my sacred longings all shall be fulfilled, and every good that I can wish for shall be mine, for all the joys of earth and all of heaven's ecstasies sublime abide for evermore in such a love.

Chapter 6

Give Your Best to the World

"We have looked far and wide for remedies, but in our search we have overlooked one of the greatest of all; and that is love. Not the love of the person; not mere sentiment or emotion, but that strong, spiritual feeling that makes every atom in your being thrill with the purest sympathy and the highest kindness; and that makes you feel that every creature in existence deserves your most tender care and attention.

When everything goes wrong with us, we blame fate, environment or the world; we forget that the world does to us what we have done to the world. When we blame the world for everything, the world will so act that it will be to blame; but when we love the entire world with the whole heart, the world will change toward us accordingly and be kind.

When you do not succeed, when no one seems to care for your service, or for your talents, there are two things to do; do your best and love much. Do not condemn the race because it is slow to appreciate your worth; when you do this you push the world further away from yourself, and its appreciation will decrease instead of increase. Love the world, the whole world, and love with all the power of heart and soul; this will bring the world nearer to you; you will enter into friendly relationship with the world; the race will thereby discover what you have to give and will come at once to receive your talent.

True achievement in any sphere of action depends upon real ability, and a strong, deep, whole-souled love. Real ability can be cultivated, and we can all learn to love much;

therefore the future of any person may become far greater and more beautiful than the present.

When others speak wrongly against you, do not permit the slightest trace of ill-feeling; anger and indignation not only weaken your own system, but also cause you to attract disagreeable people and adverse conditions. Love those who have mistreated you; love them with the very deepest power of your soul and they will soon come to you to make everything right again. Love can change the worst hatred into the deepest love; and what is more, when you love everybody you attract only the best people and the best conditions.

Love much, and lovely souls will daily come into your life; and those people who are not as lovely as they might be, will become better because they have met you and felt the divine fires aflame in your soul.

When people are going wrong, just love them; not with the person, nor in a weak, sentimental sense, but with that strong, soul-love that comes from the very heart of the Infinite. Such love will lift anybody; and whoever is lifted up into the better becomes better. When we ascend in the scale of life we enter the truer and the higher; we enter the right and thereby become true and right.

When you have reason to think that others are trying to take advantage of you, have no fear. Do not condemn; do not think of the wrong they are planning to do; take God with you and love them; love as you never loved before, and the wrong they are holding against you will change and become a great power for your good instead. Love can change any condition or circumstance and every change that comes through love is a change for the better.

Love brings us into right relations with all persons and all things; love removes inharmony, perverted feelings, obstacles, barriers and all kinds of unnatural conditions, and produces that perfect oneness through which the beautiful life can come forth. He who has placed himself in oneness with man can easily find his unity with God; but no one can find God who does not love man. When we love the whole race with the whole heart, then we shall enter the presence of Him who is love.

It is the truth that "He is nearest to God who is nearest to man;" and the nearer we are to God, the more life and power we receive from above; in consequence, the more we can accomplish in the world, and the better off will the world be because we came here to live for a while.

To be at peace with everything is one of the greatest secrets to greatness, usefulness and high spiritual attainment; and he alone can find the peace that passeth understanding who loves everybody and loves much. But true spiritual love does not love because it expects to gain thereby; when we love in the spirit of gain our love is only material emotion, and does not come from the spiritual depths of the soul.

Pure soul love loves because it is love, and must love. It loves because it is its very life to love, and could not cease loving without ceasing to be. And it cannot cease to be because the love that is love is eternal love. Therefore to awaken the love of the soul is to place in action one of the highest powers in the universe; a power that can do so much because it is so much.

To feel the interior presence of this love, with its high, strong, invincible power, perfectly blended with the sweetest tenderness, not only produces a joy that cannot be measured but also lifts you into a universe that is fairer by far than we ever imagined heaven to be. And truly it is heaven we enter when we love with such a love, when we love as God loves.

Pure love sees no evil, no sin, no wrong; it does not live in the world of illusion or darkness; it is a child of the light and radiates its spiritual glory wherever it may be. Where love is, there will the light be also; and neither darkness, sickness nor sin can exist in the light.

There is nothing that will not be blessed by the presence of love; and the soul that loves with the spirit, that loves much and loves always, will meet the good alone. He has given his best to the world, and the world will open its heart to him and be kind. As the years pass by, the world will lavish upon him the richest treasures within its power to give, and nothing will be too good to place at his door. Blessings of all kinds from every direction will come in greater and greater abundance, and his life will be full with the best that God and man can give; because he has given his best to the world, and loved much.

The practical mind may think that this is only sentiment, and therefore has no value, neither for the physical life nor for the spiritual life. But too often the practical mind looks for his treasure in the realm of effect instead of in the realm of cause; in consequence, he finds but little of real value anywhere in life. The great things in life do not come through minds that dwell merely on the surface, that cannot rise above the world of tangible results. Everything that is beautiful and of real worth, whether it appeals to the eye, the ear, the intellect or the soul, has come through the mind that had visions, the mind that could soar to supreme heights, and behold the real splendor and glory of the world.

The Pathway of Roses

To be practical is well and necessary; but there is something else that comes first. This something else brings forth the substance, the material upon which practical efforts may be applied; therefore, the practical mind cannot act until the dreamer has had his vision.

The higher nature of man must act before the external mind can find anything of value to do; the soul must live and think before the person can attain and achieve, and the greater the love, the greater the life and the thought of the soul.

Whatever has added to the welfare of man in any age has been the product of the mind with the vision. All the good things of life have come from the world of visions and dreams. Someone entered the finer realms of life for a moment and brought back a treasure. The practical mind turned it to use, and the world was richer and better than it was before.

This being true, it is the very height of wisdom to train ourselves to enter consciously and frequently into those finer realms and thus bring forth more of its hidden treasures. It is the best we all seek, and since the best comes from the ideal world, the better we understand the ideal, the richer and greater life will become. To be practical in the largest sense of that term is to so live that we can touch the sublime on the one hand and turn every ideal into a living reality on the other.

The great mind is the dreamer, the prophet, the soul with visions; the mind that can soar to empyrean heights and reveal to the race some higher truth, some better way, and thereby elevate the whole of mankind. This is the mind that brings real values to the world, that makes life worthwhile; and one of his principal secrets is love.

The Pathway of Roses

When we love in this supreme, spiritual sense, we give a power to our practical efforts that we never gave before. We give life to our work; we do more and better work; results double and more; we do this through a power that many ignore as mere useless sentiment; and we thus demonstrate that love, the deep, strong, soul love, is as practical as any tangible force in the world.

There is nothing to lose but failure, and everything to gain, when we learn to love in this strong, high, universal sense. To begin, love as much as you can; be directly interested in the highest welfare of everybody; feel in the depths of the soul that we are all working together for the greatest good to all the race; and make this feeling so strong that it thrills every fiber in your being.

But do not love for effect; love because you feel love; and train yourself to feel love by loving with all the power of love, and in the highest, purest sense you know. He who tries to ascend will go up; he who tries to become strong will enter power; and he who tries to love everybody with the deepest, highest, strongest love of the soul will daily enter more and more deeply into the very spirit of that love that is love. And when you are awakened in the world of true spiritual love, real love takes possession of all your feelings and desires; and all your love will eternally love because it is love. From that moment you will constantly receive love from all the world and constantly give love to all the world. You will gain possession of one of the highest and one of the greatest powers in the universe, and the Infinite will always be with you. God is with every soul that loves much; because it is love, the deep, pure, spiritual love that gives man the power to know that My Father and I are One.

The Pathway of Roses

When there is anything you truly wish for, do not stand passively hoping that something may happen to make your wish come true; go out and make that wish come true; have the faith that you can; believe in the power that God has given you and God will give you more. Know that all the good in the universe lies in the path of him who has faith, and who will use the power of faith to make his own faith come true. He who only hopes, will see visions of good things, but will never reach them. But he who transforms his hope into faith and his faith into living words, will reach every lofty goal he has in view. To him nothing shall be impossible, for God is with him.

Chapter 7

Giving Much and Receiving

When you have attained or received something of exceptional worth, give God the glory. Do not praise yourself, or give your own personality the credit. All power comes from above, and the more we appreciate the source of this power the more we shall receive. The path to perpetual increase is to give God the glory for everything that comes, and when we realize that everything comes from God, everything that comes to us will have exceptional worth. Every moment will be a demonstration of the power of truth, every experience will be an open door to a larger, more beautiful world, and every person, thing or event that we may meet, will add to our welfare and joy. With God all things are possible, and when we give Him the glory for everything we are with Him in everything.

To live the life of the great eternal now in the consciousness of those spiritual elements in which the real man lives and moves and has his being, is to enter the new heaven and the new earth. In the spirit all things are forever new, and the life of the spirit is perpetual ascension into the newer, the larger, the more beautiful, the more sublime. When life seems barren and useless, we are not in the spirit, but the moment we enter the spirit, a million universes are revealed to mind, and the joy of existence becomes supreme. We are not required to search the world of things for happiness, worth, entertainment or events of interest; one moment in the spirit is far more interesting than a whole life of physical existence, and one hour in the cosmic world is a thousand ages of unbounded bliss.

Depend upon the Infinite and His power will see you through. We learn that the Lord fought for Israel in ages gone by, and he will do the same now, for He changeth never. The term "Israel" means one chosen of God, and every person who chooses to go with God will be chosen of God. Go with God, live with God, walk with. God, depend upon God in all things, and you will be chosen of God. When you choose God as your leader and your King, He will fight your battles; He will be with you always, and you will never see anything but victory. We fail only when we depend upon ourselves, ignoring the presence and the goodness of the Supreme. We go wrong only when we follow the light of our own darkness, forgetting that the guiding light of the Most High is at hand. This light knows what we ought to do, and when we follow this light we will always do that which is best.

The light of the spirit never leads into sickness, trouble or want. The light of the spirit invariably lead out of that which is evil, and into that which is good. To go with God is to go into freedom, into happiness and into everything that can add to the richness and beauty of life. God is rich and can give us everything we may need without depriving anyone of anything; and when God leads us on to victory no one will lose because we have gained. The best will happen to everybody, and the greatest good will come to all. The gain of one is the gain of the many, providing that gain was secured through higher power; and when the one ascends in the scale, millions will discover the light they so long have desired to see.

This is our purpose: To live the purest, the largest, the fairest, the most useful, the most beautiful and the most spiritual life possible, just for today. To be our very best here and now, with no desire to outshine some other being, but simply to be all that we are in divine being now. To fill the present moment with all the spiritual sunshine that we can possibly radiate through the crystal walls of love, peace, faith and joy; and to live so near to the Supreme that we may touch the hem of His garment whenever we so desire. This is life, and he who lives with such a purpose forever in view, shall never know an undesired moment.

To believe in the Christ is to enter into the Christ consciousness; not simply to believe something about what He was, but to realize what He is; to feel the sublime life that He felt, and to know that touch of the spirit that He knew. We believe in the Christ only when we can mentally feel the power of His life in our own divine nature, and we believe in His name, the name that is above all names, when we can inwardly discern the full spiritual significance of that name. Belief in the Christ is not of the letter, but of the spirit; not to be definitely expressed in words, but to be inwardly felt in the soul. To ask in the name of the Christ is to enter into the spiritual understanding of that name, into the very soul of the power of that name, and in that sublime state offer our prayer. When we enter into that realization where we know what the name of Christ signifies in the spirit, we can ask in His name; and what we ask in His name we invariably receive.

When we enter into the spirit of the name of the Christ we are in the supreme power of the Christ; we inwardly know what the Christ is and what He can do; and being in His power, we are in that power that can do and will do whatever we wish to have done. We fail to receive only when we are outside of that power that can give; but we invariably enter into the power of the Christ when we inwardly know the spiritual meaning of His name. To end a prayer by simply saying, "We ask it in Christ's name" is not sufficient; we ask in His name only when we can consciously feel that divinity that is defined by the name of the Christ.

Words have no power unless they are spoken in the feeling of the spirit of that truth that the words are intended to convey. We speak to God only when we spiritually discern and inwardly feel what we say, and God answers only those prayers that are spoken to Him.

We should never try to eliminate evil. To resist evil, to give thought to evil, or to work against evil, is to give more life and power to the very thing you wish to remove. Overcome evil with good, but do not array the good against the evil, thinking that overcoming implies resistance or warfare. To overcome is to rise out of, forgetting the lesser by giving the whole of life to the greater. The purpose of life is to grow eternally into the greater good. Aim to fulfill this purpose and evil of every description will disappear. There is no wrong in the world that demands our attention. The good alone deserves our attention, and when the good receives all our attention, evil cannot exist anymore. Build for the right; inspire every soul with an irresistible desire for the right, and everything you do will add to the power that makes for freedom. Think of the good, speak of the good, work for the good, live for the good, and the good only, and your life will be a light wherein darkness can never be.

The false prophet always predicts evil, trouble, misfortune and death. He can see only the weak side, the man made, the coming and going illusions. The true prophet can see that which lies behind the illusion, that which is possible, that which is in store, that which can be done and will be done. He keeps the eye single upon the high state, and thereby ascends into the reality of that vision which previously seemed but a dream. Every person who judges according to appearances is a false prophet; he forms conclusions that are not true to real life, and by following those conclusions causes that which is false and undesirable to come to pass. Every person who judges according to the divinity that is inherent in man is a true prophet; he brings truth into expression and thereby causes that which is true to prevail in tangible existence. The true prophet can see the greatness, the beauty and the perfection of the soul of man, and knowing that the soul is the master, predicts the coming of everything that is in the soul, or that the soul has the power to do; and all such predictions will come true.

God is sufficient. When you are in sickness, trouble, sorrow or want depend upon the Supreme. You need nothing else.

Infinite power is greater than all power, and if you have perfect faith, this power will surely set you free, no matter what the condition of bondage may be. The ills of the world continue principally because we think that something else besides the Infinite is required. But to depend upon other things besides the one is idol worship. The true worship of God, the highest worship of God, is to live so near to God that we can, at all times, feel that power that can do everything, will do everything, is doing everything. When we worship God, in spirit and in truth, we do not seek help from things; we use things according to their nature, but we seek help from the Supreme alone.

There is no bondage in living according to the law; in brief, there is freedom only in that life that lives absolutely according to the law. A law is but a path to new realms, fairer than we have ever known before. To follow any law in life is to increase the greatness and the worth of life, and to follow all the laws of life is to grow perpetually into the highest good that body, mind and soul can possibly desire. And no one could wish for a greater freedom than this. To use the law is to gain our own; to misuse or ignore the law is to deprive ourselves of our own, and bring disorder, want and pain into life instead. The law never binds nor holds down; the power of all law moves eternally towards the heights, that supreme greatness that is waiting for man; and whoever follows the law will move with that power up unto those same heights.

Give God the glory for what you have and you will receive more.

Be grateful for the measure that is coming to you and that measure will increase perpetually. This is the law and it will never fail unless you fail to do to others what God is doing to you. Giving and receiving must be equal in your life. We must give something for everything we receive; nothing is free; the universe is not built in that manner; but giving does not imply the gift of things. True giving and true being are one and the same in real life.

The act of giving produces just as much joy as the act of receiving, because both add to the richness of existence. When we give much we bring forth much from the depths of divine being, and what we bring forth becomes a permanent part of actual life. When we give much we add to life from the within; when we receive much we add to life from the without; and when the richness of the within is harmoniously blended with the richness of the without, then real living begins. But the two must be equal. When we give more than we receive, or receive more than we give, discord follows, and herein we find the cause of many troubles and ills. The lesser without cannot receive the greater within, nor can the greater without be appropriated and appreciated by the lesser within. The small, undeveloped mind cannot enjoy the sublime grandeur of nature, nor can the great, highly developed mind find contentment in crude, uncultivated surroundings. The without and the within must be in harmony if the highest happiness and the truest life is to be enjoyed, and this harmony is invariably secured when giving and receiving are equal. In truth, there is no other way; if we would have the real correspond with the ideal, and the

The Pathway of Roses

capacity to enjoy be as large as the good things we have found to enjoy, we must give as much as we receive and receive as much as we give.

Before we can receive those things in the without that have worth, we must bring forth worth from the within. What we bring forth from the within we always give to the world, because no person can enrich his own spiritual life without enriching the whole world thereby. Before we can receive the best of all things in the without, we must bring forth the best of all things from the within. But to desire to give to the world from the richness of our own nature is not sufficient; many have done this and have found themselves in want, both physical and spiritual. To desire to receive is just as necessary as to desire to give. The two desires should be equally strong, and together should hourly grow in strength. The desire to receive is just as good as the desire to give, providing the two desires are equally dear to the heart. The more we receive the more we can give, and the more we give the greater our capacity to receive. Therefore, by placing ourselves in that position where we can constantly give more and more and constantly receive more and more, we not only add more and more to the richness and beauty and perfection of our own life, but we become a great power for good in the world. And this is our highest aim.

Before we can live a great life and receive from the external world those things that naturally belong to a great life, we must give forth into real life more and more of our own inherent greatness. Before we can receive as much from the world of things as our largest personal needs and desires may demand, we must unfold, develop and use those powers and talents that are necessary to the building of greater and greater things. Be of great use in the world and you give more and more to the world. In response the world will bring your own to you. He who actively is much, gives much; and he gives the most who serves the best.

To serve the human race in the largest and highest sense, we must bring forth into living expression the truest, the best and the greatest that we can possibly find in the depths of our own sublime being. And to this end we need all the inspiration we can receive from nature, all the love and friendship we can receive from man, and all the wisdom and power we can receive from God.

To become all that we are destined to become, we must receive the largest possible measure from every source, but we cannot receive the largest possible measure from any source unless we give all we have the power to give whenever we have the privilege to do so. And this privilege is ever present. Whatever our field of action may be we may give the very best that there is within us; and we will not do so in vain. Live a great life where you are; hide nothing that has worth; use every talent in full measure; bring forth into life and usefulness the highest powers that you know you possess, and you will enter into a greater and greater life, until you finally reach the supreme heights of exalted spiritual attainments. Awaken everything within you that can, in any manner, enrich, beautify and perfect the whole of life. Do not limit the giving of your greatest self to anyone part or anyone group of parts. Live for the universe and all that the vastness of the cosmos may contain.

The more we all give to the whole of life the more we all shall receive from the whole of life. We therefore have everything to gain by giving more and more everywhere, and by receiving more and more from every source in order that they may give again in still greater measure. And herein we find the secret to that beautiful life that God has prepared for them that love Him.

The Pathway of Roses

"Be not anxious for your life." Live your life according to the very highest light that is within you; use fully and well all the powers that you have received; give your best to the world at all times and under every circumstance, and depend upon the Infinite for everything that existence may need or desire. You will receive it. You need not be anxious about anything. God is greater than anything that can possibly happen. Have faith in Him and He will see you safely through. Things go wrong only when you fail to be your best and fail to take God with you in everything you do. It is therefore in your power to place yourself in that position where everything will go right. The lilies of the field are all that beautiful lilies can possibly be, and they depend wholly upon the powers divine that are within them. Accordingly, they are an inspiration to all the world.

Chapter 8

And All Things Shall Be Added

But seek ye first his kingdom and his righteousness; and all these things shall be added unto you. — Mat. 6:33.

The kingdom of God is within, and manifests through man as the spiritual life. His righteousness is the right use of all that is contained in the elements of the spiritual life. The spiritual life being the complete life, the full expression of life in body, mind and soul, it is evident that the right use of the spiritual life will produce and bring everything that man may need or desire. The source of everything has the power to produce everything, providing the power within that source is used according to exact spiritual law.

The spiritual life being the source of all that is necessary to a full and perfect life, and the kingdom of God within being the source of the spiritual life, we can readily understand why the kingdom should be sought first; and also, why everything that we may require will be added when the first thought is given to spiritual living and righteous action. Righteous action, however, is not simply moral action, but the right use of the elements of life in all action.

To seek His kingdom first, it is not necessary to withdraw from the world, nor to deny oneself the good things that exist in the world; to seek the kingdom first, is to give one's strongest thought to the spiritual life, and to make spiritual thought the predominating thought in everything that one may do in life. In other words, go to God first for everything, place your greatest dependence upon His power to carry you through everything, and live so close to His kingdom within that you are fully conscious of that kingdom every moment.

To seek the kingdom first, the heart must be in the spirit; that is, to live the spiritual life must be the predominating desire; but the mental conception of the spiritual life must not be narrow; in brief, that conception must contain the perfection of everything that can possibly appear in life. To think of the spiritual life as being distinct from mind and body is to deter the spiritual life from being expressed in mind and body; but what is not expressed is not lived. To think about the spiritual, or to feel the emotional power of the spiritual is not sufficient; but that is as far as the spiritual life has been taken by the average person; that the other things were not added is therefore no fault of the law.

The spiritual life must be thoroughly lived in mind and body; the power of the spirit must be made the soul of all power, and the law of spiritual action must be made the rule and guide in all action. When the spiritual is lived in all life, the richness, the quality and the worth of the spiritual will be produced in all life, and spiritual worth is the sum-total of all worth.

To enter the kingdom within is to enter health, harmony and happiness, because these three great principles reign supremely in the spiritual life of man. Therefore, by seeking the kingdom, health will be added, harmony will be added, happiness will be added. It is impossible to be sick in the spiritual life; and discord and unhappiness can no more exist in such a life than darkness can exist in the most brilliant light. But to seek the kingdom is not sufficient; we must also seek his righteousness. If we misuse any organ, faculty, function or power anywhere in body, mind or soul, we cannot remain in health no matter how spiritual we may try to be.

To seek his righteousness is to use everything in our world as God uses everything in His world; which means, in harmony with its own nature, in harmony with its sphere of action and in harmony with the law that tends upward and onward forever. Righteous action is that action that is always harmonious, and that always works for better things, greater things, higher things.

To enter the kingdom within is to enter more power, because there is no limit to the power of the spirit; and the more power we enter into or become conscious of, the more power we will give to mind and body. In consequence, the more spiritual we become the stronger we become, the more able we become, the more competent we become, and the more we can accomplish whatever our work may be. And he who can do good work in the world invariably receives the good things in the world. To his life will be added all those things that can make personal existence rich and beautiful.

To enter the kingdom is to enter the life of freedom. There is no bondage in the spirit, and as we grow in the spirit we grow out of all bondage; one adverse condition after another disappears until absolute freedom is gained. All bondage comes from incompleteness in living, and misuse of life in doing. But the spiritual life is full and complete, and it follows the law of righteous action in all doing; therefore, when we seek first His kingdom and His righteousness, perfect freedom in all things and at all times will invariably be added.

When we seek first the kingdom, all other things are not added in some mysterious manner; nor do they come of themselves regardless of our conscious effort to work in harmony with the law of life; that is, the law of being and doing all that lies within the power of life. We receive from the kingdom only what we are prepared to use in the living of a great life, and in the doing of great and noble things in the world. We receive only in proportion to what we give; and it is only as we work well that we produce results; but by entering the spiritual life we receive as much as we may require in order to give as much as we desire; and we gain the power to do everything that is necessary to give worth and superiority to our present state of existence.

When we enter the spiritual life we gain every quality that is required in making life full and complete in our own state of being; and we gain the power to produce and create in the external world whatever we may need or desire. In other words, we receive everything we want from the within, and we gain the power to produce everything we want in the without. We therefore need never take anxious thought about these "other things." By seeking first His kingdom and His righteousness, we shall positively receive them. The way will be opened, and we shall be abundantly supplied with the best that life can give.

Depend upon me. I will provide. This is the Word, eternally spoken from on high; and every awakened soul has learned the message, but the few alone have discerned its real interpretation.

God is rich, and nothing is too good for the children of God. The Spirit of the Infinite will provide; not bare necessities, but everything. Ask what thou wilt and I will answer thee.

It is the will of God that we should seek everything that is good, worthy and beautiful. The life of man should be full and complete; human existence should be rich in body, mind and soul, for this is the great divine purpose.

The Pathway of Roses

To think that we must live on bare necessities in order to be spiritual, is to limit our faith in the goodness and the power of God. The kingdom of God is at hand now; we are expected to enter now, and this kingdom is abundantly supplied with everything that can enrich, perfect and beautify human life.

Seek ye first the kingdom, and all other things shall be added; not simply enough to live on, but all things. The love of God is infinite, and we cannot think of infinite love as wanting to give less than all. God has the power to give all. He also has the desire to give all, and therefore every soul may, at any time, receive all that present development can take possession of.

The more we ask of God the more we please God. To give is the highest pleasure of true love, and God is true love. To ask Him for everything, the most of everything and the best of everything is to enter into the life of the highest joy of heaven; and to live in such a life is to live indeed.

When we do not have what we want or what we need, we should remember that Spirit can provide, and that Spirit will provide if we only so desire. Depend upon me. I will not forsake thee nor leave thee. I AM thy Redeemer, I will care for thee.

Take God at His word. Have faith in the message that comes from on high. Believe with all the power of mind and soul that God will do what love will do, because God is love. Open the heart to the influx of infinite love, and all that God can give will come with His love.

Do not hesitate to ask God for material things. God owns the universe. Everything is the product of His creative power; therefore it is all good, and what is good is good for man.

The Pathway of Roses

What you can use to promote the welfare of everybody, including yourself, you may receive. Only remember this, that things spiritual must come first in your thought. You may have abundances of things material; there is more than enough to provide everybody with all the luxuries of life. You will not deprive anybody of anything by accepting from God all that His love can give. Others may receive as much from the same source; but seek first the things of the spirit, for this is the law.

Consider the lilies of the field. Why should not you be arrayed like one of these? It is the will of God that you should be, and you will give Him great pleasure by asking Him to clothe you even more gorgeously than they. But we must remember that we are not to take these things from others; we are to receive them from God. There is a great difference between the two methods, and there are few in the world that can see it.

To receive from God we must love the spiritual the best, though we must neither despise nor ignore the material. All is from God, and all will minister to the joy and beauty of life when used in harmony with a life that is lived in God. When we live in God, all things will be turned to good account, and when we work with God, all things will work together for greater good.

The world tries to get from man; the perfect way is to receive from God; and the moment we adopt the latter method, the way will be opened. Spirit will lead; we will know at each step what we are to do, and what step to take next will always be clear. Live close to God and have faith; no matter what may come or not, depend upon the spirit to lead and provide, and you will always do what is best.

However, we must never think that it is best for anyone to live in poverty, trouble and pain; no, this is never best, not even for a moment. The Infinite can provide something better here and now, and it is His will and good pleasure to do so.

When days of darkness are at hand, cling to the great truth, spirit will provide. Think of it constantly; live in the very soul of its presence; believe in it from the very depths of the heart. Things will take a turn. The door of opportunity will open. The desired change will come. There is nothing in the world that the Spirit cannot change for the better; therefore we may with perfect faith ask for any change desired. The best is intended for all of us. God is ever ready to give everything. Ask what thou wilt and I will answer thee.

The Pathway of Roses

To think of thee and feel thy presence near.
To rise above the world of doubt and fear.
To enter where the many mansions be,
To hold communion face to face with thee.

To find the secret place where all is still.
To feel thy joy and life my being thrill.
To know that health and wholeness now are
mine. To see thy light within forever shine.

To feel the peace that passeth thought and
speech.
To know that I the endless heights shall reach.
That I thy Son for evermore shall be.
These are the sweetest thoughts of life to me.

Chapter 9

When Life is Worth Living

To establish permanently the living of life in the spiritual state of being is the greatest need of man. But this is not possible so long as we live in that conception of spirituality that forgets the body. The body is the temple of the spirit, and must therefore receive just as much thought and attention as we give to the spirit. To neglect the body is to make real spirituality impossible, because real spirituality is a living thing, and must have a highly developed personality through which this living may be expressed. Spirituality is not simply in thought, feeling or abstract contemplation; there is no spirituality without the actual coming forth of real soul life; but the life of the soul does not come forth into tangible personal living unless the body is trained to respond to that life.

The spirituality that we seek is that full expression of the soul that fills every atom in the body and gives the sublime wholeness of divinity to the entire being of man. To be spiritual is to be complete in body, mind and soul; to live the fullness of real life in every element of life, and to bring forth the truest, the best and the most beautiful that exists within us. To become spiritual is to refine everything, perfect everything, beautify everything, and make the ideal real, not only in thought but in every part of physical life, mental life and spiritual life. To grow in spirituality is to continue perpetually to spiritualize the body, as well as mind and soul, until the visible man is as pure, as strong, as wholesome and as beautiful as the highest state of divine existence.

True spirituality will give health and vigor to the body, power and brilliancy to the mind, strength and perfection to the character, and sublime loveliness to the soul. The more spiritual you become the more beautiful you become in person, the more refined you become in all the elements of your nature, the more powerful you become in every thought and action, and the more comfort, happiness and real satisfaction you will receive from everything you may do in life. When spirituality is highly developed you live constantly on the heights; you see all things as they are in the real; you know that you are created in the image and likeness of God; you are in constant touch with the beauty and splendor of the cosmic world, and your joy is supreme. You are living in the light of the spirit, and your mind at times is so illumined by that light that your understanding of higher wisdom becomes extraordinary. You thus enter those lofty realms from which all true prophets have received their inspiration, and, accordingly, you become one of those who are chosen to be taught of God.

To enter real spirituality is to anchor the mind in that very power that holds and guides the universe; and such a mind is always safe. Such a mind will not go wrong; and even though it be strongly tempted, it will be removed from danger before it is too late. There is something in the higher world about us that can and does protect the soul; and those who are fixed on high in the spirit are ever in the care of this divine protection. Dangers, calamities or catastrophes will never touch them; they are invariably taken out safely, no matter what may happen; they are ever in the hands of God, and all is always well.

This higher guiding power, however, does not simply protect the chosen ones from that which is not desired; but those who have supreme faith in the spirit will be led on and on into the larger and larger realization of that which is desired. The spirit contains all, and to grow in the spirit is to receive all. Not simply that all that satisfies the demands of the intellect or the feelings of the soul, but that all that fully supplies every want, desire or need of the whole man. Spirituality is the highest good of all life realized in full living expression. In the spiritual life there is no need, neither is there any false desire. Every desire is true to the great purpose of eternal life, and every desire is fulfilled. In spiritual life every prayer is inspired by the wisdom of the spirit, and such prayers are always answered. Whatever God may lead us to do He will always give us the power to do.

The spiritual state of being is the great foundation of all being, and the source of everything that comes forth into perfect being; therefore, the more deeply we enter into the life and the power of the spirit the more fully conscious we become of those greater things that real life has in store; and whatever we become conscious of we invariably bring forth into tangible existence. The spiritual life contains real life, real power, real wisdom, real love, real harmony, real health, real purity, real peace, real joy, and to develop spirituality is to realize more and more of the real of these things until the perfection of divine being is unfolded and lived in the present personal form. In consequence, when we are in the spiritual life we need sacrifice nothing that has real value, while we gain more and more of everything that has greater value. When we begin to live the spiritual life we begin to feel that we are now upon the solid rock of eternal being, and we feel absolutely secure. We realize that we are in safety, in divinity, in the protecting care of higher power. We are becoming more and more conscious of the cosmic atmosphere, and this gives added assurance of complete protection, because this higher, sublimated atmosphere is so surcharged with living spirit that no ill from the world can possibly pass through. We are absolutely out of the ills of the world when we are in the spirit, just as we are absolutely out of darkness when we are in the light. And to grow in the spirit the first essential is to take what spiritual life we can now understand and give that life full, living expression in every atom of body, soul and mind.

There can be no real spirituality developed so long as we try to make such developments a matter of the soul alone; mind and body must be included or our efforts simply result in feelings and sentiments that are neither wholesome nor harmless. Spirituality is not a matter of sentiment, nor is it wholly concerned with a future state of existence. Spirituality is a full life just for today. It is a life that is all that it is now, and those who are in the spirit know that the time that now is, is eternal.

One touch of the spirit and all is well. Darkness and pain will vanish, sickness and sorrow take flight; weakness and bondage will pass away, and troubles can exist no more. To be touched by the spirit is to be filled through and through with the spirit, and where the spirit is there evil is not. What we have seen in our visions shall come to remain. What is revealed from on high shall come and abide with us always. Therefore let the soul dream on. Disturb not the peace of those sweet celestial slumbers, for what to us may appear to be spiritual sleep is but life in a greater world. And thus something from above comes to tell us, "dream on, fair soul, dream on."

To worship God in spirit and in truth, is to so live that we can always feel that he is with us no matter what we may think or say or do. To worship God is to take Him with us in everything, ask Him for everything, have faith that He will give us everything, and be grateful to Him because we inwardly know that we are receiving everything. To worship is not to believe and adore, but to live and love; not simply to accept the truth but to make the truth the living soul of every thought and word and deed. When we worship God in truth, we enter into His presence knowing that He is divine perfection and that we are created in His image and likeness. To believe that we are depraved beings, base sinners or imperfect human creatures, is not to be in the truth, because to be in the truth we are as God is. Therefore, while we have those beliefs we cannot worship God in truth. To worship God in truth we must enter the truth, and to enter the truth is to know that man is even now the perfect image of the Most High.

To worship God in the spirit, is to forget the letter and enter into the spiritual realization of His omnipresent life. When we are in the spirit we do not worship with audible words or visible attitudes, but with that exalted spiritual feeling that enters into the very soul of the Infinite and there awakens to the great eternal truth that "My Father and I are one." When we are in the spirit we inwardly know that "God is closer than breathing, nearer than hands and feet," and we can feel that sublime nearness thrill every atom in our being. We need nothing to prove to us that we are one with God, for we can feel that it is the truth. Nor do we question any more whether God be personal or not. We know that we are with Him and that He is with us; and that is sufficient. His personal presence is more real to us than our own existence; we therefore need not reason on that subject. We have seen Him in the spirit, but that which is in the spirit, form cannot measure, nor words define.

The word of God is the word of truth. All truth is Scripture wherever found or by whom presented; and all Scripture is written when the mind is in the spirit. Therefore, to understand the Scripture we must enter the spirit, and read while illumined by the spirit. We shall then find, upon every page, "the bread of heaven," "the waters of life," "the meat that ye know not of." The key to the Scriptures is not some system of symbolical interpretation, nor some special method of metaphysical or spiritual analysis. The key is simply to enter the spirit when you begin to read. The spirit reveals everything that is sacred and true.

To live exclusively in materiality, that is, in the lower story of being, is the cause of all weakness and weariness. The remedy for such conditions will therefore be found in spirituality, which means to live in the upper story. So long as the mind is "high" in the world of consciousness there can be no weakness or weariness in the person. We cannot be weary while we are filled with the strength of the Most High, and we are in perfect touch with this great strength while the mind is living in the "high places" of the spirit. When we come down to the earth, earthy we lose this superior power and become weak as mere men; we are limited in every respect and have to watch ourselves at every turn lest we overtax the system. But when we do all things in the realization that we are spiritual beings filled with supreme power from on high, there is no limit to what we can do. Our strength is eternally renewed because we are waiting upon the Lord; we are living with Him, doing all things for Him, and in return we receive all things from Him.

When the mind lives constantly in the higher states of being, more perfect oneness with the Infinite is attained. We come nearer and nearer to the Life and the Spirit of the Supreme, and, in consequence, we are supplied with new life and power every moment. We are going into the source of all power; we are beginning to live and move and have our being in the very essence of that power, and we are becoming stronger by far than all the weakness and the weariness in the world. We are no longer subject to the laws of material existence; what holds true in the life of mere man does not hold true for us anymore; we have entered a new life and are ascending triumphantly to the supreme heights of that life. The seeming weakness of the flesh has given place to the limitless strength of the Spirit, for the very moment we begin to live in the spirit, the power of the spirit begins to live in us, and that which lives in us lives in every element of the body as well as in every attribute of mind and soul.

Spirituality is the perfect remedy for all the ills of life, and to live the spiritual life is the greatest thing that man can do. Therefore, to promote spiritual growth among all minds that are ready, is of more importance than all other objects and aims combined. Thousands realize this, and, in consequence, are ever in search for methods through which the life of the spirit may be found. Methods, however, are of secondary importance. When the heart begins to feel the need of the spirit, and all the powers of mind begin to desire the spirit, the perfect way will be opened. To promote spiritual growth we must live in the spiritual center of the divine that is within us, but that divine center is not found through methods. No system of mental gymnastics can open the gates to the kingdom within; nor can any system of logical reasoning in abstract truth cause the mind to be illumined with light from on high. Spiritual illumination does not come through a mere intellectual process, however exact; it comes only when the desires of the heart are spiritualized by a power that is infinitely greater than man.

To think the truth, even with absolute exactness, will not avail unless we think in the spirit of truth. The intellectual form of the truth has no power; it is the inner spirit of the truth that gives life, freedom and illumination to man. And when we begin to know this inner spirit of the truth our minds have entered into the very soul of the real. Then it is that we gain power that to many seems superhuman; then it is that we take full possession of our own life and our own destiny; then it is that we find the faith that moves mountains, and through the life of this faith we press on and on to the great goal we have in view, removing every barrier in the way, overcoming every difficulty, surmounting every obstacle, rising higher than ever before every time we fall, transforming every seeming defeat into a great and glorious victory, passing through the fires of tribulation without even a hair being scorched, and coming out of every trying experience with greater purity and greater strength, realizing one ideal after another, ascending from one pinnacle of attainment to one that is higher still, finding answer after answer to the prayers we prayed in days gone by, until every desire is fulfilled and every dream of the soul made true.

There is no reason whatever why anyone should become discouraged, or be tempted to give up because the good things desired are not realized when expected. That which is your own will positively come to you, and everything is your own that you can use in the building of a greater and more beautiful life. Continue in the faith that you will now begin to realize the fullness of life, and enter into the inner spirit of that faith. Some of the greatest things in the world have been gained after many years of constant faith and prayer — things that would not have been gained if those who prayed had lived in discouragement and doubt. If there is anything that you can use in the building of a great life, pray for it until you receive it no matter how many months or years may be required to cause your prayer to come true. Pray in the inner spirit of faith and when the time is ripe, be it tomorrow or twenty years from now, your prayer will be answered.

When your prayers are not answered at once, do not come to the conclusion that it is not best for you to have it; if that which you pray for will add to the welfare of somebody's life, it is best for you to have it. Therefore, continue to pray for it until you receive it. It is best that you should have everything that is good and true and beautiful. All that is good is good for man, and it is the will of God that man should receive it. But God gives us only that which we desire.

We have individual choice, and we must express our desire in the true spirit of faith. What we ask for will come when our faith is right and our life prepared to properly use the great good desired.

To promote spiritual growth the inner light must shine in the outer life, and the inner world of divine truth must be expressed in every part of mind and body. The expression of the divinity within is absolutely necessary, and must be in, every direction. Thousands today are expressing truth only for the purpose of securing health of body and peace of mind, and though they are having good results they will find ere long that in trying to perfect only a part of the outer life they have failed to bring forth the whole of the inner life. They will also find that the marvelous powers of the within have been permitted to sleep. After some years such minds will find that they have accomplished nothing more than being well and comfortable physically. But this is not all that we are living for. A genius is asleep in the subconscious of every mind; a spiritual giant is within us awaiting recognition; and in the soul is the Christ knocking at the door. These must not be kept waiting age after age while we are only concerned with being well and happy on the surface. It is not right to live a small life no matter how comfortable that life may be when we have received the gifts of the supreme life from on high.

The expression of the spirit should be universal in all the actions of man. The labor of the hands should be filled with the life of the spirit; the work of the mind should be animated with the one power of spirit, and every act of consciousness should feel the divine presence of the spirit. There are few, however, who think of expressing divine spirit in every day work, and consequently, the spiritual life becomes a thing apart. But when the personal life is separated from the spirit, darkness, confusion, sickness and trouble begin; existence becomes a burden, and though we may possess the wealth of the world, life has nothing of worth to give. There is no joy in things unless the power of the spirit is in the world of things. There is nothing to live for unless we live for the spirit, and when we begin to live for the spirit all things, from the least importance in the physical realm to the most precious elements in the highest spiritual realms — all become ministering angels, adding eternally to the worth, the beauty and the joy of personal life. To him who lives in the spirit, everything in life has much to give, and to him, the best alone is given.

When we think, the mind should be filled with the spirit, and our intellects will become brilliant in the true sense of that term. When we read, our eyes should be filled with the spirit, and our sight will ever become stronger and better. When we work, every muscle in the body should be filled with the spirit, and we should renew our strength from the source divine. We thus cause the outer life and the inner life to become one life, and it is such a life that we are here to live now. Say that life is beautiful, no matter how things may appear on the surface. Say that you are strong and well no matter how the body may feel. You will thus speak the truth about the true state of being; and what you say, you create. Say that you are well and you create health. Say that life is divinely beautiful and you create such a life. And what we create today, we shall realize tomorrow.

There are a number of methods through which the spiritual nature of man can be developed and brought into larger and larger expression, but the majority of those methods are so complex that they lead more into intellectuality than into spirituality. To develop the mind, with its many faculties, complex methods are, as a rule, necessary, but to develop the soul, the simpler the methods are, the better. The secret is to keep the eye single upon the sublime spiritual state, to form the highest possible conception of the most perfect spiritual qualities imaginable, and to think of those things. The power of concentration is truly extraordinary whenever it may be applied, and its effectiveness is nowhere as thorough as in the world of the spirit. To think constantly of things spiritual, with an effort to enter more and more into the real life of the spirit, is to spiritualize all the elements of thought, all the phases of consciousness, and all the active states of realization. In consequence, everything in human life will become more spiritual.

What we think of we create; therefore the more we think of things spiritual the more spirituality we shall develop; and when the whole of thought is concentrated constantly upon our highest spiritual ideal, we shall actually move into the real spiritual state. There is a spiritual state of consciousness immediately above the usual conscious state, and it is the lifting of mind and thought up into this higher state that produces spirituality; therefore, spiritual development will necessarily require the ascending tendency in every action in life. This requirement, however, is invariably supplied, when the power of attention is constantly directed upon the spiritual state. When we think of that which is spiritual, everything in life begins to ascend towards the higher spiritual states; that is, when our thinking of the spiritual is inspired with a deep soul desire to rise and live on the heights.

Live with the beautiful side in human nature and your own life will grow more and more beautiful until you become an inspiration to all the world. Look for the greater good in all things and you will find God in all things. And when you find God in all things God will be with you in all things.

Say that life is beautiful, no matter how things may appear on the surface. Say that you are strong and well no matter how the body may feel. You will thus speak the truth about the true state of being; and what you say, you create. Say that you are well and you create health. Say that life is divinely beautiful and you create such a life. And what we create today, we shall realize tomorrow.

The pure in heart shall see God, and to be pure in heart is to think pure thoughts the thought of sublime spiritual truth. The reason we do not see God is found in the fact that we have clouded our minds with impure thoughts thought that is out of harmony with the divine order of things. Pure water is transparent; the same is true of a pure mind. The deep things of God are easily discerned through a pure mind, just as easily as the rocks of the river bed when the water is pure and still.

Chapter 10

The Way, The Truth and the Life

Jesus saith unto him, I AM the way, and the truth, and the life; no one cometh unto the Father but by me. — John 14:6.

The great statements of Jesus Christ were never spoken from the personal, but always from the impersonal. No truth ever sprung from the personal mind because it is only the impersonal that can touch the universal, and it is only in the universal that absolute truth can be found. When the mind enters the impersonal state, consciousness comes in touch with the cosmic state of being, and in that state we realize the "I AM" of being. We discern what the "I AM" actually is, and we find that the consciousness of the "I AM" is the open door to the limitless vastness of the spiritual universe. "I AM the door." Enter through the door of "I AM" and we pass into that immense world that is found on the upper side, or the divine side of sublime existence.

The "I AM" in every soul is the spirit of Christ within us, and when we become conscious of the Christ within us we can truthfully say that "the mind that was in Christ Jesus, the same mind is in me." The mind that was in Christ Jesus knew the "I AM" of eternal being; in brief, was the "I AM" of eternal being, and therefore could say that I AM the way, and the truth, and the life. But this same "I AM" is in every soul and constitutes the real "me" of every soul, and as we grow in Christ we grow into the realization of that great truth that we are one with Christ, and that the same Christ that reigned supremely in the personality of Jesus shall reign supremely in us.

The Pathway of Roses

The Christ within us is the only begotten of the Father, and is created in the image and likeness of the Father. There is only one Son of God, but this one Son reigns in every soul, and constitutes the "I AM" in every soul. The "I AM" that occupies the throne of your spiritual being is the only begotten Son of God, and as this Son is like the Father you cannot grow into the likeness of the Father unless you do so through the Son. Nor can you enter into the presence of the Father without going through the Son, because it is the Son that unites the Father with you.

The Son of God is one with God, therefore if you wish to realize your oneness with God you must enter into the life and the spirit of the Son. In other words, you must become conscious of the "I AM" within you because it is this "I AM" that is created in the image of God, and we are not one with God unless we realize that we are created in the image of God. To be one with God is to know that we are in the Father and the Father in us, but we cannot enter into that consciousness wherein we know that we are in the Father until we are conscious of our exact likeness to the Father.

When Jesus declared, I AM the way, he spoke in the consciousness of the Christ. It was the supreme "I AM" that made this great statement, and this "I AM" is the way. The supreme "I AM" is the way to everything that man may need or desire throughout eternity, for "I AM" in God, and in God we find the allness of all that is. The "I AM" is the way to God, because it is the "I AM" in man that is always one with God. "I AM the door," and there is no other door; it is therefore evident that no one cometh unto the Father but by me.

To go to God you must go by way of the Christ; that is, you must enter into the inner consciousness of the Christ that reigns within us; you must enter so deeply into the spirit of your own sublime being that you can readily realize that "I AM," and know that "I AM" is not distinct from you but is the real and the eternal of you. "Where I AM there ye shall be also." You shall someday enter that same exalted state where your consciousness of the "I AM" will be so perfect that you will know that you are "I AM." Then the supreme "I AM" will speak in you as he did in Jesus and will in like manner declare in you, "I AM the way."

When we find the spirit of Christ within us we find the way; we then enter the path, the path that leads to the fullness of life and the perfection of being. To daily ascend higher and higher in the consciousness of this spirit of the Christ is to follow the Christ, and to follow the Christ is to enter the Kingdom.

The "I AM" is the truth because all truth has its source in the divine being of man. That the real man is created in the image of God is the one supreme truth, and the real man is the "I AM." To know the truth is to enter into the life and the spirit of the "I AM" within; that is, the Christ within, and to enter into the Christ is to enter into freedom because there can be no bondage or ill whatever in Him. This is how we gain freedom when we know the truth; not by forming intellectual concepts about truth, but by entering consciously into the spirit of the Christ within which is the truth.

To enter into the Christ consciousness is to become conscious of the real being of the Christ, and the real being of the Christ is identical with the real being of man. To become conscious of the real being of man is to know the truth concerning man, and when we know this truth we know that man is divine because man, in his eternal nature, is identical with the nature of the Christ. When we know that we are created in the likeness of truth we know that we are truth, and we can say, when speaking from the Christ consciousness, into which we have entered, "I AM the truth." And when we know that we are truth we are conscious only of that which is truth. We cannot be out of the truth when we are in truth, and as there can be no ill or bondage in the truth we must necessarily be in absolute freedom while we are consciously in the truth.

The "I AM" is the life; all life comes from God, and the life that is in us is the life of the only begotten of God. The life eternal is the life of God in us, and it is the "I AM" in us that lives the life of God in us. To gain the life more abundant it is therefore necessary to enter more and more deeply into the consciousness of the "I AM" within. In brief, the more fully we realize the "I AM" or the Christ within us the more we live, and when we enter so perfectly into the Christ consciousness that we actually know that the real in us is identical with the "I AM" in us, then we begin to live the life eternal; then we actually enter eternity while still in personal form; then we know with positive conviction that we are immortal, and we need no further evidence for any other source whatever.

When we learn that "I AM the door," and seek this door in the spiritual life within us, we shall find it; and as we pass through this door we enter the other side of life, the divine side, the eternal side. There we find the kingdom of God that is within us, and beyond is the shining shore. But we are not required to leave the personal form and the physical life in order to live on the other side of life. True being is to live on the spiritual side of life and to manifest the perfection of spiritual being in the personal side of life. Thus the Word becomes flesh and the glory of God is made visible in man.

For narrow is the gate, and straightened the Way, that leadeth unto life. And those alone who are in the spirit can find it. Follow the light of the spirit in all things, choose the living Christ as the pattern in all things, and depend upon God in all things. Do not seek the truth; seek the spirit of truth. The spirit leads into all truth. To know the truth is to know the way. To be guided by the spirit into all truth is to walk in the light of the spirit all the Way, and the Way of light leads into the kingdom of eternal life. Follow the words of the Christ until the spirit is found; then follow the spirit into the greater life of the Christ. Keep the eye single upon that light that is revealed through the spiritual vision of the soul. Where that light is shining there is the gate; beyond is the Way that leadeth unto life, and all who are in the spirit shall find it even now.

Chapter 11

To Know and Think the Truth

To mentally live in the spiritual understanding of truth, and to give constant expression, in thought, to the words of truth, is to train the mind to know the truth in a larger and larger measure; and to know the truth is to create and express true conditions, throughout the entire personality.

A statement of truth is the absolute truth expressed in words; that is, the mental or verbal expression of a certain state of perfect and divine being. Therefore, a statement of truth does not describe things as they are in the external, but describes man as he is in the spirit; and when the mind begins to think of man as he is in the spirit, the perfect qualities of the spirit will be unfolded and brought out into the personal life.

The life of the spirit is the true life of man because man is a spiritual being; the soul is the real man; the mind and the body are merely instruments. For this reason it is evident that when man thinks of himself he must necessarily think of himself as he is in the spirit. The conditions of the body do not describe the divine state of the soul; the soul is real, absolute, divine, perfect, complete, created in the image of God, while the personality is but a partial expression of the real, in many respects incomplete, and in a state of development.

When man thinks that the incomplete conditions of his personality constitute himself he is not thinking the truth about himself; his thought is false, and false thinking produces false or detrimental conditions in mind and body.

However, when he thinks of himself as he is in the divine perfection of his being, he is thinking the truth about himself; his thought is the truth, and the thinking of truth produces true or wholesome conditions in mind and body. Therefore, so long as man thinks of himself as being an imperfect personality he will cause his personality to be imperfect, weak, sickly and more or less in disorder; but when he constantly thinks of himself as he is in the perfect, wholesome, divine state of his real spiritual being, he will cause his personality to be wholesome, healthful, harmonious and in the most perfect state of order.

The truth gives freedom. To know the truth is to live in the perfect world of truth. When the mind discerns truth, all thought is created in the likeness of truth; all thought is truth; and man is as he thinks. To think the truth is to create that which is true, and when the true comes into being the false ceases to be.

There can be no darkness in the light; there can be no false conditions in the truth; therefore, when man is in the truth, the wholeness and the perfection of the truth will pervade his entire being through and through. Every part will be true to the truth, and every element will express the divinity of man.

When the mind thinks the truth, every mental conception of true being will formulate itself in a statement of truth; these statements will convey to man's intelligence the higher understanding of all that is. The mind will learn to see all things as they are in truth; the divine perfection of all things will be realized; all thought will contain the spirit of truth, and man, himself, will be the truth in every fiber of his being. Therefore, every mind should think statements of truth as frequently as possible, and with the deepest conviction possible.

The conditions of the personality are the direct effects of the states of the mind; therefore, the conditions of the personality will always be true, good and perfect so long as the states of the mind are true; and the states of the mind will always be true so long as the mind thinks the truth — thinks the truth about man as he is in the divine perfection of his real spiritual being.

To train the mind to think the real truth about man, statements of truth, of every possible description, should be employed extensively. In brief, the mind should be daily drilled, in the thinking of absolute truth; that is, the mental or verbal expression of statements of truth; and to enter into the spiritual understanding of the real significance of every statement should be the central purpose in view.

The mere mechanical repetition of such statements will not avail; the real truth of each statement is discerned only when the mind enters into the very soul of the statement; and it is the real truth that we wish to know, because it is the knowing of real truth that alone makes for freedom in life and that produces the fullness of life. To train the mind to think the real truth, the following statements of truth may be employed, though the wording may be changed to correspond with the state of each individual need, or the degree of conscious development in the spiritual life.

The perfection of my being is now realized in the spiritual understanding of truth

The understanding of truth reveals to the mind the divine perfection of all being, and the more spiritual this understanding is the more clearly can the divinity of man be discerned. Spirituality illumines, because to be spiritual is to live in the supreme light of the spirit. In the spirit there is no darkness, therefore, in the spirit all things can be seen as they are, and to see all things as they are is to see that all things are created in the likeness of God. The realization of the great truth that being is perfect, created in the image of God, will cause this perfection to be expressed. What we realize in the spirit will be expressed in the person. Therefore, when the real truth of this statement is understood, the personal life will be a manifestation of the spiritual life, and all will be well in body, mind and soul.

God is love, and in Him I live and move and have my being

To live the true spiritual life — the life of complete emancipation and high spiritual attainment, it is necessary to love all things with the pure, limitless love of the soul, but such a love cannot be realized so long as consciousness is personal only. It is when we feel that we live in the love of God that we gain consciousness of that love that loves all things at all times, and we shall invariably feel that we do live in the love of God when we know the real truth of the statement that God is boundless love, and that we have our being in Him. To realize that we live in God is to feel His presence, and when we do feel His presence we become absolutely filled with a love that is so tender, so beautiful, so high and so sublime, that we are placed completely at one with all the universe. We immediately transcend, and eliminate entirely, every adverse feeling; we are at peace with everything and that peace is animated with the spirit of that love that cannot be measured. To live in such a love is supreme joy, and it is the privilege of every soul now.

I AM fixed on high in the spirit of truth

The I AM of every soul can truthfully make this statement, for real being is permanently established in the true life of the spirit, and as every individual is the I AM of his own being, every individual, to speak the truth, must make this statement about himself. To realize the truth of this statement is to enter more and more into the fixed state of true being, and to grow in the realization of this state is to gain that absolute safety and security where the soul finds complete divine protection. To be in the spirit of truth is to be in the very life of true existence, and to be fixed in this life is to occupy a permanent place in God's own beautiful world. In other words, to be fixed in the spirit of truth, is to be anchored in God, and we can readily realize how absolutely secure such a state of being must be. When we make this statement we should try to realize what existence in the truth must necessarily mean, how it must feel to be in the consciousness of the spirit of such an existence, and what a life must hold in store that is permanently established on the very heights of that existence. The more fully we enter into the soul of the truth that this statement conveys, the sooner we shall realize the truth itself; and when we do, we shall know that we are fixed on high, permanently established in the spirit of truth, forever anchored in God.

My spiritual being is the expression of eternal life

The life eternal is the whole of real, absolute, limitless life, and the real, spiritual man is this life individualized and expressed. The life eternal contains the whole complete existence; therefore, to live the life eternal is to live all that there is in absolute existence. It is the life eternal that the soul lives, and since man is the soul, he should affirm that he is living the life eternal now, and that his true being is the perfect expression of that life. The life eternal is the life of the divinity that is in man, and the true being of man constitutes that divinity; but we manifest in personal life only that which we become conscious of, therefore the mind must be unfolded to realize the true nature of the life eternal before we can enter into life now. To unfold the mind into this conscious realization, all thinking should be animated with the highest spiritual conception of the life eternal that we can possibly form, and the great truth that the true spiritual being of man is the perfect expression of that life, should be held before the mental vision constantly. In addition, every effort we make to live the life, that is, to live in the soul of real life, will cause this statement, not only to seem true in the ideal, but to prove itself to be true in the actual.

I AM ever ascending into the greater and greater freedom of God

God is absolute freedom, and man is eternally becoming what God is. To realize this truth is to place life in that position where personal existence will, at every step in human advancement, be in full possession of that measure of freedom that present consciousness can possibly involve. This means that the life of every moment will be absolutely free, and that the measure of freedom will increase in perfect harmony with the increase of the mind's capacity for freedom. The real man is ever in possession of all the freedom that present development can comprehend and employ, and is ever ascending into the greater freedom of God; therefore, to enter into the realization of this truth is to keep the eye upon the supreme freedom, to steadily rise into more and more of that freedom, and this is the true path to complete emancipation. When we steadily grow into the freedom of God, we must necessarily grow out of everything that is limited, undesirable or adverse. The lesser passes away as we pass upward and onward into the ever expanding world of the greater.

God is health and wholeness, and I AM his image and likeness

There can be no sickness in God; for the same reason there can be no sickness in the real being of man; and as each individual is what he is in his own real being, he must necessarily be well at all times. The real man cannot possibly be sick any more than light can be darkness, because he is as God is; therefore no man can truthfully say, at any time, that he is sick, weak or disabled. He cannot be any of these things, no matter what personal conditions may seem to be. The real man is always well, and I AM the real man. I AM not the body, nor the instrument, nor the garment. I AM the I AM, the image of God, the exact likeness of the Most High. When adverse conditions appear in the personality, there are personal causes, either physical or mental, but these conditions can never enter the life of the real spiritual man. The real man continues to be well and strong at all times, and the life of the real man is perpetually a life of perfect health and wholeness. To live constantly in the conscious realization of the life of the real man is to always feel well, in body, mind and soul. There can be no sickness in the body so long as we live in the life of health, and we do live in the life of health so long as we continue in the realization of the great truth that God is health, and that we are as He is. Those adverse conditions that may exist in the body now will entirely disappear the moment we enter into the realization of real life, and begin to live in the spirit of the truth that we are as God is — perfect and whole, now and forever.

My Father and I are one

The mind that was in Christ Jesus, the same mind is in you, and this mind knows that My Father and I are One. When we enter into the spirit of the divine mind we realize that there is no separation whatever in the spirit. The spirit of the human soul is absolutely one with the spirit of the Infinite. There is no difference whatever in divine essence or soul life; only the Infinite is God while the human soul is an expression of God, the son of God, the only begotten of God.

When we enter into the very presence of God, we know that no separation can exist in the spirit, and we also learn that the Christ consciousness implies the highest consciousness of this divine oneness. The mind that was in Christ Jesus is conscious of the spiritual oneness that exists between God and man, and we enter into that mind whenever we feel that we are in the presence of God.

To realize that we are one with God, in spirit and in truth, is to realize that we are also one with the life, the divinity and the perfection of God; and therefore we are as God is; what is in God is in us; we live the same life that He lives, and since there can be no imperfection in His life, there can be no imperfection in our life.

The spiritual life of man is perfect, and when man enters fully into the consciousness of his spiritual life, his personal life will become the exact expression of His spiritual life. Then the Word will become flesh, and no ill can exist in the body any more. Nor can the untruth any longer exist in the mind.

To grow in the Christ consciousness is to grow in the consciousness of the spiritual life, and as the light of the spiritual life becomes stronger and stronger in mind, these elements of darkness, sickness, adverseness or imperfection that may remain in personal existence will entirely disappear. Then we shall realize the emancipated life, the freedom that comes from the knowing of the truth.

God is my strength. I AM strong with His limitless life and power

To dwell perpetually in the conviction that the strength of the Infinite is our strength, is to steadily grow in the conscious realization of power, and the more power we become conscious of the more power we possess. To think of weakness in any sense of the term becomes impossible when we know that the limitless power of the Infinite is just as much ours as it is His. All that the Father hath is mine. And when we cease to think of weakness we shall never again be conscious of weakness.

To think of truth we can never admit that we are weak; we cannot even admit that it is possible for us to become weak. When we feel weak we are simply permitting ourselves to be untrue to ourselves; we ignore the reality of our own being and cause the mind to create conditions in our system that are false. Thus evil begins. But so long as we cause the mind to be fixed in that great truth that God is our strength, we shall not be conscious of anything that is not strength; nor will the mind create any condition that is not true to the truth.

When we realize that the strength of the Infinite is our strength, and that the strength of the Infinite is limitless, we must come to the conclusion that we are capable of doing anything that the living of a great life may demand. Whatever we are called upon to do, we are equal to it, because, have we not the power of the Supreme with which to work?

In the light of this truth we can never say that we are unable to do what the hour may require; nor can we say truthfully that we are ever tired, wearied or overcome. Such thoughts do not belong to the truth. While we are in the truth there is nothing that can make us tired; nor is there anything that is too much for us. God is our strength, and the power of Him that is within us is greater than anything in the world.

Though the flesh may seem to be weak, it seems so only because we have not fully accepted what is truly our own, the strength of the Infinite. But when we do accept this strength, the power of the spirit will manifest in the flesh; we shall then be strong, through and through, with power from on high. Every part of body, mind and soul will live with limitless life, because God lives with limitless life, and all that the Father hath is mine.

My being is sustained in the Word of Truth

The word of truth is the coming forth of truth into life; it is truth taking shape and form in the world of being, and to be sustained in the word of truth is to so live that everything in life is shaped, formed and determined by the power of truth.

To think frequently of the great statement that we are sustained in the shaping and forming power of truth is to place the mind more and more perfectly in harmony with that power; in consequence, the mind will be shaped more and more in the exact likeness of truth.

When the mind assumes the form of truth, every action of the mind becomes an expression of truth; the mind itself becomes a true mind and all thinking will convey the elements of truth to every part of the being of man. When the mind is formed by the truth, only true conditions will be formed by the mind; and therefore, neither sickness, inharmony, weakness, adversity, pain nor want can possibly exist anywhere in the human system.

To feel that we are sustained in the word of truth is to produce that deep realization of the power of truth that is so conducive to the full understanding of truth; and as we grow in the understanding of truth we grow into the freedom that is produced by the truth.

The word of truth is the living truth; that is, the power of truth expressed in tangible action; and is therefore distinct from abstract truth, or the mere intellectual conception of truth. The intellectual aspect of truth does not sustain the true life because it has not become the word, or the power of true formation. But the realization of the world of truth takes life into what may be termed truth in action; and when we are in the truth in action we are acting in the truth.

To act, live or think in the truth is to give the sustaining power of truth to every action, and thus every action will not only be a true action, but it will contain the limitless power of truth. This is why no true action can fail, and also why no ill can possibly come to any human personality that lives in the word of truth, and that is consciously resolved into the pure spiritual essence of truth.

When the human system is sustained in the word of truth, every part of the system is fixed on high; that is, placed within that true state of being where everything is created in the image of God, and where everything is always well. In this state the good alone exists; everything has freedom because it is in the world of absolute freedom, and therefore everything will do what divine purpose planned that it should do. This is the true meaning of freedom, and it is such freedom alone that can give to every soul what the largest life and the greatest joy may need or desire.

"But let your speech be yea, yea; nay, nay." Every statement we make should either affirm that which is true or deny that which is not true. Statements that contain both the elements of truth and the elements of untruth are of the evil one; they confuse the mind, and lead to sin, sickness and death. Make no compromise with the untruth, and let no half-truth find expression in your life. Give positive expression, in thought, word, action and life, to that which you know to be real, and eliminate completely what you know to be unreal. Make your life a living affirmation of the great things that are before, and so live that everything you do will deny the lesser things that are passing away.

Spiritual consciousness is in the light of the truth, and can always see the truth clearly. To see the truth clearly is to know the truth, and to know the truth is to be free.

The spiritual understanding of truth is the direct consequence of the mind's insight into that realm where everything is what it is; where nothing can be added and nothing taken away.

When you inwardly feel what you say, you give spiritual power to your words; and what you say will surely come to pass.

Chapter 12

Finding the Lost Word

Illumined minds in every age have declared their belief in what may he termed the sacred word; or that formulated statement of truth through which unbounded power could he expressed. According to this belief, anyone who knew this secret word or statement, could, by the use of that word, secure anything he might desire. Through this word the sick could be healed, adversity overcome, calamities prevented, enemies turned into friends, earnest desires realized, life prolonged, and everything gained that would tend to promote the comfort and joy of existence; and those who were high in the scale of spiritual attainments, could, with this word, perform miracles. This was the belief, and this is still the belief among nearly all who recognize divine power in man. But what this word really is, is a mystery in the minds of the many, and therefore it is usually called the lost word.

The great word is not a word, as many suppose, nor a definite statement of truth. The great word is the soul of every word, the spirit of every thought and the inner power of every expressed statement. In the minds of the great majority it is a lost word, because their speech does not have soul, their thought does not have spirit, and their statements of truth, or untruth, are devoid of inner power.

But those who are learning to live, think and act, not as material personalities, but as Sons of God, are finding the great word; they are beginning to speak with authority, and there is hidden power in everything they say.

What they say will come true, does come true; what they think they can do they gain the power to do, and their work invariably contains some exceptional quality that the ordinary mind cannot define. The spiritually minded, however, can understand; they know the secret; they realize that the great word is the supreme power of divine being coming forth into the speech, the thought and the actions of the fully awakened soul. And if these minds will continue to enter more and more deeply into the spirit of this supreme power they will find that the great word can do everything that the ages have declared that it could do. Thousands today do, at times, use this secret word; that is, they give soul to what they say, and they give spirit to what they think; in consequence, their words carry weight and their thoughts have extraordinary power. But they do not, as a rule, understand how the power of the soul is given to word and thought, and therefore do not secure results whenever they may so desire. The secret, however, is simple, so simple that it can be comprehended and applied by anyone.

To begin, train yourself to feel inner power whenever you give expression to a statement of truth; and whenever you think enter into the spirit of your thought. When you speak, do not simply say words; say more. Never indulge in empty speech; that is, place yourself, your whole self, your great self into every word you utter. Let the spoken word be the body of your speech, but see that everybody has a great soul. The audible word itself has no power, but that word can carry all the power that you can inwardly feel at the time it is spoken. When you give soul to your speech every word will contain hidden power, and it is this hidden power of the spoken word that constitutes the secret word, the great word, the word that works wonders for those who understand. We realize, therefore, that there is nothing mystical or mysterious about the great word; it is simply a measure of supreme spiritual power taking expression in thought or speech. Jesus Christ was the greatest master in the use of the word that we know, though there have been hundreds in every age that have discerned its power and applied it to a great degree. In this age there are more than there ever were before who are consciously using the word, but as the general understanding of its nature is not clear, results are not as great as they might be. But it is predicted that we are to do the greater works, and it is our privilege to do so now because we have received the power.

There are thousands in the world today who are ready to do the greater works; they understand the law; they know the truth and their desire to live the truth is becoming stronger every hour; but there is one thing more needful. We must enter more deeply into the spirit. To believe in things spiritual is not sufficient; nor will the daily effort to conform with spiritual principles supply the necessary requirements. We must do all of these things and more. We must aim to enter into the very life of the innermost power of the spirit whatever we think, say or do. When we think the truth, we must mentally feel the inner spirit of that truth. When we desire the realization of some divine quality or perfect condition, we must mentally feel the deep invincible soul of that desire. And when we speak, we must not speak as personal men, but as spiritual Sons of the Most High, endued with limitless power from the Supreme. In brief, whatever we do in body, mind or soul, we must enter more deeply into the hidden powers of the spirit, and must try to realize that that power is the very soul of all power. When we think we can feel the soul of divine power, we must try to enter into the soul of that soul; and when we realize that a deeper soul state is being felt, we must try to enter into the soul of this deeper state, and so on, ever going deeper and deeper into the limitless vastness of the spirit. Thus we shall gain the great word, the word that gives soul to every word, spirit to every thought and inner power to every statement.

Give soul to every spoken word and you can heal yourself by saying, "I AM Well;" you can emancipate yourself from every adverse condition by saying, "I AM the Freedom of Divine Truth;" and you can cause every atom in your being to thrill with life and power by saying, "I AM the Strength of the Infinite." Give spirit to every thought you think and every condition you picture in the mind will be realized in the body. Every true desire you feel will be fulfilled, and every dream of greater things will positively come true. What you think you can do you will gain the power to do, because every thought that is filled with the spirit is also filled with the limitless power of the spirit. Give inner power to every statement, and whatever you affirm to be true you will cause to come true. The great word is creative, and if the hidden power of this word is in your statement, it will create whatever your statement may affirm. Therefore, select your statements with wisdom, and pray only for that which you know that you want. When you regain the lost word, all your prayers will be answered and all your desires come true. It is therefore advisable to pray for wisdom first, to desire spirituality first, and to seek first the kingdom of God.

The power of the spirit finds full expression only through the Word; but since mankind in general does not possess the Word, it is usually spoken of as the "lost word." To the mind that is only partly awakened this Word is something vague, almost incomprehensible, yet a jewel most earnestly desired. He feels that there is something within him that can know this Word, and speak the Word, but it seems to be lost to his mind in some mysterious manner. It is the speaking of the Word, however, that heals the sick and that makes man free; it is therefore most desirable to possess. When it is stated that the Word is lost, the idea is not that the human race possessed it once, and lost it later. The entire race never did possess the Word; never had the power to speak the Word. The Word has been lost to the race from the beginning of manifested existence in this sphere, but has been found in every age by the illumined minds of that age, and through those minds declared to the world. Instead of speaking of the Word as the "lost word," it would therefore be better to speak of it as the "hidden word," hidden from the mind of personal man, but revealed to the minds of illumined souls.

Those minds that are on the borderland of the great awakening realize that immediately beyond their present mental comprehension lies a world of wisdom and light, indescribable in its marvelousness and beauty. To some minds it is so near that at times the veil is parted, and they obtain a slight glimpse of the glory and splendor that was, is and is to be. Others have crossed the border at certain periods in their lives, and have actually entered, for a time, the Father's House of the Many Mansions. But the great purpose of every soul is to someday enter this celestial world and abide there always. Many have believed that we must leave the body before we can enter that sublime realm; the truth is, however, that we may enter today, if we are ready, and live in that higher world while still living upon earth in physical form. We shall then find that the earth is not outside of the kingdom, but that the real earth, spiritually discerned and understood in truth, is also one of His secret places.

To have the spiritual discernment to look into this beautiful world, these higher realms, and behold the sublime glory of the kingdom, the Father's House of the Many Mansions, is to regain the "lost word." "It is for you to know the mysteries of the kingdom;" and whoever has sufficient spiritual power to part the veil and see those things that are prepared for them that love Him, has found the "hidden word." Now he knows the mysteries; he has seen them as they are. He has crossed the border, he has trod the shining shore and his eyes have beheld eternity. He has seen the Word, because the One Divine Word is the revelation of all that Is Eternal. Whoever can see that which Eternally Is, that to which nothing can be added, nothing taken away, that which is the foundation of all, the life of all, the all in all, can see the Word. The Word is revealed to him; divine wisdom has inspired his soul, the light of the spirit has illumined his mind, and he speaks as one having authority. He speaks, not of that which others have told him, not as the scribes; he has seen the mysteries; he bears witness to the truth because he has witnessed and beheld the truth with his own illumined mind. The heavens have opened before him; he has not only had a vision; he has seen the truth that is beyond the vision and that truth is the Word.

To reach this sublime state the secret is faith; not the faith that believes, but the faith that knows — the faith that can see with the vision of the spirit. Every soul that has some discernment of higher things has a portion of faith. This faith increases as the soul ascends, and the soul ascends as the faith becomes larger, higher and more illumined. To feel the touch of the spirit is the beginning of real faith, and the nearer the soul lives to the spirit the larger the faith. In the first stages of faith, the way is opened for the power of the spirit to come forth and prepare the human temple for the greater things that are to follow. After this period, if the mind continues in spiritual growth, illumination begins, and will continue until the Christ state is attained.

During the first stages of spiritual illumination the mind feels the nearness of a higher world, and here is the soul's opportunity to take many steps towards the heights. Whenever these sublime moments appear, enter the stillness of the spirit, and place body, mind and thought in touch with the soul's eternal calm. Then when in the peace that passeth understanding, open the eyes of the spirit, and in faith, desire to meet Him face to face. He may not appear; but be not impatient; know that He will appear, and you can wait.

You can wait an eternity for such a privilege, for a single moment in His Presence is a million heavens in one. But when you do draw near enough to behold His shining glory, give thanks with all the power of heart and soul. The Redeemer has entered your life; you have found the way; you have entered the great climax of human existence and now you may begin to live. Henceforth, give your highest thought and attention to every spiritual experience that may appear, no matter how insignificant it may seem to be. Know that every manifestation of Divine Presence indicates that you are growing in the spirit, that your spiritual eyes are being opened, that you are beginning to discern His omnipresence and to know that He is always here, closer than breathing, nearer than hands and feet.

To know God is the beginning of all wisdom. To know and feel that God is here, everywhere, that we live in His spirit, His life, His wisdom, His power, His light and His love now, is to awaken the mind to real wisdom. Then we shall find the" hidden word;" then we shall enter the inner sanctuary of the soul and behold the Word of God manifested in the true being of man, eternally creating the true being of man in the likeness of the image divine. And then we behold the Word of truth in the being of truth we gain the power to speak the Word of truth. To know the Word is to have the power to speak the Word, and to speak the Word is to cause the Word to become flesh. Thus the life, the wholeness and the glory of the spirit is made real in the personal being of man.

To grow daily in the spirit is the way to the higher faith, the larger wisdom and the beautiful life. Aspire constantly to live the life of the spirit; turn all thought and attention to the more perfect understanding of the spirit; keep the eye single upon the divine perfection of the spirit, and there shall be many moments when His spirit will actually appear. When these moments come, grieve not the spirit away; receive its life and its power by entering into the stillness within; then open widely the door of the heart that the Guest from On High may come in. Soon He will come again. His coming will become more and more frequent, and when you are ready to actually live the life He lives, He will not go away any more.

Whenever the spirit comes and is received, the Word is being revealed to you, and you obtain a larger glimpse of that sublime state of being where you are about to enter, never to return. Never to return to the ways of the world; never to return to the bondage of sin; but to live in the light and the freedom of the spirit while still in personal form; to walk with God while still walking the earth; to be surrounded and protected by His invisible power while still living and working in the midst of visible things. In the world and yet above the world. Whenever you discern more clearly the glory of the kingdom it means that you are drawing nearer and nearer to the pearly gates. Press on; not with force and will, but with peace and faith, the eye ever single upon the Light that leads. It is the will of God that we should enter now "there is another and a better world." That world is not a future state of existence, but an eternal state of existence; it is therefore at hand here and now. To enter the "pearly gates" is to enter that better world — God's own true world where all is well. And those gates are ajar to all who can speak the Word.

The Pathway of Roses

Light within, guide thou my way,
I AM seeding truth today;
Where thou leadest I will go.
And all wisdom I shall know.
Peace and joy and truth and love
Are the blessings from above
That will surely come to me
When I gently follow thee.
Light within, thou light divine,
Thou shall never cease to shine;
Thou canst not depart from me;
We are one, for I AM thee.
Darkness flies and sins depart,
Truth is reigning in my heart;
Endless day dispersed the night
When I found I was the Light.

Chapter 13

The Royal Path to Wisdom

Solomon prayed for wisdom and received it; any other soul may do the same. God is infinite wisdom; and "all that the Father hath is mine"; we need simply go and receive our own. We may receive from the supreme mind, at any time, as much wisdom, on any subject, as our own minds can possibly appropriate, and we may also receive, from the same source, the power to appropriate more.

The wisdom that comes from God does not simply pertain to the soul or to the life of some other world, because God is the original source of all wisdom, and therefore we may receive light directly from Him on any subject whatever. Nor does the wisdom that comes from God need special interpretation; it is sufficiently clear for anyone to understand who is in harmony with God.

When higher wisdom needs interpretation, it is not from God, but is simply the mystical ideas of minds that have not found the clear light of the Infinite mind. The mystical wisdom of man is complex and confusing; the wisdom of God is simple and illuminating; the former produces darkness and doubt; the latter produces that faith that knows.

When we learn that real wisdom comes directly from God, we shall no longer seek knowledge through the training of the senses to discriminate between illusions; nor shall we depend upon experience for instruction. Real wisdom does not come from experience; experience can only tell us how it feels to live in illusions and overcome illusions, but it tells us nothing about how it feels to live in the real and ascend into the greater and the greater life of the real.

The mind that lives in the light of the Most High, knows the result of any experience long before that experience arrives; therefore, to such a mind, experience can convey no information. If the experience is pleasant, it is welcomed and received for the joy it brings, but if it is not pleasant, it is avoided, and the mind that is taught of God, knows beforehand whether any particular experience will be desirable or not.

To live with God is to gain good from every source, be the source physical, mental or spiritual; but the wisdom that comes with this good does not come from these various sources; it may come through these sources because to live with God is to touch God everywhere, and thus receive wisdom from God through every channel in the world.

To be taught of God is to pray for wisdom, to depend upon God for wisdom, and to live so near to God that we shall be in the light of His wisdom. Whatever we wish to know, we should take it to God, and let His spirit lead us, guide us, and inspire our minds with the truth desired.

The mind that is led by the spirit will not go wrong; or if it should temporarily be on the verge of taking a misstep, something will interfere. This something may seem to be special providence, and in a certain sense it is, because the Infinite is ever ready to do for man whatever he may wish to have done.

When we place ourselves in the hands of the Infinite, He will find a way, and this way will be revealed to us before it is too late. Sometimes it may not appear until the eleventh hour, but it invariably comes in time. We may therefore rest assured in this faith and know, "That I will not forsake thee nor leave thee; I AM thy Redeemer, I will care for thee."

The Pathway of Roses

The great secret of all the inspired minds of the ages may be found here; they seemed to have superhuman knowledge, they spoke with authority, and their words have been universally received as the truth; the reason being, they lived in the light of the Most High; they were taught of God.

To be taught of God it is necessary to live with God, walk with God, and open the mind completely to the great influx of supreme light from on high. It is necessary to be in such close spiritual touch with the Infinite mind that we can feel the thought of God, and think His thoughts after Him. And this any soul can do. To live with God is the simplest life of all, and also the most beautiful; and to walk with God requires no effort whatever. Any soul that can lift up the mind towards supreme spiritual realms can walk with God now.

When we place ourselves in that position where we can be taught of God, it is then that we begin to use the mind in the highest sense. It is then that the mind becomes so transparent that the light of Infinite wisdom can shine through and manifest itself in all its brilliancy and glory. It is then that the Word becomes flesh, and the truth of divine being is unfolded in the personal life of man.

The true function of the human mind is to think with the Infinite mind, because the human mind is an inseparable part of the Infinite mind. When the human mind tries to think alone, it becomes confused, and the ideas that it may form are mere illusions.

It is therefore evident that all the ideas in the world that have been formed while the human mind was trying to think apart from the Infinite mind, are illusions; and the wisdom of the world is full of such illusions. We can remove them completely, however, by turning to God, and opening our minds completely to the clear light from on high.

When we begin to receive the wisdom of God, we find that the wisdom of the world was the cause of our trouble; we were living in darkness and could not see the way, therefore took many missteps and made many mistakes; but when we open our minds to the wisdom of God we are in the light, the way is clear, and we shall not go wrong any more.

However, we are not required to ignore everything that man may say in order to receive the pure wisdom of God. God speaks through everything and most of all through man. When we desire, with the whole heart, to be taught of God, we shall constantly receive wisdom from God, and it may come through a million channels, including the mind of man, but we must remember that the mind of man does not simply mean the minds of other men; our own minds are included in the mind of man, and as we grow in the spirit we shall receive most of our divine wisdom with our own mentalities as the principal channel.

This is the great goal we have in view, but we cannot place our own minds in perfect touch with the Infinite mind unless we think of all minds and all things as being channels for the wisdom of God. When we can see God in all things, then we shall meet Him face to face. When we can receive His wisdom through all things, then we shall hear His voice, speaking directly to us, in the beautiful silence of our own soul.

When we enter this silence, as we may at any time, we know we are in communication with God, and we may learn the truth about anything that we have sought to understand. God is not a God of the future state alone. He is the God of all time, even the present, and He is at hand ready to lead us aright in everything that we may wish to do in the present. We may be taught now, by Him, in all things pertaining to physical and mental existence as well as the very highest spiritual existence. And the more we ask of God the more we please God.

Lay not up for yourself treasures upon earth." Where the heart is there our treasures will be also, and when the heart is in the earth, earthy, all that is beautiful in life will be lost. Our treasure is that which we love the best, but it is not wisdom to give our best love to things. Give your best love to the spirit of things and you will receive, not only the visible form, but also that sublime something that gives life and loveliness to the form. Seek the riches of the spirit and you gain wealth and happiness that shall never pass away. The richest man in the world is he who has found the diamond fields of the soul, while the poorest is he who is burdened with things that have not the spirit of things. It is our privilege to have abundance of all that is rich and beautiful in the visible world, but it is the wealth and the beauty of the soul that gives happiness; it is the treasures we lay up in the spiritual within that make all other treasures worthwhile.

When we know that God is life, power, health, harmony and joy, we will receive those blessings in boundless supply whenever we feel that His presence is here. When we attain the consciousness of the omnipresence of God, we will receive from God whatever we know to be in God.

Chapter 14

The Golden Path to Increase

For whosoever hath, to him shall be given, and he shall have abundance, out whosoever hath not, from him shall be taken away even that which he hath. Mat. 13:12.

The real element of possession exists in consciousness. What we possess in consciousness we inevitably will gain in the personal life; and no matter how well secured our external possessions may be, the moment we begin to feel in conscious that we may lose them, our hold on those things will weaken, and external loss will shortly begin unless this adverse state of mind is immediately changed.

To consciously feel that everything that you need or desire is for you — in brief, actually belongs to you in the real, is to be among those that hath, even though you may, at present, be empty handed in the external world. To you shall be given, and you shall have abundance both in spiritual possessions and in visible possessions. But to consciously feel that you do not have real or permanent possession of anything, is to be among those that hath not, even though you may have visible wealth in great measure. From you shall be taken away, and those external possessions that you seem to have shall pass to other hands.

This law is universal in its application and holds true in all matters, be they physical, mental or spiritual. The secret of gaining more on any plane is to consciously feel that you have more. Enter into the hath state of mind. Whether you desire life, health, power, wisdom, spirituality or greater abundance in external things, train your consciousness to feel that you have the real substance of the thing desired. Do not judge according to appearances, but continue to inwardly feel the possession of that which you claim as your possession.

When the mind enters the feeling of conscious possession, the first gain is the fuller possession of yourself and your powers; you immediately begin to feel stronger; this will strengthen and enlarge your consciousness of gain, which in turn, will increase the power of accumulation that has begun in your system. You thus not only become larger and stronger in your own nature, but you gain a more powerful hold upon everything with which you may come in contact. You awaken greater and superior qualities in your own mind and soul, and you inspire faith and confidence in the minds of others. You thus create those advantages and essentials, both in the within and in the without, that are conducive to gain.

When the mind enters the fear of loss and begins to feel that there is going to be loss, the first loss is the loss of self-possession. You lose your hold upon your own powers, and, in consequence, begin to weaken. Your faculties fail to do their best, your work becomes inferior, your personality does not attract as it did, and your power to inspire confidence in others, is on the wane. You suffer loss in all things, physical, mental and spiritual, and you are daily losing ground. Finally, everything that you seemed to possess is taken away. But the loss began in your own consciousness, and you could have stopped it there if you had known how.

The losing tendency can be stopped at any stage, but the only place where it can be immediately stopped is at its first appearance in consciousness. When you begin to feel that there is danger of loss, or when the general indications seem to predict loss, remove that feeling at once. Refuse to think of loss; refuse to admit the possibility of loss; refuse to recognize loss in any form whatever. Proceed to claim your own; give all the power of mind and thought to the great truth that you do possess now, in the real, everything that you can possibly need or desire. Give full recognition to the boundlessness of your own spiritual riches, and live in the conviction that whatever you claim possession of in the within you will gain possession of in the without.

The tide will turn before any real loss takes place; and instead of falling back into the world of the ones that hath not, you will advance farther into the richness of that world where dwell the ones that hath. In consequence, to you will be given, and you will have more than you ever had before. This method should be used with faith and perseverance whenever there is the least indication of loss; negative conditions should be replaced with positive conditions, fear should be annihilated by faith, and every downward tendency should be converted into a strong ascending tendency.

To live in the "hath" state of mind and grow steadily in the conscious feeling of possession, continuous growth in spirituality will be required. It is only through spirituality that we can grasp the reality of the inner substance of things, and we must gain consciousness of the inner substance of life before we can master those forces that make for perpetual increase in life.

To live in the "hath" state of mind it is also necessary to advance constantly into a deeper and larger conscious possession of those things that we already possess in abundance. There can be no inaction in consciousness; if we are not going forward into the larger and the more perfect we are going back and down into the lesser. Therefore, no matter how much power we actually possess, we should daily claim conscious possession of more; no matter how perfect our health may be, we should daily enter into the consciousness of higher perfections of health. When we cease to grow in health we prepare the system for sickness, but so long as we grow in health, sickness will be impossible.

The same law is applicable both to external possessions and spiritual possessions. To retain what we have we must daily develop the consciousness of more. The moment we decide to be satisfied with what we have we will begin to lose what we have. There is no limit to the riches of the kingdom of life, and it is the will of God that man shall enjoy more and more of these riches, every day, so long as eternity shall continue to be. And to do the will of God is to bring the highest happiness to man.

That the love of money is the root of all evil is true, providing we give the statement its true and full significance. When we speak of money we do not mean those things simply that pass for money, but we mean all external possessions. When we love external possessions the heart is in the without and not in the spirit as it always should be to be in the truth. When the heart is in external things, we begin to live for things; the mind comes to the surface and consequently becomes shallow and material. The mind that lives on the surface is not in touch with the deep things of life, is not conscious of the inner light of truth, and is therefore in darkness. To be in darkness is to go wrong, and to go wrong is to create evil. Every mind that is not led by the inner light of the spirit will go wrong; in fact, every wrong act comes because the mind follows external darkness instead of internal light; and it is only the love of other things that draws the mind out into the darkness of things. So long as we love the spirit the mind is in touch with the spirit and is illumined by the light of the spirit. When we are in this light we will not go wrong, we will not commit evil, because we can see the right, and we can see that the right is the very thing we have desired, longed for, prayed for.

The more deeply we love the inner life and the riches of the spirit, the more spiritual and illumined we become; accordingly, we can see more and more clearly how to do all things as they should be done; our mistakes will decrease, and wrongs and evil will disappear. To love the life is to enter into the spirit of truth, and in the truth there is freedom — freedom from sickness, evil, weakness and want. Evil can grow only in materiality; and materiality is produced simply by our own confused thinking. But when we are in touch with the spiritual life within, our thinking is not confused; we are then in the light of truth, and we think the truth. In consequence, we no longer produce the darkness and discord of materiality; instead we produce the peace and the harmony of spirituality, and all is well.

When your treasure, that is, that which you love the best, is in the without, in the earth, earthy, your whole life will be in the earth, earthy. You will thus live continually in wrong thought because you do not see how to create right thought. All mental light, even the light of reason, comes from within; therefore, when the mind is so absorbed in outer things that it ignores completely the within, all thinking will be more or less at variance with truth, and evils must necessarily follow. But when your treasure is in the spirit, and you love the riches of the soul better than anything else, you will live on the mountain top. You will dwell in realms sublime, in the very light of His infinite wisdom; all your thinking will be illumined with that light; you will thus think only the truth, and he produces no evil who always thinks the truth.

To lay up treasures in heaven is not to prepare for a heaven in the future, but to accumulate greater and greater spiritual riches now. That soul that is attaining real spiritual wisdom, that is growing daily in the love that loves everything, that is living in the peace that passeth understanding, that is being filled more and more with life and power from on high, that is gaining conscious realization of all the divine elements of pure, spiritual being — that soul is laying up treasures in heaven. Such a soul is actually coming into possession of those superior riches now, and is learning to use them today for the glory of God and the emancipation of man.

To become a strong soul, to attain the mastery of the spirit, to become a living inspiration to all the world, to unfold all that is lofty and beautiful and sublime in the spiritual life, to realize the joy everlasting and draw nearer and nearer to the Christ state — that is the purpose of him who is laying up treasures in heaven. And when we possess spirituality with all its qualities of high worth, we have the riches of all riches; we have that something that can produce all riches, not only in the spirit, but also in mind and body. That person who has found the riches of the within need never have any fear of external loss. Though all might disappear in the without, still, being in touch with the source of all supply, he could at once begin to regain everything.

When we are in the spirit we are upon the solid rock of all good; we possess the key to unbounded riches on all planes, and so long as we live in the spirit we shall not lose that key. When one door closes we can open another, sometimes several, and all that the heart can wish for shall always be ours to possess and enjoy. When we are in the spirit, we not only possess the riches of the spirit — those riches that actually make every moment of existence a full realization of the highest joys of life — but we also possess the power to supply the without abundantly, being in perfect touch with the Giver of all that is good in the world. There is no truth in the belief that we must necessarily relinquish external possessions the moment we begin to lay up treasures in heaven.

That power that produces the riches of the spirit, can, and will, produce abundance in the external world as well. All outer things will invariably be added when the kingdom within is sought — actually sought, and sought first, not only at first but always. So long as we seek only the treasures of earth we get but little of those treasures, while we get an overabundance of the suffering and pain of material existence. But when we begin to lay up treasures in heaven, we obtain the peace, the joy, the contentment, the health, the strength, the wisdom, the power and the life we so greatly desire; in addition, we obtain higher spiritual possessions without number, and an abundance of everything that is necessary to make the outer life full and complete.

Live eternally in conscious unity with the Infinite; have faith in God, have faith in humanity, have faith in yourself; then live, think and act according to principles only, and there is nothing you may not accomplish.

Great deeds in life are invariably brought about by higher power. And if we would be constantly in touch with higher power, we must live in the perfect faith and consciousness of the great spiritual within, where higher power has its center and throne. This, however, is not possible so long as we think more of the person than of the soul. To be centered in the spirit we must live in the spirit, and give the spirit our first thought at all times. Then we shall be filled with the supreme power of the spirit, and OUT strength, both in mind and body, shall be daily renewed from on high.

"Resist not him that is evil." The true path to emancipation is to give so much thought, life and attention to the building of the good that we have not the time to even think of evil. Then evil will die for want of nourishment. The mind that is absolutely full of a strong, spiritual building power, has no room whatever for evil conditions of any kind.

Chapter 15

The More Abundant Life

I came that they may have life, and may have it abundantly. — *John 10:10.*

The greatest thing that man can do is to live. Everything that appears in any sphere of existence comes from life, and therefore everything increases with the increase of life. To live more is to become more and gain the power to accomplish more whatever the field of action may be; to live more is to enter more fully into the richness and joy of life itself, and there is no joy that is greater than that which comes from perpetual growth in real life.

The purpose of life is to live more life; the principal secret of perfection in any period of life is to live as large a life as that period can appreciate and employ, and to constantly add to the abundance of that large life is to make each period better than the one that went before. Growth in life means growth in health, growth in strength, growth in capacity, growth in mental brilliancy, growth in talent, growth in wisdom, growth in power, and, in brief, growth in everything that a normal state of existence can possibly need or desire. The mission of the Christ is therefore not purely transcendental, nor solely for some other world.

The teachings of the Christ are applicable to every part of personal existence, and may be applied with great profit in every circumstance or event that can arise in the great eternal now. What is more, no person can do full justice to anything he may undertake to do unless he enters into full harmony with the great mission of the Christ. The life more abundant can come only through the Christ, and we all need the life more abundant if we are to be true to our own marvelous nature.

The coming of the Christ, however, was not confined to a short period of time some two thousand years ago; the Christ comes now to everyone who enters the spirit; and when He comes, He invariably brings the life more abundant. We may, at any time, enter the fullness of eternal life; and when we do, everything changes for the better. The life more abundant dispels the ills of existence in the same manner as light dispels darkness, and just as effectively, whatever those ills may be.

The ills of personal existence come principally from two causes: ignorance of divine law and false desire. The coming of the life more abundant gives the mind the necessary power to understand the laws of life; when we are in the life eternal we are in harmony with the laws of the life eternal, and will not misuse those laws any more. When we are filled with the richer life from within we no longer desire the lesser things in the without; we will not care for the wrong, having found everything that heart can wish for in the beautiful kingdom of the right.

To enter the life more abundant, first live the teachings of the Christ; not according to the letter but according to the spirit. The spirit is infinitely greater than the letter, and includes everything of worth that the letter may contain. Second, live now in the Christ consciousness. Know that the Christ is here, that His spirit is within you and all about you, and that you can be conscious of His presence at any time by simply opening your own mind to Hi a kindness and tenderness and sublime love. Know that "I AM with you, even to the end of the world," and think on these things.

The Pathway of Roses

The more attention we give to the great truth that the Christ is here with us now, the more we open the mind to the consciousness of His spiritual presence, and as we enter more and more into the consciousness of the Christ, we enter more and more into the limitless life of the Christ; thus we become filled, through and through, with the supreme power of that life that is eternal life.

The life eternal, however, is not distinct from any other form of life; it is the source of all life, and as we enter more and more into the life eternal we gain more life on every plane of being. We then begin to express the life more abundant through every part of body, mind and soul, and thus demonstrate conclusively that a strong soul does not mean a weak body.

The life of the soul is eternal life, and the more we unfold that life the more health, strength and vigor we give to the body; the mind becomes more brilliant, the personality more powerful, and the character more beautiful. And above all, we ascend to that sublime life on the heights that is fairer than ten thousand to the soul.

For whosoever would save his life shall lose it; and whosoever shall lose his life for my sake shall find it. Mat. 16:25.

When you lose your life for the sake of Christ, you let go of the limited life that is living in you in order that the limitless life of the Christ may live in you. Likewise, when you deny yourself and follow the Christ you remove the personal self from the throne of your being and enthrone the superior spiritual self instead. There is therefore no sacrifice; you lose nothing but your limitations and your illusions, while you gain everything that the kingdom of God holds in store for man.

The Pathway of Roses

The belief that it is necessary to lose something of actual value in order to gain the life eternal is not the truth. Poverty in the personal life does not produce spiritual riches, nor does the sacrifice of temporal joys produce the bliss of heaven. The idea of self-sacrifice must be eliminated; so long as we think that we have to sacrifice all that is good in the visible world in order to gain the joys and the riches of the invisible, we are out of harmony with the beautiful order of the cosmos. In the true order of things all that is real is good, and all that is good, man has the privilege to enjoy now.

The only things that we are required to sacrifice are our ills, our defects, our weaknesses, our shortcomings, our limitations; in brief, we are required to remove the personal self and its imperfections from our world of existence. The true self-sacrifice is that which refuses to permit personal imperfections to rule in the personal life, and gives up to the light, the power and the life of the spirit.

When you deny yourself in the true manner, you deny your outer mind the privilege of rulership. You no longer follow the desires and the beliefs of the flesh; you no longer obey the dictates of the body; you declare that the body must serve the soul and the soul must serve the Christ. You thereby permit the supreme life of the Christ to live in you; the mind that was in Christ Jesus enters your mind, and His life and His power becomes your own. The lesser life is lost, the greater life has come in its place. The mere man in you is decreasing while the divine in you is increasing and will thus continue until you are perfect as your heavenly Father is perfect.

To try to save the personal life is to live exclusively for the limitations of external existence; in consequence, the mind becomes so absorbed in the lesser life without that it is wholly unconscious of the greater life within. But we cannot receive the greater life from within unless we are in conscious touch with that life, and since the within is the only source of life, we cease to receive life the moment we are consciously separated from the inner life.

To live entirely for the personal life is to be separated from the inner life, and therefore we are not receiving any more life. The personal life, however, that we are trying to save will be gradually used up, and thus we will lose what we are so anxious to save. But when we begin to live for the spirit, and begin to follow the Christ into the vast spiritual realms of limitless life, we will find more and more life; and the more life we find in the vast within the more life we will bring forth into the without. All the life that we become conscious of in the soul we will express in the mind and the body, and the personal self, instead of growing weaker, will grow stronger and stronger as it is filled more and more with life and power from on high. And thus, by losing ourselves in Christ we gain everything that exists in the supreme life of the Christ; we lose nothing, sacrifice nothing, while we find ourselves — all that we are in the image and likeness of God.

Live a beautiful life wherever you may be and you become a living benediction to all who may pass your way. You may see no immediate results; in fact, your beautiful life may have scattered its blessings so far and wide that you cannot find the exact places where the flowers grow that you planted; but that does not matter. You have given; in consequence, the world is better off and you are a stronger soul. You know that not a single good deed can be lost; somewhere it will bless somebody. You know that every good seed that you may sow in the garden of human life, will someday take root and grow. You may not remain long enough to see the flowers, but somebody will see those flowers, and the fact that your hand planted the seed is pleasure enough for you. To feel that you have given happiness to someone else, is the greatest happiness of all; and to know that millions will be inspired by the sublimity of your life ages after you are gone — could anything give a deeper joy to the soul? And yet, this is a privilege that is not given only to the few; there is not a soul that may not look forward to such a future and to such a life.

To be perfectly satisfied to let your light shine wherever you may go without ever looking back to see if there were results or no, is the mark of a great soul So long as we do not wish to give unless we see visible results in exact places, our spirituality is not of the greatest; and so long as we require the personal testimony of those whom we have helped, to spur us on, our faith is nothing. He who has the true faith knows that spiritual living is a power wherever it is lived, and he never thinks of looking back to find if it was true. He scatters the seed and leaves results to Him that faileth not. He radiates the good and knows that that which is good can never cease to produce good.

When you realize that you are an entity through which God is expressed, and that your mind should be so transparent that the highest divine light may shine through and illumine the outer world, you have found your true place. To remain constantly in that beautiful place means that a higher power will be flowing through your being, radiating in every direction, giving the spirit of truth to everything you may think, say or do. You thus become a personal expression of the Word, and your life will be a message of truth to the race.

"Ye are the light of the world." Do not hide your spirituality in your feelings or your emotions. There is power in the spirit. Live this power, and give personal expression to everything that the spirit may contain. Then you will demonstrate to the world that the way of the spirit is the true way. When you are lifted up, hundreds and even thousands will come and go where you are going. Therefore, let the full glory of the spirit shine in your life; let power from on high manifest itself in everything that you may think or say or do, and great shall be your reward, both in this world and in the world to come. The spiritual life deprives you of nothing that has real worth, and gives you more and more of everything that has high worth.

"Agree with thine adversary quickly." There is a spiritual side to everything; enter into harmony with this spiritual side and the discord that seems to exist on the personal side will disappear. Forget those elements that are at variance and think only of those states that are perfectly at one with each other. You can easily find them; we find everything we seek, and whoever goes out to find harmony will discover that there is more harmony in the world than anything else, excepting life itself.

Chapter 16

Human Nature Becoming Divine Nature

There are thousands of people in the world today who have undertaken to live the spiritual life, and the majority of them understand, to a fair degree, the principles upon which such a life is based; nevertheless, there are too many who do not have as great results as they ought to have, and they are at a loss to find the reason why. With the spiritual wisdom which we now possess, we ought to do greater things than were ever known upon earth before; we ought to be able to overcome every wrong, not only in our own lives, but also in the lives of all who are receptive to our spiritual work; and we ought to realize an ever increasing abundance of infinite good and infinite power from on high. We ought to do all these things and much more, and when we can see distinctly where the two ways part, we certainly shall.

When we know that we have such an exceptional opportunity for higher usefulness in this age, we cannot be satisfied simply to use the power of divine truth for the attainment of physical health and personal prosperity. There are other and greater things to work for, but not many have the secret path to the world of these greater things. However, the reason why is simple; and likewise, the reason why the majority do not secure as great results as they should in the lesser things, is also simple. And the reason is we cannot serve two masters; we cannot take two paths at the same time; when we come to the parting of the ways we must take the one that leads into light and forget the other absolutely.

When we learn that man is created in the image and likeness of God, we enter a new realm of thought; we have made a new discovery, and we have found another way to think and live. The former belief taught us to think and live as a sinner, as a weak human body; the new truth has taught us to live as a spiritual being, as a child of God, as a strong, perfect, divine soul. And here is the place where we must decide which way to go, as it is not possible to believe the old and the new at the same time and have result; nor is it possible to believe part of the old and part of the new at the same time and realize that power for good that the new may contain.

There are many minds who believe in divine truth, and who accept fully the great truth that man is the image of God, but still continue to think of themselves as weak, human creatures. When the difficult task comes, and they fail, they usually become discouraged, and this is their language: "Just as I expected; but then I AM only human, only a weak, frail, being, not able to cope with these things; some day I may be able to overcome, but as yet I AM too weak; I must not expect too much of myself, as I AM only human." This is the drift of the thought in many a mind, and it explains perfectly why they have not overcome the wrong and attained the good. They are trying to realize the perfection of the divine within while recognizing the imperfection of the human without. They expect to attain divine power while persisting in living in the world of human weakness. They are trying to serve both the truth and the untruth, but we cannot realize the power of truth until we eliminate the untruth completely.

The outer has seemed to be the only reality so long that the mind naturally thinks everything existing in the outer to be reality; and here is the difficulty; we think the outer to be substantial and the inner to be "mere mental mist," but it is when we reverse this belief that we find the real truth. The statement that the flesh is weak has been a race thought for ages, and it comes natural to think of the flesh as weak; but the truth is that the flesh is weak because we have made it so, and we have made is so by claiming human weakness as our heritage instead of spiritual strength. He who lives constantly in the conviction that unbounded, spiritual strength is his inheritance now, will never for one moment feel that the flesh is weak. The flesh is what we make it, and it is just as easy to make it strong as to make it weak. Think that you are a weak, frail, human creature and the flesh will become the dwelling place of weakness; but know that you are a strong, invincible, eternal soul, and the Flesh will become the very embodiment of strength, and will be filled with life and power from on high.

We may philosophize learnedly about the beauty of spiritual thought, but that will serve no purpose unless the truth that is contained in our spiritual thought is stamped upon every word we express. We all realize the power of words; whenever we speak we send a life current through every part of the body; and if the words spoken are the expressions of material belief we give conditions of weakness to the body, and at times even disease. When we stamp every word, not with human thought, but with divine thought, every word will convey to the person the very spirit of life, power and wholeness. Through the power of speech a person can bring upon himself every wrong in the world; and through the same power he can bring upon himself every good in the world. Through the right use of words, uttered or unexpressed, a person can attain or obtain anything. Words are living forces; they create according to their nature, and they attract their kind. When we become as scrupulous about our words as we are about our clothes we shall become a superior race.

The parting of the ways is found where we can see the difference between human expression and divine expression. So long as our expressions are stamped with the belief that we are weak, frail or "only human," we shall continue in weakness and in that smallness of character that we call human nature. But human nature is simply an undeveloped condition; it is not a permanent factor in human existence; it seems to be permanent simply because practically no effort has been given to the unfoldment and expression of man's divine nature. To say that we are "human" and that we must ever remain so in this world is not only the untruth, but such expressions give weakness and adverse conditions to the personal life. We cause the flesh to become weak and remain weak by living in the belief that we are mere human creatures, and therefore when we meet adversity we "fall down," become sick, or otherwise manifest the imperfection of that life that is lived apart from the spirit.

When we take the other path, however, and begin to recognize our divine nature as our only nature, there will soon be a change in events. When this path is taken we recognize limitations no more, and the term "cannot" is forgotten. You never again permit yourself to say that you are sick, tired, limited, easily tempted or merely human. Such expressions you simply will not employ under any circumstances whatever. You know your divine nature, and every thought you think and every word you speak must express what you know to be true. Your every expression of mind, tongue or being thrills with the life and the power of eternal spirit. Regardless of obstacles or adverse events, you stand by your convictions of truth whatever may happen or no. It matters not to you what happens in the exterior. You are not an exterior being; you are a spiritual being, created in the image of God.

Nothing that happens can affect you, disturb you, or even touch you; you are in Him, in everlasting safety. You live in the spirit; you know what is true in the spirit, and you think and speak accordingly every moment of your endless existence. Ere long the word of truth becomes a living power in body, mind and soul, and your entire being becomes a perfect expression of that Divine Word that is of God.

There is a strong tendency to compromise with the undeveloped side of the person whenever we fail to demonstrate the absolute power of the spirit. But this must never be permitted. No matter how many times you fail in the person do not admit that you are weak. You are not the person; you are the soul — the perfect image of God, and the image of God is supreme strength regardless of what may happen in the person. Continue to think the absolute truth, even in the midst of sickness, failure, trouble and want, and those things will soon depart never to return any more.

The Pathway of Roses

Father I AM one with thee.
One through all eternity;
One forever In the past,
One as long as time shall last.
Thou in me and I in thee,
Life of endless unity;
This my dearest song shall be,
Father, I AM one with thee.

Father, I AM one with thee,
Sweetest thought of truth to me.
I AM filled with life divine,
Therefore boundless good is mine.
All my life is lived in thee.
Perfect life of harmony;
This my highest thought shall be,
Father, I AM one with thee.

Chapter 17

A Sublime State of Existence

There never existed an awakened soul that did not believe in a spiritual state of being; and there never existed a soul in any condition of human understanding that did not have glimpses, at times, of what appeared to be another world. To those who had simply gained the simplest form of human consciousness, this other world seemed to be far away, a place we could not inherit until we had taken our departure from this visible state of existence; but to those who were on the verge of spiritual consciousness, this other world was not a faraway place. Those awakened souls could discern that it was a spiritual realm in which all might dwell today — the kingdom of heaven that is ever at hand.

This other world is the soul of the universe, permeating the limitless vastness of the entire cosmos. It is the sublime essence of all reality, the real reality of all that is; it is the infinite spiritual sea in which we live and move and have our being, the divine counterpart of everything that was, is, or is to be. It is that world which we find on the supreme heights of all existence, and is therefore the cosmic world, orderly, harmonious, complete, perfect, transcendent, infinite, divine. To live in this cosmic world is to view the entire universe from the heights, and from that sublime view everything is beautiful and all is good. Therefore, the life of the cosmic is a life of perfected being, everlasting peace and eternal joy. It is the life victorious — the life of the spirit — that every exalted soul has revealed to man, but it is not a life that is apart from personal existence; it is the soul of personal existence.

The cosmic world permeates the physical world as spirit permeates substance; and what the physical world is to the body, the cosmic world is to the soul. According to the true purpose of life, the body should live in the physical world, enjoying everything that is good and beautiful in personal existence; while the soul should live in the cosmic world, enjoying everything that is good and beautiful in spiritual existence. This is complete existence, but the soul cannot consciously live in the cosmic until it is awakened, or until it has become conscious of its own exalted divinity.

The awakening of the soul into the world of its own spiritual nature, will not deprive the body of anything that is worthy in physical life. We are not required to leave the physical to enjoy the spiritual, nor is it necessary to sacrifice anything that can add to the welfare of the body in order to inherit the riches of the soul. The greatest good comes into the whole of life only when the body lives a complete physical life and the soul a complete spiritual life. The soul cannot fully express itself unless physical existence is all that it can be on the physical plane, and the body is not fully alive until the soul is awakened on the spiritual plane. We do not appreciate the beauty of the physical until we are illumined by the light of the spiritual, and we cannot comprehend the marvelousness of the visible world until we can see its splendor and vastness from the supreme heights of the cosmic world.

We must live in the cosmic world before we can live real life in any world. It is the soul of existence that unfolds the real beauty, the real worth and the real joy of every form of existence, but we do not become conscious of the soul of existence until we begin to live in the cosmic world. We cannot realize the fullness of life until we live in the source of life, and the source of life is spiritual. All life comes from above, therefore the nearer we live to that which is above, the more life we shall receive until we inherit real life itself — the life of the spirit — the life that is lived in the full consciousness of divine being. When we live almost wholly in the personal we live only in part, but when we live in the full consciousness of the spiritual as well as the personal, that which is in part passes away and the limitless life is realized instead.

It is then that we inherit the life more abundant, and everything that life has the power to give.

To live in the cosmic world is to realize the purity and the absoluteness of the spiritual, the divinity of man's real nature and the absolute perfection of his true being. It is to know the truth about man — the truth that he is created in the image and likeness of God, and it is the knowing of this truth that makes man free that produces complete emancipation. To enter into the cosmic world, therefore, is to enter into freedom, health, harmony and wholeness, and, in brief, everything that promotes the highest good for body, mind and soul. The cosmic life is the apex of all ascending life, the fulfillment of every true desire in life, the realization of everything that is ideal in life, the attainment of the one supreme goal in the living of divine life. To live in the cosmic is to live in the world of the great within, in the highest state of being, in the life of the soul, in tune with the Infinite, in the secret places of the Most High.

To enter the cosmic world is to ascend to the heights and live the spiritual life. The living of the spiritual life means the overcoming of spiritual death, and it is spiritual death that must be overcome before man can receive his inheritance, here or hereafter. The phenomena of physical death need not concern us; its coming produces no permanent effect upon real existence, nor is anything gained by prolonging personal existence so long as the soul is dead to spiritual existence. It is spiritual life that gives real worth to personal life, and it is the life of the living soul that prolongs indefinitely the life of the living body.

The Pathway of Roses

When the soul is not awakened, consciousness lives in a condition of spiritual death and mental darkness. The mind is deprived of the guidance of the spirit, and therefore follows blindly the changing desires of the flesh, those desires that are suggested by the world of things. In consequence, the person is almost buried in materiality, and goes wrong more frequently than otherwise, usually not knowing the reason why. The result is sickness, trouble and adversity, or the sum total of the ills of life. The real cause of all these ills is spiritual death, and the great, infallible remedy is the spiritual life. The ills of life are produced by the mind going wrong, but the mind will not go wrong when it is led by the spirit, and the mind invariably is led by the spirit when we live in the life of the spirit.

The higher we ascend in the true light of the spiritual life the more clearly we can see how to so live that we may be in perfect harmony with all the principles and laws of life. Our sins will cease, our mistakes will diminish, and consequently, ill effects will become more and more insignificant until we can truthfully say that we have gained complete emancipation. When we live in the spirit we live in the light, and when we live in the light we will not go wrong. We can then see where to find the greatest good, and no person will seek the lesser after having learned where to find the greater.

When consciousness acts almost entirely in conditions of spiritual death, nearly every action is at variance with the true order of things; in consequence, confusion, darkness and the downfall of the person follows. We always go down when darkness becomes our only guide, and as the spiritual light is the only guiding light, we will continue to go down so long as the spirit is not awakened. When spiritual death begins, downfall begins, not only in the lives of individuals, but also in the lives of nations, races and systems of thought. Therefore, the overcoming of spiritual death is the great hope of the world. It is this alone that can lead us out of the Egypt of sin, sickness, adversity and pain, into the promised land of peace, wholeness, happiness, freedom, power and truth. It is the awakening of the spirit that will take men and nations out of the powers of darkness, and place the whole of mankind upon those sublime heights where we shall live a life that is befitting the Sons of God.

The spiritualization of the world means the real salvation of the world; not salvation for the future alone but also salvation from sin, sickness and adversity now. When spiritualization begins, the mind is given a light, and that light invariably leads upward and onward into better things. To spiritualize the mind the soul must be awakened, and to awaken the soul is to overcome and eliminate the conditions of spiritual death. Then real life begins — the life of an emancipated personal existence harmoniously blended with the life of an exalted spiritual existence. To awaken the soul, every act of consciousness must be animated with a strong, deeply felt desire to reach the heights; the eye must be kept single upon the supreme spiritual goal, and very thought must be formed by the highest spiritual understanding that can possibly be realized. To live must be the one ruling purpose, and that purpose must be inspired by the spiritual touch of that life that we know to be eternal life.

To awaken the soul and illumine the mind with the light of the spirit, one of the great essentials is to live by faith. To live by faith is to place your entire life, and everything that pertains to your life, in the hands of Supreme Power. This means that your life will be drawn towards the heights, because Supreme Power is ever ascending towards greater and greater heights. It also means that all things that pertain to your life will work together for the greatest good, because it is the purpose of Supreme Power to produce the greatest good. Whatever is placed in the hands of this power will be inspired and guided by this power, and consequently will do what this power is doing, that is, working in harmony with everything to produce the greatest good.

The secret of faith is therefore simple, and we can readily understand why all things become possible to him who has real faith. Supreme Power can do all things, and he who has faith places his life, his purpose, his plans, his desires — everything, in the hands of Supreme Power. That he should fail is impossible. When the Supreme is with us nothing can be against us, and the Supreme is with us when we place ourselves absolutely in the hands of His power.

When we live by faith, we are constantly on the verge of the great spiritual world, because the power into which we have given everything, is the power of the spiritual world. We are living, thinking and acting in constant recognition of the Supreme Power of the spirit, and are therefore constantly being touched by the spirit, and there is nothing that is more conducive to spiritual awakening than this tender touch of the spirit. To feel, through and through, that His presence is closer than breathing, nearer than hands and feet, is to arouse every spiritual element in our nature, and the soul will come forth into life clothed with the sublime glory of its own inherent divinity. Then we shall ascend into God's own beautiful world, and the life on the heights will begin.

The Pathway of Roses

When the soul discerns that My Father and I are One, the door to the kingdom of heaven within will be opened. To be with God is to be in heaven, and this is a privilege that any soul may enjoy now while yet in personal form.

To simply hope for health and freedom is to remain in our present condition however adverse that condition may be. But when we have faith in that power that can give us health and freedom we enter into the very life of that power, and we are healed at once. Faith moves on and on and enters directly into the very condition that is desired; it never ceases to press on until it is in the presence of that which is wanted, and therefore we can never fail. Hope stands on the outside; faith walks in; hope waits to be guided; faith trusts its own light and proceeds; hope waits for the right opportunity; faith creates its own opportunity; hope waits to see the solid rock appearing from out the seeming void; faith goes out upon the seeming void and finds the solid rock; hope stands upon the earth eagerly looking towards the heavens; faith mounts upon the wings of the spirit and ascends to the highest heavens.

Chapter 18

A Foretaste of Heaven

How to enter the silence is a problem that confronts every earnest seeker for that higher state of being, that more beautiful world of peace and joy, that inner realm where all is well, that secret place where dwells the soul with God. Prophets, illumined minds and great souls of every age have discovered that there exists a hidden somewhere in the cosmic life of man, the finding of which means the full realization of all the hopes of human life. In this inner realm there is healing for all ills, there is the peace that passeth understanding, the joy everlasting, and light, wisdom and power without end. To enter this sacred chamber of the soul is to find the answer to every prayer, the long sought fulfillment of every heart's desire; whatever the soul has longed for, the same will be found in this inner sanctuary of eternal life; and the path has been called the silence.

The will of the Father is to give us the kingdom; but we must go to Him if we would receive what is prepared for them that love Him. But how shall we go to God? We seem to be away from Him. There seems to be a gulf between our own life and the Infinite life. To bridge this gulf is the great need of the soul, and the silence seems to answer this need. Therefore, to know how to enter the silence becomes a great secret, both in the living of daily life and in the attainment of supreme spiritual life. To simply believe availeth nothing; we must actually go to God if we would receive what eternity holds in store. All things come from God, and he who enters into the presence of God will receive all that God can give. To go to God is to enter into the stillness of the spirit, into the silence of those secret places where the Infinite reigns in glory, where the Christ is enthroned On High.

The Pathway of Roses

Be still and know that I AM God, This is the way, and no other path can be found. There are many who are trying to climb up some other way, but they will not find what they seek. The straight and narrow path alone leads to the Father's House. But there are few who find it, because the many try to reach the spirit without becoming spiritual. Man expects to gain the gifts of the spirit through methods, but never will he find the kingdom in this way. He alone receives the gifts of the spirit who becomes spiritual. He alone enters the kingdom who will live the life of the kingdom.

There are many who believe that psychical experiences constitute the "gates ajar" to the spiritual kingdom within, and multitudes have been lost in this sea of darkness and confusion. Such experiences never lead the soul to the kingdom, but they are, in many instances, the only obstacles in the way. So long as a person encourages those experiences and permits himself to be led by strange signs, he will remain in the without, and will suffer the usual ills of material man. The kingdom of heaven does not come by observation, neither tangible observations nor mysterious observations. The kingdom is found only in the spirit, and the spirit does not manifest itself in strange signs, but in the great and beautiful life. Jesus taught the existence of a spiritual realm within man, and emphasized again and again the necessity of living in this higher state if we would receive what real life can give. In this age, the entering of this secret place — the inner chamber of the soul, has been called the silence, or the true prayer of illumined faith — the prayer that not only asks of God but realizes eternal oneness with God. It is the prayer that is uttered in silence that is answered; it is the truth that is realized in the silence that gives freedom, peace and wholeness to man.

To enter the silence is to enter God's world, where everything is created in the image of God and manifests the likeness of God. To be in the silence is to know that you are spirit. To be in the silence is to know and feel that God is omnipresent and that you are one with God. To be in the silence is to actually be in the life eternal, and realize the divinity, the goodness and the perfection of all things. To enter the silence is to enter that sublime state where you know that God is in His Holy Temple and that all the world is silent before Him.

To enter the silence is not to have certain strange mental experiences for the space of a half an hour. You may have visions, you may realize the seeming reality of mystical realms, you may project thought, you may communicate with minds that are far away, you may have all kinds of super-physical sensations in mind and body; you may seemingly leave the form and be conscious of other worlds; you may imagine that your body is ether and that you can float upon the air; you may go into ecstasy and seem to receive wonderful revelations; you may have all of these experiences and many more, some of them real, some of them not, and never be in the silence for a single moment.

To enter the silence is to actually go to God; to enter into His presence and to know that He is ever with you. To enter the silence is to walk with God; to feel that His spirit protects you, leads you and keeps you, and that nothing but good can possibly come. To enter the silence is to awaken to the great truth that all that is real is good. To enter the silence is to become conscious of that cosmic state of existence where there is neither evil, sickness nor sin; where all is perfect and good; where life lacks nothing, and where the fullness of Infinite life reigns supremely through the all in all. To enter the silence is to see the soul-side of all things, to come face to face with the eternal, the changeless, the absolutely divine. In the silence you never look for experiences; you are above the world of experience; you are not in the presence of

The Pathway of Roses

the passing; you are in the presence of the sublime stillness of that whichever and ever is as God is. When you are in a quiet state and have experiences you are not in the silence; but when passing thoughts are forgotten, and you find yourself face to face with the sublime stillness of eternal life, then you are in the silence. In that state all is silent and still; nothing is passing; all is; all is in Him; and all is illumined with the light and the glory of His radiant presence. Divine moments. Beautiful beyond human comprehension. A foretaste of heaven. A glimpse of the Many Mansions. Alone with God and the Great White Throne.

To enter the silence there are no special methods, but there are many things, which if done, will prepare the way. The first of these is to live the life of the spirit every day as far as you know; live in the spirit of the prayer without ceasing, and desire eternally the coming forth of the soul. And inspire this desire with the great truth that your soul is the throne of God. When the soul comes forth the Word becomes flesh, the perfection of divinity manifests in personal form, and the Mind that was in Christ Jesus the same Mind will be in you. Every day for a few moments be alone with the Most High. Let those moments be sacred, and think only of Him. Do not permit another thought to enter consciousness. Fill your being through and through with such strong spiritual aspirations that the thought of the Infinite reigns supremely in your mind. Try to realize His presence, His life and His love. Give yourself up wholly to God, and know that you are absolutely in His care. Enter so deeply into the spirit of this realization that you can actually feel divine nearness — that God is closer to you than your own life. To feel this is to enter into the greatest joy of sublime existence. To be touched by the Spirit of God, if but for a single moment, produces a million thrills of divine ecstasy, and so great is the joy that one short moment feels as if it were an eternity. In brief, when you are in that sublime state you are in real eternity; time passes no more; every moment appears to be an eternity because it is in eternity; and being in eternity it gives to you an eternity of bliss — unbounded bliss from the highest heaven.

There is nothing that will prepare the way to this sublime spiritual silence more than this — to give a few moments every day to God, to think of Him only, and to think of Him with your whole life, with your whole strength, with your whole mind, with your whole heart and with your whole soul. To give up to God is to enter into the kingdom of God, and to enter the kingdom of God is to receive everything that God has to give. To give up everything for God is to receive everything from God. To place everything in the hands of God is to be guided and led by the hands of God, and God leads man into every good that the mind can imagine. God leads out of the lesser into the greater, out of limitations into the richness of the boundless, out of mere existence into the glories and splendors of empyrean heights. And it is the purpose of the silence to so deepen the consciousness of the spiritual life that we may live eternally in the very presence of God. Thus we shall ever walk with God and be guided by Him in all things.

To consecrate your entire being to the spiritual life and so live that everything you do draws you higher and higher into the very world of the spirit — this is another essential to the attainment of the true silence. When your life is consecrated to the spirit, all the powers of your being will constantly ascend towards the supreme heights of the spirit. Thus you become more and more spiritual, and to be truly spiritual is to be able to enter the secret places at any time. Another important essential is to live in the consciousness of the divine side of all things. Never for a moment permit the mind to forget that there is a divine side to everything in existence. No matter how imperfect things may seem to be on the surface, know that there is another and a better side, even to the least of these; and do not for a moment lose sight of the great truth that that better side is created in His image and likeness. This lofty mode of thought and life will not interfere in the least with the duties of everyday life, but will, instead, make all work and all life a great joy. To work when the mind is in the spirit is to work both wisely and well; and when you ascend to the supreme heights of the spirit your work becomes a great work. To live in the spirit is not to live apart from visible things, but to gain far greater mastery of things, and thus gain the power to do far greater things. To live in the silence is not to live in a dream; it is not to become oblivious to the realities of tangible existence, but to inspire tangible existence with all the power, with all the life, with all the truth, and with all of the beautiful that the soul can find when it soars to celestial realms on high. The purpose of the silence is to unite the world of things with the world of spirit, and thus give the fairest life in all the world to body, mind and soul.

The Pathway of Roses

Sun of my soul, eternal light,
Be thou my leader and my guide.
And I shall ever find the right
By walking truly by thy side.
Tho' clouds of doubt may hover near,
Darkness and wrong obstruct my way,
My faith in thee shall banish fear,
And give my soul the light of day.
Upward and onward I shall rise,
Treading the path of truth and right,
Passing through God's celestial skies,
Led by the Spirit of His Light.

Chapter 19

The Vision of the Soul

Faith is the "gates ajar" to the Holy City, to the world celestial, to the many mansions, to the spiritual realms, to the beautiful life, to the inexhaustible source of all that is good. Faith is the path that leads to the soul's inheritance of all that the heart has prayed for, and to follow this path is to have faith in faith.

Thousands have undertaken to live by faith, but not having sufficient faith in faith have too soon adopted a different course. In the beginning of the spiritual life it is so easy to forget the vision of the soul, so easy to follow the dictates of the senses when this vision has seemingly faded away. And the cause is we have not sufficient faith in faith.

When we begin to live by faith we must have sufficient faith to go on and on, no matter how many obstacles or failures we may meet at first. Temptations are numerous and the soul that has resolved to employ spiritual methods in all things must be able to deal with the tempter as Jesus did. But this is not impossible, because the mind that is in Christ Jesus, the same mind is in you.

The greatest obstacle is the intended kindness of friends. They have our welfare at heart, and wish to do everything they can to promote that welfare; hut they almost invariably employ the ways of the world; they do not know that faith is always sufficient. Here is a place where much strength is required. Here is the real parting of the ways, and the problem is, will you listen to those who love you with the love that knows not the way, or will you depend upon faith alone? Will you accept the kindness of the world or the unbounded love and the limitless power of the Infinite? Whoever loves brother or sister more than me is not worthy of me. Also, if thy right hand offend thee, cut it off. It is better to lose everything that is near and dear than to lose faith, but so long as we continue in faith, giving faith the first thought, and having abundant faith in faith, we shall not lose anything that we love.

The "right hand" is the sum-total of all those things in the world, that we feel we cannot get along without. They seem indispensable, and their loss seems irreparable; but they are insignificant compared with faith. We must be ready to dispense with them all if necessary to the realization of perfect faith, and we must depend absolutely upon faith regardless of the wishes of our dearest friends. But when we are ready to sacrifice everything that faith may have its way, we shall find that no sacrifice will be required of us.

When Abraham became absolutely willing to even sacrifice his own son in order to obey the spirit, he learned it was not required of him. And it is always thus; when we are willing to lose everything that spirit may reign, we find that we lose nothing, but gain much.

When we have faith in faith we find that faith can do anything; and we find that faith in the life, the power and the guidance of the spirit will take us safely through anything. If we are in trouble, faith will open the way out; if we have lost our friends, faith will give us more and better friends; if we have lost all of our possessions, faith will give us greater riches than we ever had before.

We have been told that the story of Job is an allegory; but even so, it illustrates what can be done, and what is being done in varying degrees in the lives of thousands where faith in faith is abundant and strong. He who has the faith that Job had will regain all he has lost and in addition, will receive much more. This is the law of faith and we can all prove the law by simply having faith in faith.

When we are in darkness and sin, faith will lead us into the full light; when we are in bondage to sickness and pain, faith will heal us and give us complete emancipation; and when we are in poverty or want, faith will lead us into the land of plenty.

The old thought has informed us that he who would live by faith must expect to live in poverty; many have believed this and have therefore been compelled to let go of almost everything of value and worth in the world. What we believe must come, will come. As your faith is, so shall it be unto you. If it is your faith that you must live in poverty in order to live by faith, in poverty you must live.

But it is the Father's will and desire to give us the riches of the kingdom; and to have faith is to live in harmony with Infinite will; therefore, when we begin to live by faith we shall leave the life of poverty and enter the world of abundance.

To live in poverty is not a mark of spirituality. If you are poor something is wrong either with you or with the society in which you live. But faith can take you out of that wrong and cause all things to become right. Faith can give you the best of everything that the whole of life can produce. Believe this and so it will be.

When things seem dark, and all that is near and dear seems to be slipping away from you, do not complain or weep. Have faith. Depend upon faith. Have faith in faith. Know that faith will change the course of events; turn darkness into light; turn hatred into love; turn chaos into order and harmony; and cause the best of all things to flow into your life in greater abundance than ever before. Faith can do anything. Have faith in faith and to you shall come the riches and blessings of the beautiful life.

The tendency of man is to turn to old methods when faith seems to fail; but why does faith ever fail? The reason is we have not sufficient faith in faith. When we have perfect faith in faith, it can never fail us. The power within faith is limitless, and it is our privilege to call into action as much of this power as we may need or desire.

We are called upon every day to decide upon something of importance; but how is this decision to be made? Are we to follow fear or faith? Fear declares that everything may go wrong; this is always the language of fear; but faith declares that everything will go right; and this is always the language of faith. Fear does not know; faith does know. Follow the verdict of fear and everything will go wrong, because the path of fear leads into wrong. But follow the superior insight of faith and everything will go right. The path of faith is the ever-ascending path to the greatest good that real life can give; therefore, no one can follow faith without finding the richer, the larger, the truer and the better.

Fear always expects the worst, because it can see only darkness; faith positively assures us of the best, because it can clearly see the light; and in the light the best is always found. But whether we decide to follow fear and live in darkness, or decide to follow faith and live in the light, will depend entirely upon how much faith we have in faith.

Millions are living lives that are not satisfactory; they long for a change, but they are in such complete bondage to fear that they are always afraid to even hope for something better. There is a power, however, that can break the bonds, and that power is faith. Are you living in Egypt? Are you in bondage to the king of evil, oppression and misery? Faith can lead you out. Depend upon faith, and begin this moment to follow wherever faith may go. Is there a Bed Sea of mental materiality between yourself and the promised land of peace, happiness and plenty? Take the rod of faith in your hand and stretch it out over the sea; the waters will instantly divide, and you may walk safely to the other side. Faith can do anything. Have faith in faith.

There is not a single person in the world today that cannot enter the promised land, and do so now. Anyone may find peace, health, happiness, freedom, and the very best that life can give. These things are for you in your present state of existence. It is the will of God that life should be sweet to every soul; do not believe that you must suffer. There is freedom for you this very moment; there is a beautiful life that you may enter at once, and faith is the open door.

Have faith, and the veil of mystery is no more; you may see what has been hidden, and enter the secret chambers of life. Have faith, and the clouds of darkness will completely disappear; you will behold the light of the eternal sun, and the radiance of its glory will fill and illumine your entire sphere of existence. Have faith, and the barriers of limitations will fall to rise no more; and the invincible powers of the spirit will surge through and through your entire being, proclaiming in language divine, "Nothing shall be impossible unto thee, for I AM thy strength and thy life forever."

Faith is the assurance of things hoped for, the evidence of things not seen; and the reason is that faith lives in the light. Faith knows that we may receive anything we ever hoped for, because faith discerns that power that makes all things possible. Faith is in the light, and therefore sees what has not been seen; it does not simply believe that the unseen is real, but proves the reality of everything by going out into the boundlessness of everything.

Faith is never sad, because it lives in the joy everlasting. Faith never grieves, because it knows that nothing is lost. Faith knows that what shall be united will be united; what shall be found will be found; and what belongs to us cannot long be kept away from us. Faith also knows that whatever we may need or desire now, exists for us now; and it is our privilege to enter through the door of faith and receive our own. The great secret is faith. Faith can do anything. Have faith in faith.

The Pathway of Roses

The soul never acts alone; whenever the soul acts, God acts also, in the same place, at the same time, and for the same purpose. Whenever the soul undertakes anything, there is immediate and direct assistance from the Supreme. Therefore, the soul can never fail; nor can any personal undertaking fail that is prompted, directed and inspired by the soul. My Father worketh and I work; and I AM the soul. So long as I know and feel that I AM the soul, the soul will act in all my work, and where the soul acts there God will act also, because the two are One. What the soul begins, God will finish; what the soul aspires to be, God will cause it to be.

Chapter 20

The Infinite Revealed

When we think of God as absolute and infinite, and try to picture His spirit as it fills the universe with His transcendental omnipresence, we seemingly lose, at first, that beautiful something that makes Him personal to us. God does not seem to be God unless we can think of Him as a friend, and go to Him as we would to some person that was very near and very dear. It seems difficult to speak to an Infinite Being, and there is no beauty or comfort in believing in God unless we can speak to Him at any time when we feel the need of His tender care. Nevertheless, our reason declares that God must be infinite or He would not be God; and our spiritual discernment concurs with reason upon this great, momentous theme; but since God is infinite, absolute and omnipresent, how can He be personal? And if He is not personal, how can we think of Him as being different from cold principle and law?

We cannot think of love as existing apart from personality, and God is love; therefore He must be personal; but how can God, who fills the universe, be personal? This is the problem that confronts nearly every mind that passes from the literal belief in truth to the spiritual understanding of truth. When we try to think that God is not personal, we feel as if we have lost a great friend, the very friend of all friends; there seems to be no use for prayer, because how can the limitless Soul of the universe be interested specially in one of us, a mere atom in the immensity of the cosmos? Besides, we find it practically impossible to pray to something that is nothing but changeless principle and immutable law. We therefore cease prayer and substitute affirmations; but something is lacking; the soul remains comfortless; the intellect may be satisfied, but the tender elements of love and sympathy are gradually disappearing, and finally we come to a place where nothing but cold intellect remains. Then we discover we are not on the path; we have gone astray, and everything the heart has wished for seems to be far in the distance. With God all things are possible; therefore, it is not beyond His power to be personal as well as absolute; nor is it beyond the power of man to understand how this can be. God is the great Soul of the universe. He lives and acts everywhere, and there is no place where He is not; nevertheless, He is just as personal to anyone of us as the very dearest friend; in truth, more so, because His personal nearness to us is closer than that of any friend, closer even than life itself. He is not limited and circumscribed as the form of a human personality; if He were, He could be personal only to those who lived in the same locality as He might happen to live; and therefore the vast throngs would receive no more comfort from His personal care than if they should try to worship principle and law. The very fact that God is infinite makes it possible for Him to be personal to all the souls in the universe; and the fact that He is present everywhere throughout the limitless vastness of space makes it possible for Him to give His personal care everywhere, thus ministering individually to every soul in existence.

God is individualized in every soul; that is, He actually lives in the very being of every soul. God is within us, closer than breathing, nearer than hands and feet; therefore it is not necessary to look to the great Soul of the universe whenever we think of God, to look within is sufficient. To contemplate the vastness of infinite life or the immensity of a universal soul is to lose sight of God. We can know Him only when we meet Him face to face within the sacred realms of our own divine spirit. Do not look towards the vastness of the without, but look towards the divinity of the within, and God will be there. He is always there, and His being there means that He is personal to us, ever ready to give personal attention to any need that we may have at the time. Being within us, and being in the very life of our own spirit, He is nearer than even our own personality, and can therefore give us His personal attention whenever we may so desire. Though He is not personal to anyone or any special number alone, being omnipresent, He is personal to all souls at all times, and that is a truth that is beautiful indeed to think of. The vine is united with all its branches, and gives its very life to each individual branch at all times. The vine is personal to each branch, and yet is not confined to the personal form or personal limitations of anyone branch. In like manner, the Infinite is personal to every soul, but is not localized as anyone individual soul may be.

When we state that God is in His heaven, we do not mean that He occupies a certain local heaven, because God is everywhere, and where He is there heaven must be also. Nor do we mean that He has a local throne, because the Infinite is enthroned in every soul, and all souls are spiritually one; therefore the great throne of God is the spirit of all souls united in one perfect, universal divinity. But there is also a local heaven; there is a local heaven in every soul, and God lives there eternally; there is a local heaven wherever two or more are gathered in His name; there is a local heaven wherever there is a new heaven and a new earth; there is a local heaven on the spiritual heights of every word of divine existence, and there are heavens above heavens both In the great without and the great within, the higher we ascend upon the great eternal path of endless and limitless glory. God has provided everything that the life of man may desire. There are heavens for the senses and heavens for the soul; there are heavens that the eye can see and the person enjoy, and there are heavens that only the soul can discern while on the mountain tops of its own exalted divinity. And everywhere there is God giving His personal thought to every human desire or need.

God is not a personality, but He is personal to every personality in existence. He is personal to each one of us because He is in actual personal touch with each one of us. He lives in all, therefore he is personal to all, and can give personal attention to the needs of each and all. The soul knows this; the mind in its higher states of consciousness has discerned it, and thus the belief in a personal God has arisen. The mind has discerned only the personal presence of God in the soul at certain intervals, but the soul knows that God is personally present at all times in all souls. Thus the former belief in a personal God is not lost; it is only made infinitely larger. The feeling that we can speak to God as we speak to a personal friend continues, only that feeling has become infinitely more beautiful. To realize that God lives in us and we in Him, is to know that we are personally in touch, not with a part of God, but with all of God; and that all His power, all His wisdom and all His love is for each one of us now and eternally. All that the father hath is mine; and being infinite, He is personally interested in me even though He be personally interested in all the other souls in the universe at the same time. What He can be to one He can be to all, and He is. His eye is ever upon each one of us, and His hand is ever ready to guide whenever we may so desire.

God never ceases to think of you, nor should you cease to think of Him. He is personally interested in you and your welfare; then how can ill befall you? Why should any of us ever go wrong with the Infinite Hand so near? There are no reasons why unless it should be our endeavor to understand through reason that which the spirit alone can discern. Depend upon the spirit; follow the light of the spirit and every moment shall reveal the presence of God. Everything we do will be directed by His wisdom, and His power will see us through. Nothing need disturb us, neither need we ever be anxious. God wants us to reach our goal. He is personally interested in every undertaking we have in hand, and He is working with us, placing His limitless power at our command. Therefore, we need not be concerned when unexpected changes appear; every change will be a change for the better; every turn in events will lead us into greater events, and every door that may close on the left will open another door on the right through which we may pass to a greater world than we ever knew before. This is what will happen when God is with us; and He is always with us, only we must learn to receive everything that He has to give.

To know God is the beginning of wisdom, because God is the source of wisdom. The nearer we live to the source the more we receive of that which comes from the source. The mind that is not consciously living with God may have intellect and mental capacity, but the wisdom that knows can come only to that mind that is walking with God every moment of conscious existence. The mind that does not know God thinks in the darkness; the mind that does know God thinks in the light.

The Pathway of Roses

God is my light forever,
His spirit is shining within;
My home is the kingdom of heaven,
I'm free from all evil and sin.
God is my love and power,
My being is perfect and whole;
I'm living the life of the spirit,
The beautiful life of the soul.
God is my life eternal,
My truth and my wisdom divine,
I'm heir to His riches and glory,
His kingdom forever is mine.

Chapter 21

Return Ye Unto God

Wherever we may be, whatever has happened or whatever may threaten to happen, it matters not; there is a power that can change everything. There are no reasons for sorrow, fear or regret; there are no occasions for anxiety, discouragement or despair; there is a path that leads to the world of the heart's desire, and anyone may find it. Great learning is not required, nor shall we find certain fixed beliefs necessary. The secret is simple, simple enough for any mind in the world, because it is the will of Infinite Love that every mind in the world shall know the way. None need stumble, none need go astray, none need ever be lost. All that is necessary is to follow the voice of the soul, and this voice is ever proclaiming in language divine, Return Ye Unto God.

The world has tried every imaginable method to gain freedom, but when all these methods fail, as they all will, Return Ye Unto God. The moment we return to Him, all that we have lost will return to us; and that which we do not wish for will vanish. When we return to Him we return to our own, because He is the source of everything that can possibly be our own. To be with Him is to be where we wish to be, and where we wish to be there we shall find the "gates ajar" to the heaven that is within. Before we can enter the heaven that is within us we must find perfect peace for mind and soul, and this peace we always find when we return to God. The more closely we live to His presence the deeper and more exalted the calm; and out from the silence of this calm comes the sacred symphonies of life, that music of the soul that we all recognize as the prelude to the kingdom of God. When we can hear it we know that His presence is near; we can discern through the spiritual vision those secret places that every returning soul has the privilege to enter. We learn what is in store, and life is not the same any more. We have had a vision, and all things have been glorified.

Return ye unto God. All other paths lead to sorrow and death, but in Him there is freedom and joy forever. In Him there is life, in Him there is peace, in Him there is wholeness and purity; in Him there is strength, in Him there is health, in Him there is power and truth; in Him there is all that life holds in store for man — all that the human heart can wish for. Seek no other source; follow no other path. There is only one place where the soul finds rest and contentment; only one place where every vision is realized, and every lofty dream made true. All may find it; the secret. is simple. Return ye unto God.

But Jesus answered them, My Father worketh even until now, and I work. — John 5:17.

The significance of this statement is as large as the limitless sea of divinity in which we live and move and have our being. The Infinite is everywhere and works everywhere, and therefore He is with us working with us. To know this is to know one of the greatest truths in the world, and there is nothing that is more helpful in the living of everyday life than to live, think and act in harmony with this truth. Whatever our work may he, it ceases to be difficult the moment we realize that God is working with us. When we know that His power is with us, the burden disappears completely.

The undertaking we have in mind may be very large; it may seem to be more than we alone can carry through; but we need not be alone; the Infinite is at hand ready to work with us, and with Him there can be no failure. Depend upon the Supreme; ask God to work with you; live so near to the Spirit that you will be one with God, and when you choose to go with God, He will go with you. Then the work will almost do itself; you perform the most difficult task with perfect ease, and you can work as much as you desire, weariness will not even make an attempt to enter your world.

The average person works alone; his task is therefore difficult; he does nothing well, and his work is wearing and tearing to a degree that makes his life both bitter and disappointing. But he works alone, with almost every disadvantage in his way, simply because he has not ascended in the spiritual scale. He has not arisen to that lofty realm where he can be in harmony with Supreme power, and therefore must depend upon the limited power of mere man. This, however, is his own choice; he may rise in the spiritual scale whenever he may desire and as much as he may desire; and the higher he goes in this scale the more direct assistance he receives from the Infinite.

When we reach those same spiritual heights that Jesus had reached, we can also say as he did that my Father worketh and I work, and we will receive just as much power from God as he received. We shall thereby do the works that he did, and as we go on still farther with him, we shall do the greater works. Jesus declared that he could of himself do nothing. His great power came from God, and his spirituality was so high that he could both receive and apply this power. He had reached that state where he was in perfect harmony with Supreme power, and could manifest the fullness of that power in all his life and works.

And his command was: Follow me; what I have done, ye shall do. We are therefore not to remain content with simply believing that he was what he was and did what he did; we are to go and do likewise. Nor is the way difficult; to follow Christ is the simplest thing in the world, and there is nothing that produces such great results. Though we may not reach the heights that he reached at once, we can press on, and gain ground daily. Every step will bring added power, and this power we can use now in everything that we may be doing now. Spiritual power is not only for some other world; nor is its sole use in this world to keep us away from temptations. The power of the spirit is intended to be used in the living of a great life here and now, and in the doing of great things in this present world.

Those alone will enter the kingdom who do the will of the Father, and to do the will of the Father is to live the life that He lives now. Live the life of the Spirit now, and you are saved both for time and eternity. And one of the greatest essentials in the living of the spiritual life is to live so near to God that His power is in everything that we may do. Then God works with us; not simply in what the world calls great things, but in all things. Even in those things that seem to be insignificant, the power of the Supreme is with us, and everything we do brings joy.

The first step to be taken in anything we wish to do, is to seek divine assistance. To ask God to go with us and work with us, and to enter into such perfect spiritual harmony with God that we can feel His supreme power through and through — that is the first and most important, be it work pertaining to body, mind or soul. Whether we are beginners in the spiritual life or have reached the heights, God will work with us in whatever we have the understanding to do now; and as we rise in the scale, He will work with us in doing those greater things that spiritual giants have the privilege to perform. And with God working with us, we shall never fail; all work will be pleasure, and the days of weariness shall come no more.

The mind that understands the spirit of truth knows that it is the Father that does the work; that it is the power of the Infinite that produces all power; that this power comes into our life to be directed and used by us, and that we may receive as much of this power as we desire. Such a mind knows that it will profit nothing to force the limited power that we may seem to possess, but that more power from on high comes without fail when our thoughts are very high and very still.

Therefore, the true mind creates all thought in the supreme stillness of higher spiritual realms, and leaves results to divine law. Those results will be far greater and better than the personal man, unaided, could have possibly produced, even with every external advantage at hand. When we have great things to do we are tempted to rush forward and force those things through; but this must never be permitted. Such methods are not only detrimental to the mind, but are wholly inadequate to fulfill the purpose we have in view. To be perfectly still at such times, and let Supreme Life do the great work is the secret.

To secure more power we must go up into those spiritual regions where power is limitless; and when we enter that high state our thoughts not only become enormously strong, but thinking becomes so smooth and easy that no effort whatever is required. We think God's thoughts after Him, and those thoughts are not only full of power, but also full of peace. To understand how an action can be perfectly still may be difficult to the mind that has never felt the perfect calm; but we must realize that stillness does not imply inactivity. Real stillness is the highest form of activity, where the strongest power acts in absolute harmony. To be in real stillness is to be in that power; therefore, the mind that is perfectly still thinks the highest thoughts, the greatest thought and the most powerful thought.

We may all demonstrate through personal experience that it is not strenuous metaphysical efforts that perform miracles, but the power of those high spiritual thoughts we create while in the secret places of the Most High. And when we learn to use that method only, and never permit ourselves to become mentally overwrought, we shall develop healing powers that are extraordinary — powers that will do greater things than was ever seen upon earth before. "Greater things than these shall ye do." "I AM with you always, even unto the end of the world."

When you live in the presence of the Infinite you are constantly in touch with higher power and superior guidance. You will therefore not only be able to accomplish far more in your chosen vocation, but you will be prevented from going astray. The very moment the person is tempted to take a misstep, the spirit from within interferes, and you are prompted to again proceed on the true path. When you are on the verge of doing something that is not best, higher power appears; something unexpected happens to upset all your proposed plans, and you are led to see, by the light from within, that there is something better in store. The nearer you live to the Infinite the more readily you are corrected and placed right whenever you are going to go wrong. Your seeming mistakes, therefore, are brought to naught in every instance, and you are awakened more and more to the realization of the great truth that God knows best. When in doubt or in darkness, leave it to God; the right way will open and the very best will come to pass.

The first principle in the unfoldment of the soul is to live in the spiritual attitude; that is, in the prayer without ceasing, or in that attitude where you feel that you are in the spirit. When you are in the spirit, or in the spirit of real prayer, and deeply desire certain things, you will certainly receive them. Everything that you can possibly pray for is in the spirit, and when you are in the spirit when you pray you will be in perfect spiritual touch with what you pray for. And what we spiritually touch, that we receive. Place human life in conscious contact with higher life and the latter will flow into the former. Soul unfoldment will place the being of man in higher and higher states of spiritual relationship with the Supreme Source of all things. Therefore, to unfold the soul is to open the way to every lofty goal that man may have in view. "And if thy right hand cause thee to stumble, cut it off." The right hand symbolizes that which we tiling we cannot live without, and to think that anything in the visible world is indispensable, is to be in bondage to things. He who knows that he can live whether the universe lives or not, has found life itself — the eternal life of the spirit. He is therefore no longer in bondage to things because he is in that life that is infinitely greater than all things.

Chapter 22

Prayers That Are Answered

The Infinite is changeless, therefore there is no special providence in the usual sense of that term, and yet in the higher sense, everything is special providence. Every act of the Supreme is a special act because it provides for a special need somewhere in the life of the human soul.

However, it is not necessary to ask God to go outside of His changeless laws to answer our particular prayer. Our particular prayer is already provided for; that is, God is already doing that which is required to supply what we desire. Therefore, God will not have to do something special to answer our special request. He is already and eternally doing everything; but we must do something special to secure what God has already provided for us.

What is called special providence is not the result of a special act of God, but the result of a special act of man; and this special act of man is the act of man going to God to present his request and receive his heart's desire.

The prayers that are answered are not the prayers that we express when we are away from God, but when we are with God. Our prayers are never answered when we think of God as far away; to receive an answer to our prayer we must go to God; we must enter into His very presence, and while we are in His presence there is no true request that we can possibly make that will not be granted.

The Infinite is limitless, both in power and in love; therefore, God is not only able to do everything that we ask Him to do, but He wants to do it. It is a great privilege for infinite love to do everything, and the love of God is infinite.

It is not the wish of God to withhold from us anything that we may desire; it is His supreme desire to give us everything, but we are created with a free will, therefore God gives only that which we, through our own free will, may select.

The average person thinks he is imposing upon God when he asks for much; but the fact is that the more we ask for the more we please God, provided we go to Him and receive it, and if we wish to please God in the highest measure we should pray without ceasing, pray for everything we can use in the building of a great and beautiful life.

The power of prayer, however, should not be used exclusively for the realization of what is usually termed spiritual things; all things become spiritual when animated with the spiritual life; and all things are good when used for a good purpose; therefore, we are free to pray for everything that can add to the whole of life, be it of the body, the mind or the soul.

The true spiritual life does not mean the riches of the soul combined with weakness of the body, poverty of the person and ignorance of the mind. The true spiritual life is an ideal life on all planes, and God is ready to provide us with everything that can make the whole of life ideal, if we only pray for it with the prayer that not only asks of God but also takes us to God.

The true prayer never doubts, but believes implicitly that the request will be granted; and this is natural, because we cannot possibly doubt when we know that the more we ask of God the more we please God. But it is not only natural for the true prayer to have perfect faith; it is necessary. Before our prayers can be answered we must go to God and receive what we have asked for; and it is only through perfect faith in God that we can enter into the presence of God.

The true prayer is always inspired with the thought" I know that thou wilt answer me"; and this thought is the spiritual product of faith — the faith that feels the love of God.

The true prayer is also animated with the highest form of spiritual gratitude, and is therefore always inspired with that beautiful thought, "My Father, I thank thee that thou hearest my prayer, and I thank, thee that thou hearest me always." The prayer of faith knows that God does hear every prayer, and that he will answer every prayer providing we come to Him in person with our request. In consequence, when we are in the spirit of true prayer, our gratitude must necessarily be boundless.

When we feel that God will give us anything we may ask for, that there is no doubt about it whatever, we cannot otherwise but give expression to the very soul of gratitude, and this gratitude is both limitless and endless; it is the soul's eternal thanksgiving.

To live in the spirit of that prayer that is ever asking God for everything, that believes that God is giving everything, and that is constantly giving thanks to God for everything, is, in itself, a life of the highest joy. In such a life everything is being taken to higher ground, because we are manifesting in body, mind and soul, more and more of the likeness of God. Personal existence is becoming ideal existence, while the soul is living in the full conscious realization of God's own beautiful world.

But thou, when thou prayest, enter into thine inner chamber, and having shut thy door, pray to thy Father which is in secret, and thy Father which seeth in secret shall recompense thee. — Mat. 6:6.

This is not a literal statement; the inner chamber is not some secluded place in some material structure, nor is the door referred to something that can be opened or closed with the power of physical hands. There is only one inner chamber; there is only one secret place; there is only one sacred realm where the human meets the divine, and that is in the soul of man. To enter the inner chamber is to enter the beautiful stillness within. God is enthroned in every human soul, and to enter into the secret places of the soul is to meet Him face to face.

The door that must be closed is the consciousness of the without, that something in the mind that takes cognizance of the world of things. "When we enter into secret, the visible must be forgotten; we are upon holy ground and must remove the shoes of external existence. We cannot enter the silent within so long as we think of outer things, therefore the door must be closed. And we cannot pray to the Most High unless we enter His presence. To pray is not simply asking God, it is also going to God. The most beautiful prayer is not uttered in words but is felt in the sacred depths of the soul.

When we simply ask God our prayers are never answered; we do not pray unless we enter into secret; it will profit nothing to make a request of the Infinite unless we first enter our inner chamber and close the door. And no person ever prayed in secret that was not rewarded openly. No prayer that is uttered in the sublime stillness of the soul is ever disregarded. All such prayers are answered. What we ask of God when we meet Him face to face, that we invariably receive.

When we have learned to pray in secret we should never have occasion to doubt any more. We then know that every request will be granted. Even though the answer does not come until the eleventh hour and the last moment of that hour, we know that it will come. Our faith is as perfect as the word of truth, and as high as the heavens of the spirit, and in that faith we live. God will find a way; we have asked Him to do so and every request brings that beautiful response, "I will not forsake thee nor leave thee; I AM thy Redeemer, I will care for thee."

To enter the inner chamber of the soul is to transcend everything, for the time being, that pertains to the visible world; but this requires spirituality. We cannot enter the spirit so long as we are subject to the body, and we are subject to the Body so long as we live for the body. When we begin to live for the spirit we can enter the innermost chambers of the spirit whenever we so desire, and when we are in this spiritual state we may pray for anything that is needed in the body, the mind or the soul. What we pray for in secret we shall receive openly. Therefore, to live for the body is to neglect the body and to lose the soul. But to live for the spirit is to give the fullness of life to the entire being of man.

When we pray openly we do not pray, because we cannot be in the secret chambers of the soul so long as we are in the material world of external things; and no desire is a prayer unless it is uttered in that secret place within where we meet Him face to face. We must be with God to receive of God, and as He is enthroned within us, the perfect path to Hi a presence is to enter the spiritual chamber within. There we shall find, not only the sublime stillness of the soul's communion with God, but also the secret power of faith — the faith that makes all things possible.

The secret power of faith is found in the soul's nearness to God; the nearer we are to God the more perfect our faith, the greater our power and the more beautiful our life; and when we enter into the sacred realms of the soul we are in the very presence of God. We are touched by the spirit, and to be touched by the spirit is to be filled with the spirit — to be filled with everything that the perfection of divine spirit may contain.

The prayer without ceasing is the living of that life that is so near to God that we can feel His power and His love at all times. In that life the mind is in constant touch with the soul and every true desire becomes a prayer uttered in secret. Therefore, when we so live that life itself becomes a beautiful prayer, there is nothing that we can desire or ask for that we shall not receive. When we live so near to God that we actually have our being in the spirit of His life, our every desire will be just and wholesome and true, and all such desires will be fulfilled; not in the distant future, but now. We shall begin to receive now that which is in store for them that love Him and every day the measure will increase as long as eternity shall continue to be.

If ye abide in me, and my words abide in you, ask whatsoever ye will, and it shall be done unto you. — John 15:7.

There is no stronger statement to be found anywhere in the literature of the world, and there is possibly no statement that has received less attention. Nevertheless, those who understand the inner meaning of high spiritual truth, know that this statement is not only based upon an exact scientific principle, but that any spiritually minded person can demonstrate the whole truth that is contained in that principle.

To abide in the Christ is not simply to live in the acceptance of some belief about Jesus; but this is the current idea; and being purely literal it has no power whatever; in consequence, those who claim to abide in the Christ do not secure any greater results through their prayers than do those who depend solely upon mere personal desire.

To abide in the Christ is to actually live in the Christ consciousness, and every part of mind and soul is permeated, through and through, with the life and the power of the Christ. Your entire being is in the hands of higher power; you are in a world where things are absolutely mastered by the spiritual will, and your mind is so spiritualized that it responds perfectly to the power of divine will.

When the words of the Christ abide in you, your mind is in absolute truth because those words are absolute truth. The mind that is in truth is in the true state of being, and to be in the true state of being is to be so close to God that anything desired can be received at any time. With God all things are possible, and God will do anything for us if we live as He lives. This is the secret, and we do live as God lives when we abide in the Christ with His words abiding in us.

When the words of the Christ abide in us, every thought we think and every word we utter will be animated with the spirit of the Christ; in like manner, inner spiritual power will give soul to everything we do, and that power that caused even the winds and the waves to obey will begin to work through us. Supreme power will be with us at all times to answer our prayers; our thoughts and our words will be living thoughts and words, and will carry the power of the spirit wherever they may go. We are therefore in that position where we not only can receive from God anything desired, but where we have the power to make our own prayers come true.

To be in the Christ means more than to receive from his love what our hearts may desire; it means spiritual mastership. To be in the Christ is not a mere feeling of the emotions; it is a life, and in that life the power of the Christ is supreme. Nor is this power given to us temporarily; it becomes our own, and we become able to bring to ourselves anything we may ask for. It is the promise. "What I have done, ye shall do." This promise is not mere words; it means something; it means that any person may attain spiritual mastership and cause the world of things to respond to the power of the Christ within him.

We have believed this; the hour is at hand to prove it; and those who will try will find that God is with them. But we must remember that this supreme state does not come through personal effort. "I can of myself do nothing." We must enter the consciousness of the Christ, the inner life of the Christ, the very spirit of the Christ; and our thought must become identical with His word. When there is no difference whatever between our thoughts and the sublime words of the Christ, then we can truthfully say that His words are abiding in us.

When our thoughts become identical with the words of the Christ, the same power that was in His words will be in our thoughts; and also in our words; a principle of truth so extraordinary that when we first think of it we become awestricken with thoughts so great, so wonderful, so marvelous that no tongue can ever give them utterance. And as we penetrate further into the inner meaning of this great truth we meet thoughts more marvelous still; we are face to face with the statement that we, even we, shall in the near future hold in our own hands the same power that wrought such wonder works in the hands of the Christ. Every person that is living the spiritual life is steadily moving towards that supreme goal.

When we abide in the Christ and His words abide in us, we are living absolutely in the inner spiritual world; in that world there are no impossibilities, and everything that we can possibly ask for is even now at hand; that all our prayers should be answered is therefore most evident. God is more willing to give than we are to receive; the reason why we do not receive what we may desire or need is because we are not willing; that is, our will is not in harmony with the will of God and our desire is not in harmony with the desire of God. But this harmony with God is fully secured when we begin to live in the Christ and begin to think only those thoughts that are inspired by the words of the Christ. We are then absolutely in His power, in His life, in His love; we may ask what we will; His life contains everything; His power brings forth everything; His love gives everything.

Therefore I say unto you, all things whatsoever ye pray and ask for, believe that ye have received them, and ye shall have them. — Mark 11:24.

This great statement gives positive emphasis to the law that we can gain actual possession only of that which we have gained conscious possession. Or, in other words, we must become conscious of the existence of an object before we can gain personal possession of that object. We must enter consciously into the life of that which we desire to gain, but we cannot enter into the life of that which we doubt the existence of. Doubt invariably produces a gulf between ourselves and the object of doubt, while faith produces mental and spiritual unity.

Spiritual unity is always followed by actual or personal unity; that is, what we enter into conscious possession of in the spiritual life we will, ere long, gain actual possession of in the physical life. Believe that you have already received in the spirit what you desire to receive in the person, and you will receive it in the person in a very short time. This is a law that positively cannot fail. Claim your own in the ideal world and you will receive your own in the real world.

This law gives rise to the practice of affirmations, but affirmations as usually employed do not comply with all the elements of the law. To simply affirm that we are what we wish to be, or that we have what we wish to possess, is not sufficient. Our spiritual possessions do not express themselves unless there is a strong, positive, personal desire for expression. We must pray for that which we wish to realize, but our prayer should not be mere asking. The prayer that asks in the feeling of uncertainty as to whether the thing prayed for is for us or not, is not a prayer of faith; and it is only the prayer of faith that is answered.

To pray in the feeling that knows that what we pray for is, even now, ready to be given to us, is to combine the desire for expression with the realization of possession, and we thus comply fully with the law of supply. In this attitude we have faith, and it is only through faith that we can enter into the spirit of that which we desire to actually possess. We must awaken the spiritual cause before we can secure the physical effect, but it is only through faith that we enter into the world of spiritual cause. Faith produces spiritual unity, and when we are one with the spirit we become conscious of the life, the richness and the power of the spirit. In consequence, we cause that which is in the spirit to be brought forth in the body, because what we gain consciousness of in the within we invariably express in the without.

When we simply affirm that we have what we wish to possess, the mental action is quite liable to be merely intellectual or even mechanical; and we do not touch our interior, spiritual possessions in the least. But when the affirmation is animated with prayer and desire the mental action becomes so deep that the spiritual life is reached. Or, to express the same truth in another manner, when our prayer for that which we desire is strengthened by the positive faith that we have already received it, we remove all doubts and barriers and enter at once into actual and conscious possession.

To use affirmations alone is to ignore the great possibilities of Infinite assistance. Any person may, for a while, build himself up mentally and personally with affirmations alone, but the structure is artificial; it is built upon the sand and will surely fall when the storms of environments and changing circumstances become a trifle too strong. Without the conscious and continuous assistance of the Infinite no man can travel very far on the upward path nor go very high in the scale of true being. But any man who takes God with him can overcome any obstacle in the world, scale the highest heights in existence, and what he builds today he is building for eternity.

The proper course to pursue is to ask God for everything you desire; ask Him to be with you in everything you wish to accomplish; pray without ceasing, and while you pray and work and press on to the great goal you have in view, affirm with positive faith that God is with you, that He has given you everything you can possibly desire or need. Believe that you have what you pray for, believe that you are what you wish to become; then ask God to enlarge your realization, to give perpetual increase to your faith, and to be constantly with you in working out these great supreme convictions.

The Pathway of Roses

The true prayer is a high spiritual communion with God, but it is not an inactive state. True prayer is oneness with God and a strong living desire for the full realization of all that is in the life of God. Therefore, the true prayer is the perfect way to God. If we wish to be with God we must pray. If we wish God to be with us we must pray. Live in constant prayer to God and you secure the constant and conscious assistance of God in everything you do. But a prayer is not a prayer unless it incorporates the affirmation of the truth upon which the prayer or desire is based.

To simply affirm that God is with you will not give you the assistance of God. When you affirm a truth you are talking to yourself; when you pray you are talking to God, and God listens only to what we say to Him. If we want God to go with us we must ask Him, we must talk to Him consciously if we wish His personal assistance and power.

To affirm the truth is absolutely necessary because affirmations will train our own minds in right thinking, will remove doubt and will develop in us the power to know that all that we can pray for or desire is ours now. But in order to enter into the actual realization of our own we must enter the kingdom of God, because all things that are in store for man are now in the kingdom. And it is true prayer — the prayer that goes to God that constitutes the "gates ajar" to the riches and glory of that wonderful kingdom.

And Jesus lifted up his eyes, and said, Father, I thank thee that thou heardest me. And I know that thou hearest me always. — John 11:41.

This beautiful statement was given before the answer to the prayer was received, and is therefore an illustration of the very highest form of supreme faith. To thank God after you have received what you asked for is simple; any heart can, at such a time, be full of sublime gratitude; but to thank God before you have received what you intend to ask for, and feel the fullness of that gratitude thrill every fiber in your entire being — that is spirituality indeed. Likewise, to be able to say that you know that God hears you always; only the mind that is in the spirit can make such a statement, and pray in this manner; but that alone is real prayer.

To precede any prayer with doubt is to close the door between yourself and the spirit; there must be no uncertainty in our communion with God; we do not believe that God is God so long as we are uncertain as to whether our prayers will be heard or no, and we cannot enter into the presence of God until we believe that He verily is God.

When we know that the power of God, the wisdom of God, the love of God — all is limitless, we can feel no doubt whatever, as to whether or not our prayers will be answered. Divine power can do anything, but divine love cannot refuse anything.

When we know God as He is, we know that He nearest us always, and we feel it a privilege to thank Him every moment for this great truth. And when we thank Him in this manner before we begin our prayer, we not only enter into the very love of His spirit, but we also enter into that faith that makes all things possible.

The faith that knows that God nearest us always is so close to God that it is animated with the very power of God; and therefore when we are in such a faith nothing can be impossible; we may then ask for what we will and it will be done unto us.

The more perfectly we realize that God hears us always the higher we ascend in the scale of true spirituality, because this supreme faith lifts the soul higher and higher until we are received at the very throne of the Most High. And to be in His presence is to receive whatever we may have asked or prayed for. God is everywhere, and we may enter into His presence anywhere. The Most High is enthroned in every soul, and pure spiritual faith is the "gates ajar" to His beautiful kingdom.

The Pathway of Roses

There is abundance of hope in the world, but what we need is more faith. Everybody is hoping for better things; the poor hope to get rich; the sick hope to get well; the sad hope to gain happiness; the troubled hope to find peace; everybody is hoping for something, but few have the faith that is necessary to secure that something. When we are in bondage, or keenly realize our bondage, we hope that the Great Deliverer will come; we pray that He may come; we hope that our prayers will be answered, and we are so absorbed in our hopes that we fail to hear Him knocking at the door even now. To have hope is to face the door, but hope stands still; it never moves towards the door. To live in hope is simply to face the great goal, but we may continue to face that goal for ages, and never move forward a step. "To live in hope is to die in despair," because hope remains stationary; it never gains what it hopes to gain. But when faith begins we remain stationary no more. We press on directly, and with power, towards the coveted goal; our hopes are soon realized; our desires are granted; what we wished for is withheld no more; through faith we have entered that world where every prayer is answered and every wish made true.

Chapter 23

The Faith That Moves Mountains

To him who has faith nothing is impossible. It matters not what he may wish to realize or what he may wish to do; if he has faith, it can be done. But what do we mean by faith? Faith is not a passive belief; it is a positive action. It is the power of the spirit within man acting upon the life, the mind, the body and the nature of man; and by acting through man it acts upon everything with which man may come in contact. When we have faith we do not simply believe in the form, or that which may exist in the external; when we have faith we enter into the spirit of that in which we express our faith; the secret of real faith and the real power of such at faith is therefore found in the spirit.

When you proceed with something that you wish to accomplish, do not simply have confidence in yourself; and do not simply proceed in the mere conviction or assurance that your purpose will be realized; do more than that; have faith, and when you have faith, your mind will enter into the very spirit of that which you have undertaken to accomplish. This is the reason why nothing is impossible when you have faith, because when you enter the spirit you enter the power of the spirit, and to the power of the spirit there is no limit whatever. To have faith is to enter into the spirit; to enter into the spirit is to enter into the life and the power of the Most High; and with God all things are possible. The entire world of things is permeated with spirit, with infinite power; therefore, when we enter into the spirit of anything we enter in the one spirit that lives in all things, and gain possession of as much of the power of the one spirit as we can possibly receive. The greater our faith the greater our capacity to receive of the limitless power of the spirit, and, in consequence, the greater will be our realization of whatever we now may have in view.

To have more and more faith, the secret is to enter more and more deeply into the spirit of everything in which we express our faith. Do you have faith in yourself? Then try to enter mentally into the spirit of your entire being whenever you think of yourself. Do you have faith in your work? Then try to enter into the spirit of everything that is connected with your work. Do you have faith in every person you meet? Then try to enter into the spirit of his life, into mental contact with the greater man that lives within the personal man. Do you have faith in all things? Then enter into the spirit of things, into the real soul of things whenever you think of things or look upon things. Do you have faith in God? Then enter mentally and spiritually into the spirit of Infinite Spirit whenever you think of God; whenever you think of God, think of yourself as being in the spirit of God, and try to feel that God is closer than breathing, nearer than hands and feet. The more deeply, the more fully and the more completely you enter into the spirit of that of which you think, the greater your faith; and the greater your faith the greater your power.

There is not a person in the world who may not proceed in life with the full conviction that his ideals will be realized and that he will accomplish everything he has undertaken to do. If he lives and works in faith he simply cannot fail, because faith will give him all the power he may require, and anything may be accomplished when we have sufficient power. But the average person proceeds in the thought that he may possibly reach his goal; he is not certain; he concludes he will try, and will do his best; but as to the outcome he does not know. This, however, is not faith, and without faith nothing whatever can be accomplished. To fulfill any purpose, even the most insignificant, there must be some measure of faith, and the greater this measure, the greater will be the realization desired. He who proceeds in real, unbounded faith, will place his life in touch with invincible spirit, and he will continue unmoved, untouched and undisturbed, no matter what the circumstances may be. He will place his mental vision upon the highest light of supreme faith, and whatever may happen he will never waver from that light for a moment. He will continue with ceaseless perseverance and the most positive determination; he will continue in faith, and as he continues and grows in faith he will gain more and more power until he has sufficient power to do everything he is determined to do.

Faith does not always produce the expected miracle at once; it does not always convert a life of confusion, sickness and failure into a life of happiness, harmony and abundance without much waiting and watching and prayer; it does not always change a pathway of thorns into one of roses the very first day we begin to live by faith; and it does not always remove every obstacle in a minute. There are times when it requires months and even years of constant faith to realize what we pray for; but we may rest assured in the great truth that whoever fixes his attention upon a certain definite goal and continues to work towards that goal, in faith, will positively reach it. Work in faith, in continuous faith, in the spirit of unbounded faith, and you will reach your goal, you will accomplish your purpose just as surely as the coming of another day. Therefore, though you may not have results at once, nor even for some time, continue to work in the same unbounded faith; the results you desire will positively be gained; and the deeper and stronger your faith the sooner you will reach the object in view.

When faith seems to fail, the remedy is more faith. Do not become discouraged in the midst of seeming failure; do not give up the purpose you have undertaken to fulfill; do

The Pathway of Roses

not doubt the possibilities of this purpose, nor come to the conclusion you are moving in the wrong direction. Continue to work in more and more faith, and if you should be on the wrong path, something will happen to set you right. Enter more and more into the light of faith, and all things will clear up. When you are on the wrong track doubt and uncertainty will but confuse you more, and cause you to go further into the wrong. But faith will increase your light; faith illumines the mind and clears the sky of your entire world; faith will lead you out of your mistakes and give you enough power to regain all that is lost and more. Continue, in faith, to press on towards your goal; discord will soon become harmony; uncertainty will soon become positive convictions; the crooked will be straightened out; obstacles will disappear; you will find your proper place; you will enter the work that is intended for you; all things in your life will work together for good, and you will press on and on, gaining ground steadily, drawing nearer and nearer towards the highest goal that your spiritual vision can possibly discern.

The majority of minds have many obstacles to meet, and almost invariably give emphasis to the belief that every seeming obstacle actually is an obstacle; but faith does not look upon obstacles as obstacles; faith does not call difficulties, difficulties. When a person begins to live in faith, all things that come into his life are looked upon as opportunities, and they are. We all know very well that if we had no difficulties or obstacles to meet, or what would be more appropriately termed "great occasions," we should soon become nonentities. It is the difficult things that we meet that enable us to bring into action the greater power that is within us; difficulties, therefore, are the most valued of opportunities, and if taken advantage of as such, will always be met with joy. No obstacle should ever be called by that name or ever thought of as being an obstacle, for it is, in truth, something that will enable you to prove to yourself that the power that is within you is greater than anything in the world. When we no longer call obstacles, obstacles or difficulties, difficulties, we shall not be disturbed by obstacles or difficulties any more. Whatever we meet will be turned to good account and will call forth more and more of the greater power that is within us. Accordingly, all things will work together for greater good; every occasion will be welcome, no matter what it may be; every experience will be a pleasure, and everything that we pass through will add to our welfare and joy. When a person thinks that every obstacle is an obstacle, he will frequently hesitate to proceed; and will, in many instances, on account of this hesitancy or doubt or fear, fail to reach his goal; but if he proceeds in the faith that there is something within him that is greater than all the obstacles in the world, there is no obstacle that can stand in his way. In fact, when he proceeds in such a faith, every obstacle that is met will simply call forth that greater something that is within him, and this "something" will give him all the power he may require to reach his goal.

Faith is that attitude of mind through which we come in conscious touch with the Infinite. When we are in the attitude of faith we are in the very spirit of life, and in the spirit of life God reigns supremely. The power of the Infinite is in the spirit, and when we are in the spirit we become one with that power; therefore, while we are in that oneness nothing can be impossible with us anymore. But the power of the Infinite, expressed through us while we are in the spirit of faith, is not applicable to spiritual things alone; it is applicable to all things, and may be applied anywhere in life in the attainment of the higher, the greater and the better. If you wish to change your environment, or if you wish to better certain things in your life, determine precisely what you want; then have faith. Continue to say "I have the faith," and repeat that statement as frequently as possible. Believe that you will realize what you want and believe that your belief is absolute truth. Have faith, and also have faith in faith; and whenever you affirm the statement," I have the faith," enter into the very spirit of that statement. When you say that you have the faith, and enter into the spirit of what you say, you awaken the power that can do what your faith' has undertaken to do. That is how faith can never fail; the moment you begin to have faith in what you have undertaken to do you arouse all the power necessary to see that undertaking through. And the more frequently you affirm, in the spirit, "I have the faith," the sooner you will enter into the spirit of real faith, where the necessary power will be gained.

Our constant purpose should be to become conscious of the inner spirit of faith; and when we feel this inner spirit we should try to become conscious of the still deeper spirit that is within our first realization of the spirit. To go deeper and deeper into the realization of the spirit should be the ruling desire whenever we enter the attitude of faith; and as there is no end to the depth or the height of the spirit, there is no limit to that inner world of life, wisdom and power that may be realized through faith. However far we may enter into the spirit we can always go farther still; every step that we take in spiritual realization opens the door to a still higher spiritual realization, and whenever we proceed, through faith, to enter more deeply into the limitless spirit of faith, we open another door to the marvelous kingdom within. Faith goes into what seems to be unreality and finds that the deeper we enter the world of the spirit, the more real and the more substantial the spirit becomes. Faith goes out upon the seeming void and finds that there is no void; all is real, and the farther we go out into the vastness of limitless life the more real and the more beautiful life becomes. Therefore, to follow faith is always to pass from the lesser into the greater, into the better, the richer, the larger, the more wonderful and the more beautiful.

The mind that lives in doubt can see limitations everywhere; the mind that lives in faith can see no limitations, and, in fact, knows that there are no limitations anywhere. The mind that lives in doubt is in bondage to these seeming limitations and therefore realizes nothing more of life than what is confined within these seeming limitations; but the mind that lives in faith lives in the freedom of the all of life, and is daily realizing more and more of everything that is contained in the all of life. Faith can see that no matter how large or how beautiful life may be now, there is always a larger and a more beautiful life to live for, to work for and to realize in the days that are near at hand. In the life of faith there is no end to anything; there is always something more, always something richer, always something greater, always something better. The life of faith is therefore full of realization, full of promise, full of joy. What was promised by faith yesterday is realized today, because faith is not only the power to see the greater vision, but is also the power that can lead life into the very world of the greater vision; and thus the promise of yesterday is always fulfilled today.

Every person in the world, whatever his present position may be, can begin today, and through the power of faith, work himself up into any attainment or realization he may have in mind. Whatever his goal, he can reach it, if he works in faith. This may seem to be a strong statement, but Jesus Christ declared it was so; and it is certainly high time that we begin to believe and practice the great truths this Master Mind proclaimed. If the teachings of Jesus mean anything they mean that I can, through faith, overcome anything in my life, change anything in my life, better anything in my life, and realize any goal whatever to which I may aspire to reach in life.. Though it may take months and years to reach certain things, those things that have exceptional worth, nevertheless I can do it, if I continue persistently to work in the spirit of unbounded faith. And, in the meantime, if I give this same faith to all my work, I shall be gaining ground daily, making my life larger, better, richer and more beautiful constantly. When I begin to work in the spirit of faith, I will always be in touch with the spirit; and to be in touch with the spirit is to be at one with God, because the kingdom of God is in the spirit; therefore, when I AM in the spirit, I AM with God; God is with me; God is on my side, and we two constitute a majority; we are greater than anything we shall ever meet, and we have the power to do anything we may desire, to work out anything, accomplish anything or realize anything that we may at any time have in view. Faith has made us one — the Infinite and myself, and together we hold, not simply the balance of power, but all power. Therefore, knowing this to be true, why should I ever doubt anymore; why should I ever hesitate anymore; why should I ever be fearful or afraid any more.

There are thousands of richly endowed minds in the world that accomplish nothing to speak of; and the reason is they live in the confusion of doubt, uncertainty and fear. Many of these minds would become giants in the world if all their powers were spurred to action by the invincible spirit of faith. In fact, there is not a single mind, whether naturally endowed or not, that would not come forth into a larger, richer life if inspired by the wonderworking power of faith. Faith awakens the all that is in human life, and makes that all a continuous power for good. Therefore, not a person in the world, whatever his work may be, can afford to live or work a single moment without faith, without the deepest, strongest faith that he can possibly arouse in his own soul. Faith is not for the spiritual world alone, but for every world. Not a muscle should move unless it moves in faith; not a thought should be formed unless it is filled with the spirit of faith; not a word should be uttered unless it conies directly from the limitless power of faith. This is what it means to live by faith, and such a life is a life indeed.

There is a belief among many that since every soul has the power to draw upon the limitless for any desired supply, it is not necessary to give special attention to physical or mental efforts. In other words, if they continue to live in faith they will receive what they want, their own will come, even though they be very inefficient as far as work is concerned. This is their spiritual theory, but it is a theory which, when applied, leads invariably into poverty both of body and mind. The fact that "all things are yours" on account of your divine heirship; and the fact that your spiritual nature is actually and permanently one with the limitless source of every good thing in existence, does not prove that you may receive all that you need by simply declaring, "my own cannot remain away from me." To fold your hands and wait in faith for your own to come, is not to wait in faith; hope stands and waits, but faith goes to work. Therefore, if you are waiting in faith you have no faith; and having no faith you will continue to wait; your own will not come. In the real, "all things are yours," but you can make no actual use of the riches of the kingdom within until they are brought forth into manifestation. The life, the power and the riches from within, however, will not manifest through a mind and body that is dormant; and the habit of waiting and hoping for supply to come, regardless of efficient personal effort, has a tendency to make the faculties and the elements of the human system more or less dormant.

To have faith is not simply to believe that everything will come to us, or that everything must come to us because everything already belongs to us. Faith is not simply belief; it is an attitude of mind and soul wherein you place your own life in perfect contact with infinite life; and, in consequence, when you live and work in faith every thought and every effort will be charged, so to speak, with the power of infinite life. To work in faith is to give more life and more power to your work; to think in faith is to animate and inspire your thought with a finer insight and a higher degree of understanding than you could ever receive in any other manner. The mission of faith, therefore, in practical life, is to give the individual that greater measure of wisdom and power through which he may make himself worthy of the very highest good that he may desire as his own.

All things belong to us; that is, all things are ready for us whenever we can use them; but we cannot use the greater things in life so long as we are living a small, partially dormant life. The riches of the kingdom are not for us "to have and to hold;" they are for us to use; and we can use them all only as we become alive with the life more abundant in every element of body, mind and soul.

The principle is this: Use the body, use the mind, use the soul, use every faculty, use every force, use every power that you can possibly find and arouse throughout your entire being; and use all these things in faith; that is, while you are using all these things, place your life, your mind and your consciousness in such perfect touch with the Supreme Source of life, power, wisdom and inspiration, that you become a perfect channel of expression for all that is great and worthy in the vastness of sublime existence. In this manner, you become so worthy, so competent and so efficient in your life that all that is great and worthy in the ideal can be naturally attracted and used by you in the real.

With regard to this subject, the human family divides itself into three classes. The first class is composed of the masses of men and women in the world, those who try to live and try to accomplish something in life by depending solely upon objective faculties. They proceed without paying any attention to the greater powers within them or to their relationship with infinite life; in consequence, they are constantly hemmed in by their own self-created limitations, and as a rule, merely exist. The second class is composed of those who go to the other extreme, depending almost entirely upon the power of the spirit to provide supply, while the true and full use of the powers of the personal man are either wholly or partially neglected. These people are buoyed up in the beginning with hopes and expectations, and for a time their spiritual theory of life seems to work; but ere long they find themselves drifting into adversity and want, and are forced to return to the ways of the world, as mere existence is better than annihilation.

The third class is composed of those who combine the powers of the personal man with the powers of the spiritual man; they make a special effort to turn all their powers and faculties to practical use, and to all their work they invariably add the inspiring attitude of unbounded faith. The members of this class try to develop all their faculties to the very highest degree; they try to place body, mind and soul in the best working condition; they try constantly to increase their working capacity because they are not only believers, but doers; they are disciples of work — work that adds to the welfare of the world, and they always work in faith; they try to make the best use of everything in their possession, but while trying to push to the front, so to speak, the best that is in them, they try constantly to develop a higher and a finer conscious realization of the great truth that we live and move and have our being in the limitless power of the Supreme.

That all the great men and women that have appeared in the history of the world have come forth from this last mentioned class is most evident; and that no person can ever rise in the scale of life unless he applies the method of this class is equally evident. To depend solely upon the personal man is to merely exist; to depend solely upon the spiritual man is to be a dreamer, not a doer; but when the powers of the personal man are combined harmoniously and practically with the powers of the spiritual man, we cannot only dream; we can also make our dreams come true. What we discern in the ideal we can cause to come true in the real. We provide practical working capacity on the personal side and limitless power on the spiritual side; whatever we may wish to do, attain or accomplish in the great without, we may receive all the wisdom, all the understanding and all the power required from the great within. We shall thus demonstrate the great truth that "All that the Father hath is mine," not simply for spiritual contemplation, but for actual, personal possession and use in the tangible world today.

That the powers of the spiritual man can be readily combined with the powers of the personal man, in the producing of practical results, is a fact that is constantly being demonstrated in the lives of thousands. We all know of remarkable instances where people have, when in the midst of extreme want, sickness or despair, placed themselves in the hands of higher power, and secured emancipation under circumstances that have seemed miraculous. Many a person has found himself in a position where everything was lost, where all the elements were against him, and where not a single ray of light could be found anywhere; but by placing himself in touch with the power of the Supreme, and by going to work in full conscious oneness with that power, has caused everything to change in his favor.

Many a person has demonstrated the great truth that by taking God with him in his work, he could overcome every obstacle, remove every barrier, vanquish every enemy, disperse everything that was against him, and come out victorious under circumstances that, in the beginning, seemed utterly hopeless. It has been demonstrated thousands of times that where the personal man alone was helpless, complete emancipation and victory were made possible where the powers of the spiritual man were combined with the efforts of the personal man. This is therefore a principle that no person can afford to ignore, no matter what his work may be.

Whatever we may wish to do or gain, there must be personal effort; but the more perfectly we are conscious of the limitless powers of the spirit within us, the greater will the results of those efforts be. And this is not true of certain special efforts alone; it is true of all efforts from the least significant on the physical plane to the most important on the sublime cosmic plane. It is true, not only in instances of man's extremity, but also in every state or degree of man's prosperity. If the power of the spirit, when combined with personal effort, can take man from death's door into perfect health, as has been done thousands of times, even when all hope was lost and every other method had failed; and if this same power, when combined with practical work, can take man out of the lowest depths of adversity, poverty and despair, and place him on the very heights of freedom, power and limitless supply, is there any reason why the power of the spirit cannot be combined with personal effort in all the affairs of everyday life and thus give an ever-increasing measure of health, happiness and prosperity to man? Man calls upon God when everything else has failed; but he should call upon God before he tries anything else, and he would never fail.

Though we may be strong physically now, and be in possession of exceptional capabilities and advantages, we cannot afford to ignore the fact for a moment that increase comes only from the within. "They that wait upon the Lord shall renew their strength;" none others. The present strength of the body will not hold out unless it is constantly replenished from on high. The present capabilities of the mind will shortly lose their brilliancy and power unless they are kept in the highest state of perfection through constant contact with the light and the life of the soul. It is not wisdom to use up the limited powers of the person and utterly ignore the great interior source of inexhaustible power. Yet man does this very thing; therefore, his person is weak, his days are short, and his life but a trifle better than mere existence. There is, however, a better way; let the powers of the spiritual man be constantly combined with the life, the powers and the efforts of the personal man, then shall the person of man never be weak; his days may be lengthened indefinitely, and his life will become richer, more beautiful and more inspiring, until a million joys are blended harmoniously in every moment of his endless existence.

We are all heirs to the kingdom, not only the spiritual kingdom but the entire kingdom of life; we can receive, however, only what we can use; we need only what we can use, therefore to receive more at any time would be superfluous, and there is no place for the superfluous in the realms of divine law. There are many that can use much, very much, but the majority do not receive as much as they can use because they do not live and work in the consciousness of the "all things are yours." Others receive but little at any time because they do not fully use what they already possess. We draw upon the universal for greater supply in proportion as we turn to good account our present supply; though we must remember, that no person can turn to good account the best that is in him now unless the efforts of the personal man are filled through and through with the powers of the spiritual man. The work that we do in faith is the only good work; and the faith that we apply in work is the only true faith.

The Pathway of Roses

The average person thinks that it is his privilege to continue to "hold" his possessions, regardless of use, and that he can accumulate as much as he likes; but this is not true. The true life is not lived for the purpose of accumulating things. Many have realized this and have gone to the other extreme, concluding that the only true life was the life that had no tangible possessions whatever. There are only a few, however, who have taken the path that lies directly between these two extremes, and that is one reason why the power of the spirit to combine with the power of the person in practical life has not been as extensively demonstrated as we should wish. But it is our privilege to demonstrate the true law of complete existence, and when we do, the reward will be great indeed.

Every individual is entitled to all the riches of the spiritual kingdom, and in addition, to the possession of as many things, and as beautiful things, in the visible kingdom, as we can possibly appreciate and use in the enrichment of all the realms of his own entire existence. But before he can secure all these things, he must cause his personal nature and his spiritual nature to live together and work together as one. He must work for everything that he may desire, and must work in the faith that every desire will be fulfilled.

To express the law of this principle more briefly, the first essential is to make the best use possible of everything that we may possess now. The second essential is to live, think and work in faith. He who lives in faith lives in the spirit, and he who lives in the spirit lives in God. No person can afford to do anything without taking God with him; no person can afford to think a single thought without realizing that that thought is created in the infinite sea of divine thought; no person can afford to express a single desire without realizing that that desire is the expression of some supreme, some great, some beautiful state of interior existence.

The Pathway of Roses

It is extremely important to try, as much as possible and as frequently as possible, to enter into the inner consciousness of the great truth that "All things are yours." As we grow in this consciousness we actually enter into real, limitless possession; and when we begin to "inwardly feel" that we possess the rich and the beautiful in limitless supply, we will begin to attract the rich and the beautiful from every source in the world.

Take the statement, "All that the Father hath is mine," and mentally dwell upon the very innermost truth that can be found in this statement. Try to realize what is means to possess everything that there is in the kingdom of the Infinite, and enter into the very soul of that meaning. Try to feel the spirit of limitless, divine possession, and resolve to live perpetually in the innermost life of that spirit. The consciousness of limitless supply will soon become an actual factor in mind; and we can begin to draw upon the limitless when we are actually conscious of the limitless.

When you actually realize that "All things are yours," you will never be anxious about the future any more. You know that there will be a ready way to supply every need at the proper time. You do not live in the possession of simply the barest necessities; you live in the life of abundance, and the rich and the beautiful in your life is constantly on the increase. But you are never disturbed about the greater needs that you know will come in the future. You live in the positive faith that when the greater needs are at hand, the greater supply will also be at hand. And your faith always comes true.

To live in this faith is to live in perfect peace; we are never disturbed about any threatening circumstance; we are never fearful or afraid anymore; we know that the door will open when the time comes; we shall surely have what we need — enough to supply the greatest possible need. Having done our part we know that God will not fail in His; for as much greater is His faithfulness than ours as the entire cosmos is greater than a single drop in the sea. "I will not forsake thee nor leave thee;" upon this we may always depend.

When you look into the future, do not be anxious about methods or means to carry out what the future moment may demand. When you come to that place, God will be there; the limitless powers of infinite life will be there; the wisdom, the light and the luminous understanding of your highest spiritual nature will be there; all of you will be there, and the power of your faith to draw upon the limitless for any desire or need will also be there. Then why be fearful any more. Why be anxious about anything. All things are yours now, and the now that now is, is eternal.

Though your bark may be tempest-tossed, be not alarmed. The Christ is asleep in the ship. You may call Him at any time; and when you do the heavens will be cleared, and a beautiful stillness will come over the vastness of the deep. What does it matter to you what may threaten in days to be; the Christ will always be with you; wherever you may choose to sail upon the infinite sea of life, the Christ will always be in your ship. For lo, I AM with you always. Whether He be asleep or awake, where you are, there He will be also. You may call upon Him as you will, and peace shall reign supremely in your life once more. For the winds and the waves shall obey my will. Then why be fearful or afraid any more. He can still any storm in the world, and bring the silence of the heavenly calm wherever His presence may be.

Chapter 24

The Winds and the Waves Shall Obey My Will

Then he arose and rebuked the winds and the sea; and there was a great calm. But the men marveled, saying, what manner of man is this that even the winds and the sea obey him. — Mat. 8:2327.

We all come to places at times when the sea of life is tempest tossed, and the winds of adversity are mercilessly raging about us; we are all placed in circumstances at times when everything seems to go wrong, when everything seems to be against us, and when we fear lest we perish; but at such moments we should remember that the Christ is in the ship. No matter what the ship of life may be; no matter what manner of men may be sailing in that ship, or what their purpose may be, wherever man may be found sailing upon the sea of human existence there the Christ will be found also. Wherever we may be or wherever we may go, the Christ is in the ship. "For, lo, I AM with you always." And it is our privilege, under every circumstance, to awaken the Christ. When we do, he comes forth invariably, and the winds and the waves will obey.

Whenever we enter into that higher and more sublime state of being where we meet him face to face, the consciousness of the Christ within us is awakened; we are in the Christ state; we are in the presence of Supreme Power; we are at one with God; and upon us comes a beautiful calm. The winds and the waves in our own minds are stilled, and upon the great sea of thought within us the billows are tossing no more; the storm has ceased; the black clouds have disappeared; all is beautiful and still; and the peaceful waters seem radiant with joy as they glitter in the sunbeams from the smile of God. We have opened our minds and souls to the strong and peaceful presence from on high; thus we have placed ourselves in the beautiful calm; and when we are stilled, all that is about us will be stilled also. As man is in the within, so will his life be in the without. When he can still the storms of his own mind he can also still the storms of adversity in his outer life. It matters not what is taking place in our own circumstances, all must change when we change; all must be stilled when we are stilled; and whenever we awaken the consciousness of the Christ within, upon us comes a beautiful calm.

When we know that the Christ is within at all times; when we know that whenever we call upon the Christ to come forth, the winds and the waves will obey; and when we know that the very hour the Christ is awakened, everything in life will be stilled, harmony will come out of everything, peace will come out of everything, good will come out of everything — when we positively know this, need we have any fear whatever concerning the future? Need we fear opposing circumstances or adversity? Need we fear any condition that might arise? Nothing can happen that need disturb us in the least. The Christ is always in the ship; we may call upon him at any time; he will never fail to come forth, and when he does, there will be a great calm; peace will reign once more, and all will be well again.

Those who do not know that the Christ is in the ship, are living constantly in fear; they reason that almost anything might happen to place obstacles in their way, or that certain conditions might arise to upset everything they had undertaken to do; and the things they fear usually come upon them; but when they know that there is a power within that can be awakened at any time — a power that is greater than anything in the world, fear may be banished for all time. When this great truth is realized we need never be concerned about the future any more, and anxious thought may be banished forever; whatever may happen in the future there is a power within that can change anything as we may desire, and turn anything to good account as we may desire. We may thus live in the conviction that all things will work together for good — for greater and greater good, and we may know that this conviction is based upon nothing less than eternal truth.

The Christ is always in the ship, always in every ship that may pass upon the sea of life; and he may seem to be asleep; we may not be aware of his presence within us, but our unconsciousness of his presence does not prove that he is asleep, or that he is never there. The Christ is never asleep. The only begotten son of God that is within all, within everything, that is the ruling power in every soul, the Supreme I AM in every soul, is never asleep. The statement that the Christ was asleep in the ship is metaphorical. It is not the Christ that is asleep, but our own consciousness of the Christ. When our own consciousness of the Christ is asleep we are not aware of his presence, and he seems to be asleep to us. When we are not aware of this great spiritual power within us, we are unconscious of that power; we are asleep, so to speak, as far as the existence of that power is concerned, and therefore will never think of awakening that power. But when we have attained sufficient spiritual discernment to know the power of the spirit in our own soul, we shall begin to call forth that power. From that moment higher power will be with us, and we shall no longer be victims of the tempest tossed sea; whenever the billows begin to toss or the storms begin to rage, we may call forth the Christ; he will always be with us, and will always respond to the call; he will answer our prayer with his own presence, and in his presence all is beautiful and still.

This same unconsciousness of the presence of the Christ within also explains the seeming loss of the soul. The soul is the Christ individualized, created in the image of God, and therefore can never be lost. The soul is coexistent with God, always is with God; and that which is eternally with God can never be lost. But the personal man is sometimes so engulfed in materiality that all view of the soul is lost. The soul is always there within us, ever abiding in the shining glory of the kingdom of God within us; the soul is safe, always was safe and always will be safe, safe in the life eternal; but if we are living in materiality, we do not see the soul, we do not feel the soul, we are utterly unconscious of the soul and therefore conclude that there is no soul. Or, if we are sufficiently awakened to feel the soul, but not sufficiently developed in spiritual discernment to know the divine nature of the soul, we may conclude that the soul is weak and imperfect as the flesh, and that it may go down into pain, bondage and misery at any time, now or in the future. And thus has arisen the seeming need of the doctrine of future salvation for the soul. Such a doctrine, however, is not based upon the spiritual conception of the soul, but was formed when we looked upon the soul through the confusion of materiality. The soul is never lost, never can be lost; and as you are the soul, you can never be lost. The soul is always safe with God, therefore you are always safe with God Realize this truth, and you will find the soul; you will find that you are identical with the soul and that all is well with the soul now as all is well with God now.

To save the soul is not to save the soul, because the soul needs no salvation, but to restore the power of the soul as the supreme ruling power in your whole life. Enthrone the soul in every thought and action and you save the soul, not from sin, because it is free from sin, but you save the soul from your own personal neglect. The power of the soul is no longer neglected but is saved for actual use in the realization of health, freedom and mastery throughout your entire being; thus you gain emancipation for every element in your being, and that is the salvation we seek. We are saved in the true sense of the term when the divine power of the soul reigns so completely throughout the mind and the body that all the ills of life are completely banished from mind and body. We are saved in the true sense of the term when the body is filled with the power of health and wholeness, when the mind is illumined with the light of eternal truth, and when the soul is abiding forever in the splendors of the cosmic realms. And such a salvation is realized when we no longer ignore the soul, but place the soul upon the throne of being as complete master of everything that we may ever think or do or say. To enthrone the soul, the principle is to follow, not the desires or the tendencies of the person, but the supreme purpose of the spirit, and to depend absolutely upon the power of the soul in all things, knowing that the power of the soul can see you through no matter what your life, your work or your purpose may be.

The belief of the many is that whatever we may wish to accomplish we must depend wholly upon ourselves; and that we must depend upon ourselves as far as our ability and power may go, is very true, but it is not true that we should depend "wholly" upon ourselves. We can receive power and aid from sources that are above the personal self; and what is equally true, no one ever scaled the heights in life that did not depend constantly upon these higher sources. The best ideas, the noblest thoughts and the greatest truths that have ever appeared in the world, came to man when his mind was in the upper regions, in touch with the spirit sublime; and the power with which all great things have been wrought, has come from the same source. Men and women who depend wholly upon themselves — their personal selves, are weaklings; they come and go without doing anything aside from sustaining existence; but men and women who depend upon Supreme Power as well as their own ability to work out their purpose in harmony with that Power, invariably become giants in mind and soul. It is the deeds of such minds that become lights on the path to greater things; it is the lives of such souls that reveal to the race what true, spiritual existence has in store; and it is the work, of such men and women that has given us the light, the freedom and the happiness that we now enjoy.

You may live in absolute darkness today; you may not know where to turn; your sky may be black and a raging storm may be almost upon you; you can see nothing but destruction as you have no idea what to do; you are about to give up and perish, but as this thought passes through your mind you remember the "last resort;" you remember the great statement, Call upon me and I will answer thee. You then call upon that power that should be sought first, but that men usually seek last when in trouble. You turn to the Christ that is asleep in the ship. You open your mind to light and power from above, and almost at once there is a rift in the cloud. You are in absolute darkness no more, and the threatening storm is beginning to "break." You pass more completely into the spirit of the Christ, and you realize the beautiful calm. The clouds are gone; you are in the light! You can see everything clearly, and you know what to do. You are now in touch with that upper region from which you may receive better ideas, greater thoughts and more valuable truths than you ever received before; in consequence, you will find precisely what you may need in securing emancipation from external adversity, and in building for those greater things that alone can satisfy the aspirations of the soul.

The belief that the Christ within can still the winds and the waves of every condition that we may meet in life, and change every circumstance into one of calmness, harmony and wellbeing, is a truth that can be taken into every event of daily life. No matter what may come; no matter what the obstacle or the difficulty may be, there is something within us that is greater than anything in the world. The Christ is with us in the ship; we may call him at any time; he can still any storm, change any circumstance and remove every obstacle that we shall ever meet. His power is not applicable to conditions of mind and soul alone, but no physical conditions and circumstances as well. There is nothing that will not respond to the ruling will of the Christ within, and there is no place in practical life where the power of this will may not be applied to the greatest advantage. He who lives in constant touch with Supreme Power, is always in possession of the most power, and he may apply this added power in body, mind and soul. "They that wait upon the Lord shall renew their strength;" but this added strength does not simply appear in the spirit; it appears also in the mind and the body. Therefore, it is always profitable to be in touch with Supreme Power, and to depend upon Supreme Power, whether our work be physical, mental or spiritual. It is not wisdom to depend solely upon the lesser things of the person when we may constantly receive power and aid and inspiration from the greater things of the spirit. All things are for man; and the use of all things should ever be his purpose, no matter what his work may be. We have found a perfect remedy for fear, because he who knows that the Christ is always in the ship will fear nothing. To him no ill can come whatever. Though the approaching storm may sweep everything before it, its fury will be dissipated into nothing when it comes to the ship where the Christ is awake.

But the Christ is in every ship, and he will come forth in every ship and utterly put to naught the impending danger. Whatever our position in life may be, or whatever we may be called upon to do, when we know that the Christ is with us we may proceed calmly, peacefully and serenely in the full conviction that nothing but good will come. We need fear nothing because there will be nothing to fear. The turning of the tide may sometimes be delayed until the eleventh hour, and even until the fifty-ninth minute of that hour; but the turn will come without fail. We may continue positively in that faith. "I will not forsake thee or leave thee." This is the truth, and we can, under every circumstance, demonstrate this truth, providing we never fail to call the Christ. We must go to the Christ first; then he will come to us and answer our prayer whatever that prayer may be. We must place ourselves in touch with Supreme Power first; then that power will come with us; and when Supreme Power is with us we have nothing to fear. When the power of the Supreme is on our side all things will be on our side; and God will go with us the very moment we choose to go with God.

When the day is calm, it is well; but if it is not calm, it is also well; it will soon become calm if you call upon the Christ, for "the winds and the waves shall obey my will." If the future seems bright, you may rejoice; but if the future seems dark, as dark as the blackest night, you may also rejoice; there is a power within you that can put adversity to flight and turn misfortune and sorrow into the glory of a cloudless day. When all that is good is coming into your life you may be grateful; but when all that is good is passing out of your life you may also be grateful; the Christ that is within you cannot only save your ship from every threatening storm and impending danger, but he can also guide your ship towards the shores of richer treasures and greater good than you ever knew before. Grieve not when in the midst of loss; rejoice with great joy, and be grateful from the deepest depth of your heart. Call upon the Christ and you will regain everything and more. There never was and never will be any real occasion for disappointment or tears; when the lesser disappears, turn to the greater; you will find the gates ajar, and you may enter at once into pastures green.

The power of that will that causes the winds and the waves to obey, comes invariably from the depths of spiritual existence. It is the power of the Christ enthroned in the soul, and whoever will recognize and call forth the reigning Christ within, will gain possession of such a will. But we can never gain such a will so long as we try to dominate the lives of others or try to forcefully control external circumstances or events. Nor can we gain such a will so long as we try to will with the outer mind. The real will comes from the great spiritual depths of being, and as it is coming forth it causes the being of man to become deeply calm and enormously strong. The difference between the man of real will power and the man of mere external force is readily discerned. When you meet the latter you find a great deal of domineering effort expressed through the most superficial of action; but you find the man, himself, weak and easily overcome by almost any adverse condition; when you meet the former, however, you will find yourself in the presence of a truly strong man, a man who is strong and alive all the way through to the very depths of his inexhaustible being, a man who is actually conscious of irresistible power; and» you inwardly know that such a man cannot be moved by any power in the world; he has gained possession of that something that is greater than anything in the world, and wherever he may journey upon the sea of life, the winds and the waves must obey.

To depend exclusively upon the personality of Jesus and that power of the Christ that manifested through him twenty centuries ago, is to ignore the present power of the Christ within us. Thousands are doing this, and, in consequence, continue in sickness, trouble and sorrow. To depend upon any personality, no matter how sacred or how highly developed, is to depend upon the outer form and ignore the interior spirit. Such a practice leads into materiality away from spirituality, and materiality means bondage. To follow the Christ is not to worship the person of Jesus but to follow absolutely the light and the spirit of the Christ in your own soul today. The power that can calm the waves on every tempest tossed sea does not come through any external personality; such a power can come only through the great spiritual depths of your own soul, or, to state it differently, from those sublime spiritual heights within where the Christ reigns eternally. When we follow the Christ that is here today, the Christ that reigns in the spiritual kingdom within today, we shall steadily grow in spirituality, emancipating mind and body from every form of bondage and from every condition of materiality, until that freedom that comes from the truth divine has been realized in its greatest measure. Then we may also say, My yoke is easy and my burden is light. Then we may also speak the great word, Peace, Be Still, and to us shall come the beautiful calm.

The Pathway of Roses

Rock of Ages, truth divine,
Strong foundation, ever mine;
Safe, secure, I here remain,
Free from evil, sin and pain;
Living ever in the right;
Fixed on high with souls of light.

On the rock of truth I stand,
Destiny at my command;
Filled with power from on high,
Boundless good forever nigh;
Far above the world of wrong,
Safe with truth, so firm and strong

Every height in truth's domain,
I shall reach and thus obtain
Every wish within my heart
For no blessing can depart;
All of good is ever mine.
On the rock of truth divine

Chapter 25

For I Have Overcome the World

These things have I spoken unto you, that in me ye may have peace. In the world ye have tribulation: but be of good cheer; I have overcome the world. — John 16:33.

There are two distinct worlds open to man in his present state of existence; in the one he finds tribulation; in the other he finds peace; the first is material; the other is spiritual, and it is man's privilege to choose which one he would have as his present place of abode. If he selects the material, he sacrifices everything that has real value in life; he secures a few fleeting pleasures and much pain; not a single moment gives real satisfaction, and nothing that he can do produces the results expected.

But when he selects the spiritual, he sacrifices nothing that is good; he secures all the joy that life can give; his pains are few, if any, and when they do come, they come to lift him higher; every moment is rich, every hour is thoroughly worth living, and there are many periods of time when his soul is lifted to the supreme ecstasies of the highest heavens; whatever he does he builds wiser than he knew, and he not only receives everything expected, but more.

Therefore, those who understand what the spiritual life holds in store, may be of good cheer; their sorrows and tribulations are over; better days are at hand; the words of the Christ have prepared the way, and that way leads to peace. No matter what external conditions may be; no matter what circumstances we may be in now; we may be of good cheer. "I have overcome the world"; and in Him we may live whenever we so desire. The power of the Christ can overcome anything and change anything, and that power is in us. Then why should we not rejoice, and rejoice in Him always?

There is something within us that is greater than things, and it is our privilege to claim the power of that something now. "I have overcome the world now, and every soul may live in Me now." That means emancipation now for all who will receive it. Freedom is not for some other world, but for the life we are living today. We are not required to live in tribulation at any time during present existence; the way to complete emancipation is before us at all times. I AM the way. Whoever will transcend personal consciousness and enter into the consciousness of "I AM" will enter that life that is not of this world, and he will gain that power that can overcome anything that may exist in this world.

To enter the supreme life of the Christ is to gain the supreme power of the Christ; and to steadily grow in the consciousness of that life and power is to rise out of every tribulation until complete emancipation has been gained. That supreme life is in store for us; it already exists in the supreme "I AM" of our own being; this "I AM" is the Son of God, the only begotten of God, the Christ in us; and the Christ that is in each one of us is one with each one of us. That is how "I AM in the Father, and ye in me."

This supreme oneness wherein the soul is one with the Son and the Son is one with the Father, is real; it is not merely in thought or in feeling; it is not solely an abstract state of being; it is as real and as tangible as life itself, and every element that pertains to that oneness is as real and as tangible as life itself. I AM the way, and you are that I AM; you must be or you could not be one with the Father. If you are not that I AM you would be separated from God, and no soul can be separate from God and live. Claim your divine sonship; claim your divine inheritance; claim that supreme power that overcomes the world; it belongs to you; it is you; know this truth and this truth shall make you free.

To believe that you are a mere, weak, human being is not to be in the Christ; when you live in the Christ you are filled through and through, with supreme power, and you know neither weakness nor tribulation any more. This is evidence that you are in the Christ. When you live in Him you are stronger than any adversity that is in the world; you remain untouched, unmoved and undisturbed no matter what may threaten in the world; you are in Him and in Him you have found peace. You have entered the spiritual world, and I AM the door to that world; you have risen to that supreme state of being where you can say, in the spirit of eternal truth, I AM, and through the power of that truth you have overcome the world.

The attitude of overcoming is usually thought of as being inseparably connected with resistance, and as being directly antagonistic, in its action, toward that which is to be overcome. Nearly every person, when trying to overcome anything, begins to resist, begins to antagonize, begins to work against that which is not desired. Accordingly, he does not succeed because he must work in the opposite direction before his purpose can be fulfilled. The first principle in overcoming is to give no thought whatever to that which is not desired. The more completely we can forget that which we wish to overcome, the better. The second principle is to give our whole attention to that something which we know we shall realize when we have overcome. If a person is in adversity he knows that when this adversity is overcome certain most desirable conditions will be realized. Then let him begin at once to give his whole attention to those desirable conditions. By giving his whole time, thought and energy to the attainment of that which is desired, he will invariably overcome and rise out of that which is not desired.

The Pathway of Roses

We overcome the wrong by turning completely away from the wrong, and giving all our life and power to the greater realization of the right. This is the secret of overcoming.

When we devote all the power of thought, all the power of soul, all the power of life to the constant attainment of greater and better things, we shall ascend perpetually in the scale of existence. This means perpetual growth, and, in consequence, the elimination of evil, because all evil is caused by retarded growth. The purpose of life is to move upward and onward forever; to live is to live more; but no person is actually living more unless he is living more every single moment. The moment he begins to live more he begins to ascend, and when he begins to grow into the greater he begins to grow out of the lesser. When he grows into the right he grows out of the wrong; he gains freedom from that which is not desired by entering more fully into the life and the spirit of that which is desired. But the moment he ceases to live more, he retards his growth; he violates the purpose of his life, and instead of supplying more life he supplies less life; his real nature, however, demands more and more life, and therefore, demand and supply will at once become unequal. There will, accordingly, be a lack of something in his life, and every evil that man has ever met came originally from a lack of something. Real life demands the living of more and more life; but when man fails to live more and more, the natural demand in life will not be fully supplied; the lack of one or more things in human existence will be the result, and conditions of evil invariably follow.

Real life is lived in the individuality, the soul, or the real man; and so long as we consciously live in the real man, or in the I AM of being we shall continue to live more and more. We shall thus realize the fullness of life constantly, and constantly grow into a larger measure of that fullness. Life will be full; there will be no lack of life, and no retarded growth in life; in consequence, there will be no evil in life; we shall have perfect freedom and there will be nothing to overcome. Accordingly, we shall fully comply with the great statement, the true way to overcome is to so live that there is nothing to overcome. However, when we do not consciously live in the individuality, or in the real man, but live consciously in the personality only, we are not in touch with the constantly ascending current of real life; we are not in touch with that greater measure of life that will enable us to live more and more life. A lack of life will at once be felt, and here we have the original cause of every ill, every wrong and every undesirable condition that man can know. This is the real fall; conscious living falling down from the living of unlimited life in the individuality to the living of limited life in the personality. But this fall did not take place only once ages ago; it is taking place every day in nearly every mind, and is taking place many times a day in most minds. To be saved from this fall, which is the only fall, proceed to live in the spirit, in the soul, in the real life of the I AM of being. Express the life more abundant in the personality, but live in the individuality. By living consciously and constantly in the individuality you will live in the life more abundant. You will live the limitless life, and what we live we express. We express in the personal man whatever we live in the real man; and therefore when we live the limitless life in the real man we express the limitless in the personal man; thus the personality is ever filled with the life more abundant; there will be no lack of life anywhere in the being of man; and there can be no evil where there is no lack of life.

To try to remove or overcome evil is nothing but wasted effort; evil is not a thing but a condition arising from a lack of life. When necessary life is supplied, there will be no further lack of life, and where there is no lack of life there can be no evil. To antagonize evil, to resist evil, to work against evil will not remove evil. Supply the life more abundant and evil will disappear of itself. Evil is simply emptiness, and no place can be empty when every place is full. To supply the life more abundant, live in the soul, in the real man. Do not establish yourself in the personality; establish yourself in the individuality and live in the source of life instead of in the partial manifestation of life. This is the simple secret. Go up into more life and you overcome everything that is not desirable in life. Do not try to overcome anything; simply begin to live more. Give no thought to evil; never try to remove evil; give all your thought to the attainment of the good, and direct all your effort towards the attainment of an ever increasing measure of good.

When you see evil, do not become indifferent; proceed at once to add to the good; when the good is on the increase evil is on the decrease; this is invariably the law; and the good will begin to increase the moment we begin to live more. The same principle should be applied in every thought, action or relation in human life. We should never emphasize or ever recognize that which is not desired; but that which is desired should be recognized constantly and be emphasized most positively at every opportunity. When we meet others, their imperfections and shortcomings should be overlooked, while their good qualities should be given special attention. When we think of ourselves we should apply the same rule, and we should apply it universally in all physical, mental and spiritual training. The child that is trained in this manner from birth will naturally become extraordinary. When all the power that a person may possess is employed in the building of greater things, there must be great results, even though the power originally possessed be limited. The average person, however, employs but a fraction of his power in the upbuilding process; the remainder is employed in resisting evil and adversity.

The reason why we are not higher in the scale of life, and not more perfectly developed in body, mind and soul, is because we have emphasized our imperfections, and have failed to give our good qualities special attention. You give your life to that which you emphasize; therefore give no thought to weakness or imperfection; give all your thought to those desirable qualities that you wish to build up; your worthy qualities will soon become so strong that weakness can no longer exist in your nature. Build up what you want; that is how you overcome and remove what you do not want. The more fully we can concentrate the whole of attention upon that which we desire, the sooner it will be realized; and when that which is desired is realized, that which is not desired can exist no more; therefore give all your thought, all your power, all your life, and the whole of your attention to that which is desired; do not try to remove the lesser but work uninterruptedly for the greater. The lesser is left further and further in the rear as you approach the greater goal that lies before you.

The process of overcoming is an ascending process, with the eye fixed upon the eternal mountain tops of spiritual supremacy. Give constant recognition to the very highest states of spiritual supremacy that you can possibly discern, and desire all the elements of your being to move perpetually towards those sublime states. You thus produce this ascending process; you will begin to grow out of, to rise out of everything that you have wished to overcome; and when this ascending process has been placed in full, continuous action, there will be nothing further to overcome. The wrongs that we wish to overcome have been produced by retarded growth, but when we are ever rising into more and more life, growth will no longer be retarded; and, in consequence, there will be no further wrongs to overcome. It is therefore evident that if you are still meeting things to overcome, you have not learned to live more and more; you are still permitting yourself to fall down from the world of real life into the world of temporary conditions; you are still living in the body instead of manifesting in the body; and you are still following the confused desires of the personal man, when the only true desire can arise in the real man. To go up into more life, into the limitless life of eternal being, is the remedy.

Whenever you find yourself in any adverse condition, remember you will not come out of it until you grow out of it. You may antagonize adversity and cause it to disappear temporarily, but it will soon return in some other form. Nothing, therefore, is ever gained by such a method. Train yourself to grow out of that which is not good by constantly growing into the greater good; and we invariably grow into that which we think of the most. Think constantly of that which you desire, and you will grow into it. But your thought must be of the heart; it must be deep and strong, and inspired by the invincible power of soul. Do not give personal force to your thought but try to feel that every thought you think has soul, and know that every thought that has soul has the power to do whatever it was created to do. And in all your efforts to grow into the better, the greater and the more beautiful, consider the lilies of the field; grow like the flowers and you will never fail. The flower resists nothing, antagonizes nothing, works against nothing; it gently comes out of its gross and earthly environment, and grows on peacefully, silently and serenely until it becomes an inspiration to all the world. Human life can do the same, must do the same, if we wish to realize the life beautiful and become conscious of the richness and glory of the spiritual heights.

The Pathway of Roses

Spiritual consciousness never weeps; grief comes from the feeling of loss; spiritual consciousness knows that there is no loss; nothing ever can be lost; whatever was, is, and evermore shall be. To spiritual consciousness there are no tears; not because such consciousness is cold or Indifferent, for he who has entered spiritual consciousness loves with a higher, a truer and a far more tender love than he ever knew before. He who has entered spiritual consciousness knows that all is well; and where all is well there can be no tears. Spiritual consciousness feels the existence, the presence and the unity of all things, visible and invisible. To be consciously in the spirit is to love all souls with the love of the spirit, and he who loves with the spirit is one with all souls, both in this realm and in realms beyond. He is conscious of the great white throng those who are in the form and those who are in a higher form. His sublime love has given him a sublime vision, and through that vision he can see that nothing is lost, that all is well, and all that is well is eternal.

Chapter 26

The Supreme Purpose of Life

The beliefs of the past have told us that we are now living in time, and that later on we shall enter eternity; but we are rapidly discarding this idea; first, because it is not true, and second, because we have discovered this idea to be one of the chief causes of age and premature death. By premature death we mean the passing away from this sphere before we have fulfilled the purpose for which we came, and since we are here for some special purpose, we must permit nothing that will take us away before our work is finished.

That we are living here for some great purpose we must all admit; that we have something very important to accomplish in this world we are all beginning to learn; and that we must necessarily remain here for a long time to rightly promote the divine plan is becoming more and more evident. When we think of this great theme from every viewpoint of consciousness we invariably come to the conclusion that man should remain here until he reaches such a high spiritual state that nothing in the world of things can serve him anymore; and we shall find that when we begin to live for the attainment of this sublime state, every moment of existence will be perfect bliss. It is truly sweet to live when we live to promote the great divine plan.

We find, however, that but very few live a good life, and that only a limited number reach a high spiritual state before taking their departure. But what might the reason be? We all realize that old age is unnatural; and none of us require logic to demonstrate the great advantage of a life where eternal youth and eternal ascension in life are blended into one. Therefore we wish to find the fundamental cause of those conditions that produce age, that produce sickness, and that take us away from this sphere before our work is done. And this cause we find in the fact that man thinks he is living in time; when he should know that he is living in eternity.

When man fully realizes that he is living now in the great eternal now, and that he is already in eternity, he shall know age no more. Man grows old because he believes in the passing of time. He believes that he is living in a world where time is ever going, and that he is going with it — to the grave. He is conscious of the passing of years, and believes that the further he goes with the years the more years will be added to the burden of his life. He therefore thinks of himself as so many years old; but here he is mistaken. Time is not passing; time is; and the time that is, is eternity.

What we call time is only that period in eternity that we are conscious of now, and in truth we cannot call it a period of any definite length. To some it is long, to others it is short, to some it passes quickly, to others it drags, and it is variously interpreted by various minds; but the time itself continues to be the same — the eternity that we are conscious of now. It may be stated, however, that time must be passing because something certainly does appear to come and go. But this is only the changing attitude of consciousness as man ascends in the scale. We look at the sun; it appears to move, but we know that the sun is not moving from the earth's point of view; it is the earth that is moving. In like manner, we have looked upon time as passing, but now we know that time is standing still; we are moving upward and onward forever.

When man becomes conscious of the fact that time is standing still, that he is moving, and that the further on he moves the larger his life becomes, he will have attained the secret of that life that is ever young. It may be stated, however, that if man believes he is moving, that belief will cause him to think of advancing age; but the truth is that when man realizes that he is ever moving onward he will know that he is growing into life; and he will never pass into age so long as he is growing into life.

The many believe that time is passing — coming to man and going away from man, and that man himself is passing, not into life but out of life; in consequence, the life more abundant is not realized. What the race does realize in growth, advancement and higher attainment is produced partly by the natural power of life to ascend in the scale and partly by the efforts of great souls. The race belief, however, concerning time and man's relation to time, is a constant obstacle, both to emancipation from the imperfections of the lesser life, and the ascension into greater life. To secure emancipation now, to realize that youthful life now that is a necessary part of the spiritual life, and to rise daily into the greater spiritual life, the usual conception of time must be reversed. But we cannot accomplish this by trying to change our relations to those external devices that measure the movements of nature; nor will a denial of nature avail in the least. The change that is required must take place in our own consciousness.

Realize that time is, that the time that is, is eternity, and that eternity is still, always here, forever giving forth her riches to man. Realize that there is no time except the eternal, therefore time does not pass because there is neither time to pass nor passing time. Realize this great truth in the depths of consciousness, and years will only add to your power, your youth, your life and your spiritual attainments. Then you shall remain upon earth until your work is finished — until you have reached the Christ state.

When this truth is realized, you will consciously feel the stillness and the calm of the eternity that forever is. You will no longer feel that you are passing on and on to some undesired end where adverse forces will rob you of the life you are here to live; you will no longer think of death or those periods of inability that have formerly preceded death; these mean nothing to you; they do not belong to your life; you are living in eternity; time is not adding years to your life; your life is eternal, and that which is eternal cannot be measured by years. The movements of nature in their circles and spirals may be measured; but that has nothing to do with life or time. Nature is forever moving around the great eternal now, and the eternal now is living in the deep silence of the life that forever is now. The life that you live — the real life, the eternal life, is the same life that is now; and in that life there is no time, no years, no age — only eternity.

Ascension in life means the appropriation of more and more of real life; it does not mean the changing of life from one state to another, nor the passing through periods of time. Growth does not come from the passing of time; growth comes from appropriation; besides, there is no passing of time. When we think of growth we usually think of so much gain in so much time, but that is a mistake. The soul that truly lives, appropriates all that it needs each moment; no more, no less; it does not deal with time; it deals only with that which has real, eternal existence; it never thinks of tomorrow because in eternity there is no tomorrow; it lives now, and it knows that the life that is now will never pass away.

When we become conscious of eternal life we no longer question the immortal existence of the soul. To feel eternal life is to know that life is eternal, and that every soul that lives, lives the life eternal now. We cannot separate the life of the soul from the life that is eternal, and the moment that we discover that the two are one we know that we shall live forever. We need no external demonstration to prove to us that those that have gone before are still alive; we now know that no soul can possibly cease to exist, and we spiritually discern the immortal existence of all the souls in the world. We seek no visible sign because we are in the presence of that something from which every sign must proceed. We no longer ponder over the life after death; we know there is no death. That which is eternal life can never die, and to become conscious of the soul is to discover that the soul is eternal life. The soul is coexistent with God; what God is the soul is; the soul is the real man, the man that is forever in the image and likeness of God.

When we ask "If a man die, shall he live again?" we prove to those who understand that we are still living in the person, and that we still think of ourselves as being persons. The person passes away, and therefore so long as we think that we are persons we think that we shall also pass away; but we are not certain whether we shall pass into nothingness or into another life; we do not know because we are not awakened into that consciousness of eternal life that does know. We doubt no more, however, when we discover the real life of the soul, and find that we are not persons but spiritual entities, sons of the Most High. If you wish to convince yourself that you are to live after you have removed the physical body, do not seek after mysterious signs in the without; seek rather the real life in the within. The more deeply you enter into real life the more fully you realize that there is no end to your own life. The outer consciousness informs you that you have life; the inner consciousness informs you that there is no end to your life, and the one is as convincing to the mind as the other.

You know that you are living because you are conscious of life. Enter more deeply into the reality of your being and you become conscious of eternal life. Then you will not only know that you are living, but you will know that there can be no end to your living. To be conscious of life is to know that you are living now; to be conscious of eternal life is to know that you are living in eternity now, and that to live in eternity is to be eternal. To develop the consciousness of eternal life it is only necessary to grow daily in the spiritual life. Seek to understand the reality of your own divine being, and you will not only develop that spiritual discernment that knows the immortal existence of your own soul, but you will also develop that discernment that knows the present continued existence of all souls. You will know that you are destined to live eternally, and you will know that all souls, from ages past, are now living eternally. You know this, not through signs from without, or evidences that may appeal to physical senses or psychical senses, but through that spiritual understanding that is in conscious touch with every soul in God's unbounded cosmos. Neither the physical senses nor the psychical senses can know the soul; it is therefore impossible to demonstrate to any of those senses that the soul is immortal. Spiritual consciousness alone can know this great truth and to be spiritually conscious is to live in that sacred, interior realm where we know that man is perfect and divine, as God is perfect and divine. We know this when we are in the spirit, for nothing can be hidden in the light of the spirit. In that light we see all things as they are; therefore we know, and we speak with authority, not from ourselves but from God. In the spirit we are with God, and His thought becomes our thought, His word our word, His life our life.

The Pathway of Roses

When you see someone leaving the body you do not weep if you are spiritually awakened; you know that the leave-taking is but seeming; there is neither going nor coming in the spirit; there is no separation in spirit; in the spirit all are one in His love. Though the soul that seems to depart becomes invisible to physical sight, still that soul is ever visible to spiritual sight. To be consciously in the spirit is to see all those who live in the spirit whatever the form may be. In the consciousness of the spirit the manifestation of the form is secondary; whether the form be physical or ethereal is not of first importance; but to know the spirit, to be conscious of the spirit, and to know that all souls are eternally in the spirit — that is the first importance. That soul that seems to have gone, has not gone; you who are in the spirit, can feel her life, her presence and her love just the same; and you are wide awake to the fact that she still lives. Her existence is just as real to you as it was before, because in the spirit all is real. To you, who are in the spirit, all souls are real whether they manifest in this world or in some other world. They are all in God's sublime world, and when you are spiritually conscious your eyes are opened to the splendor and glory of that world.

Chapter 27

The Psalm of Rejoicing

The Lord is my shepherd; I shall not want.

When we are led by the spirit of the Most High, the condition of want is removed completely; which means that we shall want for nothing. There is nothing that we may need or desire for the living of a complete life that we shall not receive when the Lord is our shepherd. We shall have abundance in every domain of existence, and no matter how great our demands may be the adequate supply will always be at hand; provided, however, that our demands are in accord with the ascending life — the life that leads to the heights.

We are not required to place limitations upon our demands or desires; the Supreme is not limited in His power to supply; it is our privilege to desire everything that we may need to make life as large, as perfect, and as beautiful as we possibly can; in brief, the more we desire the greater becomes the life we live, and the greatest life is the most acceptable life to God as well as to man. We do not please God by humbling ourselves into insignificance, the Infinite does not ask us to be small because He is great; He does not demand that we be satisfied with little because He has everything. This is not the nature of God because God is love, and love eternally declares, "Be as I AM; come and enjoy everything that I have to enjoy; what is mine is thine; what is for me is for thee, and nothing shall be withheld whatever."

To want for nothing means that we shall be in possession of everything — everything that is necessary to a life that is all that real life is intended to be. This means that we shall have all the peace that the soul may require, even the peace that passeth understanding; we shall have all the wisdom and all the power that we may need to attain in life whatever our highest aspirations may have in view; we shall have sufficient joy to satisfy perfectly every element in the whole of being; we shall have happiness without measure, harmony as beautiful as the symphonies of heaven, and health in perfection forever. Not a moment shall your body know any ailment whatever, and not a moment shall your mind know sorrow or pain. This is the truth. It could not be otherwise when the Lord is your shepherd. God is love, and love leads away from ills and pains into the infinite delights of sublime existence.

God is equal to all your needs; He can give health and strength to the body; He can give peace and power to the mind; He can give wisdom and joy to the soul; He can surround your personal life with all that is rich and beautiful in physical existence; He can surround your spiritual life with all that is gorgeous and sublime in cosmic existence; and when you select Him as your shepherd He will. Take God at His word. Do not believe in His goodness and power and then act as if your belief was not true. Believe that He will actually supply your every need, then act accordingly. Have faith in abundance and expect your faith to come true. You shall not be kept waiting, nor shall you long remain empty handed Your prayers shall be answered, your needs shall be supplied, and all that your life may require shall now become your own.

Do not depend upon yourself alone. The belief that man must depend wholly upon himself to rise to the heights of being is not true. Man alone can do nothing of real worth; it is only when we work with God and God works with us that we can do what the ideal within us desires to do. The greatest things in the world are done by those who constantly depend upon God, who walk with God and live with God, and then make the fullest, the largest and the best use of those powers they are eternally receiving from God. Wherever you may go, or whatever you may wish to do, take the Lord for your shepherd and you shall positively gain what you have in view. Failure becomes impossible because God is equal to any condition that may arise, and so long as you are with God, God is with you. Though you may meet adversity, you need not be disturbed; something will happen; God will cause something to happen so that things will take a turn; you shall be led into pastures green where all your desires shall be granted. Then you shall want for nothing. Remember, you shall want for nothing. This is the great truth to understand fully and demonstrate fully in the actual living of life.

The secret is absolute trust and faith in the goodness and the power of the Supreme. Believe that God is your shepherd; believe that you can want for nothing so long as He is with you; then act accordingly. Live as if you actually believed that your belief was true, and you shall find it to be true. It is only when we live the truth that the truth proves itself to be the truth. Do not wait for external evidence before you proceed to act upon your faith. Real faith has any amount of internal evidence, and any principle that proves itself to be true in the within can be demonstrated to be true in the without. What the vision of the soul may declare, the powers of the personal man can supply; and daily life can be made as true, as beautiful and as sublime as the life that is lived on the heights.

He maketh me to lie down in green pastures; he leadeth me beside the still waters.

To be led by the spirit of the Most High is to pass through perpetual change — to pass from the good to the better, from the better to the best, and then higher and higher into those richer realms that infinite love has in store. In such a life there is always something new to live for, always something higher, something better to enjoy. Such a life can never be wearisome nor monotonous, for it is nothing less than a continuous feast — the richest imaginable feast, and all the elements of that feast are changed as often as we desire. It is in this feast that we partake of "the meat that ye know not of," and it is in this feast that the soul is nourished unto eternal life. Then comes the great spiritual strength that gives us the power to transcend the seeming and enter into the realms of existing sublime. And how beautiful to enter the pastures green of those lofty worlds, there to lie down and rest in the peace that passeth understanding, in the deep eternal calm that touches the soul with the symphonies of heaven. And how beautiful to be led beside the still waters, the living waters of celestial kingdoms on high, peacefully flowing onward and onward into that fairer kingdom, wherein we shall enter some golden morn, there to behold what eternity has in store for man.

When we follow the spirit, countless worlds are constantly opening before us, and in those worlds there are pastures green everywhere. In these we shall find nourishment for the soul; in these we shall find rest for the spirit. Then shall the soul come forth with new strength; then shall the spirit arise with power, and the spiritual life within us shall begin its great eternal reign. And when the spirit begins its reign, the outer world takes upon itself the peace, the wholeness, the harmony and the perfection of the beautiful life within. Adversity disappears; wrongs give place to the purity of the life divine; imperfections are lost in the dimness of the past, and the richness that we find in the pastures green of realms sublime, is reproduced in personal existence. Then we shall realize in the without what the soul has discerned in the within; then the joys of the spirit shall be made known to the person, and life in this world shall become the image and likeness of that other life that our most lofty moments have so beautifully revealed.

When the Infinite leads you and guides you, you will constantly be led into the larger, the greater and the better. Pastures green will always be ready for you the very moment you are ready for a larger, richer life. You will never have to remain in the lesser for a single moment after you are ready for the greater; the Most High will open the way for you, and the increase you desire in your life shall speedily become your own. All the world rests upon the Great law of perpetual increase; and the pathway of all life is upward and onward forever; therefore to follow the law of life is to ever ascend into a greater and a greater measure of the highest good that life can give. The great law of life is the law of infinite life because God is the source of all law and all life; and since God lives as His own laws direct, we understand that when we follow the laws of life we shall live as He lives. And we always follow His laws when we are led by Him. We therefore conclude that all life that is led by the spirit of infinite life will ever live in perpetual increase. In such a life the greatest good in life will be enjoyed now, and that good will become higher and greater without any end.

The great truth to remember is that God always leads into the greater, never to the lesser. When the Lord is your shepherd you will eternally be led into pastures green, and every new pasture will be richer than the one you knew before. Walk with God; live in the presence and the power of His spirit and follow the light of the Supreme in all things; then you shall be led eternally into greater and greater things. The boundless will ever be at your door and your faith will open that door. This is a great truth; it is a truth that we must always remember and always apply because we can receive from infinite supply only what we believe that we will receive. Believe with heart and soul that you will receive everything that is necessary to the fullness and completeness of ideal living, and you will receive all these things if you have taken the Lord for your shepherd. He will lead you into pastures green, and your faith will open your life to all the richness that those newer worlds may contain.

The Infinite never leads into trouble, sickness, adversity or pain. When we enter such conditions we are not led by the spirit of the Most High; we are simply going away from His spirit, and thus create the very ills from which we soon must suffer. When we go away from God we create evil; this is the only way that evil can be created, and the evil we thus create is the only evil that can ever come to us. Therefore the one great remedy that can heal all the ills of human life is found in that wonderful statement, "Return Ye Unto God."

When people who claim to be spiritual, are led into sickness and trouble, they are either mistaking emotionalism for spirituality, or their spirituality is as yet but a negative quality. When we begin to walk with God we begin to gain real spirituality, but such a spirituality is not simply a beautiful vision of the perfect and the divine; nor is it simply an esthetic feeling or a tender sentiment; it is the great spiritual life within coming forth with living power. Spirituality is sweet and tender and beautiful, but it is also immensely strong. Therefore when we are in possession of real spirituality the ills of life must vanish just as darkness disappears with the coming of the light. No ill can exist in the living power of the spirit, and we are always filled through and through with that power when we are in the spirit, when we are living in that life that God lives. And when the Lord is our shepherd He invariably leads us into His life, His world, His kingdom, and into His light, wherein we shall know the truth — the truth that gives freedom to all that is in the being of man.

The Pathway of Roses

When you are led "beside the still waters" everything in your life will move smoothly, and all your efforts, experiences and modes of existence will work together harmoniously for greater and greater good. At first, or for some time, there may be conditions in your life that are not as they should be, but these will soon pass away, and while they do remain you will be so strong, if you live in God, that no adversity can disturb you in the least. When you are led by the spirit of the Most High, adversity will become less and less, while you will gain in strength, more and more, so that whatever adversity you may for awhile meet will be as nothing in your life. You thus become able to master whatever may appear in the present, and you are, at the same time, rising out of every condition that is in any manner undesirable or adverse. You are led beside the still waters into the peace, the contentment and the joy of complete emancipation.

The life that is led by the spirit is the most peaceful, the most comfortable and the most sweetly serene of all life; it is ever beside the still waters, and is ever in touch with the great eternal calm. But it is also the most interesting as well as the most beautiful, for it is ever moving onward and onward. And here we find a great secret. The great life is not the life that imitates the storm-tossed sea, but the life that is deep and strong and yet always peaceful and still. Such a life is great in power, limitless in capacity and wonderful in efficiency, but in all things and at all times, is forever sweetly serene. Such a life sounds the very depth of real being and calmly brings to the surface the rich treasures of those inexhaustible realms within. And thus the entire domain of human existence is made larger, richer and more beautiful without any end. We shall ever find pastures green both in the within and in the without, and beside the still waters we shall be led into that peaceful life that we have sometimes felt when the soul was attuned to God.

The Pathway of Roses

He restoreth my soul; he leadeth me in the paths of righteousness for his name's sake.

When we enter into the life of the Infinite, all that is high, all that is perfect and all that is beautiful in the soul will be restored to consciousness. The glory, the divinity and the sublime majesty of the soul will be revealed; the veil of mystery will be removed and we may behold the gorgeous splendor of the spiritual life as it truly is. The soul is no longer lost from view; we are no longer ignorant of the wonderful life within us; the heavens are opened, so to speak, and we may see most clearly and most perfectly that eternal something within us that is created in the image and likeness of God. Our divine nature is restored to us; we learn what we are; we discover our great inheritance; we find that we are not mere human creatures, but sons of the Most High, destined to reign with Him on the heights of glory, and to live in His sublime kingdom during countless ages yet to be.

When the soul is restored, our inner spiritual nature becomes the ruling power in life; mind and body becomes servants to the soul, and we no longer live for circumstances, conditions and things; we begin to live for life itself, and we thus gain, in an ever increasing measure, all the richness, all the beauty and all the power that life can give. When we live for life we can gain everything of worth that is in life, and we invariably live for life when the soul is the ruling power in life. In the life of the soul all is perfect and all is well because the soul lives the same life that God lives. Therefore when the soul becomes the ruling power in personal life, we will live as God lives in our entire domain of life, and throughout that domain all will always be well. When the soul is the master in human life, all will be well in human life, and the soul is always restored to its high place in life when we elect to be led by the spirit of God.

The Pathway of Roses

The soul is perfect, being created in the image of God; therefore, the elimination of the imperfect in life must begin when the soul becomes the ruling power. When the soul rules in mind and body it will live in every part of mind and body; and where the soul lives there can be neither sickness nor pain, neither weakness nor want. When the soul is restored to its high place of majesty and power in life, all the ills of life must inevitably disappear. When the light returns, the darkness is no more. When the wholeness of the spirit becomes a living power in mind and body, the life of the person must necessarily become as clean, as strong and as wholesome as the life of the soul. And such a state of being is invariably secured when the soul is selected to reign in the wonderful kingdom of man. The ills of life come only when we follow those desires of the person that are not inspired from within; but when the soul is restored, every desire of the person will be true to the life of the spirit. We shall then no longer follow darkness into wrong and distress, but we shall follow divine light into peace, wholeness, freedom and joy. We naturally follow our desires in everything that we may think or do; therefore when all our desires are born from above, we shall naturally keep the eye single upon the light from above, and in consequence, will ever be led by the wisdom of God.

When the soul is restored to complete mastership in the human domain, everything changes for the better; a new life begins and all the elements of this new life contain possibilities for greater things than we ever knew before. We actually enter a new world, and the former things are passing away. What was against us either disappears or changes so completely that all its power is given to the promotion of what we have in view; and those things that always were for us become stronger and stronger until we feel that limitless power is on our side. When the soul rules the destiny of human life all the forces of life will build for a greater and a greater destiny; all things will move towards the heights; want will give place to perpetual increase; sickness will give place to wholeness and strength, and adversity will give place to harmony and joy. Restore the soul to mastery in your life and your entire being will be restored to its birthright divine; all that is worthy and beautiful in sublime existence will begin to accumulate in your world, and life to you will be rich indeed. Follow the spirit and you will always go right. He will lead yon in the paths of righteousness, and whatever you think or do will always be for the best. In brief, nothing but the best can happen to you because the Lord is your shepherd and He will surely care for His own. The spirit never leads into anything but that which is right, that which is good, that which is best. When you do not follow the spirit, you are either going wrong or you are drifting into channels that will finally take you into the wrong. You may not be consciously following the spirit now, and yet you may be seemingly going right now, but this does not mean that you are on the true path. Those who are not following the spirit now are going wrong, and to them adversity will come sooner or later. Present conditions, however favorable, do not prove that you are on the path that leads to freedom and the greater life. You are on that path only when you know that you are led by His spirit in all things and at all times. We cannot judge according to appearances; the truth comes only from the supreme light within; and when we know the truth and live accordingly, we know that all will be right — in the within and in the without — all will be right.

We all follow the inner light to some degree; the soul is awakened in us all and is prompting us all; but in many instances we are led by those personal desires that are not in harmony with real life, and we are influenced by external conditions and things; thus we go wrong, and here is the cause of our troubles and pains. Whenever we go right, we go right because we have followed the higher promptings from within; and whenever we go wrong, we go wrong because we have followed those external conditions that are not in harmony with the real life within. But do we know when we are prompted by the soul? Do we know when we are led by the spirit T Do we know when we are guided by the Infinite and by Infinite Wisdom alone? At first we may not know; we may follow the spirit at times without knowing that it is the spirit, and at times we may think we are led by the spirit and yet be mistaken. But every person who fully and absolutely decides to follow the spirit in all things, henceforth and forever, will not long remain unconscious to the radiant presence of the Most High. If you will take this great step your spirit will soon be attuned to the tender music of the still small voice, and your mind will be illumined more and more with the glory of His sight. Then you will know, and never be mistaken, whenever He speaks to you; then you will see His light at all times and you will always know that it is the light divine. You will readily discern the meaning of His will in all things, and you will find that to follow His will is to go where glory is waiting. Not to some other world, but to His world, here and now. "There is another and a better world" here and now wherein we all may dwell in the never-ending today; and the light of His spirit leads directly into the freedom and joy of that beautiful world.

Yea, though I walk through the valley of the shadow of death, I will fear no evil: For thou art with me; thy rod and thy staff they comfort me.

When God is with us nothing but that which is good can happen. It matters not what we may meet or what we may be required to pass through, good will be the final outcome. We need fear no condition that can possibly arise; Supreme Power is with us, and we may overcome and surmount anything. "We shall come out of every experience uninjured and unharmed; nothing can hurt us because there can be no hurt in the presence of infinite goodness, infinite power, infinite love. Wherever we are called we may safely go; whatever we are expected to do we may proceed. So long as we feel and know that God is with us, all will be well. We shall be led, guided, directed and protected; we may, without doubt or fear, proceed to do our part, and leave results to higher power; the very best will come to pass. Even though things happen for a short time that seem adverse, the outcome of everything will be good, very good. The light of divine wisdom is guiding our life, our thought, our actions, our destiny, and therefore all things will work together for the very highest good that we can possibly realize in every state of continued existence.

What is here spoken of as the valley of the shadow of death is the most extreme condition of danger that a person can possibly pass through; there can be no worse state of threatening calamity than the "dark valley," yet even there "I will fear no evil, for thou art with me." It matters not to what extreme we may be taken by circumstances or fate, God is equal to all our needs. He can protect us and guide us anywhere, and He will. He can take us out in safety, and He will surely do so if we have selected Him as our shepherd. And not simply because His power is supreme, but also because where God is there can be no evil. There is no evil to fear where God is because there can be no evil where God is. Be with God and God will be with you; and when God is with you, you are ever in the presence of the good and the beautiful. You are in a world where freedom is complete, where truth is omnipresent, and where all the elements of life are in touch with higher and better things.

When we are in the presence of danger we almost invariably shrink into dread or fear of some kind; and when called upon to do what seems beyond us, or what we personally dislike, we usually hesitate, or refuse absolutely; but this is all a mistake. God is with us; we need fear nothing, for He will protect us in everything. God is our strength, and with His strength we can surely do anything that life may require of us. When we feel weak we should remember that His rod and His staff are at our service. If we must have something to lean upon, His staff is ever at hand, and with such a staff we shall not fall down; no matter how heavy the burden, or how difficult the task, we shall not fall down. His staff will support us whenever we may need support; His rod will hold us up whatever the circumstances may be, and the power of His presence will give us all the strength we may require to reach any goal we may have in view. We should rather look upon difficulties as opportunities through which we may demonstrate to others the great truth that nothing is impossible when God is with us. And when called upon to do what seems beyond our capacity, we shall proceed nevertheless, pressing on in the full faith that we can. God is with us, and when He is with us we can do anything that our present sphere of existence may require.

If we have a great purpose to carry through we need never hesitate. Though the opposition may be great and the obstacles seemingly insurmountable, we may safely proceed. We need fear neither danger nor defeat, for Thou art with me. God will see us through. The Lord is our shepherd; we shall want for nothing; indeed, we shall receive everything we may need to accomplish what we have undertaken. When the task seems hard and the flesh seems weak, then we should remember, Thy rod and Thy staff they comfort me. And in that comfort our strength shall return, even more than enough to carry through the task that lies before us. We are equal to any occasion when God is with us, and God will always be with us if that is our deepest prayer of the heart. Therefore, we should never complain, and never give up to weariness or defeat. When it seems as if we could do nothing more, God will do the rest; and if we take heart again and proceed in unison with Him, we shall become stronger than we ever were before. When it seems as if everything would be lost, we should refuse to judge according to the seeming. "The Lord is my shepherd." The seeming loss will not take place. The tide will turn. God can turn anything in our favor, and if we accept Him as our shepherd He always will.

When God is our strength how great indeed is that strength. With Him at our side we have our own life in our own hands, and may do with it whatsoever we will. The present is ours to enjoy, the future is ours to create. Adverse indications mean nothing; threatening ills or failures mean nothing; we need fear none of these things. God is greater than all outward indications, and His greatness is with us, on our side, working for our happiness and welfare. We should never recognize that which seems to be against us, for when God is with us His strength is our strength, His life is our life, and the wisdom that illumines His mind the same wisdom shall illumine our minds also. We therefore can never have any occasion to fear, to hesitate or to entertain doubts in any form or manner. The Lord is our shepherd. He will surely care for His own, and whatever is necessary to give fullness, perfection and completeness to the great eternal now, that we shall all receive.

God is with us when we choose to be with God. This is the simple secret. When we select Him as our shepherd, then we become His own; then He will care for us, guide us and protect us; then He will place the gates ajar so we may enter into pastures green; then He will lead us beside the still waters into the peace and the joy of the beautiful life. It will all be as we desire. The Infinite is ever ready, and it is our privilege to accept His goodness today. But to accept Him as our shepherd does not mean that we must completely relinquish our own will and our own way. When we decide to go God's way we shall find that He is helping us to gain our way; and when we decide to follow His will we shall find that He is giving us all the power required to carry out our will. Thus we shall find that the goodness of God is far greater than we thought, and that His love is as boundless as the infinite sea.

Thou preparest a table before me in the presence of mine enemies: Thou anointest my head with oil; my cup runneth over.

When God is with us we shall continue to enjoy the best that life can give regardless of what surrounding conditions may be. Though things may seemingly be against us, and though we may be in the presence of enmity and adversity, nevertheless, those things shall neither touch us nor disturb us. In the midst of such circumstances, or any kind of circumstances, God will prepare a table of everything that is rich and desirable in life. Whatever may happen in the world in which we live, God will protect us from loss. His table will always be richly laden, and it will be our privilege to partake according to our largest and most heartfelt need. When the Lord is our shepherd we need fear neither persons nor things that may seem to be against us. When God is with us, nothing can be against us. We have a place at His table, and those who are guests at His table shall want for nothing. He will provide for Hi a guests and provide richly; therefore if we accept Him as our everlasting host we need never be disturbed about any condition, circumstance or event. The best will happen, and all will always be well.

When things go wrong with those who are living only for the world, things will go right with us. Misfortune cannot overtake us. In His presence the power of evil is powerless, and we are ever in His presence so long as we elect that we so shall be. When we take God with us, and leave all our plans and desires with God before we decide, there will not even be indications of misfortune or adversity in our world. He will continue to prepare His table before us, and we shall continue to enjoy, both the good things of this world, and "the meat that ye know not of." We shall continue in prosperity even though all who live in the material world go down into adversity. The Lord is our shepherd, and we shall not want. However, if we should meet what would seem to be the indications of a threatening misfortune, we need not be disturbed. There may be temporary losses, and adverse conditions may come so near as to almost enter into our very lives, nevertheless we need not be disturbed. Whatever may threaten to happen, we need fear no evil, for Thou art with me. The entire experience will simply prove to be an open door to better things and greater things than we ever knew before. Such experiences sometimes come to those who are in His care; not often, but sometimes; and they come to test our faith, our spiritual strength and our dependence upon Him; they come to prepare us for a greater life, for pastures green, for new fields of endeavor and for a higher mission in the world. Count it all joy; so long as we are with God, God will be with us; and He will cause all things to work together for greater good than we ever dreamed.

Whatever may come to the world, the best alone can come to us. And we shall thus, not only realize the richness and the beauty of that life that is lived in God, but we shall become living examples to the world, proving to the world that God's way is best. We shall then demonstrate to all who have eyes to see, that to follow the light of the spirit is to follow that light that leads into everything that is worthy and beautiful in endless existence. The world believes that the spiritual life leads away from happiness and abundance; we must prove to everybody that the spiritual life leads into greater happiness and a richer life than we have ever known before. And we can prove this when we take the Lord for our shepherd. When we accept a place at His table, we shall demonstrate in the most tangible and the most convincing manner that to go with God is to go where every person may supply his every need; and not only be supplied, but supplied in the richest, the most worthy and the most ideal manner conceivable. To go with God is to find everything that heart can wish for in this world, and in addition, the infinite glory, the gorgeous splendor and the supreme joy of His kingdom on the heights.

To be anointed with oil is to have everything that is worthy and superior come down upon us. The oil of all things is the richest essence of all things, and when we are anointed with this richest essence, our minds become enriched with all that has quality and worth, all that is high in the scale of being. And it is but natural that that mind that lives and thinks with God, should be constantly enriched. Everything that comes from God has quality; everything that we receive from God has high worth, and everything that pertains to the spiritual life contains all the elements of real superiority; therefore, to follow God is to rise eternally in the scale of superior being. When we elect to go with God we leave behind us all that is common, ordinary or inferior; and we put on the royal garments of true quality and high worth. We become superior in body, mind and soul, and every element in our being becomes a living expression of that quality that reveals the royal presence of God.

When we are actually living in the spirit, and can fully appreciate all that is good and beautiful in real life, we become so filled with gratitude and joy that neither thoughts nor words can express what we feel. It is then that we wish as never before "that the mind could fathom and the tongue could utter the thoughts that arise in me." Our cup is running over; we have everything that can fill the fullness of life with the richness of life, and our joy is great indeed. Words fail us, but that something within that is far more eloquent than words gives utterance to what we wish to say. And as we listen, this language divine becomes heavenly music, repeating again and again that tender refrain, "God's beautiful gift to me."

To always live in the realization of that sublime state of being where our cup is running over, is to become conscious more and more of the great truth that real life has everything that man can wish for, and infinitely more. And as we grow in the conscious realization of this truth, the power of this truth will manifest itself in our external world. Then we shall find increase everywhere; wherever we may go in the physical world, in the mental world or in the spiritual world, God will prepare His table before us, and we shall enjoy the richest feast that His infinite goodness can possibly provide. In every domain of existence His bountiful hand will be our supply, and our cup will always be running over. What we feel and realize in the world of the spirit that we shall gain in the world of things. Thus our joy becomes complete; all that we need is always at hand, all that we desire for a greater existence shall be speedily supplied, and wherever our place in life may be, God will appear and prepare His table before us. He will be our supply always and everywhere; and existence will be rich indeed.

Surely goodness and mercy shall follow me all the days of my life; and I will dwell in the house of the Lord forever.

When the soul enters the faith that leads eternally into the kingdom, the entire being of man is placed in the keeping of the spirit of goodness. That power that works for the good and the good only, will henceforth be with man under every circumstance and condition; and all his actions will be attended by the angel of mercy. His life will be lived in the consciousness of the Infinite presence, and this consciousness is the open door to the house of the Lord. The moment we feel that God is closer than breathing, nearer than hands and feet, we are upon the threshold of the sublime spiritual world — the Father's House of the Many Mansions, and from that moment we may dwell in His house forever. From that moment all will be changed; life will never seem ordinary, commonplace or mere existence anymore; we have seen the House Beautiful, we have felt the touch of the life that God lives, we have been on the heights, and we have had a glimpse of the glory that eternity holds in store. Henceforth, there is so much to live for, that simply to think of the ever ascending destiny that lies before us, is in itself a source of unspeakable joy. Then who can measure the peace, the joy, in brief, the unbounded ecstasy that must follow the living of the life? Those who have been led beside the still waters know the meaning of such a life. Those who have entered the house of the Lord know what is prepared for them that love Him. But tongue can never tell, and only the mind of the soul can understand.

To follow the spirit is to enter the glorified vastness of the great spiritual mind within; and here is wisdom. Spiritual things must be spiritually discerned; we must enter spiritual light in order to know the reality of our own divine being, and the mind of the soul is eternally illumined with this light. There are no mysteries in spiritual consciousness; all is clear; the meaning of life is perfectly understood; the purpose of it all is distinctly revealed, and the soul knows what it is about every step of the way. Every soul that goes with God in all things and at all times, will ever live in this consciousness, and will ever rise higher and higher into the greater brilliancy more sublime beauty of the spiritual light. To live such a life is to dwell in the house of the Lord, and whosoever will, may dwell in that house forever.

The Pathway of Roses

The world in which we live may not, at present, contain everything that the heart can wish for; but "there is another and a better world" that does contain everything. Our human dwelling place may not be perfect, it may not be complete, it may not satisfy the soul's longing for the ideal and the beautiful; but the house of the Lord can satisfy. We therefore need not be unhappy; personal life need not be incomplete because there are seeming limitations among external conditions. The fact that we manifest in visible form does not mean that we should live wholly among visible things. The law of true being is to manifest in the personal but to always live in the spiritual. The house of the Lord is our true dwelling place now and forever. And as there are many mansions in the Father's House — innumerable mansions, we shall not be confined to one place, or one state of existence; we shall live in each of these mansions; we shall enjoy them all, we shall pass through them all as eternity goes on. No matter how lofty the present abode of the soul, there is always something higher; no matter how unspeakable our spiritual joys today, or any time in eternity, there are always greater joys coming in days that are yet to be. We thus realize what it means to dwell in the house of the Lord forever.

When we have entered to dwell permanently in the house of the Lord, existence, both personal and spiritual, becomes perpetual joy. Whatever external conditions may be, or whatever may come and go in personal life, we are always in the joy everlasting, in the peace that passeth understanding, in the world on high where all is forever well. We no longer depend upon things, and we are no longer moved by things; we have transcended the world of things; we have gained the power to perfectly use things, and we are attaining the mastery of all things. We are living in God's world — the world of limitless richness, happiness and power; therefore, the world of things constitutes but a small part of our vast and wonderful domain. We have found so many sources of joy, so many states of being that can add to the value of life, that though other things should sometimes fail, we are never affected in the least. Confusion and failure in the outer world mean no more to us than the loss of a penny would mean to a man who owns a mountain of gold. Things may come and go in the outer world, but we are living in the house of the Lord. In that house there is never confusion, trouble nor pain; in that house there can be neither failure nor want. The Most High provides for that house; therefore so long as we dwell in His house we shall want for nothing. Whatever may come or go, we shall always have abundance, both in the within and in the without. We need fear nothing; we may rejoice always, for in His house all is well, and for evermore shall be.

The Pathway of Roses

Dream on fair soul, dream on. Thy visions are not in vain. Other and greater worlds are waiting for thee. Dream on fair soul, dream on. Let thy spirit ascend to the supreme heights of those greater worlds where thou shalt behold the glory and splendor of that sublime existence that is in store for thee. And let nothing that may come or go in thy wafting hours cause thee to forget what thou hast seen. For the time is near when the dreams of the night shall rise with the morning but shall not depart with the setting sun. What thou hast seen in thy visions shall come to remain; and what thy lofty moments have revealed to thee shall become thine own forever.

Chapter 28

God's Beautiful Gift to Me

The great goal is cosmic consciousness, and every soul that endeavors to live according to the highest light that is known in the world, is daily drawing nearer and nearer to that sublime state. To such a soul the heavens may be opened at any time, and the splendors of the cosmic world revealed. Then everything will change. Life will not be the same any more. The meaning of it all will be discerned, and no fault can be found anywhere. When we look at life from the heights of the cosmic realm we can see only the divine side of existence; we therefore can see no evil; in brief, when we are in the cosmic we have absolutely forgotten everything about evil; we do not know that there is such a thing as evil because we are in that exalted world where we can be conscious only of the good. And here is the real evidence of cosmic consciousness. When you have entered the peace that passeth understanding and the joy that can only be described as a million heavens in one, you are in the cosmic state, providing you have forgotten every ill and every wrong you ever knew. In the cosmic world everything is as God made it; nothing has been changed in any way; absolute perfection and absolute divinity reign supremely, and the glory of it all no power in man can ever attempt to picture. It is beyond all the powers of the personal man; it is for the soul only to understand and enjoy.

When we enter the cosmic state we transcend that part of man that takes cognizance of the imperfect and incomplete; we enter a realm that never knew anything less than absolute, divine perfection, and therefore when we are in that realm we can know no evil. In the cosmic state our eyes are too pure to see evil, and the mind too high in divine consciousness to even think of evil. We are thinking the thoughts of the Infinite and everything we are conscious of is manifesting the shining glory of the Most High. In the cosmic state we think the truth, the absolute truth, because in that state everything is the expression of absolute truth. Therefore, the more frequently we enter into the realization of cosmic consciousness the more fully will the mind discern the truth, and the more readily can we think the truth whatever the field of our thought may be.

There are many minds that think that they have frequent experiences in cosmic consciousness, but not all of these have judged those experiences correctly. The great within is filled with wonderful realms of every description, and some have mistaken one or more of these realms for the home of the soul when the body has been removed. Many have thought they have seen heaven after beholding the gorgeous splendor of these inner realms, while others, after meeting the beautiful thoughts that take human shape in the great within, believe they have conversed with angels. But this is not the cosmic world. Though we may find peace and joy and ecstasy without measure in many of these beautiful interior realms, still we also find imperfection in one or more of its many forms. We do not forget evil while we are in the ecstasy of the great within; nor do we become unconscious of everything but that which is pure shining divinity. This, however, is precisely what happens when we are in the cosmic state; we meet only that which is wholly in the likeness of God, and our joy at times becomes so great that our feelings cannot contain themselves. Our cup overflows and the person bursts forth in tears. We have found that for which we have waited and prayed so long; we are inwardly moved as never before, and it is but natural that the person should weep for joy. We have found eternal life, we have felt His presence, we have touched the hem of His garment, we have met Him face to face.

The Pathway of Roses

The greater number of those who are spiritually inclined are almost constantly on the verge of the cosmic state, and at intervals they receive glimpses of that wondrous world. Could they but see themselves at such moments, they would discover that their faces are also shining as the sun, for their minds are illumined with radiant glory from on high. But such moments do not usually come when the senses expect them, nor can they be produced at will. We gain glimpses of the cosmic only when the soul occupies the supreme state in consciousness, and we begin to live within the pearly gates of the cosmic when the soul has gained full supremacy in every domain in consciousness. Therefore, to attain cosmic consciousness, we must give the spiritual life the first place in everything; we must do everything to the glory of God, and follow the light of the spirit in everything we may think or do. The eye must be single, and to see and to know only that which is wholly divine must be the one supreme desire.

The ruling spirit in the cosmic world is divine perfection; therefore the more we think of divine perfection, and the more we try to see divine perfection in all things, the more we develop the consciousness of divine perfection; and the development of this form of consciousness will finally culminate in divine consciousness which is synonymous with cosmic consciousness. To keep the eye single upon the great truth that every creation of God is good is to draw nearer and nearer to that state where we became conscious only of the absolutely good; then follows the limitless joy of the cosmic world. But when we permit the eye to become double, and begin to see the evil as well as the good, the unreal as well as the real, we fall from our lofty state; and this is the only fall of man. When we partake of the fruit from the tree of the knowledge of good and evil, we fall from the cosmic world, and we have to leave paradise. We cannot live in the garden of bliss, in the joys of cosmic consciousness, so long as we know evil as well as good; but when we become unconscious of evil, with the eye single upon His supreme goodness alone, then the gates of paradise shall open for us once more. Then we shall forget everything but that which is good and beautiful and true; we shall enter the new heaven and the new earth, the new heaven in the within, and the new earth in the without, and while still in personal form we shall live in the cosmic world.

To rise daily into a higher and better understanding of the reality of the cosmic state of existence is to become conscious, more and more, of the real sweetness of existence. Life becomes so rich and so beautiful that to live is in itself absolutely sufficient. In the cosmic state every moment seems to be an eternity of bliss, and every movement of consciousness produces a million pleasures. In comparison, the joys of sense have no significance whatever. Therefore, when the mere living of life gives all the joy that heart and soul may desire, it is evidence conclusive that the cosmic state has been reached; and the joys that are to follow, the soul on the heights alone can know.

The cosmic world is that highly refined, spiritualized world all about us, permeating everything, encompassing everything; the great divine sea in which we live and move and have our being; a world of pure light, gorgeous splendor and celestial brilliancy. The cosmic world is the world sublime; it is everywhere, and we live in it now and eternally, but only those who are spiritually awakened can discern its reality and behold the shining glories of its fair transcendent realms. When the true spiritual awakening begins we discover the cosmic world, and we enter cosmic consciousness. The heavens are opened and the vision before us reveals splendors and glories that tongue can never describe, joys that cannot be measured, and life that is a million heavens in one.

The Pathway of Roses

When we are in the cosmic state the entire world is clothed with the sun; the waters of the deep reflect the radiant glory of celestial kingdoms, and the mountains proclaim the majesty and the power of the life that is lived on the heights. Nature sings the everlasting praises of Him who is closer than breathing, nearer than hands and feet, and every human countenance beams with the beautiful smile of God. The flowers declare the thoughts of the Infinite: the forest chants the silent prelude to worship, while the birds inspire the soul to ascend to the vast empyrean blue. We are speechless with ecstasy, but as we behold the beauty and glory of it all the spirit within speaks from out the fullness of the heart and sweetly proclaims in language divine — "God's beautiful gift to me."

There is an upper realm in the spiritual life of man where the reality and perfection of divine existence is revealed. In this realm all is truth, all is purity, all is love. To enter this realm is to become conscious of eternal truth and understand the truth as it manifests everywhere. In the cosmic state the spiritual understanding of truth is complete, therefore every step in the spiritual understanding of truth is a step towards cosmic consciousness. All understanding is spiritual that discerns the spirit of truth as well as the reality of truth; and the mind develops in the discernment of truth when every effort to understand truth enters into the very innermost life of truth. When you think of truth, think of the spirit of truth; that is, that spiritual life or soul that is within truth; and desire with all the power of life, thought and feeling to enter into the soul of truth. To enter into the soul of truth is to enter into the cosmic state, and you not only gain an illumined understanding of the truth itself, but you become conscious of the entire cosmic world. The heavens are opened, for I AM the door, the way, the truth — the spirit of truth.

The Pathway of Roses

To enter the cosmic state is to become conscious of that divinity within us that is too pure to behold anything but that which is absolute purity. "To the pure all things are pure," and in the cosmic state we become pure; we enter into the world of shining purity; we do not recognize evil, and to us, iniquity has no significance whatever. While we are in the cosmic state we are in a pure state and can know only the boundless world of sublime purity that is all about us and all within us everywhere. Therefore, to enter the cosmic state the mind must be pure; that is, the mind must face the divinity that is in all things, and must, at all times, keep the eye single upon the shining purity of that divinity.

The cosmic realm is filled through and through with love, and to enter this realm is to love every living creature with all the power of heart and soul. When you are in the cosmic state you are in the universal; all life is divine to you; all life is beautiful, all life is precious, all life is sacred; your sympathy is as large as the universe and as touching as the innermost tenderness of the soul. To love everybody, no matter what they are or what they have done, is a part of your own life. You are above personal conditions; you are above personal deeds; you can see through the imperfect and behold the shining glory that reigns supremely in all that is. You see the divine reality in all things and you love it with all the tenderness of heart and soul. This divine loveliness in all things is the all in all in all things; to you it is beautiful, "fairer than ten thousand to the soul."

To love in the spirit of the universal is not to disregard the person. You love the person infinitely more because when you are in the cosmic every atom in the person is glorified with the presence of Him who is closer to life than breathing, nearer than hands and feet. You love the person because all that is true in that person is the coming forth of the divine. That which may not be true you do not see; your eyes are too pure to behold iniquity; besides, the imperfect in any person is insignificant and does not belong to the real person himself. Even in the most sinful of persons the evil is but a fragment compared with the good that is inherent in every fiber of his being. Take the worst person in the world and you will find the good and the right in him a thousand times greater than the wrong. When you are awakened to the truth you know this; therefore it becomes so easy to love; and since your heart is simply overflowing with love, you must love — love everything and everybody. And what a supreme joy is found in such a love.

To enter the cosmic state and develop cosmic consciousness, the soul must be given perfect freedom to love in the universal. It is a part of the life of the soul to love everything in existence, therefore the physical senses must not interfere with this love by impressing the mind to think that some things are evil and not worthy of love. Everything is worthy of love because in everything the good is infinitely greater than that which appears not to be good. The senses must be trained to recognize this great truth and the mind must be trained to harmonize all thinking with the sublime desires of the soul. When you meet a person see the all in all in that person; you will then see the shining purity of divine loveliness animating every fiber of his being; his countenance will be glorified before you, and you will love him with that beautiful love that reigned in the tenderness of the Christ. Meet all things in this sublime spiritual attitude, and the material veil will be removed more and more until all the splendors of the cosmic world are revealed to your vision.

To develop cosmic consciousness, place yourself in the hands of higher power. Depend upon higher power in all things; do nothing without first calling upon higher power; and so live that every thought, word and action is inspired by the spirit of higher power. Feel that higher power is always with you; deeply desire higher power to direct you, and open consciousness so completely to the limitless life of higher power that you actually realize that you live, move and have your being in the infinite power of the Most High. To enter the cosmic state you must transcend all belief in limitations; you must enter the universal where you clearly discern that all things are possible, for God is everywhere; and when your life is filled through and through with the presence of higher power you are lifted to the mountain tops of this lofty state. You rise above personal conditions and enter the limitless — where life is limitless, where power is limitless, where truth is limitless, where light is limitless, where the good is limitless, where love is limitless — where everything is limitless; and that is the cosmic world.

To live by faith is another supreme essential in the attainment of this sublime state. It is the very nature of faith to go out upon the limitless, and wherever faith may go, better things, higher things and greater things are found than were ever known before. Faith invariably leads upward and onward; faith always inspires the soul to ascend; while the spirit of faith illumines the way. To enter into the true spirit of faith, have faith in the innermost life of faith. There is a hidden power in faith; this power is the power of the Infinite; it is the soul of faith, the spirit of faith, and is eternally one with the spirit of the Most High. To enter into the spirit of faith is to enter into the spirit of the Most High, and thus be filled through and through with the power of the Most High. And this is the reason why all things are possible to him who has faith.

When you use the power of faith, have faith with the spirit of faith. You thus enter into the real power of faith and the illumined world of faith. In consequence, you not only gain the power to make all things possible, but you also enter into the spiritual light, and in the spiritual light the shining glory of the cosmic is revealed. To have faith with the spirit of faith, think of that supreme spiritual life and power that is in faith. Mentally dwell upon this inner life of faith, and whenever you use your faith, which should be every moment of existence, enter into the spirit of faith with all the power of feeling, thought and soul. You thus place yourself in perfect spiritual touch with the world of celestial light, with, the world of divine wisdom, with the world of eternal life, with the world of limitless power, with the world of shining purity, with the world of that love that loves everything and everybody with the most touching tenderness of the Most High. You are in the Mind that was in Christ Jesus; you are in the same Spirit that He was when His face did shine as the sun and His garment became white as the light.

Poise and Power

Poise and Power

Table of Contents

Chapter 1 -   470
Chapter 2 -   473
Chapter 3 -   476
Chapter 4 -   480
Chapter 5 -   485
Chapter 6 -   491
Chapter 7 -   496
Chapter 8 -   502
Chapter 9 -   507
Chapter 10 -   512
Chapter 11 -   519
Chapter 12 -   524

Poise and Power

Chapter 1

WHATEVER we wish to attain or accomplish, power is required: and since it is our privilege as well as our desire to attain much and accomplish much, any method through which we may increase our power will naturally receive our most direct and most thorough attention.

The newest science of life has discovered such a method, and it is the purpose of the following pages to elucidate its principles and laws so perfectly that anyone can apply them with the greatest possible results.

The method under consideration we shall call Poise, because Poise conserves energy, and conserved energy accumulates energy.

The path to increase is to save what you now receive, and to constructively use what you have saved. This we accomplish through Poise.

When we attain Poise, all the energy generated in the system is saved; that is, all loss and waste is prevented. This fact means much — so much that months of experience may be required to realize its import in full.

Some conception of the value of being able to save all the energy generated in the system will be gained when we learn that the average person loses from three fourths to nine-tenths of this power. Even the mental giants in the world are actually wasting nearly three-fourths of the energy generated in their systems. The one-fourth which is saved and employed makes them great: then what might they not become if they saved and employed all this power?

Poise and Power

The human personality may well be termed a living dynamo, because the amount of energy generated in the average healthy person is simply enormous. We may therefore predict great things for the race when the art of saving and using all this power is learned.

But the importance of the subject does not end with attainment and achievement; in fact, the art of saving one's power is of value in every department of human activity.

Modern physiological research has demonstrated conclusively that it is practically impossible for anyone to become sick so long as the system is full of energy. And it has traced the great majority of the ordinary human ills to one cause — lack of vital force.

It is therefore evident that sickness •could be wholly prevented had we some method through which all the energy generated in the system could be saved; because there is enough energy generated in the average person to perform several times as much physical or mental labor as the average person does perform. At the same time he can keep the •entire personality full to the brim with vital force.

These are startling facts; and since Poise will prevent all waste and loss of vital power, there can be nothing that is more important than the attainment of Poise.

When we enter the field of industry and witness the numerous failures on every hand, we find more evidence to prove that our subject is one which deserves the most profound attention; because is not a large number of these failures due to a lack of mental capacity;. and is not mental incapacity almost invariably caused by a lack of energy?

When the system is full of energy, physical endurance and mental capacity will both increase; and the mind with' its faculties and talents will be constantly pushed forward. The result cannot be otherwise than advancement and greater success.

The energy generated in the system, when saved, will push the individual, forward to higher attainments and greater achievements, even though nothing else be done to promote progress.

Everybody knows through experience that nothing can hold down the person who is literally charged with enormous energies, and we are all being charged every hour with enormous energies, but we do not retain them. We let nine tenths of this power slip away because we have not acquired Poise.

Power simply must press on to greater things; and he who is full of power will positively enjoy the privilege of continuous advancement.

Add to the possession of power the constructive use of power and we have the real secret of greatness.

Chapter 2

Poise may be defined as peace and power combined; a state of being wherein you feel perfectly serene and exceedingly strong at the same time. Why peace and power must combine in the formation of Poise is very evident when we realize that all disturbed action of power means loss of power.

The mere act of being quiet, however, is not sufficient to prevent the loss of power. A quiet person is not any stronger than a restless or strenuous person.

The fact that both peace and power may exist in the system at the same time does not prove that the person has Poise, nor that any power is being saved. To acquire Poise, peace and power must combine in consciousness, and not simply exist, side by side.

A person may undertake to live the serene life, and may become so quiet in mind that a large number of the faculties become dormant. During all this time enormous energies are being generated in his system; but his peace has not been united with his power; therefore, the power is lost.

Power is saved and Poise attained only when the energies of the system work in a state of calm. It will therefore be seen that practically all the mental and physical actions of the average person are wasteful. Even the three most valuable actions of mind in the formation of advancement scatter forces to an extent that is startling. These three are ambition, enthusiasm and determination; all indispensable, but most detrimental, as ordinarily employed.

The ambition that is not calm produces a stir in the mind by a letting loose of mighty forces. A sudden determination to do something remarkable is usually a similar phenomena, and is followed by reactions of "what's the use."

Periodical outbursts of enthusiasm belong in the same category; simply another way of getting rid of energy that we do not know how to hold nor employ. When the natural enthusiast acquires Poise and learns how to use his powers constructively, he will become a genius.

All forms of nervous feeling and nervous action indicate a lack of Poise, and are therefore channels through which a great deal of energy is lost.

That phase of joy which is usually called ecstasy is another channel through which energy slips away; and the fact that practically all emotional minds run frequently into ecstasy, makes the matter serious indeed.

That we should lose energy by being happy may not be pleasant to think of; but since ecstasy is not true happiness, we are far better off without it.

All forms of passion and nearly all ordinary expressions of love waste energy to a great degree; another fact that may not seem altogether pleasant; but since no action of mind is true unless it is in Poise, we do not love with true love unless we love in Poise.

When we learn to love in Poise we shall never return to the old, semi-insane, wasteful method, with its shallow, fleeting joys and its pangs of misery and despair.

When we love in Poise there is neither pain nor disappointment; and the joys are as deep as life itself.

Poise and Power

To desire in the present those things which we cannot gain possession of in the present is a cause of waste and loss that is practically without an equal. The reason is readily understood when we learn how universal is the habit of desiring what we cannot get.

Why this habit wastes energy is due to the fact that whenever we desire anything, a great deal of force rushes to that organ in the body or that faculty of the mind, that would be gratified should the desire be granted. When the desire is not granted, all this energy finds itself on a fool's errand. There is nothing to act upon; and if the mind does not know how to transmute those energies and call them back into use elsewhere, they are lost.

The habit of desiring what we cannot get must not be confounded with aspiration, or the desire for constant improvement; because in the latter we are daily working up towards the goal in view, while in the former we simply desire, doing nothing to reach what lies beyond.

There is only one true course for desire, and that is the constant improvement of yourself. Such an attitude of mind gives all the energies of the system something to work for now; and the energies that are put to work are never lost.

As the individual improves himself, better and better things will constantly come to him of themselves. He will not have to desire better things; he will daily attract better things, because he is daily becoming better.

Chapter 3

One of the first essentials in the attainment of Poise is to gain conscious control of the circulation; the object being to establish a perfect equilibrium among all the vital functions of the system.

Poise is not possible so long as the circulation is too weak in some parts of the system, and too strong in other parts; therefore, the mind must learn to control and regulate the circulation according to the requirements of a balanced state.

That the mind can increase or decrease the circulation in any part of the system is a well known fact; and since a great deal can be gained through this accomplishment, every effort should be made to perfect it to the highest degree.

To control the circulation the mind should not use will-force, but should concentrate with feeling upon that part of the body where an increase of the circulation is desired. When a decrease of the circulation is desired anywhere, attention should be directed to the opposite side, or opposite extremity of the body.

When you are in a "keyed up" condition, too much blood is being drawn to the brain; the equilibrium of the system is disturbed and you are entirely out of Poise. The result is a great loss of energy as well as the formation of a number of undesirable conditions.

To overcome this condition, direct the entire attention upon the feet, and gently pass thought vibrations down through the body. Mind should feel deeply and serenely during this process, and should hold in consciousness the thought of accumulation. In a few minutes a balanced state will be realized, and a fullness of life will be felt throughout the system.

There are a great many people who are "keyed up" nearly all the time; and there are many more who permit themselves to get into that state whenever anything extraordinary is about to transpire; but since the system is practically emptied of energy during such a state, no one can afford to permit even a slight tendency in that direction. When such tendencies are felt they should be counteracted by gently passing the circulation down through the body.

To hold the thought of accumulation during this process will prevent further loss at the time, because the energies always obey the desire of the predominating thought.

When you are in a dull, stupid, inactive state, the system is out of balance and you are out of Poise.

To overcome this condition, the circulation should be gently and moderately drawn towards the brain, until a condition of increased activity is being felt throughout the system.

To draw the circulation towards the brain, direct attention with deep feeling upon the back brain, and desire gently the forces of the system to move upwards. A few minutes practice is usually sufficient to restore normal activity. A dull condition of the system should never be permitted for a second, because it not only means loss of energy, hut it indicates that disease of some kind is brewing. The threatening evil, however, can be "nipped in the bud" by the simple method just given.

A condition of weakness indicates that the system has so completely lost its Poise that it is unable to retain any of its power, and is consequently something which requires immediate attention.

The remedy is to concentrate upon the abdominal region, and cause the circulation to increase in the vital organs. Immediately this is done, there will be a sensation of returning strength, and if the process is continued at frequent intervals, the normal conditions will soon be restored.

Though you may be too weak to get out of bed in the morning, at noon you will be strong enough to go to your work, through the proper application of this method.

Whenever the circulation is in an unbalanced condition, we should try to restore equilibrium by these methods, and after a little practice we shall find that we can increase or decrease the circulation in any part of the body by simply wishing to do so.

In preserving the health this accomplishment will be found of extreme value; and in addition we shall learn to remove a number of physical conditions through which energy is wasted and lost.

Our object is to prevent all loss of energy; therefore, we must remove every cause of such loss. An unbalanced circulation is one of the most serious of these causes.

When we try to control the circulation, we shall find that we always have results during states of mind that are very deep in feeling and absolutely still. Therefore, when such states are realized we should watch carefully the mental steps that were taken in bringing about that realization. We will thus discover a way of our own, which is always the best way.

Poise and Power

Results in the control of the circulation are indicated by an increase of warmth in that part of the body where our attention is directed; and also by a delicate sensation of energy accumulating in the same place.

Though there are nearly a score of direct benefits to be derived from the conscious control of the circulation, our principal purpose in the application of this art should be to prepare the system for perfect Poise, and the greater power which will positively follow.

Chapter 4

Cultivate the calm attitude. Learn to pass through all kinds of experiences without deviating for a moment from the true state of living serenity.

All forms of restlessness waste energy, and must, be overcome ere perfect Poise can be attained. The same is true of everything that agitate mind, or disturbs consciousness.

It is possible to reach a state where nothing disturbs you; and it is possible to live constantly in that state while being in the very midst of the hustle and bustle of the industrial world.

This state is not attained by a deadening of the sensibilities; because a mastery of the forces of life always causes the sensibilities to become finer and keener than ever before. You are consequently aware of everything, but disturbed by nothing. The harmony of your life is so deep, so positive and so strong that discord cannot affect it.

To attain this serene state, be absolutely quiet for twenty minutes every day, or twice a day if possible. Do not simply be quiet; try to feel the life and the power of the calm state. It is not the peace that is simply still that we seek, but the peace that is both strong and still.

During this exercise picture in mind the most perfect conception that you can form of the calm attitude, and mentally feel that you are in that attitude. After a few days you will begin to become conscious of the serene state. This means that the serene state is being established in you.

The value of mind-picturing in this connection is very great, as it is in nearly everything that we accomplish in life.

We may not have thought of it before, but the fact is that practically everything that has ever been done by man, began in a mental picture.

Mind-picturing is rapidly becoming a great art, and those who neglect to study its principles will be left in the rear.

Before you attempt to enter this quiet state, relax body and mind; turn attention upon the depth of your being, knowing that the depth of your own being is still — absolutely still, just as the depths of the sea.

After giving a few moments to the deep silence within, give up your entire personality to the silent thought that will naturally follow; but never try hard to be quiet. The serene state comes through the absence of trying. We reach this state not by trying to be still, but by being still.

In this connection it is well to remember that the greatest capacity of mind comes from the strong, silent life force; and that this life force comes into expression only when we are in the calm attitude.

The idea that one must become strenuous in order to do things should be eliminated completely, because it is the opposite to the truth. The mind that remains constantly in a serene state will do a great deal more work in a day than the mind that is strenuous; and what is better still, the serene mind will do better work and live much longer.

The reason is that the serene mind not only saves its power for actual, constructive work, but is also in touch with the depths of real life; and there is nothing that has greater power than real life.

Twenty minutes taken once or twice a day for the purpose of being absolutely quiet, will if properly employed, produce the calm attitude in a few weeks, after which it will be second nature to be always serene.

Every night before going to sleep, concentrate quietly upon the brain center for a few minutes. During this process gently draw all the finer forces of the mind towards this center. The effect of this method is truly remarkable, not only in a general way, but in several particulars.

All forms of nervousness can be cured with this method, and it has never been known to fail in the cure of insomnia. It is a present help in the overcoming of all "kinds of physical or mental disturbances, and can cure all kinds of aches and pains of the head almost instantly.

It is a well-known fact that all kinds of nervousness, including nervous prostration, are produced by discordant vibrations in the nerve-forces; and that all these nerve-forces proceed from the brain center. Therefore, when a mental state of perfect peace and harmony is concentrated upon the brain-center, the vibrations of the nerve forces will be made harmonious. The result will be relief in a few moments, with perfect harmony throughout the entire system.

Nervousness wastes energy to an enormous extent; therefore, if we wish to save our power we must proceed to remove this condition at once. The method just presented will absolutely remove every trace of nervousness and is so simple that anyone can apply it correctly.

The brain center may be located as a point midway between the opening of the ears; or at that point where the spinal cord unites with the brain. Nerve force is generated in

Poise and Power

the brain and passes from the brain to the spinal cord, and thence to every part of the system.

The condition of the vibrations of this nerve-force is formed as the nerve-force passes from the brain to the spinal cord;: that is, at the brain center. Therefore, if we wish to change the vibrations of the nerve-force, we must act upon the brain center. Remember, as the vibrations of the nerve-forces are at the brain center, so they will be all through the: system.

It is, therefore, readily understood why nervousness will disappear from the entire system the very moment that peace and harmony are established at the brain center.

When concentrating upon the brain center, the object should be to impress the calm attitude in such a way that stillness is established throughout the depths; of mental action. That is, the entire center of the brain should be made calm to the very center of every atom. This, is accomplished by concentrating calmly with deep, serene feeling.

To gently draw all the finer forces of mind towards the brain center at the time is absolutely necessary, because it is quiet action that produces peace. When forces are made to act in calmness, they will produce calmness in that place where they are directed to act.

Should difficulty be met in drawing the finer mental forces towards the brain center, the cause is a lack of feeling. This may be corrected by gently thinking about those finer forces that permeate the substance of things. The mere thought of the finer forces will usually bring consciousness into touch with these forces; and whenever any force touches consciousness, it will follow the desire of attention without any effort being made in that direction.

To enable the beginner to apply this method at once, he may associate this concentration with physical breathing. While inhaling with the lungs make a gentle mental effort to draw the finer mental forces to the brain center. While exhaling with the lungs let the finer mental forces pass down through the body.

The physical breathing should be very quiet and easy, as well as deep and full.

To combine in this way the physical "breathing of oxygen with what might be called the mental breathing of finer energies is an exercise that cannot be equaled in value by anything that man can do. It is, therefore, the height of wisdom for everybody to learn this method perfectly and apply it constantly.

The best time is in the evening after you have retired, because the process will make the entire system so perfectly calm and restful that a most delightful sleep will follow.

The exercise, however, can be taken at any time during the day, and should be taken whenever a tendency to nervousness is felt. Any adverse condition in the nervous system can, in this way, be nipped in the bud, and the amount of energy that will be saved will be simply remarkable.

Chapter 5

The calm attitude is indispensable to the attainment of Poise, but the fact that the calm attitude has been attained does not prove that Poise has been acquired.

Poise is more than serenity: it is a serenity which is filled with a strong inner life. Therefore, when you are in Poise, you not only feel perfectly calm, but you also feel immensely strong. And it is perfectly natural that you should feel immensely strong while in Poise. You could not feel otherwise while all the energies in your system are being retained.

This fact gives us a simple method for ascertaining whether we are in Poise or not, and will enable us to correct the matter at once.

Since our object is to hold in the system all the energy that is generated in the system, it will be necessary to practice the art of holding energy until this "holding attitude" becomes subconscious, or second nature.

Consequently, a few moments should be taken at frequent intervals for the purpose of trying to hold in the system all the energy generated in the system.

The method is simple and consists in expressing a deep, quiet feeling throughout the system, with the idea of "holding" all the power that you feel.

After a few moments of this practice, the consciousness of added power is realized; sometimes becoming very strong. When a great deal of power accumulates in this way, it is well to direct it to some part of the body or brain that you wish to develop. This is done by concentrating attention upon those parts.

Poise and Power

When trying to hold energy in the system the results will increase considerably if the mind is made to think serenely in every part of the entire personality. In other words, think with every fiber in your being. Think serenely; think the holding of power; think Poise.

When full consciousness is attained, one will naturally think with the entire personality, and not simply with the brain. Then it is that one will develop a powerful mind. Then it is that genius will begin.

By expressing deep, serene thought in the entire personality while trying to hold the energy generated in the system, three great things will be accomplished. The process of holding the energy will be promoted to a very great degree; the mind will be trained to think through the entire personality; and the mind will gain conscious control of energy in every part of the system.

The last accomplishment is of extreme importance, because to attain perfect Poise the mind must control every part of the system. This is possible only when the mind thinks in every part of the system.

Such thinking, however, must not be superficial, but must be of the heart; that is, it must be subconscious thought.

To learn to think subconsciously, concentrate attention upon the substance of the personal life. Try to consciously feel the real essence of your being.

To express such thought throughout the entire personality will also produce what may be called interior action — the deep feeling of real life. This is extremely important because it is the real life, the calm, strong, invincible life that is the actual foundation of Poise.

When subconscious thinking begins, the imagination will become far more active, a fact which must be dealt with wisely; because the imaging process is creative, and creation employs energy.

Whenever we imagine anything we create images in mind that are in the exact likeness of that which we imagine; imagination is therefore plainly seen to be a creative process. But is this creative process of any value? If nothing comes of it, both energy and time have been wasted. It is a fact to be remembered that the average mind wastes an enormous amount of energy through useless and aimless imagination.

To prevent this loss, we must learn how to use the imagination constructively; to image only those things in mind which we wish to retain as permanent factors in our advancing existence.

To imagine that something is taking place that is not taking place is to create an artificial structure for the purpose of tearing it down again — a pastime that seems both innocent and harmless, but it wastes energy to a degree that is startling; there are millions of minds that indulge in it daily.

To image upon mind the inferior side, the imperfect side, the dark side, or the disagreeable side of anything, is to create mental structures that will ever be an obstacle to the welfare and the growth of the individual. Therefore, this practice not only uses up creative energy for nothing, but in addition creates mental states that are against us in every shape and form.

To imagine ourselves in the past or in the future is also to use energy to no good purpose. We are not in the past; therefore, to create mental structures after the likeness of past events is to create something which we cannot use, and which will have to be torn down. Neither are we in the future; and since we do not know in detail what the future is to be, we cannot picture anything in mind that will be true to our future. Therefore, what we now imagine about the future will have to be taken out of mind as a false structure, when the future comes.

It is not necessary to illustrate any further. The fact that imagination employs energy is sufficient to cause every mind to exercise caution in the use of the imagination henceforth; and to never permit the imaging faculty to construct what is neither real nor possible now.

To employ the imagination constructively, image yourself in mind as you desire to become through orderly development. Image all your faculties and talents as they are in the ideal and perfect sense; picture upon mind the larger, the higher, and the better of everything that now exists in your life.

By this process energy will be employed in promoting advancement, growth and progress. It is a joy to know that energy employed in this way is not really used up, because the more we advance, the larger becomes our conscious scope of life; and the more life we are conscious of, the more life and power we gain possession of.

Therefore, to use energy for the purpose of growth and progress is to multiply energy. The law is, "to him that hath, shall be given." We shall understand this law perfectly when we realize that we possess in consciousness only that which we constructively employ.

Poise and Power

Since our object is higher attainments and greater achievements, it must necessarily be our desire to constructively employ everything that comes into our states of existence. For this reason we must learn to hold in the system all the energy that is generated in the system; to have it ready for the hour of extraordinary action.

The secret of great achievement is to hold all energy in Poise until required; and when required, to direct it through concentration into the proper mental channel.

The advancing mind may be called upon to do something remarkable at any time: therefore, it is the height of wisdom to learn how to hold all the power in the system so that there will be abundance of energy to apply when the occasion demands.

After we have employed, with thoroughness, the various methods for holding energy in the system, we shall find that a great deal of energy will begin to remain naturally in the system; and it is then that we shall begin to become conscious of real Poise.

Such consciousness will aid remarkably in the further promotion of Poise, because when we learn what Poise really feels like, the mere thought of Poise will increase the Poise. We shall then find more evidence to prove the great law, "to him that hath shall be given."

It is therefore of the highest importance to learn to detect the attitude of Poise, and to attain a fuller and deeper realization of this attitude.

Poise holds in the system all the energy generated in the system; consequently, by frequently trying to hold this energy you steadily work yourself into the attitude of complete Poise.

Chapter 6

Be virtuous in thought and action. The gain of power through virtue is truly remarkable.

Never think of sex relations; to do so will turn energy towards functions that cannot be used now, and all such energy is lost.

Energy should be turned only into those organs, functions and faculties which can make constructive use of energy now; therefore, no thought should be given to functions which must of necessity remain inactive. There may come a time when these functions can be used legitimately and properly; and when that time comes, energy may be turned into those functions, but not before.

If you are unmarried, never think of sex at any time. Never permit even a mental tendency toward such desires. Every time you think of sex, a certain amount of sex desire will be expressed; and the expression of such desires mean that creative energy will flow towards the sex-functions. But what becomes of this energy?

The law is that all energy that, is caused to accumulate in a function that is not' used, is lost. It is therefore evident that an enormous amount of energy is lost through the lack of virtuous thought.

In the average person there is a subconscious tendency to give up a certain amount of energy every day to the sex-function. Through this tendency energy is constantly flowing into the sex-function, to be utterly wasted and lost. We are not making extravagant assertions when we declare that a very large number of people lose nearly one-half of their energies in this way. We are also keeping strictly within the bounds of fact when we declare that the world would have ten times as many great minds as now if real virtue was generally lived. By real virtue we mean the prevention of all loss of energy from the sex-function.

To bring about this complete prevention, three things are necessary. All illegitimate sex relations, physical or mental, must be discontinued entirely. No thought of sex should be permitted whatever, except during actual, legitimate sex-relations. The subconscious tendency to cause a constant flow of creative energy towards the sex-functions must be overcome.

The first essential is not at all difficult to comply with. This is demonstrated by the fact that nearly all unmarried women, and a great many unmarried men do comply with it already. The second essential may be more difficult, because it is easier to control action than thought. However, this second essential simply must be complied with because every thought of sex deprives the system of energy. The third essential can be complied with through transmutation only, which will be considered in another chapter.

Subconscious tendencies can be changed or reversed only through subconscious action; and the required subconscious action in this case is transmutation.

The subconscious tendency under consideration is hereditary to a greater or lesser extent in everybody, but is intensified by every unvirtuous thought that the individual may create.

Being hereditary, and quite deep seated in the subconscious life, persistent effort will be required to remove it; but the recompense for such effort will be very large. In the average case it will mean that physical strength and mental capacity will be nearly doubled.

If you are married, reserve all thought of sex for the hour of true and legitimate functioning. At all other times refuse absolutely to think of sex. Keep mind in a pure, virtuous attitude under all circumstances, and counteract all impure suggestions with the thought of spotless virtue.

To be conscious of virtue is to save a great deal of power, because through such consciousness a tendency to retain all the creative energies in the system is established.

When we feel the real life of virtue, the mere thought of virtue will add power to the system. Such thought will also neutralize the temporary effect of every unvirtuous suggestion that may be met in the outer world.

When you meet people, never permit yourself to think of whether they are males or females. Meet people as people; or rather, as minds with unbounded possibilities. Whether they express themselves as masculine personalities or as feminine personalities should not concern you. Your object is to associate with the superior side of all personalities that you may enter into a deeper sympathy and a higher understanding of everything that has quality and worth.

This leads us to another phase of human relationships — the meeting of mind with mind; and it is a study of the first importance in the attainment of Poise.

When we meet other minds, a certain degree of mental activity takes place. Since all action employs power, the nature of such mental activity will determine whether this power is to be lost or no.

Poise and Power

There are only two ways of meeting other minds: the one is to meet them in a state of sympathetic harmony; the other is to meet them in a state of cold resistance. True, there are many grades and vibrations of these two, but they are all modifications of one of the two.

When we resist we lose energy; all fighting attitudes are wasteful. Even righteous indignation, as it is called, destroys as much vital power as ordinary anger. The same is true of all antagonistic attitudes, arguments and disputes. Never argue with anyone. Nothing is ever gained through arguments or disputes, where mind is arrayed against mind; but much is lost, because all such attitudes of mind scatter forces.

Be in harmony with all things and all persons at all times. Relate yourself harmoniously to all circumstances and conditions and be at peace with all creatures, all elements and all forces.

When you are out of harmony you are out of Poise.

When antagonistic forces are felt, they should never be permitted to follow their inclinations. The tendencies should be turned, and the energies directed into channels of construction. When on the verge of anger, think of something you love, and your power will be saved. When on the verge of fear or anxiety, have faith. When people present their inferior side, make a special effort to see the superior side. When things seem to go wrong, enter into mental contact with the ideal, which is always right. In brief, be in harmony, regardless of what may transpire.

When "trying" occasions are met, the perfect Poise will be tested. If we come out victorious, Poise will be more firmly established than it ever was before. It is therefore to our advantage to meet such occasions, if they are met in the right way; and the right way is to hold attention upon deep thought and feeling. So long as thought is in deep feeling, we can remain in Poise, providing we are conscious of Poise, no matter how trying or adverse the circumstances may be. However, the very moment we permit thought to run towards the surface, Poise will be lost.

This state of deep consciousness or feeling is one of the characteristics of Poise; therefore, so long as attention is held in deep thought, mind will be in the attitude of Poise.

This attitude of deep, "serene thinking is indispensable to harmony while we are in contact with other minds, because everything that comes from another mind has the tendency to modify the attitude of our minds. But it is only the surface states of mind that can be modified at first by what comes from without; therefore, by remaining in the attitude of deep, serene thought, Poise will be retained and nothing can change our way of thinking or acting unless we give conscious permission. Neither can anything disturb our equilibrium at any time.

Chapter 7

Be composed and self-possessed. Forget the outer self by thinking deeply about the inner self. This is extremely important, because complete self-possession is the result of mild surface action, and a full, strong, serene interior action.

To forget the outer self does not mean to ignore the objective and the physical life, but to establish the center of conscious action in the larger interior life. What we become conscious of, that we shall express; therefore, when we consciously live in the larger, interior life, we shall express a larger measure of life, and consequently the outer self will be far better supplied and cared for than if we lived on the surface.

In the attitude of complete self-possession the mind has full conscious control of every action of the personality, and can therefore prevent every unnecessary movement of thought or muscular activity.

It is a fact to be well remembered that every unnecessary movement of mind or body is an uncontrolled movement; and that every uncontrolled movement wastes energy. In the average person, restless, nervous, uncontrolled action is almost a habit, appearing especially in unnecessary movements of hands and feet. This is a lack of Poise and must be overcome.

However, when we try to remove unnecessary surface action, we are liable to be drawn to the opposite extreme and become too quiet. In this age, when the inner life is being studied so extensively, a great many arrive at the conclusion that the serene life is the only true life. This conclusion is based upon the discovery that the higher consciousness can be attained only through the perfect calm; but though the perfect calm is necessary to the attainment of any larger or higher state of mind or consciousness, still, the perfect calm alone will not bring these things.

Too many students of the new life have aimed at simply becoming quiet, acting upon the belief that both wisdom and power will come in the silence; but in their efforts in this direction they have overlooked one of the greatest principles of attainment in existence, viz: no attainment is possible without power; and power cannot act constructively unless it acts in peace.

A person may become quiet in a superficial way without preventing in the least the constant waste of energy through the various sources mentioned. In this, quiet state he may expect to gain power, but no power will be gained until he stops the waste of power, and consciously unites peace with power.

We must remember that the consciousness of peace and the consciousness of power are two distinct states of consciousness. Though both states may exist in the mind at the same time, still, if they are separated nothing will be gained as far as the gaining of power is concerned.

The quiet person has the consciousness of peace: the strenuous person has the consciousness of power; but neither has Poise, and both are wasting their energies to an enormous extent. The strenuous person scatters his forces broadcast by forceful action; the quiet person fails to hold on to any of his energies and permits them to gently slip away.

When the consciousness of peace and the consciousness of power are united we have a new state of consciousness, and this consciousness is Poise.

Poise and Power

Therefore, when we proceed to change the center of consciousness from the plane of restless surface action to the plane of serene interior action, we must not forget to keep power in mind, as well as peace.

In this connection, the attitude of deep soul satisfaction should be cultivated to the fullest extent; also a state of uninterrupted contentment.

This may seem difficult to do when everything in life is the way we do not wish it to be; but we must remember that happiness does not come from circumstances or things.

Happiness does not come from having much, but from being much. And he who is much will inevitably possess much.

Contentment and soul satisfaction hold power in the system, and thus aid directly in giving the person the greater power required to make everything in life become the way he desires it to be.

Deep soul satisfaction will also promote the consciousness of Poise, and give to mind a clear conception of what Poise actually is. In other words, Poise will be felt; and we do not understand Poise until we feel it.

After we have felt Poise, we know the way to the mental attitude of Poise, and can successfully enter this attitude at any time and under any circumstance.

When we have learned to do this, we should always act in Poise, whether our work be physical or mental, or both. To act in Poise does not require slow, measured movements, as too many suppose. You can work with lightning speed and still be in Poise. In fact, the more perfect your Poise, the more rapidly you can work, and the higher will be the quality of your product.

It may appear to be a startling fact, nevertheless it is true, that when you work in Poise you will never feel tired, providing you secure eight hours sleep out of every twenty-four.

Always think in Poise, and feel every thought to be calm and strong. If every thought does not produce a calm, strong feeling in mind, you are out of Poise and are losing mental energy.

To think in Poise is a very high art, and will aid remarkably in developing ability and mental capacity. To cultivate this art, give the feeling of Poise to every thought, and gradually you will think more and more in Poise without trying to do so.

There are few attainments that are of greater value than to be able to speak in Poise. The public speaker who can speak in Poise will reach the very soul of his audience and every word will carry conviction. The same is true of the musician who can sing or play in Poise; also of the actor who can act in Poise. In our daily association with people we shall find that the word spoken in Poise is the word which produces the results desired. In brief, if we have to depend upon our voice for success, we shall never fail when we speak in Poise.

To cultivate this fine art, speak gently, calmly, and with serene power. It is not necessary to always speak slowly, but every word should have soul — a strong, silent soul.

Another great attainment is to be able to read in Poise; though the average person is never in Poise while he reads.

The cause of this is the habit of rushing through an article to get the main points, or skimming over as much matter as possible in a given time.

When we read something which is not interesting, we pass on as rapidly as possible to get through with it. When we read something which is interesting, we are constantly on tiptoe to discover what is coming next. The result is nervousness, restlessness, waste of energy, and the formation of tendencies which lead mind into the shallow, the superficial, and the inferior.

To cultivate the art of reading in Poise, select the best, or that which is absolutely necessary for you to read, and read very quietly at first. Realize that it is not how much you read that counts, but how much you gain from that which you do read. Express the feeling of Poise in every word that is mentally spoken, and try to discern the inner meaning of every statement made. This will develop depth of feeling in connection with your reading which is so necessary to the attainment of Poise.

In a very short time you will naturally enter the attitude of Poise whenever you take up something to read; and you will be able to read with considerable speed without losing your Poise in the least.

To read in Poise not only saves energy, but it develops depth of thought, lucidity of intellect, and evolves a much clearer understanding of that which is read.

Among all great attainments, that of going to sleep in Poise is by no means the least; because no one can fully gain that for which lie goes to sleep unless he goes to sleep in Poise. This is very important, as we cannot impress the subconscious with any satisfactory results unless we go to sleep in Poise.

Recent investigations have demonstrated the fact that the subconscious will respond to any idea or desire held in mind as we go to sleep; and also, that the great possibilities of the within can in this way be gradually brought into expression. But we must go to sleep in Poise to have these extraordinary results.

To go to sleep in Poise, relax mind and body; feel the soul of Poise, and realize the fullness of the silent life.

Chapter 8

The attitude of Poise demands perfect concentration, because all mental energies that are not concentrated are scattered; and scattered energies are always lost.

To be able to focalize all the power of mind and body upon the one thing that we desire to accomplish now is one of the greatest secrets of success; even more than that, it is indispensable. No one can succeed without concentration.

Thousands of brilliant minds have failed because they lacked in this one essential; while a great many ordinary minds have succeeded remarkably even in the midst of all kinds of obstacles, simply because they possessed a perfect concentration.

Before concentration can be developed, we must understand what it is: we must learn that it is not the mere fixation of will, nor the ability to hold thought riveted upon some object or subject as long as one may desire. Neither is concentration indicated by absentmindedness, nor the state of being oblivious to one's surroundings. In absentmindedness the mind wanders; and when the mind wanders, forces are scattered.

A tendency to absentmindedness indicates that attention is not under control, and consequently drifts at the call of suggestion or unconscious mentation. In concentration, however, the attention is under complete control of the conscious desires of mind, and can be focalized anywhere for almost any length of time, or changed to any other point instantaneously, without the slightest use of forced mental action.

True concentration is always smooth, easy, and even soothing in its effect, being absolutely free from "wrought up" or "strenuous" actions.

The purpose of concentration is to draw all the forces of the system into that faculty which is being used in the promotion of present objects; but this purpose is interfered with if forceful actions are employed. Let it be remembered that all forced actions of mind or body waste energy, because what is forced is scattered.

Another fact to be well remembered is that so long as we try to concentrate, we shall utterly fail to concentrate.

Concentration is not the result of trying, but of being: it is a state of consciousness that is not actual until it becomes permanent. The foundation of this state of mind is a wide-awake attention; not simply attention nor a wide awake mental state, but wide-awake attention. A mind may be wide-awake without giving particular attention to anything; and there are many grades of attention that are by no means wide awake.

The wide-awake mind is the mind that is in full action; and when this full action takes place in one single faculty we have perfect concentration. Concentration, therefore, implies undivided attention, and full mental action where the attention is directed.

To give undivided attention to any subject or object, a living interest must be taken in that subject or object. This is possible by viewing those things from an interesting point of view, then giving your whole life for the time being to the idea gained from that view.

There is something about every subject and every object that is extremely interesting to you, and you can find it by looking for it. Examine all sides with care, and that something which can positively attract your interest will appear.

To try to concentrate upon something in which you are not thoroughly interested is to waste energy as well as time. Therefore, to create interest is the first step. To employ time in finding the viewpoint of interest is to gain time.

To promote a full mental action where attention is directed — that is, to make that part of mind wide awake — consciousness should act in what might be called the upper story.

It is a well-known fact that all the forces of nature become finer, stronger and more rapid the higher they ascend in the scale; and the forces of mind, being natural, are no exceptions. Therefore, every action of mind should be expressed through the highest, the brightest and the finest mental vibrations that consciousness, in its present state of development, can discern.

Those actions of mind which are expressed through the finer feeling of thought, belong higher in the scale than ordinary objective thinking; consequently, if attention would always act through these finer feelings, we should permanently establish the wide-awake attitude. This is extremely important, because the wide-awake mind is not only in a superior state of ability, but is giving action to this ability.

To develop the faculty of being interested, direct attention upon something of interest every moment. This practice is most profitable, because everything develops through use.

Should you fail to find anything of interest at any particular moment, the mere fact that you are looking for an interesting point of view will keep the mind in a state of wide-awake interest, and your purpose in mind will accordingly be fulfilled.

While directing attention upon various points of interest just for practice, the point of interest may be changed as frequently as desired, though it is well to give attention to one subject as long as the interest is naturally full and strong, because this will develop the tendency to see everything through to a complete finish.

While concentrating upon the work we have in hand, it is well to seek the various points of interest connected with that work, and to give attention alternately among these various points. This will broaden the scope of attention, and consequently increase the capacity of the faculties employed. These changes of viewpoints, however, should not be too frequent, but how frequent, the individual must decide; the object being to promote a full, strong interest in every phase of the work, and to give our individual attention to every part when that part receives attention.

All objective or mechanical methods for developing concentration should be entirely avoided, because such exercises will simply tend to draw mind to the surface, and thus produce shallow thinking, as well as scattering and wandering mental states.

Real concentration has depth; therefore, to develop real concentration, depth of thought, depth of feeling and depth of consciousness must be employed. We must seek to enter into the spirit of things instead of simply gazing upon the surface of things.

When we realize that we are in touch with the spirit of that upon which we are directing our attention, we should give our whole life to that attention, and the development of real concentration will be thoroughly promoted.

Chapter 9

The object of concentration is to turn all the energy of the system into any channel desired so that the full power of mind and body may be given to the work in which we are engaged now. Experiments have demonstrated that all those forces in the system which do not follow fixed tendencies will, of themselves, accumulate wherever attention is directed. Therefore, those forces can be gathered at any time and at any place by simply concentrating in the proper way. But there are a great many forces in the system that follow fixed tendencies, and that flow steadily through the channels of these tendencies, practically undisturbed by the ordinary processes of thinking, feeling or acting. They are not affected by concentration. No matter how perfect concentration may be, they absolutely refuse to turn in their paths and go where attention may be directed.

This, however, is a serious matter, because a large amount of energy is hourly being thrown away through such tendencies that lead to the surface, towards inferiority, or towards functions that are not being used at present.

In a previous chapter we mentioned the fact that every person is born with the tendency to give a certain amount of energy every day to the sex-function, whether that function is being employed or not. We also stated that when the sex-function was not actually and legitimately employed, all such energy was lost. It is therefore evident that a certain amount of energy is constantly being lost through this tendency, whether the person be single or married, moral or immoral. And it has been demonstrated that some persons lose as much as one half of all the energy generated in their systems, through this one channel.

But this is not the only fixed tendency through which energy is lost. Every habit which exists for mere gratification is founded upon a tendency that leads energy away into nothing. Temper is another; worry still another; likewise, the tendency to become depressed at every indication of reverses.

The person who becomes angry whenever he is antagonized has a fixed tendency towards anger, and energy is being lost through this tendency every hour.

The person who worries whenever things look dark has a fixed tendency towards worry, and is hourly losing energy through this channel. The person who becomes easily depressed has a fixed tendency towards depression, and is every hour giving up energy to this channel of waste.

In this connection we must remember that every fixed tendency conveys energy: that is, energy is constantly flowing through every fixed tendency, and if the tendency is one of the many just mentioned, all that energy is being thrown away. Why the average person loses fully nine-tenths of his power is therefore easily understood.

Since concentration does not affect the forces which follow fixed tendencies, we must find something which does; because we cannot permit this great loss to go on.

The remedy is found in transmutation, which is the power to change forces into different rates of vibration.

The law is whenever any force changes its vibration it changes its channel of expression, and is at once distributed throughout the system; but it will readily follow any other tendency in mind that may be strong at the time. Therefore, through transmutation all the energies that are flowing away will be checked and converted into different forces, and be

Poise and Power

drawn into those new channels where concentration is acting at the time. In this way transmutation places all the forces in the system in the hands of concentration.

To the beginner, transmutation may seem to be something extremely difficult, if not impossible; but it is really very simple, and is of such extraordinary value that it should be mastered at once. The principle is to change the rate of the vibrations of all the forces in the system so as to divert their courses. This is done through a simple act of consciousness.

To proceed, realize fully that you are the supreme master of all the forces in your system, and that you can change them and direct them as you like. Have full faith and confidence in this conviction, keeping the idea before mind constantly for some days.

When you are ready to begin experiments, place yourself in a quiet attitude and remain perfectly still for some moments. Breathe deeply but quietly, and through the control of your mind produce a balanced condition of the circulation throughout the system. Then turn mind towards the subconscious, concentrating gently upon the deeper consciousness of life in every atom in your being. Picture in mind the life that permeates every fiber in the body and try to feel the mind that thinks in every part of this life. In other words, try to deeply feel the life that permeates your being. When this deeper feeling is felt, pass a wave of thought gently through your entire system, and when you feel that this thought-wave fills every part of the system, draw this thought-wave gently towards the deeper, finer life that permeates the system. Repeat this several times until you can actually feel the forces of your being responding to this deepening of thought.

When this is felt, turn your attention upon some faculty that you wish to develop, and concentrate with full interest in that direction. While doing so you can feel the system being filled with forces you never felt before, and you can also feel them moving with your attention, accumulating where attention is directed.

This practice taken every day will in a few weeks increase your power to a remarkable extent; and you will find that your false or perverted tendencies will have practically disappeared, of themselves. By turning the forces of these tendencies into other channels, the tendencies cease to be.

It is well, however, to give each perverted tendency special attention whenever it becomes active. Should you feel the inclination to worry, proceed at once with the process of transmutation, and when you feel the chemical change in the vibrations, enter into a deep interest in the attitude of cheer, brightness and faith. When you feel anger approaching, transmute the forces you feel and concentrate upon love, kindness and sympathy with the whole heart and soul. Whenever you feel the sex-function becoming active and you do not wish to employ that function at present, transmute the energies which you feel, directing your attention especially to those parts of the body where you feel the energies very active, and then gently draw all the refined forces towards other parts of the body, or to special parts of the brain. Such creative energies are very powerful, and to transmute them into physical vitality or mental force will prove most highly beneficial.

All these fixed tendencies are subconscious; therefore, these forces cannot be changed except through a change in the subconscious mind life. This is effected through the process just presented.

To remove a habit, take up the process of transmutation whenever the desire becomes strong; and when you feel a chemical change in the system, turn attention upon some other desire — some desire which you wish to cultivate.

No habit will remain in the system after the vibrations of the forces that expressed themselves through the habit have been changed. Likewise, the desires for certain unwholesome foods may be permanently removed. Discontinue taking those foods, and when you feel a desire for them, transmute all the energies of the system into finer subconscious vibrations and turn attention upon the desire for some food which is wholesome.

In fact, any desire can be removed in the same way. If you have a strong desire, or love for something or someone that you know cannot be fulfilled at present, you can remove that feeling, by transmutation. Anything can be changed in mind or body through transmutation. It is a marvelous art and is so simple that anyone can employ it. What is more, nothing but good can come from its use. The reason is that it works only towards the finer and the more perfect.

Chapter 10

To save energy, to accumulate energy, to transmute energy, and to concentrate energy — all these are desired because we wish to use energy; and we wish to use as much as we can possibly secure.

Our object in life is progress, advancement; but nothing moves forward without power — the constructive use of power.

To use power constructively is work; therefore, in the last analysis the purpose of Poise is to fit us for better work.

To the majority the term "work" means wear, tear and weariness; but it ought to mean pleasure, strength and development.

The industrial world is out of Poise; therefore, the waste is enormous, and the weariness is pitiful, while the laborer wears out like inanimate machinery. The majority imagine they are overworked and have good reasons, from the old point of view, for such conclusions; but the real trouble is not too much work; the real trouble is too little Poise.

So long as you are working in Poise, it is practically impossible to overwork. It is not work that furrows the brow, whitens the head, ages the body and weakens the mind; it is nervous rush. To work without Poise is one of the greatest mistakes of the age. The result is premature death to the worker and inferiority in the product.

The person who works always in Poise will live longer, accomplish more, do better work, improve constantly, and enjoy every moment of existence.

Poise and Power

When we work in Poise, works, gives strength, never weariness. This is a statement that may seem absurd, but you can prove it to be true.

Poise prevents all waste of energy; and to work in Poise will accumulate energy, because energy constructively employed multiplies itself.

When we are out of Poise, we dislike work, and work only because we have to. When we are in Poise, work is a pleasure, and we work because we want to.

If work is a drudgery to you, you are out of Poise, and are consequently losing nearly nine-tenths of your energy every day.

We view work as something that exhausts energy. We approach work fully expecting to become exhausted and tired; and what we expect generally comes, later, if not sooner.

The abnormal desire to get something for nothing, so prevalent in this age, is caused directly by the almost universal dislike for work. We dislike work because we do not know how to work. When we learn how to work, work will become our greatest pleasure, and we shall far rather work for what we require than get it for nothing.

The object of work is twofold; to produce something of worth; and to develop greater worth in the producer. The latter purpose has been wholly neglected, with detrimental results both to the artist and his art.

We must remember that the worth of the product increases as the worth of the producer is developed.

Poise and Power

Products of high quality bring high prices. It is therefore profitable, for the producer to develop himself perpetually. But the average person complains that he has no time for self-improvement; most of his time is required at his work, and when he is not working he is too tired for study. Such statements, however, indicate that Poise has not been discovered.

The fact is that when you work in Poise, all the faculties that you employ at your work can be developed while you work. Then when your evening comes you will not be too tired for study; you will not be tired at all; therefore, a few hours of study will be thoroughly enjoyed.

To work in Poise does not mean to work slowly. While you are in Poise you can work with great rapidity "without losing any power whatever. To work in Poise is to express all your energies through the attitude of supreme serenity.

The most powerful forces of nature, electricity in particular, move in absolute stillness, but with an enormous speed. The creative powers in man can do the same — would do the same if mind was always in Poise.

By working in Poise you can therefore supply both quality and quantity.

Should you be engaged in a work that is neither pleasant nor profitable, you will not remain long in that position after you have begun to work in Poise; because you will constantly improve and will soon be wanted elsewhere in a better place.

That improvement of mind and body should follow the constructive use of energy is perfectly natural; and to work in Poise is to employ all energy constructively.

Poise and Power

Exercise promotes development in every case; and what is work but exercise?

When we go to our work we expect to tear down the system; and through that attitude of mind we get out of Poise.

When we proceed to take gymnastic exercises for mind or body, we expect development — construction; and through that mental attitude we enter to a degree into Poise.

Any physical culturist who understands Poise knows that all exercises taken while the system is out of Poise are wholly detrimental; and that a certain degree of Poise is indispensable to physical development. The same is true of the mind and all the various faculties of the mind. There is no development when Poise is absent; but when Poise is present any exercise of mind or body promotes' development.

It is therefore evident that all work, physical or mental, that is expressed through Poise, will develop the worker himself; and that that part of mind or body that is employed directly in the work will receive the greatest amount of development.

That all work can be made a developing process as well as a producing process is a far-reaching statement, and means a great deal more than the average thinker will at first understand. But it must be readily admitted that the industrial world will be revolutionized — remarkably changed for the better when the twofold purpose of work is recognized and applied.

The individual, however, will not be required to wait for the industrial world at large to adopt the new system; he can begin now to make his work a developing process as well as a producing process, and thus improve himself and his environments perpetually.

It has been stated that deep feeling is one of the essentials to Poise; but to this we must add good feeling. To be in Poise is to feel thoroughly good through and through, and to enjoy a grade of happiness that is infinitely superior to anything that the restless pleasures on the surface can give to man. This gives another reason why Poise is so valuable in the process of development: viz, that no action of mind or body can promote growth or development unless it is exercised in joy.

Advancement is the result of what we like to do, what we want to do, and what we derive pleasure from doing.

Mental sunshine is as necessary to the development of the talents of the mind as the outer sunshine is to the growth of the flowers of the field.

To work in Poise and to promote development through your work, a new mental attitude towards work must be formed. Look upon your work as a channel through which you may pass to a better environment and a superior personal development. Do not go to your work with the sole idea of earning wages, because that is not your purpose. Recompense comes as a natural result of work well done, and the better the work, the larger the recompense. But to improve your work you must go to your work with the object of improvement in view: in fact, the whole of attention must be concentrated upon improvement — self improvement and better work. The person, however, who simply works for wages will not give his first thought to improvement; consequently, there will be no improvement, neither in himself, his work, nor his salary.

Poise and Power

Work for something else besides wages, and better wages must inevitably follow. Work for improvement both in yourself and in your product.

Go to your work with the idea that you are to spend a whole day turning energy into constructive use; and that you are to pass through a series of exercises which will develop your entire personality.

Realize that whenever you move a muscle in joy, that muscle grows; and that every time you think in Poise and harmony, your mind becomes stronger. Work because you desire to exercise muscles and brains in such a way that you may daily grow and develop into a stronger man, a more competent man, and a more able man.

Never go to work with the idea that you are working for a living. To simply work for a living with no thought of improvement is to continue to work where living will be meager and hard to get. But when you look upon all work as a constructive process in yourself and use all work for building up mind and body, you will not only make a living, but you will make a better living every year. What is more, you will at the same time be making for yourself a better life.

It has frequently been stated that it is only those who love their work who work well; but the majority have answered by saying that it is practically impossible to love work under present industrial conditions; and from their viewpoint they are correct.

However, anyone can love his work when he knows that it is always a means to greater things; and it is. Work in Poise; work in the right mental attitude and your work will positively be a means to something better.

Think of growth while at work; feel the expansive process of development all through your system, whenever you move a muscle or think a thought.

Work in the spirit of joy; this becomes easy when you know that every action is a stepping stone to greater advancement.

Do not work in the belief that you have to decrease in life or energy in order that your products may increase. Work in the realization that the more you produce in the world, the more power, life, ability and capacity you produce in yourself; and that the greater the things that you construct, the greater you yourself become.

The same building process that you apply upon things should simultaneously take place in yourself; and it will, if you make work a developing process as well as a producing process, and always work in Poise.

Chapter 11

That the ordinary strenuous methods of working causes the system to lose a great deal of energy can be easily understood; but that almost just as much energy is lost through the ordinary methods of resting, may seem difficult to believe; nevertheless, it is the truth.

The cause of this strange phenomena is found in the fact that no part of the system can rest until conscious action is completely withdrawn from that part. The average person when trying to rest tries to place himself in a restful attitude by consciously acting upon himself to make himself quiet. Therefore, instead of withdrawing conscious action, he continues to apply conscious action, and consequently fails to secure the attitude of rest.

Before any part of the system can rest, complete inactivity must be secured for that part; but so long as consciousness acts upon that part, complete inactivity is impossible, and consciousness continues to act upon everything that we are conscious of. It will therefore be readily understood that by trying to make yourself quiet, you will prevent yourself from becoming quiet.

The art of resting is consequently based upon the ability to withdraw conscious action from any part of the system when desired, and to become wholly unconscious of any plane of action when desired. This is something that anyone can do without any effort whatever.

True rest is not promoted by trying to do nothing, but by proceeding to do something else. To do nothing is impossible; therefore, to try to do nothing is to resist nature; and to resist anything is to lose power.

The conscious ego never stops action; it always acts upon something. While awake, this action is directed upon the objective personality; while asleep, it is turned upon the subconscious. Therefore, if you want conscious action to cease in one part of being, you must direct that action to some other part. You cannot stop the action itself. The secret is to give that action something else to do.

When you wish to rest one group of muscles, go and exercise another group. When you wish to rest one part of the brain or mind, think of something entirely different. When the whole brain needs rest, go and take some physical exercise that requires no constructive thought. Such exercise will rest the brain more quickly and far better than to lie down and think about how tired you feel.

When the entire body needs rest, read an entertaining book, or listen to quieting music, or think about something which takes you entirely away from physical existence. To enter the loftiness, the beauty and the silent life of spiritual thought will recuperate the body in less time than any other method that can be employed.

When you wish to rest anyone faculty or function, do not try to force consciousness away from that faculty or function. Simply direct your attention elsewhere, and become thoroughly interested in the new object of your attention. Consciousness will then follow, and all action be completely removed from the part that is to rest.

When you wish to rest the entire outer personality, go to sleep; but do not go to sleep in the ordinary way. To go to sleep properly is a fine art, and one that will prove most profitable when mastered.

Poise and Power

When we go to sleep, we enter the subconscious mind and carry on a form of activity in that state that is absolutely necessary. Everything that we have received during the waking state is carried into the subconscious when we go to sleep, and while we sleep, these things are made a part of ourselves.

During sleep we build character, ability, desires, motives, states of consciousness, etc., always employing the material that we have gathered during the waking state just preceding.

During the waking state we gather material: during sleep we take that material and rebuild ourselves. It is, therefore, of the highest importance that we gather the best material possible, and promote the subconscious reconstruction under the best conditions possible

All construction, however, requires energy; therefore, all the energy generated in the system should flow into the subconscious during sleep. This is accomplished by going to sleep with a definite purpose in view. A definite purpose in consciousness, as it passes into the subconscious will produce a mental tendency towards the subconscious, and all the active energy in the system will follow that tendency.

Every form of restless or disturbed sleep is produced by a portion of the active energy remaining in the outer personality during sleep. This condition, however, will be entirely removed by employing the method just mentioned. Therefore, to secure a sleep that is sound, peaceful, restful and recuperative to the very highest degree, we should go to sleep with a definite purpose in view. This purpose should form itself into a clear conception of what we wish to develop, and should be filled with a strong but gentle desire to promote that development.

Through this method, perfect rest for mind and body will be secured; a great deal of energy will be saved from loss, and subconscious development will be more thoroughly promoted.

From the foregoing it is therefore evident that the art of resting is mastered by giving the conscious ego something definite to do in another part of the system, while those parts which have been acted upon, are to rest. In this connection it is well to remember that at those moments when the conscious ego has nothing definite to do, all the energy generated in the system at the time, is lost. Consequently, during those moments when we are not engaged in regular constructive work, we should turn attention upon those latent faculties or talents which we wish to develop. Wasted time means wasted energy; both are prophets of failure.

The belief that we are resting and recuperating during those moments when we are generally inactive, is not true. General inactivity is impossible. What is called general inactivity is simply the scattering of forces, letting all the energies slip away, because they are not directed into something constructive.

Energy is being generated in the system constantly and if this energy is not given constructive work, it will scatter and disappear. Therefore, when we are through acting constructively in one line, we should immediately turn to another.

Every moment should be devoted to some constructive work either on the physical, metaphysical or spiritual planes. To devote certain regular hours to these three planes, alternately, every day is of the highest value, because such a practice will not only give regular rest to each plane but will employ constructively all the energy of the system every moment of existence. The result will be the higher development of the whole man — the one perfect goal we all have in view.

Chapter 12

Poise is peace and power combined. Therefore, if we wish to increase the degree of Poise we must increase the depth of the peace and the greatness of the power. Every method through which this can be accomplished should be employed.

Though our Poise may be perfect now, and though all the energies we now possess may be preserved and constructively employed, that does not mean that we have come to the end of Poise and its possibilities. There are degrees of Poise — any number of degrees; and after we have become conscious of Poise, the higher degrees should be sought with untiring perseverance. The greater the Poise, the greater the capacity of mind and body; and the greater the reserve force of the entire system.

To attain higher degrees of Poise, the realization of peace should be deepened, and the consciousness of power should be enlarged.

To bring these things about, the subconscious mind should be employed extensively, because it is always the wise way to go direct to the source when we know the source; and the subconscious is the source of everything.

When we daily impress the idea of peace upon the subconscious, we will daily receive a deeper and deeper realization of peace. When we daily impress the idea of power upon the subconscious, we will daily receive a larger and larger consciousness of power.

What we sow, we reap; and the subconscious is the field wherein everything may grow and flourish.

Poise and Power

To impress the subconscious, turn attention to the depth of life, thought and feeling, and think about what you desire to bring forth from the great within. The deeper the feeling of this thought, the deeper will be the impression made, and the sooner will results appear.

To think deeply of peace while concentrating attention upon the depth of mind is to impress the idea of peace upon the subconscious; it is to sow the seed of peace, and the harvest will invariably be peace — thirty, sixty or a hundred fold. All ideas or impressions that enter the subconscious multiply, just as a single seed placed in rich soil, produces a multitude of seeds.

To think deeply of power while concentrating attention upon the inner mind is to impress the idea of power upon the subconscious; and by daily impressing the desire for more power upon the subconscious, we arouse and awaken more power in the subconscious, and thus increase the capacity of power to a very great degree.

This practice if continued cannot fail to produce most remarkable results; in fact, it is something so extremely valuable that it has but few equals.

To those who do not understand the nature of the subconscious and who do not know where to turn attention while trying to concentrate upon the subconscious, we will state that every desire which is deeply felt will impress itself upon the subconscious. This impression will become deep and well established if that desire continues to be deeply felt for days and weeks.

When the desire is directly concentrated upon the subconscious mind itself, the results will naturally be greater and will appear in less time. To exactly locate the subconscious mind is not necessary, neither is it possible because the subconscious is practically unbounded. We can, however, form in mind some idea as to the sphere of subconscious action, and it is upon this sphere we must concentrate.

The mind does not simply occupy the brain, but the entire personality; and as the subconscious permeates the essence of the mind as water permeates a sponge, we understand that the subconscious thoroughly fills the entire being of man, though acting upon a finer plane of life. Therefore, to concentrate upon the subconscious, direct attention upon the finer plane of life, not at one particular part of the system, but through the entire system.

To gain a larger and a better consciousness of the subconscious so that we can constantly feel this immense state of life and thought within us, is of the highest importance; because when this is gained, every thought that we deeply feel enters subconscious life and will produce results accordingly.

All psychologists agree that the subconscious is immense beyond comprehension, and that the possibilities which are latent in the subconscious of every mind are marvelous, to say the least. To unfold these possibilities is therefore to take a direct path to genius and extraordinary ability.

That genius does exist in the subconscious of every mind is no theory, but the conclusion of the most careful research in this great mental field. Therefore, we are not making extravagant statements when we declare that genius and extraordinary ability can be developed in anyone. But it is not possible to take any decided steps forward in this respect unless we have Poise. So long as we lack Poise the greater

Poise and Power

talents from within will simply scatter whenever we try to bring them out into fuller expression.

In the beginning, therefore, the subconscious should be called upon to deepen the realization of peace and enlarge the consciousness of power so that a more perfect Poise may be attained. Nor should this effort be discontinued at any time. The attainment of higher and higher degrees of Poise must be inseparably connected with every other attainment, because higher attainments in special lines are impossible without a corresponding degree of Poise.

Consequently, the desires for more peace and more power should be daily impressed upon the subconscious. If this is done, each day will bring a greater supply of these two indispensable qualities. You will find yourself becoming more and more serene and will daily grow into the perfect calm — the calm that is not only very still, but exceedingly strong.

The consciousness of power will steadily enlarge until you feel that the power within you is unbounded; when this feeling comes your future is your own. Henceforth nothing can hold you down; nothing can stand in your way; nothing can prevent you from reaching the heights.

When you feel that unbounded power is within you, you will press on and on, regardless of obstacles or environments, and your destiny is to do great and wonderful things in life. You have touched the real source of greatness; therefore, greatness is assuredly in store for you.

When this deeper peace is realized, and the greater power is felt; and when these two are united into the one perfect state — Poise — the consciousness of real life begins. It is then that we realize that the greatest thing that man can do is to live; not to merely exist, but to live; and Life is the greatest thing because all great attainments and all great achievements come from Life — abundance of Life.

He who has found Life — the strong, calm, invincible Life, has found the peace which passeth understanding. He has placed himself in the sphere of that power which knows no bounds; and he has entered into that state of being that is greatness itself.

He strives no more to become; he is. All that he has longed for; all that he has aspired to reach and attain, he finds in Life.

All about him is Life — the calm, beautiful Life; within him is Life — the same strong, serene Life; and before him is Life — eternal Life, unbounded Life, a Life so rich, so marvelous, that eternity will be required to reveal it all.

Everything seems new; everything seems possible. To simply live is supreme joy; and to think of the future is to have beautiful visions of the greater riches still in store. But will these visions come true? Yes, they will; and he who has found Life knows that they will.

He who has found Life has discovered the limitless possibilities within; he knows that whatever man may undertake to do, the same shall be done, providing he lives, thinks and works in Life.

The mind that has learned to Be Still and Live has found the secret of all secrets. He has found that from which everything comes; that which can supply sufficient wisdom and sufficient power to do anything that man may desire to have done.

Poise and Power

To any mind that thinks, these things are true; that man can attain anything and accomplish anything is positively true. But how? The first step is that wonderful something we call Poise; the peace of the soul and the power of the soul united into the one perfect state of Life — calm strong invincible Life.

www.ingramcontent.com/pod-product-compliance
Lightning Source LLC
Chambersburg PA
CBHW031358290426
44110CB00011B/205